the journeying self

a study in philosophy and social role

maurice natanson
university of california, santa cruz

addison-wesley publishing company

reading, massachusetts
menlo park, california
london · don mills, ontario

126

IV191j

0053886?

for kathy, nicholas, and charles

preface

This essay is an approach to philosophy and social role from a phenomeno-logical and existential standpoint. It is chiefly indebted to three thinkers: Edmund Husserl, Jean-Paul Sartre, and above all, Alfred Schutz. By design, I have drawn upon and utilized many of their fundamental concepts and theories without crediting them—indeed, without even mentioning them—page by page in the body of the text. What I have tried to do instead is to present a systematic statement of relevant problems free of historical com-mentary, almost entirely without quotation, and liberated from all recourse to the formula: "as so-and-so said." Thus, the reader is thrust directly into the philosophical fray. He must decide whether this strategy is rewarding. My hope is that what is lost in qualifications will be repaid by unencum-brance. But a preliminary caution is necessary: although I have raided the writings of Husserl, Sartre, and Schutz, I have adapted as much as adopted their thought for my own purposes. In paying respect to my sources, I must absolve them of any part in my sometimes aberrant use of their ideas and be held solely accountable for any conceptual misdemeanors. In the terminal notes I have seated all the references, quotations, and bibliography so arbi-trarily denied admission during the regular performance.

The writing of this work was made possible by a University of California Senior Faculty Fellowship. At the University's Santa Cruz campus, Mrs. Joan Hodgson of the Library was generous with bibliographical assistance, and Mrs. Phyllis Halpin and Mrs. Charlotte Cassidy of the secretarial staff of Cowell College were extremely helpful. Mrs. Cassidy typed the manuscript with patient skill. The editorial staff of Addison-Wesley gave their full co-operation. Indirect assistance came from Professor Nathaniel Lawrence, who, after reading a brief outline of the plans which I had submitted to the publisher, suggested the addition of a chapter on science and, without realizing it, gave me a title. In the body of the outline, I had casually used the phrase, "the journeying self." Mr. Lawrence pointed out that my words translated Gabriel Marcel's *Homo Viator*. Although I must confess that had I thought of Marcel, I would have started with the pedestrian "Man the . . . ," I am as happy to credit Gabriel Marcel for the provenience of my title as I am to acknowledge Mr. Lawrence's tacit guidance in naming my book. Responsibility for its contents is mine alone. The book's first reader was Lois Natanson, and my final thanks as well as love belong to her alone.

Santa Cruz, California   M. N.
December 1969

contents

introduction

"Who reads the language of direction? Where may we pass
*Through the immense pattern sheer as glass?"**

James Still

Philosophy is both inviting and forbidding. Reflection on the world and on oneself in the world is part of common-sense existence, yet radical, *root* reflection, which is the mark of true philosophizing, is on the far side of daily life. There is nothing more commonplace than "philosophy" and nothing rarer than philosophy. Something of the same paradox exists in the study of the subject, for it is quickly apparent to the student that if a choice between the concreteness of his own experience and the seeming abstraction of analysis is avoidable, there still remains a distance between the reality of his individual experience and the texts of the classroom. The dualisms of life and thought, experience and theory, specificity and abstraction are hardly new, but they are experienced anew by the individual who sets out to study philosophy in the urgent hope of finding in its discipline answers to what concerns *him*. All readers do not fall into this category; those that do, however, deserve a guiding answer to the question, "How can I *begin* in philosophy?" To be sure, a great many answers have already been provided by textbook writers, editors of anthologies, and, of course, by the philosophers' original

* From James Still, "Pattern for Death," in *Hounds on the Mountain*, New York: Viking Press, 1937. Copyright 1937 and Copyright © renewed 1965 by James Still. Reprinted by permission of the publisher.

1

works. This book is neither an alternative to those options nor an oblique criticism of them. Hobson's choice is neither necessary nor intended. Rather, I offer this essay for whatever use it may serve to those readers who may find in it a new approach to old problems. Before getting on with the problems, I'd like to say a word about the approach.

Phenomenology and existentialism are efforts to explore man and his existence by placing primary emphasis on the self, understood as consciousness confronting a world and engaged in human action. The "confrontation" and "engagement" involved need further explanation. Within the career of day-to-day, common-sense existence, each of us goes about his business without philosophical worries. It is simply taken for granted by all of us that the world in which we move about and act is real, has a long history, has not only a physical being continuous with the realm of nature but a conceptual and emotive reality assumed to have force and consequence for others no less than for ourselves. Further, we assume that our world has a future which will be more or less like the past, societal and cultural institutions and practices which have always marked civilized beings, and men in action, steeped in practical affairs and proceeding to discharge their duties and obligations in typical ways. All these assumptions—and many more—*are* assumptions in the sense that unless we stop and think, reflect for some reason on them, they do not ordinarily become explicit objects for thought or investigation. In the midst of *our* world, the very idea that it is *ours*, yours and mine, theirs and ours, does not present itself as something to be considered, something which might be entertained as a theme for inquiry. All the manifold problems of our world are set, as it were, in the framework of "our" world, and however carefully and thoroughly we consider those problems, the quotation marks around "our" never flicker into relief. As taken for granted, the philosophical problem of intersubjectivity, the ground of the "our," remains not only moot but undiscovered. Within the horizon of involvement in the world, the individual is thrust into a field of action which seems to encompass him as the city cloaks its denizen.〔All the signs of mundane reality lend implicit support to the assumption that the model of the physical object in the quantified space of nature is a paradigm for the being of man in the world.〕Accompanying this conception of physical insertion is the related assumption that the encompassing world is "out there," on its own, while the individual is "over here," looking out. The phenomenological and existential notions of "confrontation" and "engagement" are a repudiation of this physicalistic model. They turn to both man and world in a new way.

In man's consciousness of the world is to be found the new orientation. But it is essential to realize that by "consciousness" much more is meant than "awareness" or a purely psychological conception of the content or activity of the mind. Consciousness, as understood here, will refer to all of perceptual experience, to man's thinking, believing, willing, remembering, anticipating, deciding, and choosing. To be conscious is to be conscious *of* something, a something which then stands to the activity of consciousness as the meaning of its performance. That which is *meant* by consciousness is not to be understood as a thing, an "object" in the physical sense, but as a significative content, a something closely bound to the acts of consciousness that are responsible for its being meant yet also having its own independence. To be aware of a fellow-man, for example, is to be in relationship to him as someone there in my field of vision, someone standing next to a painting, someone discussing that painting with a friend, someone trying to communicate his aesthetic enthusiasm to me. The someone of whom I'm conscious, then, is a being who is first of all there for me as an "object" of my response as well as of my sensation, thoughts, and imaginings. Moreover, he is himself a center of consciousness, a being like me who is not only someone for me but one for whom I am also a someone. I "confront" the Other as a being among other beings, as, truly, a fellow-man. What matters here, however, is not the quality or nature of my response to him but the character of the confrontation. In being conscious of the Other, I live in the immediacy of our relationship, in the perception of him *as* living, vital, and friendly or dull, listless, and hostile. The Other is not outside the acts of consciousness which present him as loving or fierce but the very content of those acts. Man and fellow-man have their being within the limits of their consciousness of each other.

By "engagement" is meant the involvement of the individual in his world, his action in it as distinguished from his observation of it. Although we may and indeed do sometimes stand apart from a scene and regard it with relative detachment, we are first of all actors in mundane reality, the arena of our striving and our accomplishment. It is the character of engagement rather than a theory of its purpose or importance that concerns us here. In the midst of action, the choices we make and the results of our choosing are to be understood in unitary fashion, as involving a being for whom the perception, evaluation, and definition of the situation are aspects of an integral self, a being at the center and source of a world. It is the self, then, which is the clue to the meaning of engagement, and that brings us to the existential dimension of our approach to human experience. Let us set aside, for the moment, the task of providing a definition for the term "self" as we employ it here. Instead, we will assume that in an ingenuous yet remarkably penetrating sense, each of us is aware of himself as a being in the world, a self for which experience is coherent and possible. Within the compass of common sense, the self is both a presence in and a concealment from the world. Perhaps the most striking feature of the self, in this sense, is its cunning, for each of us commits himself to the world with but a part of his being, and each of us holds back from the world that fraction of the self which remains secretive or dormant. Whatever the style of the person, the division holds true: the braggart and the aesthete, the neurotic and the Rotarian, the patriot and the embezzler, the fox and the goose all present themselves to the world in fragments of total exposure and unities of partial expression.

Confrontation and engagement are themselves merely aspects of the phenomenological and existential philosophies from which they originate. Rather than turn to an historical or systematic account of the larger positions at issue, I prefer to restrict myself here to a foretaste of what will be developed in the chapters which follow. To understand the phenomenological and existential approach to human experience, it is essential to realize that the image of Man which is projected is that of a being whose presence in the world is a unitary reality in which self and object are taken as integrally grounded in consciousness, understood as a directional force sustaining the entire range of perceptual life. Individual and action, self and situation, person and world are then bound to each other not only in their implications for each other but in their fundamental structure. Man is "in" the world as the lover is in relationship to the one he loves, not as the bearings are "in" the motor. The new vantage point which results from seizing man and world as integral is difficult to grasp precisely because we are the heirs to over three centuries of a philosophic and scientific perspective based on contrary assumptions and committed to the basic idea that man can be understood in qualitatively the same terms as all other objects and events in the natural order. Congruent with that attitude is a methodological persuasion which looks for causal explanations of all events. In our inquiry, however, the "what" rather than the "why" of experience is the first concern. In the end, it may be that the "why" of events can be understood through a reconstruction of the "what" of experience. But that demands a searching out of the meaning of sources, a rebuilding of forgotten or apparently inaccessible origins, and a tracing out of the routes we traverse in becoming "men of the world." The approach to the self involved here requires something of a movement, a development or odyssey of reconstruction to which the reader is invited. It is only fair, then, to indicate the general itinerary.

Stating it bluntly, I propose to trace the philosophical history of the individual from birth to death. Were the "history" involved here an account of "what happens" to each of us, his life history, as we say, then the notion of detailing the story of man would indeed be foolish if not absurd, particularly in the confines of a small book. What I'm after, obviously, is "history" in a different sense: not a chronicle or the reporting of events but the location and elucidation of their "inner" anatomy, the fundamental structure in terms of which the meaning of autobiography is possible. What are the most general, truly the most *abstract* features of any human life? What elements must be present in the conceptual and spiritual development of man in order for a "life" to be possible? To put the question in a more nearly philosophical manner: Given a human career, what are the conditions necessary for accounting for its coherence? In contrast to evolutionary, traditionally historical, or religious modes of explaining man's origins, the approach taken here turns to the *situation* of the concrete individual, you or me, and tries to elucidate the meanings bound up in that situation in their most general character. If a physical model is to be thought of at all in this connection, it is the sciences of geology and archaeology which come closest to providing a clue to what we are about. Just as the geologist discovers in the stratification of rock the physical signs of early mineral deposits and just as the archaeologist digs for hidden evidence, so, in a way, the phenomenological philosopher is interested in "sedimentation" of meaning and in the lost genesis of our meaningful world.

The procedures we are concerned with, then, presuppose a discovery, an *un-covering* of the meaningful history of the individual's world. The one who undertakes the voyage of discovery must be the reader himself, for the world to be explored is, in the first place, *his*. The stance of the observer must give way to that of the participant; the spectator must be replaced by the actor. Nor is a bare, surface assent to this procedure sufficient. What is necessary is the willed agreement and persistent continuity of intent which make it possible for the individual to render problematic aspects of his taken-for-granted reality which are, in fact, epistemically precious to him. The individual who undertakes the discipline we propose must be open to the most hazardous and revealing form of travel, the movement of the person inward, the journey of the self. The advance will be from the alone ego, the beginnings of the individual, to the fulfillment and finality of death. Each of the chapters which follow is a stage in the journey; the series ascends in terms of its own logic. We start with the very concept of the "self" as the experientially primitive basis for man's philosophical history, move on to the discovery of other selves, the fellow-men with whom we share that history, and to the "sociality" or social reality within which the self and his fellow-selves act in the typical ways of the everyday world. Science, history, art, and religion then follow as the great symbolic systems and constructions founded on the experience of man in daily life and, in turn, making that experience place-, time-, as well as person-transcendent. We start with the self and move toward the social. But isn't the individual born into the social world? Aren't history and society prior to the person? And isn't the fact of language enough to cast suspicion on any venture which would try to reach the intersubjective through the trap door of the ego? Clearly, our procedure calls for some preliminary defense.

There is a difference between logical and chronological priority. In the sense of genealogy, the parents antedate, are prior to, their children. Similarly, in the chronicle of history, a society is prior to its newborn member.

No infant creates his culture or invents his language. Yet there is a logical order to the structure of sociological affairs, a syntax of history no less than a grammar of language. And these structural elements are presupposed in the systems and states of affairs which exemplify them, despite the fact and quite independent of the fact that logicians and grammarians postdate the instrumentalities they study. In this sense, mathematical logic is prior to the rest of mathematics, despite the fact that it developed quite late in the history of mathematics. Similarly, the codification of a language is prior to its spoken and even written form, whether that formalization started fairly early in the history of the language, as in English, or rather late in its career, as in Yiddish. The principles, the conceptual arteries of a body of knowledge, are first in the order of systematic analysis, wherever else they stand in the development of a subject. An analogous situation pertains in the realm of experience: the fundamental principles which underly our consciousness of the world and our action in it are systemically *a priori* to the actualization or exemplification of those principles in the flow of historical events. When we fix our attention, then, on the self as the first element in the development of man's social and historical reality, we mean to strike out for what is philosophically first in the creation of man; there is no hint of denial of the ongoing reality of social order or the validity of an historical past. *Given* the fact of man as a sociohistorical being, we ask, "What are the primordial philosophic conditions which account for the actuality of our world?" The journey of the self is a search for its philosophic genesis.

If the starting point in our quest is to be the self approached in phenomenological and existential terms, then the dynamism and mobility of what is basic to individuation must be stressed and accounted for. If we remember that the phenomenological-existential standpoint repudiates the idea of the individual as set over and against the world as well as the notion of consciousness as a container closed off from an "external" reality, it is possible to appreciate the new conception of the self to be presented here: the self understood as projected toward a world it helps to constitute. That "projection" will be initially interpreted through the directional activity of consciousness, but its specifically intersubjective dimension we propose to treat under the rubric of "social role," a term which is better known to sociologists and social psychologists than to philosophers. Role and role-taking are also, of course, familiar features of common-sense experience, where they are most often understood in dramaturgical terms. A social role is taken or "played" in a host of situations in which it is deemed appropriate to act in traditionally established and approved ways. Not only professional people but all individuals, at least on certain occasions, are expected or required to act *as* befits an officer of an organization, a pedestrian in busy traffic, the father of the bride, the applicant for a job, the sentry on duty, the child playing "house," or the politician greeting his constituents. Less banal examples are not scarce, but they might properly be reserved for more detailed treatment later on. For the moment, we may say that social roles and the taking of roles permeate the human scene not only in their obvious, full-fashioned character but in their more subtle and elusive shape, in the realm of the private, the secretive, and the opaque. Hitherto, most discussions of social role have emphasized its importance at the sociological level; we intend to extend its function and implications in a far broader and more demanding manner, considering the very notion of role to be an intimate part of the fabric of human involvement in the scientific, artistic, and religious domains no less than in the sphere of sociality. With that extension a warning must go: there is no need to pretend that man and history are products, in some simple sense, of role-taking. Rather, the point is that man and history seen in their *becoming*, as features of the development of the self and its social allies, are expressions of the ego's mobility, its capacity to confront and engage mundane existence through the constructions of consciousness. In this context, social role may be understood as a clue to what is both hidden and manifest in the self's encounter with the world.

What follows now is the first step in the journey. If this sketch of our approach has helped at all, it should be evident that the one who begins in our way must commit himself to doing more than following what is said in the way a tourist tags behind his guide. The reader must be both investigator and investigated, both pursuer and pursued. The hardest point in philosophy is exactly this one, for at the outset the very familiarity and coziness of the taken-for-granted guards us against the intrusions of sharp reflection. What has always been "ours" in the common-sense world must be made thematic, and what we have always relied on as the indubitable truth of things must be invaded and searched. If there are no assurances about results, there is at least something that can be said about the prize of the venture. The point of *this* approach to philosophy is to bring the individual to the existential recognition that the familiar everydayness of our experience in the world of daily life is the result, the creation of an immensely complex apparatus of consciousness and that consciousness, far from being divorced from the real, is the secret of its practicality and power. The goal of our investigation cannot be understood apart from the journey which brings us there.

chapter
one

the
self

We begin with an experiment. Ordinarily we believe in the reality and validity of our world, its history, and its likely future. For practical purposes,
we trust in the machinery of commerce and the efficacy of societal procedures.
We know who we are, where we come from, and the business we have at hand
in daily life; from the rooftops of the world we look down at the enactments
of men. Geared into mundane action, we harness our excitements and resent-
ments into codes of force and legends of consequence. Our experience is both
of the world and in the world, bound to the chain of events which causally
preceded and produced it and linked to the resultants of action which herald
the future. Ordinary, matter-of-course believing in the reality of the world,
then, is not only an aspect of public life; it is a fundamental presupposition of
mundanity, a philosophical ground for the organization and character of our
experience of the world. The experiment starts this way: Let us—the reader
is asked to follow suit—set aside our knowledge and preacquaintanceship
with history and science, interpretation and valuation. Speaking egologically,
I will, for the sake of the experiment, put aside what I know, think, and feel
about my past, my family, my ancestors, the cultural milieu which produced
me. Further, I will make no use of my knowledge of my environing world,
including fellow-men and the sciences of social structure. I am going to
suspend my believing in the most basic features of experience: the reality of
the world, its independent physical being, and the causation which undergirds its elements. Origin, relationships, and expectancies all fall under the
decision to place in abeyance those central beliefs and that cardinal believing
which are the fundament of reality. The immediate question, "But what's

left if you do that?" is most likely to come from the individual who has read about but not actually attempted the experiment. We do not need to damn the question, but separating it from the questioner creates an artificial puzzle. Before we can advance we will have to move downward. To understand the experiment it is necessary to realize that certain things are *not* called for. First of all, I am not suggesting that there is some magical way of erasing or eradicating knowledge, a categorical brainwashing by means of which time and causation can be canceled out and overcome. Second, the suspension and abeyance recommended have nothing to do with the obliteration of the world and its contents. Finally, there is no call to eliminate anything, fellow-men least of all. There is nothing arcane or violent in these proceedings, though they do involve a shock to common sense. Perhaps the quickest way to see the point of the experiment is to compare it with the act of trying to take a fresh look at something or someone you already have quite fixed ideas about. Looking at the face of someone you know intimately and have seen daily over a period of years may mean not really seeing that individual at all. One responds to what one expects to see, not what is there. A sudden change in the appearance of a friend may cause us to look closely, to "take a second look," to peer at what is new as though it were placed side by side with what was expected. Or, on occasion, we suddenly *see* the Other because of the glance of a third person. The man who has escorted a woman for years may find his taken-for-grantedness about her shattered by the look of another man. The question "What does he see in her?" may be taken in a somewhat new way when the seeing gives back the original vivacity of the person to one whose proximity to it tends to obscure it. A place as well as a person may be recovered in this way. Moreover, a situation may in fact call for a strategy of *review* in an almost literal sense of that word. The fervent nationalist may need to transcend his emotional involvement in a cause at times when the advancement of that cause requires coolness and objectivity in judgment. In some professions, a "distancing" of the self from its involvement with Others is essential to the success of a relationship. In many cases, then, a form of suspension of belief is utilized within the focus of daily life. Yet no one would charge that the world is being denied or negated. The philosophical problem, though, goes deeper.

Placing our believing in the world in suspension means, most importantly, becoming explicitly aware of the character of that believing. Two elements are involved: first, the believing is focused on, reflected on, made an explicit theme of analysis; second, the scope of the believing must be comprehended, for its range includes all perceptual experience. We can readily question someone's beliefs about politics or religion but not his believing-in as the precondition for the very recognition of politics and religion as spheres in which beliefs are appropriate. The philosopher's task, then, is to get beneath not only the rug and the flooring but the foundation that supports them. It is the very obviousness of our believing-in the reality of things which makes it so difficult to come to terms with the meaning of our experiment. We turn to the directions already perched on the shoulders of belief. The reversal that is quintessential to the new attitude demands a liberation from the familiar in order to regain the familiar, to see it *as* familiar. Seeing-as may be a clue to our problem. Again, the notion is not entirely separated from common-sense experience. There are odd moments in our lives when our involvement in activities lapses, when we are aware of ourselves *as* attending a lecture, performing a duty, witnessing an event. Self-consciousness at those times is rather strange precisely because the flow of our action is stopped and the scene of our involvement itself becomes explicit to reflection. Yet those moments are comparatively rare, and more importantly, the limit of our seeing-as is circumscribed by the event. If those limits could be infinitely expanded and our total believing-in brought into view, we would approach the meaning of radical suspension in the sense in which we have been utilizing that strange notion. Now, perhaps, we are ready for a second try at the experiment.

We begin again, then, by placing in suspension our believing in the world as existent, real, historically grounded, causally determined, and valuationally interpreted by men who are aware of each other and who assume that what is typically true for their own experience holds equally well for all other "normal" perceivers. But now it is possible and pertinent to note that no item of experience is lost to consciousness in the process; rather, everything thought of and entertained in perception is taken *as* thought of and *as* entertained. Everything specifiable in the ordinary attitude is retained in the new, but retained *as* an object of perceptual experience. The world has not changed; our experience of it has undergone transformation. What remains after suspension is everything seen in the philosophically neutralized perspective of consciousness in direct touch with its world. Past predications and present interpretations are stripped of their presuppositional grounding in what "everybody" takes for granted as the character of our experiential world.

Before it is proper to ask for an inventory of what manifests itself to consciousness thus conceived, an unfortunate caution must be introduced to spoil what the reader may have regarded as a bit of experimental progress. After suspension, we are left with our experiential world as directly given to consciousness. *Our* world? Wasn't one of the chief features of the taken-for-granted world we set out to undercut the assumption of the individual that the world is also known by fellow-men? How radical can a procedure be when it claims to make explicit what common sense presupposes, yet proceeds in terms of the vast assumption that ours is indeed a shared world? Obviously, a circle of sorts exists: *we* cannot analyze *our* experience when the meaning of "we" and "our" is a leading issue supposed to be included in the investigation itself. It is necessary, then, to move from the "we" to the sphere of the ego, the "I", to the ultimate ground of what is inescapably "mine." Before undertaking that step it should be understood that believing-in as it undergirds mundane existence is indeed intersubjective in its intent. We *do* perceive our world and act in it with the immanent belief that it is *our* world. The trick, then, is to make that "our" an explicit theme for examination, an object for consciousness in its most basic dimension.

Within the radical attitude of suspension, I discover what is "mine" in the strictest sense through three elements which undergird all subsequent experience but do not derive from experience: for the time being, let us call them time, space, and body. A bit later more precise language for what is represented by these terms will be introduced. Very simply, in suspension, I am presented with the immediacy of what I am aware of as "now" and "here." Before we turn to the status of "body," time and space need analysis. In the "now" of my awareness-of experience I find a locus of streaming incoming and outgoing perceptions. The Now is whenever I attend to that stream, its limits being self-defined, that is, defined by me. At any moment I choose to fix on, the Now presents itself as the ongoing quality of all my perceptual experience, its consistency. "Now" is, of course, a quixotic notion if taken apart from the givenness of perceptual life. Is there one Now or many? Can Now repeat itself? A distinction is called for between the Now as form and as content. The Now-character makes any particular perceptual content possible but does not vary as the content does. The Now is one and unrepeatable as form; the particularizations of the Now are infinite in possibility. Furthermore, the Now is naively given to me. There is no hint of "outside interference." I discover the Now *within* my experiential immediacy. Although it is an aspect of time, the Now is structurally prior to the measurement of time through clocks and watches. No dial shows "Now" as part of its face, yet at any time of its being read, the time is always Now. Perhaps a change in terminology is appropriate. Instead of "time," we can say "temporality" to indicate the subject-bound character of such elements of time as Now. Within the public time of newspaper deadlines, stockmarket closings, and railroad schedules, Now has no existence; at best, it is a hypothetical term brought into actuality by translating some fixed part of a timetable into the purview of an actor on the social scene. As a feature of temporality, however, Now is preeminently mine, defined by me as I move through the experiential world that I find continuously unfolding for me and before me. Temporality is sometimes spoken of as "inner time" or "lived time." At least, it is time centered in the immediacy of my consciousness-of reality, a consciousness and a reality which are discoverable before any predications are made regarding the historical or intersubjective world. Temporality is a constitutive force in the construction of what is distinctively *mine*. It leads to a similar concept of space.

If instead of time, we say "temporality," so instead of space, "spatiality." Along with the Now goes the Here of my immediate placement in intentional experience. And with the egocentricity of the content of the Now goes the subject-bound nature of the Here. The place or geographical location of the Here changes as I move about, but wherever I find myself, I am Here. Over and against my Here I discover what is There, at a distance from me. How close or far There is from me cannot be measured abstractly, for distance is a function of my *insertion* in the world. The term "spatiality" is designed to suggest the sense of personal placement in a perceptual reality defined by the individual. "There" may be interpreted in terms of the distance of the stars or the closeness of wrestling. What matters is that my consciousness-of There is defined by the givenness of my Here. In turn, that Here is defined by my experience of my own body. The continuity of terminology suggests, and properly so, that if time and space are translated into temporality and spatiality, body needs an equivalent formulation. Perhaps "corporeality" will do. It means the location of my physical body, the body studied by anatomists and physiologists, as *mine*. Within the suspension, I know nothing of the results of scientific study of "the body"; I do experience my body as the means, the instrument through which I act in the world. Before that, however, I find my body as the central point at the source of the Here. In fact, Here is where my body is. There is where my body is not. A further exploration of "my body" is necessary. The immediacy of my experience of corporeality should be understood as an indication of the interior perspective I occupy with respect to "my body." I am neither "in" my body nor "attached to" it; it does not belong to me or go along with me. *I am my body*. There is no distance between my hand and its grasping. The pulsation "within" me which I am aware of when my heart beats rapidly upon extreme exertion is the way in which my corporeality expresses itself and discloses the world. Instead of the common-sense way of thinking of the body in space at some time, I am a corporeality Here and Now whose being in the world is disclosed to me as *mine*. A final return to the experiment is now possible.

In the egological attitude of the suspension fully realized, I find myself Here as I am embodied, incarnate in the world. Each Now presents me with a perceptual world *there* for me as either over and against my body or as *with* my corporeal existence. The immediacy which has been stressed is not evanescent or illusory; rather, it is the fullness of my perceptual being. Within that fullness appear the awareness-of the past and the expectancy of the future which are mine. Not the past but my awareness of it, not the future but my expectancy of it, not the transcendent world of causal and valuational efficacy but my appreciation of it—these are the phenomena of my egological sphere. And within that same sphere is to be found the sense of the inter-subjective and the "worldly." *Our* world, then, is grasped as "our-world-as-I-intend it," our world as it is revealed within my immediate perceptual givenness. It is the meaning of the "our" which I find in my perceptual experience; but the "objective" status or ontological character of what is meant is placed in judgmental abeyance. The reality and truth of what is meant as far as its actual historical or physical existence is concerned, are not at issue in the egological attitude. Of course, if I predicate reality of my intended meaning, that predication may be considered descriptively within the suspension. Nothing more. The ego, then, is thrown back on its own resources, left to its conceptual devices. Nothing is denied in the suspension but everything must be reconstructed for two purposes: to see its structure and to comprehend its becoming. Only within the solitary confines of the ego's immediacy is it possible to display the grounds of its construction of reality. Solitude presents its own problems, however, and its demands on philosophy as well. If "our" world is rooted in "my" world, then the sociality of the intersubjective must be sedimented in the aloneness of the ego.

What is mine is mine alone. For the Here and Now of my being that "alone" is the condition for regaining the suspended predication of history, causation, and intersubjectivity. It is not a substitute for the social world but a means of retrieving it in philosophical lucidity. In this sense, the alone-ness of the egological sphere includes in a most pointed manner intentional awareness of Others. In fact, it is the very consciousness-of Others (of "our" world) which gives to the solitude of the ego its existential force. My Here-and-Now being presents itself to me as mine alone, the "mine" no longer the familiar fact of possession and preacquaintanceship but of founding or estab-lishing power, and the "alone" no longer separation from Others but the *originary* status of the ego for which intersubjectivity is problematic. Illustrations are hazardous at this level, but it may help to retreat for a moment to the common-sense world. The childhood experience of being lost may serve at this stage. The very young child who has lost his parents in a crowd, who has strayed far from home and his neighborhood, who is truly lost from all familiarity and recognition, *may* experience the terror of aban-donment. From the standpoint of the adult world, being lost means being momentarily or temporarily "strayn." For the child, being lost means being powerfully confronted with alien faces and surroundings, each aspect of which announces itself as explicit documentation of what is not familiarly there. The reassurance of friendly adults, the "Don't worry we'll find them" of authorities, the diversionary tactics so often transparent to the child, are all marks of precisely what is *not* present: parents, home, and love. In the extremes of terror and inconsolability we have evidence of the straining of the child to maintain his bonds with the familiarity of home. The scalded heaving of the deserted, his misery spilling out toward the circle of strangers about him, his passion for recovering his just-past cycle of crying and calling are, we might say, the mode of his aloneness. Instead of simply expressing his fear and anxiety, his tears and cries are his recognition of something quite reasonable in its own young terms: the permanent, once-and-for-all severance from home. Perhaps in the quality of that ruined orientation, for at least the time of being lost, we can recover something of the experiential impact of aloneness. Fellow-men are all about the child; blandishments, endearments, and encouragements are pressed upon him; but the solitude of the moment is absolute and impenetrable in its initial character because the ordinary, taken-for-granted frame of home is shattered. It can be reconstructed only from within. When the searching parents return or the child is escorted home, the appearance of the familiar is merely (though to the child overpoweringly) the external occasion for the renewal of an interior pattern, the return *of*, not *to* home.

The aloneness of the ego is both a means for the experiment and a result of it. As a means, a methodological procedure, radical suspension requires the solitary ego because all other bases presuppose the philosophical grounding at issue here: the constitution of self and world. Taken as a result, a product of suspension, aloneness is an existential feature of the condition of man as a being in the world. For existential philosophy, the primordial aloneness of the individual is accompanied by the experience of anguish. Although I am not concerned at this point with trying to trace out or develop the meaning of existential anguish, it is relevant to point out the connection between suspension and anguish. In the orientation of common-sense existence, the individual may be said to be alone in several senses. For instance, he is or may be isolated from his fellow-men, for various reasons, whether for a long or short period of time; or there may be situations of moral choice in which advice from others ultimately falls back to him, in which the decision must be his alone. In the extremes of love and violence, in both personal and political contexts of some urgency, the alone individual must, at times, come to his own conclusions and act on his own principles. That "anguish" sometimes accompanies such moments of choice is a fact of mundane life. However, existential anguish is a different matter, and the aloneness of the ego is also another affair. The most harrowing choice in daily life, one which calls truly for individual decision, is made *within* the frame of an ongoing, intersubjectively valid world. However isolated the chooser may be, he is isolated *from* his fellow-men or *from* some situation which is presupposed as part of mundane life. The isolation, then, must be understood as taking place in a horizon of communal and fellow-related existence. In the phenomenological suspension, however, the ego is seized in its bare being, without the assurances of the sustaining notions of world and sociality. The awareness of being truly an ego "on its own" is the experience of anguish. In some ways, social existence is a means of translating that anguish into a self-acceptable form of balance. Far from there being a resolution of the condition or philosophical circumstance of anguish, mundanity is a constant and only partially successful accommodation the ego makes in order to mask the implications of its aloneness.

Philosophy, we might say, begins with the recognition of aloneness in the existential sense. Obviously, there is no demand that the individual make the experiment of suspension or even bother about the significance of conceptual experimentation. The alternative is not ignorance but unwisdom. In fact, the force of mundanity is such that radical reflection on it is, if not a rarity, a rather scarce commodity. In these terms, anguish may be understood as the threat of placing in fundamental question everything which assures *our* placement in the world. The force against philosophy can be measured by two components: first, the protection of common sense against "outside" invasion; second, the insulation of common sense against "inside" erosion. If fundamental doubt is understood as a danger coming from what is not the ego, then being on guard means refusing admittance to certain ideas which are deemed or suspected to be dangerous. But if the problem is within the individual, then being on guard can only mean a refusal to be placed in the situation of choice. In this event, danger is not overcome but avoided through an immanent strategy of self-denial. It is as if the ego were telling itself: "What seems to be the case is the case; to doubt that is to commit philosophical suicide." How does philosophy begin then? How is it possible for the individual to escape the circle of mundanity and gain access to an Archimedian point from which the mundane world can be examined as problematic? We are back to the meaning of "beginning" which was called the hardest step in philosophy. If the experiment has helped at all, some answer to what "beginning" means is now possible, at least in a brief and promissory way.

I propose to leave aside the question of "motives" for the choice of philosophy as radical suspension and instead explore the occasion of choice. Most simply, the choice is made when a fundamental feature of experience emerges from mundanity as strange and cannot be explained, resolved, or expunged in terms of the framework which contains it. It may also be the case that elements of the framework either contradict each other or are found to be irreconcilable with each other. Finally, the occasion on which the discovery of strangeness or contradiction occurs may be powerfully different from the individual's previous experience, or stand out in such a way that nothing short of a vast re-viewing of the self's reality would tolerate the emergent experience. The clearest examples of such reality-rending events are the simple yet fierce nouns of man's existence: birth, love, suffering, joy, redemption, death. The discovery of death in the world, for example, is commonplace enough to be considered part of mundane education, yet the implosion of death in the experience of a concrete individual may be an entirely different event, one so unlike all other knowledge of death as to be transforming. The experience of such an event, one which cannot be sent away by the avenues of common-sense traffic, may place the mundane itself in relief, give a perspective to the taken-for-grantedness of daily life. The exact "how" of such a happening is not at issue here; the "what" of the occurrence alone is at issue. Nor is there any claim to universality. The experience of death, far from being an existential upheaval, may in fact be taken by some individuals as part of the normal course of affairs—sad, perhaps, and upsetting, but something "one will get over in time." That phrase is a stark reminder that a decisive feature of mundanity is its incorporation of death as a typified event. Whether it is death or love, such typicality is the mortar of sociality, the sustaining bond of the refusal to admit philosophy into the company of common sense. The individual who does philosophize in serious terms is the one who breaks through mundanity to the paradoxical recognition that radical reflection is one of the possibilities of the mundane world.

It might be argued, of course, that there are much simpler explanations for why the individual philosophizes: that experience no less than science is cumulative in character and includes in any present what has gone before in the development of man—that the individual inherits the insight of his tradition. The nongenetic approach I have adopted precludes such appeals, of course, but there are reasons other than those of method for taking a different tack. Most importantly, I would urge that philosophy, like experience, is not an evolutional or "additive" phenomenon if we consider the becoming of the person. Each of us can profit from advice, from the tips and warnings of those who have "been through it before," only within narrow limits. Although it may be true that there are overarching patterns of problems which confront almost all individuals in similar fashion, the career of the concrete person is embedded in a "once-given" reality which makes each choice an original event, a world-creating occurrence. Some of the reasons for this have already been indicated, by implication, in the discussion of the structure of the Here and the Now of consciousness centered in the corporeality of the ego. All egos have Here-and-Now placement and are embodied in the world, but each ego defines its situation according to its present location; that present, in turn, is linked uniquely to the temporal dimensions of that ego's history. I am Here at this moment, but I was There, a There which was at that earlier time a Here for me. Furthermore, my body is the unique instrument through which I experience my insertion in the world and know its past design and efficacy. My body has its interior history, which I have lived through in my becoming, an evolutionary intimacy which is sedimented in my present life. Thus, the ego participates in the universal possibilities of having a world, but it defines those possibilities through its own temporality. Neither the history of philosophy nor the history of Man can provide comprehension of any moment of choice or interpretation in the life of the individual in a sense analogous to the cumulative development of a science such as physics or a discipline such as mathematics. The young physicist or mathematician can, in a very direct way, find out the status of knowledge in his profession. He can start with what's known or what has been demonstrated. Whatever revolutions of thought may develop in his field, the status of what is known with certainty or what is accepted as having a high degree of probability is available through the major treatises and the professional activity in the field. Philosophy is profoundly disanalogous because the philosopher is a beginner; he must go through, live through, the experiential world which includes him at the same time that it disturbs him. The philosopher's "materials" are inseparable from his own existence; he is his own subject matter.

If we have succeeded in locating the ego, we are still at some distance from the self. There are, in fact, a number of related terms which will have to be clarified in the course of the discussion: not only "ego" and "self," but "person" as well. Our initial experiment is done with, but we are now faced with the problem of tracing out the development of the individual from the ego discovered through phenomenological suspension to the socially and culturally weighted individual who acts in the space and time of history. Let us call the historicized ego the self. It is the ego which has a concrete biography, a continuous experience, and a specific orientation toward the future in terms of projects and dispositions. The self is the ego clothed with the garments of society.

In examining the self we leave behind the strictures of our experiment and turn to some of its consequences. To begin with, the self has a twofold aspect: it is at once the unified history of its past performances and the agency which gives valence to immediate action. In one direction, then, the self is continuous, memorially directed, and indexed with clues and keys to past action; in another direction, it is the force which moves action at any given time. On the one side: the organized accumulation of what happened to the individual; on the other: the present moment which may either call some aspect of the past into question or ignore it. In common-sense terms, the two aspects of the self are known under other labels: the traditional and the impulsive. The stability, continuity, and general reliability of the individual presuppose traditional action and a seasoned performer, whereas at each moment of experience, action can also be given a new and perhaps different interpretation. The solidity of tradition is paired with the spontaneity of decision. The two factors are basic components of the self which have been termed the "me" and the "I." Their dialectical interplay helps to constitute the self as a social structure.

The Me represents societal stability and continuity by providing the matrix for the self's action. Anything entertained by consciousness, all possibilities of action, and all perceptual acknowledgments are pieced into the province of the Me. Is an idea considered new or stale? It is in reference to the Me that the answer is decided. Is a projected action suitable or not for a particular purpose? The Me receives the inquiry. Beyond that, however, the Me is the reservoir of everything the individual has done. Whatever new action is contemplated appears over and against the backdrop of the Me. The I, on the other hand, is forever renewing its appearance; it turns up each time a choice is necessary. When the individual reflects on the choice, when he considers various options, it is the Me which handles the procedure, but in the moment of active performance, the *deed* is sprung by the I. Thus, the Me is the object, but the I is the subject of all action. The time-involvement of both polarities of the self sustains this ambivalence, for the Me is past-dominated whereas the I is in the spontaneity of a present which announces the future. Rather than as separate regions, however, the polarities of the Me and the I must be understood as functional aspects of the self. To speak, as we have, of their dialectical relationship is to recognize that the integrity of the self is sustained in dynamic fashion by its temporal development. This means that the terms "Me" and "I" are merely conveniences for a complex development in which each "I" of a present becomes incorporated into the "Me" of a later state of the self. If the Me is the reservoir of the past, it includes the spontaneities of former moments of action which have been fulfilled in action and are now remembered events. In these terms, spontaneity is destined to a middle age of stability if not respectability.

The I, then, is continually absorbed in the Me of a later phase of the self's career. Yet the way in which that absorption occurs is defined by the spontaneity of the I which undergirds each new action. If the Me has the ring of familiarity about it, the I smacks of the Bohemian; its essence is a freedom which societal stasis requires. The Establishment of social structure presupposes an elusive agent if only to be recognized and heeded. The Me is the source, then, of what is typical and habitual in experience; the I, of what is innovative and audacious. With this we come to a very large dimension of the self: its involvement in the types and typifications of mundane reality. One way of understanding the Me is to see it as a vast container of patterns of action, largely evident in common-sense experience, which are known as formulas or recipes for practical affairs, as typical techniques for handling whatever problems turn up in the course of daily life. There are typical ways of dealing with the demands of personal as well as public life: ways of assessing, gauging, interpreting, predicting, and orienting oneself toward the problematic elements in mundane existence. Well-being and illness, normalcy and emergency, reassurance and threat, renewal and innovation are all treated in typified form. There are even typical ways of handling the utterly unexpected and atypical. From childhood to death, the individual is embedded in schemas of action through which he is able both to translate and respond to the world.

Thus, the student who goes off to college for his freshman year enters a world defined by his academic work, his teachers, his contemporaries, and the particular milieu of the campus. Whatever advice or recommendations, however detailed, have been given to him by parents, high-school teachers, advisers, or friends, it is evident that no amount of preparation will give him the concrete reality of his new situation in anything but rather general terms, in loose outline. Nevertheless, he is able to organize his life and get on with the business at hand. He has never met a particular professor before, but he knows, in a general way, how to act with respect to him, how to arrange a meeting during office hours, how to prepare his course work for him. To be sure, he has done similar things before in his secondary- and even elementary-school experience, but to consider those is simply to push the example back to an earlier phase of life. At the college level, the student is able to organize his social life, join organizations, attend cultural and sports events, take part in meetings or demonstrations, and share in the public character of what is happening on the campus. Moreover, he has some knowledge of individuals and groups related to college life, groups which he has never met and may, in his undergraduate career, never meet: administrators, members of the board of regents, alumni. To each of these rather distant forces, the student takes up attitudes and may involve himself in consequential positions, urging pressure or trying to persuade or attempting to influence decisions and policies. Within his status, he knows that there are expectancies, responsibilities, and powers which he shares in quite uneven ways with a host of relatively anonymous or distant factors and factions. Certain lines are open to administrators which are, in principle, closed to students. The latter have prerogatives which the faculty could hardly employ. In all, action in the world of the college is open to the student in ways which are available to all other students on the campus—or at least to all members of the freshman class—insofar as they are actors on the social scene performing in routine ways. The "general" and the "routine" modes of behavior are, in fact, nothing but types of action; they are the typifications through which the self is inserted in the world and gears into its ongoing development. To utilize such typifications

—and there is little choice in the matter—is to respond to a situation in terms of the Me, which bears the inventory of types available to the student. Paradoxically, even in the midst of dramatic and agonized insurrection, the rebel acts in accordance with the typification he has of how rebellion is to be effected, how academic war is to be waged. In the fall of 1964—a time of troubles—the University of California went through a student rebellion whose tremors of disturbance have continued to be picked up elsewhere on academic seismographs. For the rebel, we might say, the decisiveness of action was the emergence and forcefulness of the I over and against the Me. Yet, remembering or looking back on those days, glancing at photographs of the events which took place, the student who witnessed or participated in the Berkeley rebellion necessarily perceives those days and himself as a Me which has internalized the panorama of what occurred. The photographs are frozen blocks of raw and passionate acts. The figures and faces caught by the camera are now, after the action, I's which have been engorged by Me's. In short, the vivacity and uniqueness of those days as they were felt and experienced by the participants themselves have suffered the typification of time and returned to the cycle of historical development which inevitably translates spontaneity into stasis.

The self, then, lives in a social reality defined through a complex of types, constructions of typical elements and aspects of possible action. The stockpiling of such types starts in childhood and continues throughout the life of the individual. The integral action of the Me and the I aspects of the self are means through which both typicality and the *fiat* of action are achieved. However, they are neither the sole means nor the total content of the functioning self. There are two other features of the self's performance which give it the mobility necessary to understand the diversity of the individual's activity. Let us call them reflection and role. It is perhaps the definitive feature of consciousness that it is capable of reflection, and within that generic attribute it is a decisive fact that consciousness is able to reflect on itself, to take its own activity as an object of examination. Within the stance of common-sense behavior, self-reflection most often takes the form of thinking-about one's problems and considering various ways of coming to terms with them. The more radical form of self-reflection, however, involves something common sense seldom engages in: seizing the Me in its structural aspect, taking it *as* a facet of the activity of the self. If such self-reflection is uncommon as a philosophical procedure, it does occur in a different form, at a less rarefied level, in the form of self-typification. If the present I grasps itself as a Me, it is as a particularized type or through a specific construction that the Me is known. Not the Me as a vast resource but the Me of this moment, in this particular situation, at this juncture of my life is presented in the act of self-reflection. The Me articulates itself through roles, and with the notion of role we come to a critical point in the discussion as well as in the journey we have undertaken. The concept of role is familiarly known in mundane experience through the model of theatrical performance. The actor on stage plays a role, he acts as though he were someone else, and he presents himself to the audience as the character in the play. Taking a role in this sense means not only learning the lines and pieces of stage business necessary to build the role, but also creating the character, making the lines and the action live in the aesthetic reality of the drama. The dramaturgical model for role-playing is of central importance to the entire theory of social role and has vital implications for role-taking as a mundane reality, but it is only a part of the total machinery of role structure. It might be prudent to turn to the nature of role not in the context of the theatre, but as it is found initially in the sphere of mundane existence, within the compass of daily life. Our discussion, furthermore, will at this stage be limited to role as it can be understood and appreciated from the vantage point of the self, the individual rather than the group. At this stage in our development, we are restricted to the egological standpoint, but it is precisely from that standpoint that the roots of social role can be ascertained. Let us begin, then, with role and role-taking within the reality of the taken-for-granted world of daily life. There role first manifests itself in terms of the schemata of typified perception and interpretation, through the constructs of the experiential world. Not only are the formulas and recipes of action included in such constructions, but perceptual experience itself is a subtle part of the typified world. Imagine:

I have fallen seriously ill, suffering from nausea, violent headaches, and severe stomach pains. After weeks of trying drugstore remedies, home-fashioned diets, self-prescribed rest, and efforts to relieve the symptoms by a change of place and attitude, I decide to see a doctor. Perhaps I should have visited a physician earlier but I have a dread of doctors, a fear of hospitals, a hostility to nurses, technicians, and orderlies. I am not what can be called a "good patient." Each time I get involved in medical circles I become enraged by the arrogance and ignorance of the doctors; in turn, I enrage them by my medical disobedience, my campaign of noncooperation, and what I know shows itself—despite, believe me, my best and honest efforts to be considerate and responsive—as repugnance and condescension. Yes, condescension! I know they are doing their best, that their professional lives are difficult (partly because of people like me), that they are harried by impossible schedules and must work under fantastic pressure. I *want* to be cooperative but I end up in scenes of abuse, recrimination, and name-calling (I'm ashamed of it, but I must admit that at the most delicate moments in the course of being examined, I have insulted specialists to their faces). So when I'm sick, I wait. If the pathology is urgent I call for an appointment at the last minute. As soon as I arrive at the doctor's office I'm ready to go home. The truth of the matter is that doctors are badly educated (I have yet to find one that understands Kant) and confuse themselves with God. Can I help it that as soon as they ask to see my tongue I clamp my jaws tight, refusing to let go of the spatula? I admit to being a difficult patient and I know that they have names for people like me. In any event, I'm sick again, and now I'm off to the doctor's.

"Mr. Grisney!" the nurse calls, poised for me to follow her. That ruse has been tried before, and I'm on to it. After waiting an hour and twenty-five minutes, I'm supposed to follow meekly and bless the doctor for his service to mankind. What gall! You could die in their waiting rooms, and the janitor, after closing time, would clean up around your feet. Let the others take it!

"*Doctor* Grisney," I say and say loudly, "Doctor, not Mister!"

"I'm sorry," the nurse replies, "I didn't know you were a medical man."

"Precisely! That's it! You didn't know. Well, I'm not a medical man. Do you know what the word 'doctor' means in Latin? Do you know that in England surgeons are proud to be called Mister? Am I to apologize, then, for being a Doctor of Philosophy? Should I return my diploma or keep it a secret?"

Well, it's that sort of thing that tends to get me off on the wrong foot. By the time I see the doctor they're all poisoned against me and anxious to get me out of the office as quickly as possible. They say I upset the other patients. Upset them! If they grew grass on the waiting-room floor those sheep would graze. But what's the use of belligerence and where does it get you? In the end I tighten up and avoid all communication. The doctor can't get a word out of me. He has to repeat the same question three or four times and is even forced to look at me. I reply in a growly whisper, clenching my breath or merely nodding instead of speaking. I'm nobody's medical fool and I'm a sick man. . . .

It is not necessary to repeat the story in the language of role theory. If the illustration is successful, it brings into view the host of types as well as self-typifications which constitute much of the ground-pattern of common sense. Each of us knows in more or less typical terms what it is to be in the role of the patient, what forms of behavior are typically expected of adult patients, how nurses and doctors are to be treated, what one should and should not do in waiting and examination rooms. What is a bit more subtle, perhaps, is the self-typification of my invalided self. Not only am I aware of myself as patient, but I have a rather complex image of the way in which that image appears to others. There is no preciousness in suggesting, furthermore, that the hero of the illustration is the master of two correlated constructions: his self-typification as patient and his awareness that role-repudiation lands him squarely back in the camp of typification. The decisive feature of the role-playing involved here is its fictivized character, its essential capacity to project a style as well as a model of deportment to meet generally expected and recognized demands which confront "the patient." Although the illustration includes fellow-men, it is the self which interprets their actions and, just as importantly, anticipates their actions in typified terms. From the vast storehouse of schemata for interpreting experience and acting in the world, the self mechanically or impishly chooses those patterns which will define its situation and its placement in the social world. The center of choice is the self, which we have approached in egological terms.

Now it is necessary to realize that the dominant phase of the self's action resides in the span of action in which the individual expresses the meaning of his own act. From the egological standpoint, then, typification is rooted in self-typification: the individual's interpretation of his role is grounded in his understanding of himself. The prime level of typification is that of the self constructing for itself the shape of the world it then finds and acts in. The conclusion this line of analysis demands is that the self is constituted through the agency of role-taking, the original form of which is the act of reflection in which the self becomes an object for its own inspection. On this account role and reflection are bound to each other and may prove to be ways of illuminating each other.

Thus far we have used and considered the terms "ego," "self," and "individual" without much sense of the existential force of the identity of the agent. Our experiment may have succeeded in locating the phenomenological ground of the ego: its startling loneliness. The emphasis on the phenomenological genesis of the self should not lead to the conclusion that subjectivity as an existential theme is lacking and must somehow be "added" later in the discussion. The loneliness of the self is a fundamental dimension of the aloneness of the ego, but it is not yet possible to see the problem clearly because "loneliness" is commonly understood as a mood or feeling which envelops or descends on the individual. The existential problem, however, arises at a different level and concerns a qualitatively separate aspect of the self. Instead of defining loneliness as a mood, it would be more appropriate to suggest that moods are ways in which the self discovers itself in the world and defines its way of being there. This reversal of approach is quite consonant with the repudiation of the interior-exterior model of the self, for there is no "inside" of the ego for an enveloping force to surround. Loneliness is prior to moods and antecedent to dispositions. In one sense it is also prior to the world of fellow-men, the absence or distance of Others. We may understand the loneliness of the ego as its immersion in the anonymous and purely typical stream of perceptual life in which neither the *person* nor the alter ego has yet emerged as a true identity. Once again, please remember that there is no denial here of an historical and intersubjective world; the account offered moves at the structural level, seeking to disclose the *a priori* conditions necessary for the possibility of experience. In these terms, the alone ego suffers the loneliness of deprivation of the sociality it has not yet achieved. We are speaking of an anticipatory lack. We are speaking also of a new concept, that of the *person*.

The ego and the self are universals in the biography of the individual. Even the I aspect of the self, with all its spontaneity and freshness, is a formal feature of the functioning self. In a way, the entire discussion of self so far has operated free of any specifying individuation by means of which what is unique or simply *alive* in the character of some actual fellow-man—*you*, for example—can be expressed. We are, to be sure, selves; but we are also distinct selves. The biographical actualization of the self is the *person*. Accordingly, persons are selves whose identities have achieved expression. It would be misleading to think of the person either as somehow encapsulated in the self or as developed by the self in its interaction with its surrounding social world. The person is not an "essence" precontained in the self, nor is the self a blank slate as far as identity and character are concerned. If we drop the language of both "original attributes" and "conditioning by environment," we may begin to speak in phenomenological terms.

Without a variety of physiological and psychological mechanisms functioning properly, the individual would be stunted and incapacitated; yet such necessary conditions should not be confused with the operation of the self approached from the standpoint of consciousness. Without a proper supply of oxygen, the human brain would cease to function in a very short time. However, it would be a hideous mistake to assert that the validity of logic or mathematics depends on the logician's or mathematician's oxygen supply. In a sense, the brain has nothing to do with consciousness. Odd as it may appear, I am suggesting that the emergence of the person is independent of the causal laws which govern the empirical self. Some of the implications of this conception of the person may now be seen.

Within the egological sphere, the concept of the person can be expressed, but the emergence of the person can be understood only in anticipatory fashion. The reasons for this will become clear as we go along. The pure ego which grounds the self is concerned only with the typified aspects of experience, with types of events or phenomena in general. What is *mine* in these terms is indeed bound to my Here and Now and articulated within the stream of inner time, but it remains subject-bound without that subject's springing into biographical specificity. The question is whether what is *mine* differs significantly from what is yours, apart from the obvious disparity of the pronouns. I suggest that the initial condition of the self is such that no difference is discernible and that the typicality of "sameness" is appropriated by the ego. In fact, the self experiences its world, including fellow-men, as it constructs its self-typification; it discovers the world through the same typifications by means of which its own experience of the world is constituted. Looked at in this way, the medium of consciousness through which the self organizes its experiential world is isomorphic with what might be called "consciousness in general," that is, consciousness comprehended by way of the typifications of a self-typifying ego. Where, then, is identity found? Where is the person? The situation of the ego is one in which the sheer quality of typification is given as the texture of immediacy, *given* in the sense of being presented to consciousness. The loneliness of the ego may now be understood as the realization that within the terrain of consciousness the self is limited to the abstractive world created by typification. The concrete

realization is that types are the conveniences of *anyone*. The power of typification is precisely its capacity to create anonymous reality. Within such
anonymity, the self finds its loneliness, paradoxically, as the isolation of
uniformity. The conclusion is strange: the loneliness of the ego is its synony-
mity with the typified world, the loneliness of complete anonymity. The
existential moment in which self-recognition occurs, over and against the
typified world, is the point at which the person is born.

As we noted earlier, a variety of situations in the life of the individual
may provide the occasion for self-recognition: the immediacies of friendship
and love or the experience of death. Whatever the occasion, however, it is
the loneliness of the ego which is presented and penetrated in existential
self-awareness. That typicality may point back to the individual in a way
which is *not* synonymous with selves in general, that being at the Here-and-
Now center of the world may *not* be experienced in the same fashion by
every individual, that the very stance of man in the world as the being who
organizes and sustains coherent experience may *not* be the intersubjective
unity it appears to be—the very possibility of these acknowledgments may
search out the loneliness of the ego in a new and violent way and reveal it to
itself as being a determinate structure. The moment of such self-revelation
is forceful enough to disassemble the organization of the ego's experience and
pierce its insularity. We are speaking, of course, of a transformation of the ego
from within its unity. In fact, such a transformation is a possibility of the ego,
just as philosophy is a possibility of the taken-for-granted world of common
sense from which we started this long ascent. And the reference to mundane
experience provides a further clue to the nature of existential self-recognition,
for both the wonder which makes the philosopher possible in the midst of
mundane existence and the grasping of the typified world *as* typified by the
ego are wrenching experiences for which the individual is solely responsible.
The individual who recognizes himself as both alone and lonely within a
typified reality is already a person. The transformation occurs in the experiential moment when type gives way to the emerging identity of concrete
existence. That moment, however, transcends the bounds of the egological
standpoint or at least involves a transegological reference which carries decisive importance for the development of the individual. Self-recognition
implies Other-recognition. The egological gives way to the social.

From the beginning, we realized that it is within our shared world that
the philosopher sets about questioning the meaning of "our" and "shared"
and "world." Adopting the phenomenological standpoint has meant acknowledging rather than denying the historical, cultural, and scientific horizons
of mundane existence. Language itself testifies to the public dimension of
private experience. At the same time, it is of crucial importance to understand
that respecting intersubjectivity is not equivalent to analyzing it, that

appreciating the communal character of everyday life is far from comprehending the structural conditions which make sociality possible—in short,
that insisting on what we all know as familiar and certain may be the quickest
way to ignore both the philosophical grounds of experience and the very
phenomena which form the substance of our world. The turn to the egological
sphere, then, is necessary for any analysis of man's mundane experience
which seeks to trace out the foundations of his conceptual and emotive career
as a being in reality. The journey we have commenced is committed to
uncovering the egological basis for the entire range of human achievement.
Nevertheless, it is clear from the first stage of our development that within
the egological sphere it is possible to find the clues to the rest of mundane
experience, including, most powerfully of all, the reality of fellow-men. If the
existential discovery of the person is the threshold to the social world, it is
because the consciousness-of Others is given within its remarkable confines.
As we will see, by virtue of the typifications of role-construction, the self is
able to transcend its solitude and gain the company of other human beings.
It is perhaps the happy irony of a typifying consciousness that the illumination of its own dynamic is a condition for the achievement of identity.

chapter
two

other
selves

There is an old exercise in logic textbooks which goes like this: "You like to walk alone; I like to walk alone; so why don't we walk alone together?" For something as private as solitude, there appears to be an enormous communality associated with the concept of aloneness: if it cannot be "shared" it is at least available to everyone to be dispensed in his own terms. Indeed, common sense has no difficulty in accommodating itself to the remarkable puzzle of intersubjectivity, for mundane existence is at once energetically shared and individually assimilated. The puzzle is "remarkable" in common-sense terms only by virtue of its unproblematicity, its epistemological domestication. It becomes necessary, then, to explain the philosophical problem of other selves. The problem presents itself, of course, from the very egological standpoint taken from the outset of this essay. In first-person terms, the question is, "How can I have knowledge of fellow-men?" Some immediate but misleading answers have to be set aside quickly. First, undoubtedly I am aware of Others as parts of my stream of perceptual experience. The Other appears to me as there, as having determinate physical characteristics, and as behaving in certain ways. Second, within the taken-for-granted terms of mundane reality I do not seriously doubt the existence of fellow-men; I do not ordinarily entertain the idea that they might be illusions or fictions. Finally, in the course of my everyday experience, I act on the unproved and largely unexamined conviction that I share the world with fellow-men and that they take my existence and efficacy for granted in the same way I do theirs. So far, then, there is nothing problematic about the Other. The philosophical issue arises when I try to clarify the meaning of intersubjectivity, when I concentrate on what *knowledge* of fellow-men consists of and how that knowledge is gained and warranted. That I have knowledge of Others is not contested; the nature of that knowledge together with the very possibility of there being knowledge of Others *is* a matter of profound conjecture. Whatever else may be secure from the prying glance of the philosopher, it is safe to say that the problem of other selves has traditionally been subjected to the most searching inquiry with some of the least satisfactory results. Some of the reasons for the disproportion between effort and conquest will be seen as we proceed.

Starting with the individual rather than with the social order places the self in what has been called the "egocentric predicament." Within the immediacy of the self's perceptual experience, there is appreciation of sensations and ideas of the surrounding world which appear to be limited to the subject for whom there is experience—the individual. The colors, noises, tastes, odors, touch-sensations, as well as kinesthetic experience are all aspects of the individual's sensory apprehension, as are, it would also seem, the multitude of ideas, concepts, interpretations, and other constructions of cognition. But if the perceptual experience of the self includes the awareness it has of the rest of the world, how does the individual ever manage to go beyond his own subjectivity, how does he break out of the circle of his own consciousness? The "egocentric predicament" is nothing less than the question of whether the self is sealed off in such a way as to allow only self-knowledge. If this were in fact so, it would not be necessary to deny existence to Others, but it would mean that each individual would be an island cut off from every other island of consciousness—a metaphysics without a mainland! If each of us shares such a predicament, it might seem unnecessary to trouble ourselves with so common a complaint. Indeed, why should it be the subject for complaint at all? Suppose we grant the claim that each individual is in the egocentric predicament. What then? Since no suggestion has been made so far that mundane existence is unreal, what motive is there for trying to resolve the situation or transform it in some way? It would seem that there is an artificiality about a predicament which is universally shared and which appears to upset very few of its subjects. Here is a predicament with a very high boiling point. The central force of the problem of other selves still needs to be located and expressed. Only then will the meaning of the egocentric predicament be clarified.

For common-sense men in daily life, each individual is in touch or may come into relationship with his fellow-men. That is the birthright of mundane existence, an article of its bill of rights. This truth holds not only for me but for all men; it is true from the standpoint of the Other no less than from my own. Moreover, an essential part of the truth of intersubjectivity is the immanent thesis that the way in which it holds for the ego is identical with the way in which it holds for the alter ego. Once again, this is *our* world. Now the difficulty with this assumption is that it is far from clear. Within common sense, there is every reason to hold that the Other shares our world in the same way I do, but the meaning of sameness here is not to be found either in the claim or in the world of daily life in which it is made. If I examine the sphere of my own perceptual experience, I find elements which appear again and again in the same way. I assume that your experience is like mine, that you too have experience of elements which are the same. However, the fact that I know what "same" is in my experience and you in yours does not establish that *we* experience the world in the same manner. In order to show that sameness of intersubjectivity it would be necessary to account for the very structure which is here taken as the starting point for the claim to communality: intersubjectivity. The circle is a curious one. If the trick is to clarify the meaning of a shared, *same* world, it is not possible to begin the clarification by positing the identity of your and my individual experience. Thus, the *egocentricity* of the predicament is understood properly when it is evident that the self has access only to the *claim* or the assumption of intersubjective sameness but has no direct grasp of what is presumed to be shared by the Other. Egocentricity is a *predicament* when taken-for-granted mundane activity either gives way to reflexive analysis or, in certain situations, demands such analysis. It is important to realize that the predicament in question here is not the feeling of tension or upset which might be thought to derive from the individual's fear that he is isolated or that the rest of the world may not be as he thinks it is. Rather, the predicament is a distinctively philosophical impasse, one, however, which has serious consequences for not only our knowledge but our interpretation of experience.

The difficulty of understanding how "sameness" is intersubjectively constituted reverberates in a variety of other issues in our experience in the mundane world. In fact, there is hardly a serious aspect of daily life which does not bear the weight of the commitment common sense makes to the intersubjective reality of its field of action. For the moment, the question of "sameness" is enough to launch us into the consideration of the general problem of other selves. It helps as well to bring into focus some of the major philosophical stances which have been taken with respect to the problem of other selves. In disparate and uneven ways, I will outline five approaches to intersubjectivity, including positions which in some ways deny the problem of other selves, absorb it, claim to solve it, offer an alternative to a proof, or, finally, reapproach the entire question of the self by way of social role.

Denial. One way of understanding the egocentric predicament is that of solipsism, the view that only the self is real. By the most radical conceptual upheaval, the position of the solipsist manages to turn the predicament into a fortress of certitude (though what need there might be for a battlement is unclear in solipsistic terms). If the sole reality is the self, then clearly it is necessary to explain other selves as facets of the solipsist's experience. On the surface, this procedure leads to difficulties only if the independent reality of the alter ego is affirmed, along with the rest of the world, of course. To the fervent claim that mundane experience (let alone historical and physical reality) is intersubjectively experienced by a plurality of selves each of which has its own reality, the solipsist replies that it is only through the self—himself—that this can even be asserted. The charge that solipsism denies an obvious truth and cannot be taken seriously is met with the very forceful rejoinder that the "obvious" is hardly a satisfactory criterion of truth and that "to be taken seriously" is always the result of the individual's judgment of some state of affairs. "I can't take him (or it) seriously" is a sign of the hauteur of the judger, never the report of the judged. It works both ways, however, and the dismissed offender always has available the countercharge: "He doesn't understand me (or it)." In the philosopher's argot, "He's confused" means to the speaker, "He doesn't understand the issues"; to the accused it means, "He disagrees with me (though I'm right and he's wrong)." None of these thrusts and parries upsets the solipsist, who maintains with the even tone born of long experience with the philosophically underprivileged: "Charge and countercharge are nothing but presentations to consciousness, givens to the experiencing self, and, ultimately, grist for the solipsistic mill." Brilliantly consistent as this position is, its very insularity points to its cardinal limitation: solipsism is essentially a *denying* philosophy. Even its affirmations prove to be negations, for it begins with a deprivation of mundane existence and ends with the *hubris* inevitable to any thinker who denies the works of Others under the guise of original authorship. The one commandment the solipsist cannot follow without self-contradiction is: Honor thy father and mother. If it is true that the solipsist has no trouble handling the problem of other selves, it is because solipsism defines itself through a denial of sociality.

2   Absorption.   The reverse of solipsism is a position which holds that the fundamental reality is social relationship, men with fellow-men, individuals who are, to begin with, part of an intersubjective world. I don't know of an antonym for "solipsism"; perhaps a neologism such as "socism" is needed ("socialism" being no longer a candidate). In any case, with or without a suitable label, the philosophical position at issue is easily described. It maintains that human reality is essentially intersubjective, that men are part of an interconnected network of relationships, and that knowledge of other selves is built into this social web. Thus, there is no problem of how one individual comes to know another. Knowledge of fellow-men is possible because knowledge

is socially grounded; its very meaning lies in the fact that ego and alter
ego are aware of each other and respond to each other in their simple function
as human beings. To be human, on this account, is to be *social*. There are,
to be sure, different philosophical systems of explanation for the grounding
of this position. Some hold to a metaphysics of the social which is ultimately
contained in God; others see the tensions, splits, and separations of individuals in the world as merely temporary moments of divorce from a transcendent harmony or as dialectical features of an historical development which
holds together competing and even contradictory elements of social structure.
Whatever the metaphysics, the result is a philosophy of man as an intersubjective creature, as a being for whom there is no *problem* of knowledge of
other selves because such knowledge is in his possession as soon as he enters
the social world. If the solipsist denies that bridges to Others are necessary
because Others are taken as aspects of the self, the "socist" argues that such
bridges are unnecessary because there is no separation between selves to be
bridged, or, to change the image, if we insist on thinking of the social corpus
as divided, all parts are linked by connective tissue and united by a single
nervous system. Such a view does not save socism from criticism. Like all
"built-in" arguments, it avoids stress and complication at the cost of assuring
its principles by decreeing a world cut to their pattern. The solipsist tele-
scopes the "we" into the "I"; the socist flushes a covey of "I's" from the
"we." For neither is there a battle of pronouns.

3 Solution. Perhaps the most radical effort to come to terms with the
philosophical problem of other selves requires a commitment to the epistemological questionability of both the self and the Other as they are located in
mundane existence. The self cannot be taken for granted as an operative
being in the world nor can the alter ego be accepted at surface value as one
with whom the self is in communication. Instead, both polarities must be
subjected to fundamental doubt. The phenomenological procedure of suspension offers a way of carrying out that doubt in systematic fashion and in a
form which does not fall into the solipsistic trap of swallowing the Other down
an infinitely expandable gullet or join the "socistic" reunion of a society
whose roster includes everyone. The solution of the problem of other selves
demands a rigorous proof. Here is one version of such a demonstration in
very simple terms: Going back to the experiment made at the beginning of
this book, the reader is asked once again to place in abeyance his believing in
the world as an intersubjectively lived and validated reality. In egological
terms, I (the reader must speak for himself) locate my believing-in as a consciousness-of Others, a consciousness which seizes the Other as a "someone"
like me. In becoming aware of my body as a corporeality, I also become
aware of the body of the Other as being *like mine*, that is, as pointing toward a

stream of consciousness unified in temporality. Rather than suggesting that the experience of the body of the Other gives evidence on the basis of which an induction or claim can be made about the similarity of the Other to me, the phenomenologist argues that, within the suspension, the Other is *presented* as an incarnate being, a body integrally related to a mind. Here we have a case of analogical experiencing rather than the more familiar reasoning by analogy. But the Other as presented is not some reflection of myself; the other self is genuinely Other and not a duplication. This shows itself in the fact that the Other is *There*, whereas I am *Here*. Furthermore, the Other is disclosed to me as being There for my Here but also as being the center of *his* sphere of awareness. In other terms, There and Here are reciprocal concepts: what is There for the ego is Here for its alter. The exciting point for the phenomenologist is that the elucidation of the presentation of the alter ego makes it possible to understand the elements which make intersubjectivity possible; and, at the same time, the procedure of phenomenological suspension makes the elucidation possible in terms of consciousness disclosed in but not limited in validity to the egological sphere. Once again, the position is not without some substantial difficulties: first, even if the phenomenological analysis of intersubjectivity clarifies the way in which knowledge of the alter ego is constituted, it is doubtful whether the existence of the alter ego is thereby proved; second, the location of the ground of intersubjectivity in pure consciousness involves a "transcendental ego" which raises at least as many questions as it resolves; third, though the alter ego may be seized directly in the phenomenological suspension, it is not as certain that the way in which the ego grasps its perceptual reality is identical with the way in which the alter ego grasps its reality, for there is a qualitative distance between direct presentation and hypothesizing. But if the phenomenologist's effort to demonstrate how knowledge of other selves is possible is not definitive, the large question which follows is whether a proof is possible at all or whether the attempt to explore intersubjectivity by way of a proof is not mistaken in principle.

4   Manifestation.   Without trying to prejudge the issue, we might reverse the line of analysis which searches for a proof of intersubjectivity and ask instead whether the ego's knowledge of and relation to his alter is not *experienced* rather than known. It may be time for another example:

I pride myself on having social finesse. There is no reason to be hesitant or indulge in false modesty. Certain very objective indicators point unequivocally to the fact that I do well on the social scene : I am not only a constant party-goer but have more invitations than I can accept, and whether or not I repay these promptly I am still in demand. Vanity aside, the reasons are easily explained. To begin with, I enjoy people ; it's no effort for me to join a group, no strain to be with strangers. Besides, I work hard at being a guest. Not only do I circulate at gatherings, I make every effort to divide my time among all sorts and at all echelons: women as well as men, the elderly no less than the youthful, the great and the meek, and so on. After all, I'm interested in everyone and in everything. The longer I live the more I realize that there are no boring people; it's all a matter of hitting the right note at the proper time in the appropriate situation.

I insist: there are no bores, only inept conversationalists. Given any natural talent at all, a dunce can be turned into a charmer under the proper tutelage. Were I not otherwise engaged, I would start a school for sociability. The main thing is consideration. Just that! If the person next to you is shy, take the initiative. If your neighbor at the cocktail hour is expansive, take a back seat to his eloquence. Compete only when a challenge will bring out the best in everybody. Above all, give your complete attention to the person you are with. Avoid the hovering eye, the appearance of being just about to fly off, or the pretense of being *too* interested in your interlocutor. Balance, reasonability, patience, a dash of old-fashioned decency and, as I say, *consideration*: there's the perfect human cocktail!

Still, finesse does not preclude discrimination. To be utterly frank, I have my preferences and reservations when it comes to people. Enjoy them? Of course. But as you would wine. Champagne is not for frankfurters, and it would be equally criminal to mix the wrong people. Notice that I don't say mix *with* but mix. That is, there are occasions when it is necessary and even appropriate to spend some time with those with whom one could have no real connection, but it is hardly a social commandment to cultivate such relationships. In the end, true consideration means taking the trouble to arrange your social life so as to avoid the unpleasantness which inevitably comes from indiscriminate socializing, unpleasantness most intensely felt by those who know they are out of place. It all comes down to the Golden Rule: treat your neighbor as you would yourself. I wish to associate with those who are at home with someone of my background and position. Accordingly, I assume the same principle to hold good for those with backgrounds alien to mine. Like tends to cluster with like. Of course, I'm far from alone in this view, and, as I say, I lead a rich social life. My friends insist it's a gift; I know better.

5 Role. In contradistinction to theories of the alter ego which either deny the problem of the Other or seek somehow to overcome it by means of some proof, the conception of social role accords a sovereign status to fellow-men but argues that the Other is both known and experienced by the self through role itself; that is, the self comes into awareness of the Other by taking his role: assuming the standpoint of the Other, responding to an event as though one were viewing it from the vantage point of the alter ego. In these terms, the genesis of both the alter ego and the ego is seen in a unity of interaction in which structural priority is granted to neither element of the social order. Instead, becoming a self means taking the role of the Other. Concomitantly, awareness of the Other involves the discovery and formation of the self.

What does role consist of? Most simply, what is typically conceived. To say that in the Other I find someone like myself is to say that I can put myself in his place, see things in the same way he does, respond to events as he does. That the uniqueness of the Other's experience is *not* given to me, far from limiting the possibility of my taking his role, is the necessary condition for role-taking. Not uniqueness but typicality is the stuff of roles. Accordingly, it is possible to view the problem of other selves in essentially abstractive terms. The Other is given to me *as* and *through* a series of perspectival possibilities: my fellow-man is he who can perceive and respond to events, for whom an object can be placed in the categories of the useful, the beautiful, or the holy, for whom communication is an open medium which leads out to *his* fellow-men, including me. Such knowledge of the Other is gained by way of the situations in which I find myself taking his role. Clearly, "role" is an abbreviation for a constant plural. The Other's "role" is in fact many roles, and to say that the individual is a player of roles means that the structure of role is involved in the plethora of performances each individual rehearses as part of his routine of daily life. Understanding the Other as a manifold of role-perspectives both presents the Other's role-reality and illuminates my own. The act of recognition points two ways: in one direction my fellow-man appears as his possibilities; in the other it is I and my possibilities who manifests himself. The alter ego does not stand behind the perspectival matrix nor at its center like a spider in his web; rather, the Other presents himself as a nexus of role-possibilities conjoined with my own lines of action. Becoming aware of the Other is, then, becoming aware of my own points of access to the social order.

But in addition to grasping the Other *as* a set of perspectives, I also come to know him *through* role-perspectives. This might be understood, in highly condensed form, in the following way: it is by means of role-structure that a conception of the Other is formed. What I know of you is initially a function of the situation within which we are related: as strangers, as just having been introduced, as sharing an airport limousine, as new boys at school, or as attending our first meeting of the League for Scottish Separatism. You are role-defined by me as being anything from someone who also enjoys browsing in antiquarian bookstores to a comrade in a fervently held cause. At both these extremes, the Other is typified by the self through the role played by the defining self. In essence, it is because I am capable of playing the role of stranger that I can understand you as stranger. The typification which establishes the alter ego has a critically important function in constituting the ego. Thus, social role makes possible the presentation of fellow-men as role-structured and role-oriented and in relation to selves who are no less role-bound. The conjunction of self and Other in the dynamic of the role constitutes the union of sociality. Some of the problems of role will appear later; for the moment, it is enough to say that role is a way of avoiding at least some of the difficulties encountered in approaches to the problem of other selves which either presuppose intersubjectivity or negate it.

Approaches to the problem of other selves involve methodological conceptions of how communication is possible. Related to but distinct from the philosophical positions we have examined so far, there are at least four methodological types or avenues of understanding between men: dialogue, analogy, behavior, and interpretation. Each mode requires its own statement.

1 **Dialogue.** Including but much more than speech, "dialogue" stands for all elements of address and response between man and fellow-man. The paradigm situation involved here is that of the face-to-face relationship in which the individual shares a spatiotemporal community of meaning with his neighbor. Beyond the root of confrontation, however, lie many patterns of dialogue which involve communication at great distance (as in letter-writing) or by indirection (as in the creation of art works) or through thematic communal activities (such as performing together in chamber groups or in theatrical companies). Moreover, the fundamental face-to-face relationship is experienced in protological form in a vast range of communicatory awareness which antecedes speech (the responsive smile the infant gives its mother) and which accompanies all subsequent human expression. The phrase "face-to-face relationship" tends to narrow the focus of dialogue, as though it meant cranial proximity, a sequence of heads turned toward each other in minuet formation. We must think rather of individuals directly aware of each other through their sharing of a segment of the spatiotemporal world. In this sense, face-to-face may mean in reality "ear-to-ear" or "hand-to-hand" no less than "eye-to-eye."

Broadly taken, then, the face-to-face relationship may be said to undergird or provide a substrate for all other forms of communication, including speech. In its simplest (though by no means uncomplicated) aspect, the face-to-face relationship expresses itself in individuals speaking to each other. Greeting and countergreeting, question and answer, remark and reply are the primitive instruments through which dialogue is constructed. In the story of intersubjectivity, then, the beginning word announces the reality of the Other. Most simply, I know the Other because he speaks to me. And beyond that, I know the Other because I reply to him. Speech itself may be understood, in this context, as the means by which mundane existence recognizes the difference between ego and alter. Not the question but the possibility of questioning, not the response but the potential for response marks the grounding force of dialogue. At the same time, the privacy of the alter ego and the immediacy of the ego's own awareness, its instant accessibility, as it were, are immanently acknowledged in speech. To the philosophical puzzle of other selves, common sense might suggest: "I may not be able to offer some theoretical explanation of how I know about someone else, but at least I can speak to him. In that way I can find out something about him, how he is, what he thinks, his attitudes and opinions." Although this claim has the merit of forthrightness, it hardly succeeds in facing the issues. What

it does do, however, is to point to an unintended truth: the accessibility of the
Other is proved, for common-sense purposes, when I speak to him. It is not so
much the answer but the addressing of the question which is the clue to dialogue. If I know the Other because he speaks to me, it is no less true that he
speaks to me within a shared microcosm based on the possibility of address and
response. Even if I don't know the language the Other speaks, I have no difficulty in comprehending his recognition of me as a partner in the social world.

2   Analogy. Perhaps the most common argument for the way in which we
have knowledge of other selves is that the Other is *like* me; he acts in the same
way I do. Most simply, a given movement of the Other—his turning the page
of a book—is like mine because it is taken to signify essentially the same
thing to him as it does to me. Much of the realm of overt action is interpreted
in this way but the force of analogy is extended and directed toward those
responses in the Other which are not available to direct observation by me.
For years, the classical example for this has been the Other's aching tooth.
With all of philosophy's turns and changes, whatever fortunes variant schools
and movements have met, in prosperous or desperate times, that toothache
has always been raging, a constant torment in the otherwise variable corpus
of philosophy.

It is, of course, the outward signs that indicate the Other's pain: his
moaning, jaw-clasping, and occasional cries indicate "toothache" to me
because I have gone through the same sort of thing when my tooth ached,
and just as the side of my face swelled up so now the Other's face is swollen.
The signs themselves do not give me either the reality the Other suffers nor
proof of his distress; rather, it is an analogical experience which provides that
foundation necessary to the awareness of the Other. Nor should the conditions
or limits of analogy be narrowly construed. There are instances of the Other's
suffering when, strictly speaking, it would be impossible for me to have an
analogical counterpart to the experience of the Other: I cannot as a man experience the labor pains of a woman. To be sure, every male gynecologist
has detailed knowledge of the nature of those pains, yet he has not experienced
them personally. Are we to conclude that he has no analogical basis for appreciating their reality in the body of the Other? Obviously, there are other
forms of pain which may be similar. From the male's having once had
severe abdominal cramps he may at least approximate the *kind* of pain
involved in childbirth. We might say, then, that there are two versions of
the analogical mode: a strong and a weak form of experience, the first moving
from "same" to "same," the second from "similar" to "similar." The
possibility of the weaker case is contained in the stronger, for just as tooth-
aches and pain in childbirth vary from "mild" and "easy" to "severe" and
"difficult," so approximating experiences (one is tempted to call them

analogies of analogies, or analogies of the second degree) have a wide range
of intensity and verisimilitude. Analogical extremes may be further apart
than powerful approximations. And even very strong, analogically close
experiences may be weakened by the lapse of years between what is now
being undergone by the Other and the "same" thing I underwent 35 years
ago. "I know just how you feel," "I went through the same thing myself,"
may spring forcefully from the white heat of analogy or from the dank odor
of lapsed memory.

Perhaps the most interesting aspect of analogy, however, is what might
be called "extrapolative understanding," the sympathetic grasp of the Other's
experience when even approximations are too weak to give any real sense of
what is at issue. Here the force of analogical experience itself drives the individual forward from the fringes or connotative possibilities of the sources
of his experience toward a grasp of what lies beyond them. An analogical
leap results: the swift seizure of the Other's experience in its essence through
the horizonal features of my past, understood in terms of its possibilities
rather than the history of my actual experience. The alien, the strange, the
pathological, the demonic, the freakish, and the hellish may be analogical
possibilities we come to by way of the outskirts of the familiar. If we proceed
along this line, we find a deeper meaning to the analogical than pains and
itches suggest: what we shall consider later as the presentation (or "appresentation") of the hidden by way of the given.

3   Behavior.   Activity, in the broadest sense, which presents itself to the
Other may be called behavior. Understood in this way, my behavior is an
object for the Other's perception and vice versa, but I have no access or
only indirect access to my own behavior. It is possible to regard the activity
of Others sheerly in terms of overt performance, without concern for questions
of the egological meaning which action has for the actor. The psychological
doctrine which holds that knowledge of the organism consists in the observer's
perceptual report and analysis of the organism is called behaviorism. However modified the classical version of that doctrine has become in recent times,
the anchor of behaviorism lies in its insistence on the observer's observation
of the observed—and the observer and the observed are never the same person.
This position carries both a negative and a positive charge: the ego has no
access to its own being and the observer is raised to epistemic eminence. Put
together, this means that consciousness is translated into behavior.

There are some immediate implications of such a translation which may
be considered apart from the history of psychology. Whatever may be
"going on" in the mind of the Other, I observe, attend to, and respond to
his behavior. If instead of saying, "This movement of his hand means that
he wants to greet me," I simply take the outstretched hand as *being* the

salutation, then the means of locating the Other is in the proffered hand. Leave aside the many difficulties such a line of argument raises. For the moment, let us look more closely at the mode of interpretation of the Other's activity which is implied. If the extended hand *is* the greeting, then perhaps it is equally true that the raised fist is the anger, the stooped shoulders the disconsolateness, the bent knees the prayer, and the smile the pleasure. Alternatively, of course, the scream is the pain and the spittle the contempt. The domain of language undergoes a similar transformation: *what* is said (the meaning conveyed) is molded in the act of speech, welded to the rhetoric of discourse. It is not necessary to separate the speaker from his speech; both may be taken as unified elements of human behavior in which events have the ontological status of independent units, happening not so much *to* as *through* individuals. The observer is the Other even when he is a participant in social action. In this way, response to a fellow-man is rendered into a mode of overtness on a par with the activity of the alter ego. "My" action becomes activity as though it were witnessed by the Other, and when I "look" at myself, question myself, reflect upon my own action, it is as though someone else were responsible for what is seen or understood. For instance:

I've had a rather nasty accident: getting out of a car, a companion slammed the door too quickly and caught my thumb in the jamb. We promptly got back in the car and rushed to the emergency room of the nearest hospital. The throbbing, bloody pulp held between the fingers of my other hand is that digital ally, my thumb. What colors that otherwise pale member is capable of assuming! And what havoc is played on the field of the palm when its lateral guardian becomes unopposable! Here comes the intern, summoned by the nurse. I throw them both a grateful and winning smile, talking a mile a minute, joking to beat the band (someone whispers out of me, "bouncy language-buster: throwing, rushing, beating!").

"Wow!" grins the intern. "Call Dr. Kildare!" (he means the resident in surgery).

Pretty soon Dr. Kildare joins us. By now we're a tidy bunch. They've permitted my friends to stay in the emergency room, and now we're together—a circle around me—cut off from the rest of the room by a folding screen. Cozy, comfy, and a real party, including rubbing alcohol. After Doctor No. 1 (assisted by Number 2 and several nurses) washes the hand with liquid soap and then some special antiseptic, he takes a small green sheet with a cut-out hole in the middle and pushes my hand through the hole. Now only the hand shows, the damaged thumb hoisted up, almost grinning at the world, the flap of a large piece of the nail hanging like a ruined crescent. Then the doctor gives me a hypo, and we all wait for the injection to take effect. Waving my other hand in a sorcerer's gesture, I say, "Thumb, be numb!" I've gotten very witty in the camaraderie of the accident.

But now the doctor starts his surgery, his repair job, and we all watch intently and silently as he expertly goes about his business: snipping, tacking, folding, dabbing, sewing, and binding. As we watch—our little sewing circle—the thumb has taken on a stolid life and station of its own, and as the others crane to see it treated, so I, in a final act of separation and union, join the group of onlookers. And as though my thumb were nailed to a support under the sheet, I become one of the circle, peering in quiet concentration at the surgeon's performance. At the last moment I just manage to rejoin the thumb so that I can take it home with me.

4 Interpretation. In contrast to "behavior," there is activity which is meaningful to the actor, to the individual who performs the action. At issue here, of course, is not merely another facet of human activity but a radically different conception of the meaning and nature of human action. "Interpretation" (or what has been called "interpretive understanding") is the contradictory of "behavior." Instead of turning to the overt activity on its own and in itself, in interpretation I attend to the meaning the activity has for the one who performs it; I turn to the human agent who is the source of the act. It is the Other who greets me by offering his hand or it is I who welcome the Other with my outstretched hand. In either case, the hand expresses the intention of the actor; stripped from that intention, the hand is the appendage anatomists study, not the flesh politicians grip. By itself or in itself the hand says nothing. Open, it may signify mourning; clenched in a fist it may mean friendly greetings. But apart from the cultural frame within which the gesture takes on its distinctive meaning, the signification of action varies with and is, in many respects, a function of the intentional character of the actor's project. The smallest or meanest activity cannot be understood apart from the actor's intent. A wink, for example, may be conniving and flirtatious or the result of a facial tic or sensitivity to light. *Qua* wink, we have only the blinking eye; as human action, though, we have something meant. If a wink be defined as a purposeful, a voluntary blinking of the eye, then it may be said that though every wink involves a blink, every blink is not a wink. Similarly, nodding the head signifies approval or affirmation when the nod, typically done, is *meant* to indicate agreement. A palsied nonagenarian at the Board meeting may be taken as going along with a proposal if a characteristic tremor of the head is interpreted as a nod, not a reflex. Nor is verbal performance free of similar ambiguities. At a critical juncture in the same meeting, the Chairman turns to a member with: "Are you in favor of the motion?" "I . . .." begins the member and is immediately interrupted by the Chairman's "The Aye's have it then and the motion passes!"

It must be realized, however, that interpretation is concerned with the fundamental dimension of the actor's intention, the meaning he bestows on his own act, rather than marginal misunderstandings of gesture or surface tricks and manipulation. In "behavior," the responsibility for translating action is passed to the observer; in interpretation, the actor himself shoulders the essential burden. This shift does not eliminate or sidestep the role of the observer. Rather, the task of the observer is to grasp the situation of social action as defined primordially by the actor. We are faced, then, with two realities: the situation as defined by the actor and as interpreted by the Other. Later discussion will be concerned with the question of how the two spheres are reconciled; for the moment, however, it is necessary to consider a further complication, involving a distinction between the Other as observer and as participant in social action.

In mundane existence, my alter ego is first of all someone who responds to me, who not only attends to my action but who is geared into a shared world of interpretation which carries with it a horizon of expectancies and demands. To my greeting within the situation of typical introduction, my alter ego responds with appropriate words and gestures. Not to do so would indicate impoliteness or hostility. The response is an act of social participation, and it presupposes the shared situation within which the meaning of the actor's greeting is embedded. Now the respondent may indeed also be curious about the actor and may observe him carefully and critically, but the initial demand of the situation calls for the Other's response, not his analysis. The movement from participant to formal observer is a qualitative one, however mixed those functions may in fact be in the actuality of a concrete situation. As a lawyer being introduced to my client for the first time, I may be more than curious about his personality. Clasping his hand may involve the most searching intuitive appraisal of his character: Will he make a good impression in court? Has he the backbone to withstand cross-examination? Could that pudgy, cold finger have pulled the trigger? Am I stuck with a loser? My professional glance may or may not tell me a great deal about the individual I am to represent, but whatever I learn about him, it is as a fellow-man that I am introduced to him in the basic context of the greeting. "I want to introduce your lawyer" necessarily implies "and here's a fellow-man about to enter your life in a special way." Interpretation is primarily rooted in the reality of daily life; it is the native commerce of mundanity. Secondarily (though crucially), interpretation implies that mode of observation which moves from casual inspection to scientific detachment. Its career will be of continuing interest to us.

The philosophical theories of our knowledge of other selves and the various ways in which we secure that knowledge have provided us with a sketch of the conceptual terrain in which man encounters his fellow-man. It is now possible to pursue the theme of the discovery of the Other in a fresh way. At issue in all of the approaches we have explored so far is the implicit assumption that in the relationship between ego and alter ego, the perceptual grasp of one by the other involves an object for a subject. However object and subject are related, accounted for, or understood, the difference between being he who is perceived and he who perceives remains to be considered. I discover the Other and I am discovered by the Other. We will consider each in turn.

To discover the Other is to be a subject for which the Other is object. In quick but not easy terms, "subject" may be defined as the consciousness within whose coherent and dominant centrality the Other appears. "Object" may be understood as that which has no unity of its own (so far as it is initially grasped by a subject) but which functions within the definition of its status provided by the subject. Subjects are dominant; objects are dependent. The domination in question refers to the subject's field of perception, understanding, and action as centered in the Here and Now as well as in the biography and projects of the individual. In first-person terms, I find myself in a world set forth from the zero point of the coordinates of my spatiotemporal placement. As we saw earlier, what is There for the ego is There as over and against my Here. Similarly, the temporal placements of before and after, earlier and later, yesterday and tomorrow are all defined by the Now of the ego. The discovery of the Other as occupying this or that position in my field of perception is a vindication, in some ways, of my stance in the world. Above all, the world is given coherence by my organizing power, the power of subjectivity. To be subject, in this sense, is to dominate the scene, to be master of what consciousness surveys. For the Other to be object for my subjectivity is for his freedom to be contingent on my assertive authority.

It might be thought, of course, that such perceptual grandiloquence is a kind of madness and that the subject who takes the Other as his epistemic vassal is simply deluded—that to use the word "freedom" in this way is either semantic irresponsibility or linguistic bizarreness. Be patient. There is a useful and instructive ambivalence in the terms "object" and "subject." To be an object means both to be something given as that which is intended (the use of the term "object" in grammar is perhaps the simplest instance of this relationship) and also to be something presented, something there for consciousness to be aware of. The dependency of object in the first sense is evident; its status in the second sense needs qualification. To be aware of the Other as object is first to take the Other as before me, near me, or as within hailing distance, or as almost out of sight. In any of these placements, the Other is *not* someone defining my Here, someone organizing my perspective. Despite the many qualitative differences between the Other and an inanimate object, they have something essential in common: their mode of presentation is defined by me; they are objects given in my experience. From that givenness, it follows that another and more subtle characteristic of the object is its status of dependency within the context of my perceptual reality, dependency on me and dependency for me. And in that dependency I discover that which allies the Other as object with the inanimate thing as object: the degraded status of being-for-another. Taken simply as for-me, the Other not only resembles a thing but is rendered thing-like. As we will see shortly, the dialectical continuity of the reality of the Other, his freedom—indeed, his subjectivity—makes it utterly impossible to move from the Other-for-me to the conclusion that the thing-like character of the Other constitutes his full reality. To the contrary, the dimension of the Other as object is merely a part of, a moment in the relationship of the self to its alter ego. That moment, though, calls for the most serious consideration, for it constitutes the first stage of the ego's organization of a world. Moreover, the object-aspect of the Other as he is for me reflects itself in a variety of ways at many levels of societal experience.

As object for me, the Other may be taken simply in his bodily presence, as a "thing" in the sense of a body. Whether that body is faceless as part of a crowd or noted almost minutely in the police lineup, the Other is severed from his subjectivity insofar as his being-for-me is reduced to the presentation of his body for my gaze. Beyond the confines of the Other's physical body, his presence includes a host of other modes of presentation: his voice, his gestures, his "look." To the drill sergeant's command, "Sound off!" there will be a flood of voices which are sprung from the throats of men like jack-in-the-boxes. The momentary identification of the roll-call voice is the fixing of the Other as object, an auditory "to be paid on demand" note. When the Other is taken purely as object, his freedom is negated or at least temporarily robbed by the subject because he is *there* for me completely within the confines of *my* centrality. The familiar examples of master and slave have been used in classical accounts of the situation. Whatever the model or paradigm, however, it is important to realize that the Other is not simply being dominated or controlled or taken advantage of; he is being removed from *his* perspectival centrality and dragged off into mine. His loss of freedom is not so much a lack of power as a loss of subjectivity. That loss has its implications for me as well as for my fellow-man. In fact, there is a reciprocity to the entire relationship of subject and object which demands that attention be paid to the reversal of the situation in which the Other is made object for my subjectivity. I, in turn, may be considered as object for the subjectivity of the Other.

Before turning to that possibility, a caution is necessary. There are two senses in which I may be understood as being an object for the subjectivity of my fellow-man. First, the reverse of the description just made may be introduced to suggest that what is true of the Other's being object for me is also true for my being object for the Other. This reversal may be quite possible and correct in principle, but it is essential to recognize that it cannot be made from the standpoint of the ego; it can be effected only from the vantage point of the alter ego. If I make the claim for reversal, then, I do so on the *assumption* that what holds true for me also holds true for you. As we have already noted, such an assumption has profound implications for the entire problem of intersubjectivity. But there is a second and different way of understanding the meaning of reversal. It is perfectly consistent with egological experience to say that I discover myself as being an object for the

Other. In this case, the "evidence" is immediate and absolute: I am reporting my own experiential reality, quite apart from claims about the way in which the Other may be presented with my objectivity. Whether or not the Other experiences me as object in the same way as I do him, I am certain that I am object for his subjectivity, for here it is the ego's experience, not the alter ego's, which is at issue. It is in this second sense that we will consider the problem of the reciprocity of subject and object.

I discover myself as object for the Other when his glance, his order, his decision constitute the field within which my presence irrupts. I am discovered at the end of his glance, as the target of his action. Again the double meaning of "object" is involved: I discover myself as object for the Other in the sense of being that which he attends to (that toward which his perceptual concern is directed) but also, at times at least, as a *thing* which the Other handles or manipulates. It may, of course, be in shame that such discovery is attained, or it may be that a relatively isolated moment is the occasion through which my object-ness is revealed to me: an epiphany of humiliation. Whatever the depth or the extent of the discovery, the experience of being bereft of my own center of action, the loss of my freedom, reveals the subjectivity of the Other. I find myself in someone else's world. Of course, the changing and dialectical character of the relationship between fellow-men precludes any imprisonment of the individual, either as ego or as alter ego, in the role of subject or object. Nor should the struggle and antagonism between men be reduced to an artificial thesis that man's relation to his fellow-men is a "nothing but . . ." kind of reality. What has been said so far about the relationship of subject and object points to fluid development of the self and transitions it follows from stage to stage in its career. In reality, the individual is both subject and object; indeed, even at the time of his complete dominance over the Other, the self may falter and relinquish its freedom. It is one thing to find the Other at the far periphery of my field of action; it is something else to dangle him there. Once again, it is in the playing of social roles that this truth becomes most evident.

Although roles may be considered as types, as variables in the equations of social action for which specific individuals and performances may be substituted, they allow for aspects of the subject-object distinction Within societal structure, some roles are highly specified; others are rather loose and free-floating, providing the possibility of a considerable degree of improvisation on the part of the role-taker. The orthodox priest conducting Mass has carefully defined and prescribed procedures he must follow; the taxicab driver transporting a passenger may adequately perform his occupational role in a variety of styles. The priest's administering the sacrament to the communicant is role-demanded; the cabdriver's getting out to hold the door open for his passenger is rather optional. To the hack who either forgets or decides not to do me the courtesy of opening the door, I may chidingly say that service is not what it used to be. "Neither are tips what they used to be," he can reply. A bluffer sort may also indicate alternatives to my use of his cab, which brings to mind the contrasting example of the priest. Communion cannot be a matter left to the whim of an individual. At the critical moment, it is inconceivable that the priest about to give communion would say to the supplicant, "Well, maybe I will and maybe I won't!" In the range of role-requirements there is, broadly speaking, an inverse relationship between the importance of the role in the scale of societal preferments (professional men nearer the top and unskilled workers nearer the bottom, for example) and the freedom of the role-player. A teacher has greater scope for interpreting the meaning of his role than does a laborer, but he must follow a greater set of requirements in order to function professionally than must the laborer, and he must follow them in more rigorous fashion. Yet it would be wrong to say that the one has less or more freedom than the other without specifying freedom in some regard. The problem at issue here, however, is not that of the relative flexibility of different roles; it is instead the freedom of the role-taker in his role. Even there, a special emphasis must be respected. The question is that of the subject and object aspects of the role-player: In what ways and to what extent is the subjectivity of the role-player sustained, enhanced, liberated or compromised, threatened, or congealed in his role? We might look first at the Other in his role:

The small neighborhood store which depends for much of its business on the fact that it seems never to be closed apart from a very few special holidays during the year is a familiar if disappearing bit of city life. The small grocer seems to be riveted to his counter, equally at home to the latest caller or the earliest riser. Entering his store expecting to see him becomes almost as automatic as picking up the telephone, expecting the voice of the operator. When I was a child, I was a constant courier from home to such a store, clenching in my fist a short list and some coins or a bill. The grocery store was no more than a large cell, with shelves up to the ceiling, tubs of butter behind glass-and-wood doors, sacks of dried beans and stacks of bottle racks on the floor, and the proprietor fixed behind the counter, bundled in seemingly endless layers of sweaters, the whole covered by a long white apron, his face waiting for me as though news of my coming had just been received over teletype.

"My mother wants . . . ," I would begin listing, and in response to each request, he would secure or cut the appropriate item, always adding the same legend:

"A half-pound butter, the best in America! . . . one box raisins, the best in America! . . . two pounds sugar, the best in America! . . ."

The routine was frequently interrupted by one or another of the grocer's many children, an appearance which invariably sent him into a paroxysm for reasons I was never able to determine. Their guilt was not in their appearance (the family lived behind the store and traffic to and from the store to the house was unavoidable), but rather their appearance seemed to be a reminder of their guilt.

"Did'n I tell you!" he'd scream at one of the brood. "Ha! Just wait! Will you get it! Will I give it to you!"

At which the child would break into a shattering lament, bringing out the other children. At that point the grocer would return to my list and resume his chant as though nothing had happened:
"One dozen eggs, the best in America!"
Throughout the years of my childhood the routine was much the same. Going to the grocer was going not only through the routine but to the routine.
Then, one day, the familiar latch failed to yield to my insistent grip. The store was dark at midday, bolted tight. And pasted to the glass was a ragged piece of wrapping paper on which had been written in pencil:

Closed because of death in the family.

For no reason I rattled the door. Perhaps the butter and cheese, the boxes of cereal and toilet paper high on the shelves, the bottles of milk cold in their stalls would rouse the grocer to his chant and return the store to its life: What right does a grocer have to die?

Of course, we have been speaking of the Other in his role, the reduction of the Other to his role. Unquestionably, the Other is far more complex than any one role he plays, and certainly my point of access to the Other playing a role is necessarily narrow and, in many respects, an insufficient basis for knowing him. But there is no moral judgment being made. Rather, the point is that in the typicality through which role-awareness is lived we find a matrix of action, a way of seeing the Other and ourselves as drawn into a social reality in which we are at times masters and at times servants of and for each other. Even if I am the buyer in a buyer's market, I find myself caught up in the requirements and limitations of a typified role. In a way, my domination of the field in which the Other appears in his role is affected by the harassment of subjectivity by typification. Although I am subject for the objectivity of the Other, although the Other appears as part of the field of action defined by me, still the I of subjectivity, the I whose existential core constitutes the person, is threatened by the anonymization which the role brings to the role-player. In command, I am yet in danger of becoming an officer of cognition, a bureaucrat of mundanity. That which threatens the self by fixing and desiccating the subject has been called "Bad Faith." We shall examine it later in other contexts, but for the present we may say that one vast form of Bad Faith consists in the individual's moving from subject to object in social roles which have congealed consciousness into routine expectancy and which have made of intersubjectivity a masked and masking reality.

We are still in the region of description and not evaluation. To speak of "Bad Faith" may appear paradoxical, but nevertheless it is essential to understand that the self which has become routinized in its role activity is not a "bad" self but merely one which articulates its experience in a certain way. Our task is to comprehend that way, not to appraise its moral worth. That understood, it is then possible to suggest that along with the dangers of anonymization, there are also remarkable possibilities, a freedom which roles and role-taking make possible. In effect, the cardinal achievement of roles is that they permit consciousness, understood as a typifying agency, to construct a social world. That mundane existence, the taken-for-granted world of daily life, is *ours* is the creation of a consciousness intrinsically capable of abstracting from the manifold particularity of experience to its typical character. In taking a role I am able to give an intersubjective weight to myself both as subject and as object, for the demands and rewards of role-taking are based on the lasting truth that I can make sense of the Other and he of me by allowing for a meaningful order of typification in which the *form* of experience is intended in such a way that it can be grasped apart from the experiential immediacy of concrete, individual existence. Roles are types; role-taking is a mode of typification; and from these roots arises the social world.

chapter
three
sociality

The experience of the self with other selves is the meaning of "sociality." *With* is the operative term here, for we are speaking of a relationship which creates the social, which gives the participants in social action the sense of their being not only in touch with each other but mutually aware of the reality-creating force of their own responses to each other. Sociality, then, is what happens *between* selves. To understand it we must examine the prime location of the "with" in what has been called the "We-relationship." Quite naturally, our movement from "I" to "you" brings us next to "we." Fortunately, in some respects the We-relationship is no stranger to our discussion, for in unexamined form, it was the starting point for the analysis of the self. At the beginning, as you recall, the effort to locate the sphere of egological experience in its radical force presupposed a context, a milieu of the taken-for-granted world of *our* experience. That profoundly assumed ongoingness of the social world is centered in the public or shared communality of man and fellow-man in the We-relationship. There is a circle, then, in any attempt to analyze sociality: We are before I am. Or, to paraphrase a classic pronouncement: We are, therefore I am. The circle includes as well as describes the connection between the We and the individual who tries to undercut the We by making it an object for investigation. The circle, of course, is larger than the problem of sociality; it is at the base of all efforts of philosophy to reflect on the world which includes it. The special quality of the problem of sociality, as far as circularity is concerned, is that the individual who analyzes the We participates in one of the possibilities of the We

47

at the same time that he transcends it. Circularity aside, however, it is possible to turn to the immediate character of the We and to survey its bounds and style. As we do so, the nature and implications of the circularity will, in turn, achieve some clarification.

The most striking feature of the We is its taken-for-grantedness. Whatever the problems of the social world, that there is such a reality is simply assumed by men in daily life. We are speaking of something so fundamental that it is difficult to focus upon it. In its most simple and evident aspect, being in a world *with* others means perceiving them in situations where mutual action is possible: acting together constitutes the frame within which the We appears. One example of mutual action is work. Two men lifting a heavy object involves a root mode of shared activity: effort. In the lifting, the common object is girdled and opposed by both men. The assumption underlying the enterprise of lifting is that the force exerted by each partner is directed toward the same task, that effort may indeed be shared. The We of this example is limited in several ways. Most immediately, the We is taken for granted by the workers precisely because *work* presupposes the experience of shared effort. It is important to realize that adeptness at the task is not debated here. Undoubtedly, there is a history of learning to work together; such activity is not assured in its procedures or outcome by the We-relationship. But just as relevant is the recognition that the We is shared by the partners within or over against the larger framework of the ongoing world of everyday life. In a sense, each We fits into a larger We, the broadest horizon being that of the sense of mundanity itself, or what we have called the taken-for-grantedness of everyday life. There is no problem for common-sense man in locating the We because the search for any aspect of sociality already takes place within the We of the encompassing social world. Just as this piece of work, this job, is done within the framework of "work of this type," so "work of this type" is a part of the larger matrix of "all work." The push and pull, the hefting and budging of lifting has its counterpart in the striving involved in all action in which men move about in the social world. The primitive fact of man's "upright posture" presupposes a countervailing force to that of gravity to keep him standing. Analogously, social action demands a force of effort, a straining to accomplish, a fundamental volition of the social.

Man *with* fellow-man in the We-relationship establishes a domain of "betweenness" which characterizes social action. To say that something happens "between" men means that the field of action involves a primal sharing of experience in which my awareness of you and yours of me express themselves through the We and are, indeed, We-dependent from the outset. Examples of the "between" of the We-relationship are not difficult to come by:

1   Our new party—the Progressive Workers United—has just been formed by five of us, a splinter group from the older United Workers Freedom Party. We split because of theoretical differences. *We* say we split ; *they* say we were expelled. Why trouble about semantics? The fact is that a party with a total membership of 125 people must be very careful to keep its theoretical center free of corruption. Parties with larger labor bases in membership have greater freedom. We must have discipline. Theoretical factionalism was in truth the reason the United Workers Freedom Party originally broke with *its* parent organization, the Allied Workers Party. Since then various efforts have been made to reunite the groups. Such a possibility seems remote at the present time, given the world situation. In any case, the Central Committee of Progressive Workers United controls the ideologico-theoretical field of operations : we have possession of the mimeograph machine. An organizational meeting is the first order of business. Posters will be made and a newsletter written. Spies and political recidivists will find no chink in our armor. We are searching for a suitable motto.

2   March 6, 1968

Mr. Walter P. Hovelander
General Manager
Community Center Recreation and Education Building

Dear Mr. Hovelander:

As Secretary-Treasurer of the Aron Nimzovitch Memorial Chess Club, I have been instructed to write to you on behalf of our membership both to bring to your attention and to protest the interference at our last meeting (March 4th) caused by a group which calls itself the Progressive Workers Party (or some such name). I will not trouble you with a detailed report of the events of the night of the 4th. Suffice it to say that our weekly round robin was suddenly interrupted by an uncouth person who shouted at the top of his voice that the Carefree Room had been reserved for his group. As you well know, Mr. Hovelander, the Nimzovitch group has been meeting in the Carefree Room every Monday night for more than six years, from the time the Center was built. Needless to say, I politely informed the intruder that there was a mistake on his part and that the Room was reserved for the Chess Club. The verbal abuse which I met after that remark would be unbelievable except for the fact that I have witnesses. To report only the printable epithets, I was called a "crypto-fascist" and a "warmonger." Needless to say, the constitution of our Club prohibits political action; we are strictly chess players, nothing else and nothing more. We have never caused any trouble and ask, in turn, only to be left in peace and quiet.

With the hope that you will see to it that further invasions by the Progressive Workers Party will be prohibited, and with thanks in advance from, I'm sure, all the members of our Club, I remain

Respectfully yours,

D. Rudolph Rasmussen

3   I get all the headaches, the complaints, the accusations, the warnings, the vilification. And don't tell me about the Walter P. Hovelander Testimonial Dinner three years ago! Were you honoring me or yourselves? You'd take any occasion to stuff your bellies. When the affair was over I had to tiptoe between the bodies to get to the elevator. The Community Center needs me more than I need it, I assure you. If I had ten dollars for every time I thought of quitting I'd be a wealthy man. It has been nothing but heartache for six years with that enterprise. Now the last straw: some lawyer representing an organization called the United Workers Freedom Party is threatening to sue the Center unless we reimburse them for $175.00 plus expenses—something about a stolen mimeograph machine discovered on our premises. Nuts, kooks, cranks! On top of it all, some government agency is investigating the Chess Club! How tangled can things get? How confused can everybody be?

I warn you for the last time that unless some sanity appears, I wash my hands of the whole mess; you can have my resignation. I spend over twelve hours a day at the Center or involved in work connected with the Center. No man can survive such a schedule. When I go home I want to be free of Center business. It's coming out of my ears. I want privacy; I want freedom; I want reasonability; I want the Center to serve its original ideal of providing a meeting place for all community groups, regardless of race or creed. Is it too much to ask or expect that we honor that ideal? Unless some changes are made around here, and damn soon, you can find yourselves a new general manager. I've had it!

What lies "between" men in the We-relationship varies from the paradigmatic force of love and friendship, the communality of work, the strength of mutuality felt in playing together and being together in face-to-face relationships to, at a far remove, the "between" of interests, involvements, and associations in which fellow-men are neither directly perceived nor immediately encountered in a present. It is necessary to realize that the domain of sociality extends far beyond the perimeter of direct confrontation. It includes dimensions of the past and the future as well as a larger field of the present, one which is not restricted to direct sensory perception of the alter ego. The social world is built out of all these temporally as well as spatially variant elements of relationship between selves, each of which requires special description.

1   **The past.**   Within the biography of the individual, his personal history, the past includes all that which was directly experienced; in the development of the person, however, there is much which is indirectly given, presented by way of the reports of others or known by construction and interpretation. The personal past includes intentional reference to the prepersonal history which is presupposed in social life. I have not only memories and the reports of others but also a considerable understanding of the larger historical past of my ancestors and our ancestors, all fellow-men who lived and died before I was born. Of those who preceded me on the historical scene, some are memorable in a public sense, that is, their lives and deeds are described in historical or other works and there is a general interest, more or less, in their affairs. A few individuals are known to me but not to the world at large because they are my family antecedents. For the most part, though, the vast numbers of human beings who inhabited this planet before my time are and will remain unknown to me. They form a truly massive cemetery of the imagination in which the epitaph is simply: they were! It is possible to posit a great

deal about the life of a miller in colonial America or of a serf in medieval days
or of a soldier in the eleventh century or of a fisherman at the time of Jesus.
But the concrete lives of the very great plurality of millers, serfs, soldiers, and
fishermen of those times (and of all times) remain lost to my personal reconstruction apart from what I know or surmise about the typical features of
lives of those types in those ages. The force of the fugitive character of this
aspect of the past shows itself in the orientation of the individual to his
fellow-men in the social world, for to know intimately or generally only a
segment of the past is to interpret, immanently at least, mundane existence
as centered vitally in a present which can recover its past only in fragmentary
and typified form. Whether we are aware of it or not, the irrecoverability of
the past as far as its anonymous masses are concerned implies the typification
of the present, the founding of what occurs now on the legend of what came
earlier. The essential point, however, is that despite our knowledge of the
past's being limited to grossly typified terms, we can and in many ways
must take up attitudes toward what preceded us historically. We are, then,
oriented toward those who came before us and to their acts. Being in a
present means, in part, being turned past-ward.

2 The present. In the Here and Now of face-to-face encounter we have
the most striking presentation of the We-relationship. But the present
includes much more than what is given directly; there is the larger sphere of
fellow-men who are alive at the same time we are but whom we never meet
face-on and with whom we share little more than the fact that we overlap in
time as inhabitants of the earth. One point of difference between my relationship to a living fellow-man whom I otherwise would never meet or communicate with and an ancestor I know little or nothing of is that I can, in principle,
influence the former, never the latter. As a being alive in the world, acting in
social reality, I can arrange to meet the otherwise anonymous Other who
is my contemporary, I can write to him or telephone him; in other ways, I
can bring some weight to bear on him through my political action. The
dead are beyond the sphere of influence as far as my action goes, though they
continue to exert influence on me, in subtle and indirect ways, and find their
way, curiously, into the present. Furthermore, to say that I am influenced
by but do not influence the historical past means that there is a doubling or
reflexive movement in interpretive experience in virtue of which the influence
of the historical past is constituted by the individual. It is in "recognizing"
or even in "understanding" the history of eighteenth-century Jewish life in
Poland that I discover the force of, let us say, the spirit of Chassidism.
There is, in fact, a movement between the larger and the more focalized
senses of the present. Not only do fellow-men I have not met before come
into the ken of my face-to-face experience but some of those I encounter

directly pass from the intimacy of shared space and time and, phantomlike, move outward into the twilight or darkness of the larger present. It must be recognized that the experience of man in the We-relationship of direct encounter in the present provides the axis for all larger constructions of the present.

Despite this, much of our knowledge of the larger present remains strangely aloof from the forms of direct experience and is closer in some respects to the orientation to the historical past. Although I "know" that I can influence a rice farmer in mainland China and be influenced by him, the *I* who has this knowledge recognizes—*I* recognize—that the likelihood of this coming to pass is infinitesimally slight; it is, to all real purposes, as "impossible" as throwing 25 straight sevens in craps. The knowledge of such "influence," then, suffers trivialization: I know that it is true in the same way that I know that the Tropic of Capricorn passes through Mozambique. Neither item has the slightest relevance to my life. That I *could* hurl from my fist 25 consecutive sevens, that I *could* go to Mozambique, that I *could* visit that Chinese farmer are possibilities on the far side of reality. Whether or not my circumstances change suddenly and radically, at *present* I discount the thesis that such distant Others can influence or be influenced by me except in highly historicized and typified form. The present includes not only the vivacity of the We in direct encounter but the remoteness of Others who remain perpetually at distance from the reality of our lives.

3 The future. Just as we distinguished between the narrower and larger senses of the past and present, so it is necessary to examine the proximal and distal meanings of the future. Most simply, the near or "personal" future is the intended field of my projects: this afternoon, next year, graduation time, in my late thirties or early fifties, retirement, my grandchildren, and so on; whereas the "historical" future transcends my life and concerns those who will be born after I and those I know die. The far future is then anonymous to me in the same way as the far past. And it is also the case that I am oriented toward the historical future despite the fact that it lies on the far side of my activity. Of course, I can influence the far future by my present actions, though it is necessary to delimit and clarify the precise nature of my orientation toward the future. Although the far future cannot influence me in a strictly causal manner, my interpretive awareness of what will happen long after I die has an important reflexive meaning: I appropriate the future to the extent that my orientation toward it becomes part of my present reality. The far future, then, has a way of manifesting itself in the present, not as something done but as something I am intentively aware of and oriented toward.

It might be suggested that such orientation is true of individuals who have some special commitment to the distant future: conservationists, scholars, religionists, and similar pilgrims of transcendence. For many individuals in these categories what is important in our present actions is that we plan for and assure not only continuity of resources and tradition but the liberty of far-off future generations to live significantly. The present, then, has a double aspect, for our action in it implies an attitude toward the historical future, an attitude which may involve the most practical and mundane decisions. What would appear to be a lack of concern or a refusal of responsibility for the future may in effect be a covert decision or the unwillingness of "Bad Faith" to confront the full meaning of the present. My orientation toward the future as it concerns those who will flourish long after my death is a central dimension of my definition of the present because it introduces the cardinal feature of transcendence into the meaning of mundane existence. My being in a present includes the recognition that my death is followed by the lives of Others necessarily known to me only in highly typified form. At this point death is not taken as an existential theme, nor is my death understood as a problem. Rather, transcendence implies an intentional or directional movement of man's action toward something given only by way of its openness, indeterminacy, or, as we have suggested, its typicality. Being oriented toward the historical future means that the individual creates the present as a reality whose interior meaning intends what it cannot directly experience in perception but which will be reconstructed by fellow-men to come.

In a way, then, intending the historical future is constituting the present from the phantom standpoint of transcendent fellow-men. *They* will be able to pick up the clues sedimented in the present insofar as we are concerned or unconcerned with them. There is no assurance, of course, that their reconstruction of their past—our present—will in fact be true to our interpretations and intentions. They may misread us just as we may or do misread our past. It is an essential feature of transcendence that misinterpretation is a permanent possibility for all reconstruction. Even more, "correct" interpretations may be lost or give way to subsequent interpretations which confound the meaning of the presents with which they are concerned. We are all familiar with the "time capsules" deposited in cornerstones or at sites in international exhibitions to be opened a hundred or two or three hundred years hence. Newspapers, instruments, devices, cultural artifacts, and other items are included to give future fellow-men an idea of what things were like—and hence what we were like—in our time. The movement of interpretation is from thing to man. Our discussion goes in a different direction: the transcendence of the present by way of the intending of the historical future leads from action to man. In fact, the entire discussion of time and transcendence introduces the enormously complex theme of the meaning of social action.

Involvement in the We-relationship signifies a "between" in the life of man with fellow-man which both emphasizes and reflects the temporal panorama of mundane existence. The paradigmatic force of the face-to-face encounter in a vivid present of shared space and time contains within it the orientation of the individual to the near and far reaches of the past and the future as well as the transcendencies associated with our ancestors and descendants. The "between" is shared, then, not only by the living but also by the dead and the unborn. And this means, in turn, that *action* in the social world has a far wider reach than the face-to-face model intimates. Indeed, social action—the crux of sociality—includes almost everything relevant to Man as a being whose interpretation of the world is the clue to his mundane existence. If to understand sociality is to understand social action, then the first order of business is to turn to the meaning of the term "action" as it is introduced here. By "action" is meant all interpretation, behavior, and conduct in which an individual is concerned with Others. "Action" throughout this discussion must be understood as "social action."

Of course, our definition is condensed; unfolded and developed it includes indirect as well as direct relationships with fellow-men. It might be helpful to ask immediately, "What would *not* qualify as action according to this account?" Answer: all reflex responses at the physiological level as well as all involuntary movement and behavior of the organism. Some responses which do not qualify on this account as action may, in time, develop into more nearly social behavior. The cry of the newborn infant will later on become part of the schema of social interaction. In its initial phase, though, it is an automatic response. Along with the individual's concern for Others must be included a principle of self-awareness or reflexiveness, that is, the possibility of the individual's becoming aware of the concern he has for the Other. Individuals are not related to Others in automatic terms. We are not dealing here with a higher form of simple reflexes. Instead, the concern of the individual for the Other must be capable of being interiorized so that response is significant. Of course, it is quite possible to respond to the Other as one responds to a stone; what we are trying to elicit is the meaning of the *social*, and to achieve that it is necessary to probe the domain of human action, not postulate it. Nor is it appropriate here to examine the "natural history" of response. The notion of "interiorization" does not imply a sharp cleavage at some evolutionary point between Man, the being who reflexively appropriates his relation to Others, and the "lower animals" for whom this is somehow ruled out because they lack sophisticated language powers or symbolic systems informed by a symbolizing consciousness. Human action needs reflexiveness because in responding as man to fellow-man, the individual becomes aware of himself through his concern with the Other. The denial or failure of interiorization leads to the anonymization of human relationships: the conversation of robots, bits and pieces of linguistic machinery. As much in need of qualification and explanation as this statement is, and as wrongheaded as it may seem to students of comparative animal behavior, let us boldly say: Man is the only being capable of social action. A defensive maneuver is needed before we can continue with the exploration of our theme. Blocking the understanding of action is a very deeply rooted conception of common sense (with no small correlative in more scientific spheres) that putting quotation marks around "action" will never change the brute fact that it means force, deed, exertion, physical power. Even when it is recognized and granted that such a phenomenon as judicial action— sentencing a man to death by electrocution—initially manifests itself in the judge's *pronouncing* sentence, it is still maintained that the judge's action is real because it portends physical change effected in a most compelling form. If the words pronounced shock the defendant or others in the courtroom, it is because they carry a tiny load of the electricity which will destroy the convicted. In mundane terms, "men of action" are usually thought of as men of power whose decisions are quickly or eventually translated into raw transformations of human lives or conditions: major political figures, leading soldiers, business magnates, and even, on a lesser scale, athletes and adventurers. It may be that the word "action" understood in this way is so connotatively entrenched in linguistic consciousness that no amount of explanation will dislodge or liberate it for other purposes. But there are compelling reasons for insisting on freeing "action" for larger work that needs to be done. It is not simply a matter of the word or even of the fact that it has already been utilized as a technical term in the classical vocabulary of the social sciences. There are philosophical reasons for insisting that action not be restricted to overt physical behavior. Most simply, even in pragmatic terms, what is effected and accomplished in mundane life is as much the product of negative decision as of positive determination. Deciding *not* to attack is as much a military action as sending men and machines against enemy lines; deciding *not* to run for office can be a devastatingly efficacious political act; deciding *not* to sell at a certain time may have profound reverberations on the stock market. There is an entire domain of such negative or covert action which is essential to the career of mundane life. It is necessary, then, to overcome the prejudice of common-sense men who roar their approval for action as overt power and turn away in disdain from the modalities of action as intentional response. We are searching for the generic ground of action, a fundament inclusive enough to account for Man as a social being. It is in interpretation that an adequate approach to action can be found.

In the midst of daily life, common-sense men interpret each other's action. As we have suggested, such interpretation is itself a prime dimension

of action. It is important, though, to understand how interpretation functions
in the social realm. At the essential level of the taken-for-granted world of
daily life, the individual actor on the social scene has some conception, some
translation of the conduct of his fellow-man. What he knows of the Other,
as we have suggested, is based on a set of constructs or typifications, largely
set into motion and energized by the dynamic of social roles. Now a closer
examination of typification is needed, and it must come by way of the problem
of interpretation. To say that the individual interprets the action of his
alter ego means that he takes the Other's conduct as meaningful or significant
to *the Other*, that is, I take your action to have meaning to you, the one who
performs the action. Although there is no assurance that my reading of your
action is adequate, that is, that I correctly interpret the meaning your action
has for you, I nevertheless make *some* translation, project *some* interpretation
of your conduct. What takes on the face of social reality for me is, then, the
construction I in fact create of the meaning which action has for the fellow-
men who perform that action. My response to the Other is in strong measure
the way in which I show (or refrain from showing) the construction I have
placed on his conduct. In the vocabulary of the philosophy and methodology
of the social sciences, it is in the "subjective interpretation of meaning" that
the basis of sociality is to be discovered. As we proceed to a closer examination of the problem, remember the starting point for the entire conception of
sociality to be developed here: it is the initial character of social reality—of
men in action related to fellow-men—that the response of one person to
another presupposes that each partner interprets the other's action as
meaningful to him, his alter ego.

Just as the term "action" carries the public connotation of overt and
forceful behavior, so "subjective" is commonly understood as referring to
the personal, the idiosyncratic, and the unreliable. To say of a judgment that
it is "subjective" is often to mean that it merely reflects the predisposition
of the judger. Thus, "subjective" is the antonym of "objective," where the
latter means true to the facts. The sad result of these usages is that otherwise
useful terms have suffered linguistic contamination. Since we are stuck with
them, connotations and all, we must make the best of the situation; we may,
indeed, take advantage of the looseness of language. What started off as a
liability may prove to be a flexibility sedimented in the language of daily life.
For the sake of clarity, we will understand "subjective" to mean related to
a person, a "subject" in the sense of an individual. "Subjective" then means
subject-bound. That understood, it is possible to describe the context in
which subjective interpretation takes place. Let us imagine a scene:

Mr. Bono, a mass observer, is making his rounds Tuesday morning, the day for ringing
doorbells, assessing tithes, leaving notes for solicitors, and assisting those caught in
chancery. A full day's work! Now he calls on Mrs. Dorfman, Apt. 1 in a modest duplex.

"Ring," says his finger.

"Yes?" replies Mrs. Dorfman.

Mr. Bono stands poised and open to all possibilities, his sensory gate ajar, his cognitive throughway green-lighted.

"Yes," he notes aloud, "affirmative."

"If you're looking for Harry," Mrs. Dorfman says, "he's not here."

"Harry," says Mr. Bono, and smiles.

The delight of relevancies, the superb pattern of interconnections. A moment ago, Harry was a possibility; now Mr. Bono and Harry are joined in the infinite web of actuality. And Mrs. Dorfman too: a piece of the puzzle, a voice of reassurance and union in the silent interiors of streets and viaducts. O jacks of selective trades! Artists of mass-construction!

"Mrs. Dorfman," says Mr. Bono, "I congratulate you and Harry too on your contribution to the What of things, the magnificence of mass."

"I'm sorry, we're not Catholics," Mrs. Dorfman replies.

Another line sent tingling into the net of circumstance, a bird for paradise, the innards of creation.

"We are all just men here," quotes Mr. Bono from recent reading.

"You mean the ecumenical thing?" asks Mrs. Dorfman.

"I refer to Leviathan," says Mr. Bono, "the vast summation whose integers we are, whether hidden in homes or conversing al fresco."

"You must have the wrong house," Mrs. Dorfman says. "Nobody by that name lives here."

And closes the door. Mr. Bono makes a notation in his blue notebook, the color of Tuesdays, and turns toward the next house.

Within the rational world, expectancies are always typified. Even the irrational is recognized and given its place in the orderly scheme of things. But rationality implies the significance of all action. The word or the deed, the look or the movement all intend some purposiveness whose source is the Other's consciousness and whose meaning therefore is given in his interpretive life. The initial response to the Other, as we have seen, arises in the context of interaction, not observation. I am, first of all (in terms of the social world), a man *with* my fellow-men, a responder to the actions of Others. To be sure, I observe the Other. It is in the role of actor, however, that such observation takes place. Observing the Other means perceiving his action as already significant in terms of what that action means to him. We are speaking of observation as a part of the process of response, not as a formal perspective in scientific procedure. As an actor on the social scene, the individual observes and is observed by the Other in the flow of interaction. The interiorization or reflexive aspect of consciousness which is essential to action may now be understood as the structural element in observation. When I perceive the action of the Other as meaningful, I observe his performance as having been or being *intended* by him. The interiorization which is at work here is the moment of consciousness in which intention and performance are united through the schema of type. The meaning I associate with my action is located in the unity of consciousness, not in a "behind the scenes" purposing. To understand that action when it is performed by the Other, I turn to the typification of "an act of that type." My own projecting of action is dominated by the essential fact that what I know of the world I have learned and continue to know through my construction of it, that is, by the typifying agency of consciousness. Mrs. Dorfman expects, with the reasonability of typification, that a caller will state his business, that if he doesn't immediately it may be because of some mistake or confusion, that what he says must make some sense in *some* context, that one does one's best to discover that context, that if the confusion persists and there seems to be no urgency in the caller's business, it is reasonable to call a halt to the proceedings and suggest that he take up whatever concerns him with somebody else. All of these assumptions lie below the threshold of formal statement; they are recipes of typification which are relied on continually in common-sense life and which serve as the secret language of sociality. All action depends on some basic congruency between the recipes of the members of society, the citizens of the everyday world. Mr. Bono, that metaphysical busybody, is an insult to the unity of typification, a threat to all recipes. If *everything* is relevant, then nothing can be said. If any sign immediately flashes its connectives to the world and if consciousness revels in every sign, then the mass Mr. Bono celebrates is an obsessive's nightmare. The inventory of items appropriate as entries into the Bono notebooks, being all-inclusive, goes from whatever happens to pop forth at some chance moment to the galactic implications implied in that bit of an event. The familiar images of the hurled pebble which disturbs the universe as it skips across the pond and that wretched flower in the crannied wall do not even begin to approximate the mischief done when Mr. Bono's lists start accumulating. The possibility of sociality rests on a principle of selection. Consciousness is an abstractive instrument; it makes possible the coherence of the world because it assures the status of relevance. In turn, social action achieves validation.

We have been following a course of inquiry concerned with understanding the foundation of the "subjective interpretation of meaning." Our result, expressed in the simplest and most direct way, is that what is "real" on the social scene is that which is defined as real by the individual. All of us, then, as actors on the social stage, live within the arc of our own interpretations of our roles. The reality of social life for the individual is the sphere of his interpretation of the meaning of his own action. What is it for individuals, each of whom defines his own social reality, to be related to one another, to be *with* one another? Isn't the "We-relationship" splintered to solipsistic bits by the individuation of the "subjective interpretation of meaning"? Quite the reverse! A very central aspect of "interpretation" is the way in which the individual comprehends his alter ego and the way in which the individual thinks his alter ego comprehends him. As we have seen, such "interpretation" is by way of the typifications and constructions the individual makes of his world and, indeed, ultimately of himself. To be *with* Others is to share those typifications. Furthermore, to be *with* Others is to respond to them, to participate with them, to assume that they typify in the same way I do, in the same way *we* do. When such typification breaks down or is for certain reasons denied or severely circumscribed, then we have, at least in descriptive terms, evidence of fundamental differences or basic prejudices. When I say that you simply don't understand this country, that your thinking is outside the categories proper to its comprehension, then the "we" of that conversation or exchange is limited to the far side of typification, to the recognition that even if communication is just about impossible, announcing that impossibility and stating the reasons for it are possible in typified terms. When I say that *we* are incapable of understanding *them* or vice versa—that "white consciousness" is outside of "black consciousness," that white Americans can't *really* understand black Americans at this point in the history of the United States, or, to say it more divisively, that "honkies" can't understand "Afro-Americans"—what I mean is that not only has language broken down but the undergirding structure of shared reality has collapsed. It is customary to speak of a failure in "communication" and to call for a new or renewed "dialogue" between the alienated groups. But when the typification on which sociality is founded is damaged, what is alienated is social reality itself, not simply groups or classes. Ordinarily—normally, we say—such fragmentation is not the case or else reflects merely a segment of social reality. When breakdown is far-reaching in the society we have some form of anomie; when it is true of the individual, we have disease of the mind, pathology of the person. Our present concern, however, is still the nature of typification in the ordinary situations of daily life, within the taken-for-granted reality of mundane existence.

If the meaning of sociality lies in the shared character of typification, then it is necessary to see how such sharing functions. What aspect of the Other presents itself to me in social relationship, and how is typification a means for grasping what appears and then moving beyond it? First, to ask what *aspect* of the Other appears is already to have a clue to the meaning of social presentation, for it is through aspects or adumbrations that we come into touch with fellow-men. To speak of an aspect or adumbration is to say, most immediately, that there is both a *situation* and a *perspective* in terms of which the Other appears. The situation is the large set of conditions which circumscribe any individual in action. And the conditions include metaphysical no less than historical and political forces which exist or have existed in the foreground or past of the particular problem at issue. Thus, the present situation of the American Negro, to return to an earlier point, is to be understood not only in terms of hundreds of years of American history but, more immediately, in the focus of the last fifteen years and even the last five years of American experience. The situation includes the history of slavery and civil war, of reconstruction and industrialization, of twentieth-century wars and continuing warfare. It includes the history of Congressional legislation and the history of the courts, the civil rights movement and urban dislocation and disaster. The situation of the Negro is nothing less than the history of American consciousness. The *perspective* from which and through which that situation presents itself is the insertion of the individual at some place in the social fabric: as a white man or a Negro, as employed or unemployed, as in one's twenties or one's sixties, as a man or as a woman or as a child, as class-oriented in a variety of ways, as politically implicated in one or several of many permutations of action. The perspective is the dynamic moment through which the situation is defined by and for the individual. To go a step further:

When questions are raised about the situation of the Negro in current American life, it is essential to know *who* is asking the questions. Is it "we" or "they"? From the white perspective, the Negro is a problem; for the Negro what is at issue is reality, himself in the world. Obviously there are "problems," recognized readily enough by both whites and blacks, but such recognition hardly confronts the reality of lives in movement. In effect, the very statement of a "problem" may tend to draw us away from the living experience to a debating of conditions, causes, and options for choice. To sympathetically and progressively intended statements on better housing made by a highly placed government official at a conference on urban power, a woman shouted out: "Stop calling us ghetto people. We are not ghetto people. We are colonialized Africans." Is it merely a matter of language? Would that woman really have responded differently had she been addressed as a "colonialized African"? The breakdown of language is merely a symptom of a fractured sociality. The question is one of recognition that though a situation may be ours—black and white—in the broadest sense of mutual responsibility, the perspective of the actor on the scene is qualitatively different, depending on who he is, where he "comes from," where he belongs or is said to belong. Clearly, situation and perspective are bound to each other and intersect each other. Together, they offer some access to the meaning of the concept of "aspect." Most directly, the Other presents himself to me *as* someone I know or a stranger, *as* someone "like" me or not, *as* someone "who speaks my language" or not, *as*, very simply, "one of us" or not. Put in this way, everything seems to be remarkably conclusive, as though in a glance the Other were spotted, identified, and pinned like a collector's butterfly. We must start at a different extreme, that of the epistemological access of man to fellow-man. There, in the perceptual bedrock of recognition, we will begin to find the emerging history of typification.

Let us start with a simple kind of object, a building block from a child's playroom. Instead of using the procedure of suspension we followed at the outset of our inquiry, we will begin by taking for granted everything we, as adults within our cultural orientation, know about toy blocks. I am looking, then, at a typical specimen: I see the capital "R" in bright red as I look out and down at the side of the block facing me. From this angle a clown greets my eye on another face of the cube, and I can glimpse the bare outline and color of a number on still another side. The underside is completely hidden, of course, and two other sides are visually lost to me. I see the object as a toy block; I know it is a cube whose sides are covered with the usual sort of designs inscribed on such toys: letters of the alphabet, numbers, pictures of animals, little words, and similar devices. Occasionally a side is blank or colored in. It would not surprise me to find a block with the outline of George Washington's head, an American Eagle, a patriotic saying, or the geographic outline of one of the States. Although I haven't looked at the latest models, I wouldn't be shocked to find pop art-style blocks, blocks which come only in red, white, and blue and with enough stars to form the flag, or sets with sayings such as "Legalize Potty." Little surprises us today. But inured as we are to the shocking, it would be a perceptual extravagance, to put it mildly, to find a block—no tricks now—all of whose sides are presented at once to the viewer. Without any training in the history of optics or epistemology, we know in mundane terms that this is impossible. We know that each time we see a three-dimensional, opaque object, we will be able to view only some of the sides at a single glance. That we can rotate the block, that we can then remember what is on all the sides, that we can remember from previous occasions what is on all the sides, that we can anticipate or imagine what is on the unseen sides—all that is as obvious as it is irrelevant to the selectivity of perception, the permanent, in-principle limitation of all perceptual experience. Nevertheless, when we see the block, we see it *as* a full-bodied, integral thing of its sort. We don't see it as a three-sided givenness which *may* have or might be imagined to have other sides. We see it in much the same way as the child utilizes it: cubed in its little hunk of wood, turnable, multi-faceted, *sided*. If the "R" is the aspect of the object presented, "R" co-presents other sides of the block. Now such co-presentation may prove to be false in terms of subsequent perception. What I took to be the underside, a normal facet of the block which "R" co-presented to me, may turn out to be nonexistent: the block may have only five sides and be hollow inside (the "no tricks" we asked for may not have been honored; the ukase is ineffective in the nursery), or the block may be made of plastic and have one of its sides broken off. Whatever the later perception may prove to be the case, it remains true that, initially, I *intended* the block as having an honest, run-of-the-mill underside. To say that I intended the block in this way is to understand something of the machinery of adumbrative awareness. The selectivity of perception and its co-presentational force are the beginnings of the typifying activity of consciousness.

To go now to the most complex of objects, human beings, we may say that they too present themselves in aspects or profiles which co-present their unity. We see the Other in his full embodiment, not as a slice of some sort of perceptual pie. But clearly, "full embodiment" is intended, not actually given in any perceptual glance. At this point, the force of learning and conditioning may intrude despite all phenomenological barricades. Don't we in fact *learn* about the embodiment of the Other from past experience, from the accumulation of a vast range of observation from childhood through maturity? There is no need to deny the meaningfulness of the past or the inescapable and enormous significance of learning. We are, however, not asking about the genesis of historical events in the psychological development of the individual but about the genesis of essential conditions for the very possibility of there being perceptual experience at all. Given any event, any perceptual experience, how is it possible that the object is recognized, apprehended *as* object? In nonpsychological terms, it is in the structure of intentional consciousness that such essential features of perceptual life can be located and examined. And there we find quickly that intentional experience —thinking of, knowing about, being concerned with—is abstractive in its very nature, first because it points to an "object" which merely corresponds to the activity which proclaims and announces it, and second, because the "object" so intended is *typified* in its generality and in its independence of the personal history, the biography, of the individual. What is essentially true of the aspect-bound reality of perception is not based on an induction from a sampling of perceivers; it is true of perception at the same time that it holds for all perceivers. To say that the individual cannot see all sides of the block at once establishes something of critical importance about human reality: each of us is open to the possibilities of a typifying consciousness and, at the same time, bound by the gravity of mundane perception.

It is a long but not a discontinuous road from the perception of objects to the perception of persons. If it is only aspects of the block which I can see at any one time, so it is only facets of the Other which present themselves to me on any one occasion. Unlike physical sides, however, the facets of a person are presentations of his character, ways in which his interpretation of the world and plans for action are revealed or concealed. And if it is necessarily only adumbrations, profiles of the Other, which are available to his fellow-men, then the large theme of the fragmentation of human reality inevitably makes its appearance in this discussion. There are a number of reasons why the Other presents himself to me only in partial guises. First, in a sense it is obvious that the Other intersects with me at some point in our history when some circumscribed event or problem limits and helps to define what is relevant to our interests and possibilities. Since everything cannot be expressed, selection must follow as an implication of social structure. Second, all the Other has available to him as far as I, his alter ego, am concerned, is an aspect of *my* reality. Can the Other be expected, even if it were possible, to present himself fully when I don't? Third, the Other has "control" of only part of his presentation to the world of fellow-men. A consummate actor or one highly disciplined in a social role may indeed succeed completely in presenting himself as he wishes to appear. Clearly, the narrower the role and the shorter the duration of the role-playing, the greater the chances for thorough success. But in the vast range of action we have neither remarkable actors nor tightly scripted roles; the margin for improvisation, indeed the demand for improvisation, is great, and the consequence is that most of us succeed only in degree, often limited degree, in appearing as we wish to. To the extent that we fail or cannot adequately gauge our success, a fragmentary presentation of man to fellow-man follows. Fourth, the *means* of presentation—language, gesture, intonation, as well as all the subtle inflections of attitude—are themselves imperfect and often fragmented instruments. The very typicality of language and the general intelligibility of gesture are attributes which work in opposite directions; they tend to assure universality precisely because they cloak or obscure the idiosyncratic and individual connotations of meaning which may be of decisive importance in communication and response between fellow-men. The price of clarity may be fragmentation. Fifth, and perhaps most instructive of all, the reason for the essential adumbrativeness in all social reality is the recognition that the individual is, in some measure, a stranger to himself, that each of us knows himself only in aspects, and that every person, therefore, is a partial expression both of his accomplishments and of his possibilities.

Between the typification of roles and the fragmentation of the person, it would seem that the choice is either anonymity or schizophrenia. Such alternatives are neither exhaustive nor fairly formulated. It would be misleading to reduce this discussion to the claim that human interaction is a matter of robot-like behavior in programmed roles or a game of hide and seek played by masked selves. We are speaking instead of the conditions of action and response which make communication possible. Anonymity is a feature of communication itself, not a judgment of the value of communication. Similarly, fragmentation is endemic to the possibilities of men in action, not a repudiation of action or a confession of its failure. The point is that even when men *do* understand each other thoroughly, even when they *do* succeed in presenting themselves as they wish to, and even when they *do* achieve the results they strive for in the arena of practical affairs, they still must operate from the inalienable ground of their limits as human beings bound to time and space, incarnated in the world as psychophysical beings, having to live *with* fellow-men in a shared world, and having to grow older and die. Such "constants," as they have been called, are as relevant to problems of the presentation of the self as they are to man's relation to history or to God. Indeed, man, as we hope to show later, is able to fulfill his role in history and achieve a significant religious dimension precisely because anonymity and fragmentation point beyond themselves to transcendent realities. For the present, let it be enough to say that a very substantial measure of mundane existence is made possible as well as infected by the force of typification.

If sociality begins and remains rooted in typification, it does not stagnate in anonymity nor remain confined to social fragmentation. It is time to turn from the phenomenology of sociality to some of its existential implications. The argument for the uniqueness of the person, for his existential fervor and identity, for everything opposed to the anonymity of roles can be put straightforwardly: We can and do distinguish between the Other who confronts us as a distinctive, fully individuated person with his own character and flair and, at the other extreme, someone whose grayness, conformity, almost built-in uniformity assures a sovereign mediocrity. That we do differentiate between the two means that a counterprinciple to typification is at work and that it succeeds in giving to the human scene evidence of vitality and originality of mind and character. There are a number of reasons which help to account for the existentially vibrant and definitive quality of the person: First, just as we acknowledged the "We-relationship" to have a self-generated reality, so we must say that in the immediacy of face-to-face encounter there is a *Thou* experienced which also has undeniable and irreducible force. "Encounter" demands its own account, but quickly put it means that there is a domain of relationship between *persons* just as there is a shared reality of selves. This entire discussion indicates a qualitative shift in the dialectic of involvement of man with fellow-man. From the analysis of self and Other in terms of adumbrations and aspects, we have come to a principle of the *person* which presents a once-lived-through existence given not simply to "the Other" but to a concrete flesh-and-bone creature who stands before me now as my love or my indifference or my antagonism reveals him at *this* moment. As distinguished from the "you" of syntax or the "you" of distance (as in writing a business letter to someone), the "Thou" of encounter in, let us say, friendship is a specified and restricted recognition of an ongoing and mutual responsibility of self *for* self through person being *with* person. Nor is it a matter of closer or more intense relationship that constitutes the person. Such calibrations tend to quantify the reality whereas what is at issue is the irreplaceability of the partners, a quality in each which manifests itself, constitutes itself only in the relationship. *Being* friends means recognizing the Other as Thou for a relationship which is unrepeatable because its temporality—what we referred to as its "ongoing" character—constructs, step by step in shared time, the recognition of person by person. To be sure, we have been speaking of friendship as a paradigm; no doubt, such a relationship is rare in contrast to "having friends," in the casual sense of Others we know rather well, are involved with, and whose lives are connected with our own in obvious ways. It is the prize won by the paradigm, however, which gives us the meaning of the Thou.

A second reason for the existential reality of the person is to be found in the *situation* of encounter. The Other, as imperatively a *person*, appears or is at least sought in the urgencies of mundane existence, in radical human need, in the terrors of exposure and sudden affliction, in the insurrections and aggrievements of the spirit. We must realize, of course, that to speak of the existential reality of the Other is necessarily to be concerned with the identity of the self as person; to say Thou is to locate the existential I. That understood, we may turn to the situation of encounter with the awareness of complicity. At a turning point in the life of my friend, *I* find myself confronting him with the core of my own being at issue. It is impossible to say in effect, "All right, I'll listen attentively and sympathetically to your problem, but don't expect all of me to be risked. Be reasonable and settle for the kind of sensitive and discerning advice which can come from that part of me which allows for our friendship." Encounter demands an all-or-nothing response, but it remains uncertain what "all" signifies. It is a necessary if not a sufficient condition for the "all" to be at issue that I or the Other understand the emergency of the situation as placing in question or endangering both the history of the person's past development and his prospects of continuing as he has been or changing in some significant way. To say that the *person* is at issue in encounter is to look at both temporal realities. A sufficient condition would be the actual risk his partner in friendship must take in making himself utterly available as a person, in *his* identity, to the needs of the Other. In fine, the difference between operating as an individual in a social role and acting as a friend in a critical circumstance is that limits can be ascribed to roles but none to friendship. That does not mean that I will "do anything" for my friend or that I will expect him to do anything for me. It does mean that whatever demands are called for will be confronted and assessed by a person limited only by what he judges to be ultimately valid for his friend, a validity which necessarily must impinge powerfully on his own existence.

Finally—though far from exhaustively—the existential quality of the person is rooted in the vivacity and spontaneity of the individual. Earlier we spoke of the distinction between the "me" of stability and the innovative "I" of subjectivity. That "I" has an existential dimension and may be understood as the principle of self-action through which the person is free to invent, to express himself in a world he will live through only once, to shape the course of his existence even if he cannot determine the history of his time. Improvisation, experiment, risk, and flexibility are features of mundanity no less than of large-scale human action in politics and war. A belly dancer has a sphere of manipulation no less than a brigadier general. Within the current of concrete existence, the person has a margin of decision about the way in which he will present himself: to repeat the same routine in the same way, to play the same role in the same way, to promise the same style of action, or—and this is the moment of freedom—to transcend the boundaries of the typical, to lash into a role with originality, to announce through fresh action that the " I " is still not captive or tame. There are, after all, significant ranges of experience in which spontaneity is valued dearly because it is the life of the person which is constituted through small but striking choices. It would be false to portray the choice between dreariness and vivacity as either a climactic decision or a once-and-for-all affair. Rather, the area between public, standardized role-playing and personal, private action is a zone inhabited by both the "me" and the "I" of the individual's action. It is, in fact, a highly complex domain in which the style of an individual's daily existence is enmeshed in a continuous flow of attitude and interpretation. The source of that flow is consciousness understood as an intentional structure, a continuous streaming forth of perceptual life. What is noteworthy is the vitality of the person which enables him to make himself seen and felt in the midst of typified awareness, to be a *person* in an otherwise anonymous world. Our discussion of the existential reality of the person and our analysis of the phenomenology of typification bring the discussion of sociality to a problematic close by presenting a troubling paradox.

If phenomenology depicts the typical, existentialism shows the unique; if phenomenology deals with essence, existentialism handles concreteness; if phenomenology is interested in the structure of consciousness, existentialism is concerned with the reality of the individual. It would seem that these philosophies represent divergent standpoints rather than complementary approaches to human reality. That they are congenial, indeed intimately intersustaining and supporting views of Man is the methodological thesis on which we have proceeded. What appears to be a paradox is a metaphysical duality which affects all philosophizing as it does the reality which all philosophizing is about. In classical and traditional terms, the duality has been called the Universal and the Particular, or Thought and Life. The question is how the truth of the world in general is related to the truth of individual experience and how a theoretical system can understand the immediacy of the person. I do not propose to try to respond to these problems at this point. Instead, I will try to show the utility of my thesis of the unity of phenomenological method and existential analysis in the chapters which follow. Being aware of the paradox, however, provides a service as well as a warning. The phenomenological examination of sociality by way of typification needs to be extended from the level of the individual-Other relationship to the larger order of society with its components of groups, institutions, and politics. The place of the individual in that social matrix, the role of the hero in mundane existence, inevitably is grounded in the meaning of such fundamental social phenomena as "classes," "parties," and the rest of the basic vocabulary of political sociology. We are back to the problems of *type*, whose philosophical foundations we sought to clarify. In fact, to speak of "groups," "heroes," "classes," and "parties" is to be concerned with the root of typification, despite the transposition of the problem. The question is how it is possible to move from the individual to the group without losing the existential reality of the person and without denying the trenchancy of typification. The promise of phenomenology must be matched by the warning of existentialism. We want to retain both structure and person. In certain ways, the next stage in our journey is an attempt to see whether such a methodological integrity is possible or whether Thought and Life are irresolvable.

chapter
four

science

So far it would seem that our story has been restricted to a very small gathering: two people, ego and alter ego. Even the We of sociality turned out to be chiefly the two of us, I as ego and you as Other, concerned with larger questions about the rest of the social world. Of course, we cannot do everything in this book; still, our quarters are rather close. It is time for a third man to appear on the scene, or for one of us to act in his place. In short, it is time for the entrance of the "observer," the individual whose function it is to describe and analyze but not to participate, or whose participation is defined by an ulterior loyalty: the scientific enterprise which dominates and determines his professional action. To start at the very beginning, we should say that it is one of the cardinal features of sociality no less than of mundane existence that reflection upon it emerges as one of its possibilities. The reflexive dimension of the ego is, as we have seen, essential to the practice of philosophy, to the individual's philosophizing. In the case of science, reflection means attending to that which is outside the scientist's egological sphere, a field of observation specified by the history and status of his discipline. By "status" I mean the present state of development rather than prestige. And status is most simply defined by what is known at a certain time as well as the methodology and theoretical grounding for what is known. A convenient means for determining what is known in the field of optics, for example, is to study an acknowledgedly major and highly regarded treatise on the subject or a series of recent works on detailed aspects of the subject. If not only recent but "up to the minute" information is needed to supplement textbook and treatise study, such material is available in the periodical literature in the field, found in research libraries. Ongoing investigation and experimentation are more or less open to professionals and graduate students in colloquia, meetings of scientific societies, and advanced seminars at universities. A student setting out today to study optics takes on the responsibility of learning what has already been accomplished by his predecessors. In a way, his initial task is to find out where he comes in.

We have been pointing to the "additive" nature of science, a progression in which determinations and results can be utilized without the student's having to place in radical question the whole history of his discipline. Of course, the history of science is not that of a continuous accumulation; there have been revolutions and upheavals in the natural sciences which have resulted in fundamental reassessments of the question of where one is properly to begin the study of physics or biology. But such upset is concerned with a conceptual framework; it is not a residual feature of the student's own experience. In philosophy, on the other hand, it is impossible to follow an "additive" path, for the object of inquiry, human experience, is not only perpetually renewed in its temporal problematicity but the investigator, the philosopher-student, is himself profoundly entangled in that temporality. Once again our paradox makes an appearance: the reality which the philosopher investigates has general characteristics, yet the course of his inquiry is specific and, for him, unrepeatable. Certainly there is the history of philosophy to build upon, but the materials, the problems which that history has assumed responsibility for, must be discovered, recovered by the individual in the history of his own development, in the uniqueness of his own human career. One of the decisive differences between philosophy and science is found at this point; it is the qualitative distance between work which can be done by all suitably trained men, more or less picking up the burden at the point reached by their predecessors, and the reconstruction of experience defined by an inquirer whose beginning point is forever fixed in the confines of his own concrete existence. In both philosophy and science, the novice enters an intellectual scene which has been affected and altered by his predecessors, a scene which continues to change as his career advances. Nor is there any suggestion intended here that philosophy's problems are somehow unaffected by world history. Rather, the point is that *within* the evolving history which the scientist and the philosopher inherit, the professional obligations of the former are intrinsically untouched by the existential commitments of the latter. Part of the difference may be seen by examining the role of the observer.

We are distinguishing between the individual as an actor on the social scene and the scientific observer as abstracted from social action. Before we can turn to the contrast in the framework of social science, it is necessary to make a preliminary statement of the role of the observer in natural science, *vis-à-vis* the objects of investigation in the realms of matter, energy, and other features of, first of all, the nonhuman world. *Things*—inanimate objects—are in our world; we are not in theirs. If it makes no sense to say that I am part of the world of a stone, it is because "world" has no meaning in this context. Stones are without "world." Later we shall turn to a more extensive probing of the meaning of "world"; for the time being, we mean by it the articulation of a coherent order of experience within whose limits the intentional organization of and reflection upon reality are possible. Obviously according to these criteria, "world" is ruled out for stones and cabbages. It might be asked whether the same is true, or as readily evident, for colonies of ants and bees or for dogs and cats. Frankly, insects and animals are always causing trouble for philosophers. Even Noah, that benefactor of the animal kingdom, must have been concerned about termites. The embarrassment over animals is far-reaching, and I'm not convinced that it is possible either to rule out the primordial elements of "world" in certain respects (dogs and cats have a memorial continuity in which "Others" and "events" have some placement) or to ignore the very forceful differences in other respects (in addition to language and history, the place of what is *not* immediately given in sensory experience) which include what we have called the reflexive dimension of human subjectivity, perceptual sensitivity of the second degree, or "awareness of awareness." In any case, the resolution of the problems calls for a Saint Francis of philosophy. There is reason to suspect that such an emancipator will come from the ranks of the biologists and "animal anthropologists" rather than from philosophy, and that his insight will be nourished by a very rich sense of descriptive detail in animal life, a brilliance and patience of interpretive observation which was characteristic of Charles Darwin. Admitting some disturbance and confessing to a sense of dissatisfaction with the state of things, I take leave of the animals.

What, then, is the role of the natural-scientific observer? First, he stands (that is, is scientifically situated) outside the field he observes. He is not part of the action or interaction but an uninvolved witness of its dynamic. I am suggesting that if there is in fact involvement by the observer, then another, uninvolved investigator must be called in to do the job originally planned for his predecessor. Second, the observer *qua* observer has no identity apart from the professional requirements his discipline demands and his particular assignment presupposes. *Any* competent observer—that is, any individual successfully trained for the job—is able to perform with equal facility and with equivalent results. If abilities and talents vary, as they do, then we need speak only of equal competence at any level of the scale. A Nobel Prize winner is not needed to read a gas meter, nor is it certain he would be especially good at the job. Third, the observer defines the beginning, duration, and termination of the events he studies; they are specified by the stipulations of the experiment or the purposes of the investigation. When the work is done the observer departs from the scientific scene. His responsibility is not to what he studies but to the scientific community to which he ultimately reports. Finally, the scientific observer is free of value commitments in his work. All of the questions of the worth or moral validity of what he is doing as an observer are methodologically excluded insofar as he performs his job in traditional form. One might say that the scientist is an observer when he typifies his role completely and functions solely in accordance with role-expectancies and role-requirements. The doubts or indecisiveness he may feel as a person do not enter his formal activity. The observer is a victory of role over person. It would be simplistic to assume that, in psychological terms, every observer and every occasion of observation are evidence of or an exemplification of a total compartmentalization of the individual, that an antiseptic atmosphere obtains in all scientific work, and that the scientist lives during working hours in a hermetically sealed tube. We have been speaking of the formal aspects of the observer and have been trying to locate his operational stance. If no scientist can live by methodology alone, neither can science survive without it. The tension created by what seems to be an unnatural strain between role and person is intensified when we move from the natural to the social sciences.

Broadly understood, the social sciences (and we shall be emphasizing the science of society) take as their object Man. In effect, then, the social scientist is a man observing Man. It would seem reasonable for him to set about his business as the natural scientist does his work, that is, as an objective observer utilizing the methods so successfully worked out by the natural sciences. The history of the development of the social sciences has, in fact, moved along these lines. In the discipline of sociology, for example, those following the tradition of Comte maintained that the methods of physics and mathematics could be applied with equally satisfactory results in that social science. Indeed, the history of sociology is incomprehensible apart from the effort to make it a science. For many years it was maintained that the inexactitude, theoretical uncertainty, and lack of rigorous predictive power characteristic of sociology, in sharp contrast with physics, were functions of the youth of the discipline, that maturity would come in time and with it exact science. The underlying thesis of this argument was that science is fundamentally power, that knowledge is validated by its capacity to control. There were, of course, countermovements to this position, and a methodological controversy began in the first part of this century which is still unresolved and which has had important implications for the entire development of the philosophy of the social sciences. The issues were fundamental: on one side the claim that the proper model for the methodology of the social sciences is that of the natural sciences; on the other the view that the social sciences are qualitatively different in nature and demand their own approaches and techniques. The arguments, in transposed and more sophisticated form, are still going on. At the center of the controversy is the problem of social action, its meaning and its status. We shall examine it without entering into an historical analysis of the various theories of social science.

When a geologist studies a sample of a rock formation, he is concerned with it as it reveals its structure and characteristics, its properties and its implications for the region or place from which it was taken. Depending on the professional mission of the geologist, the sample may indicate a possible area-source for petroleum, suitable foundation soil for a building, or a likely spot for an archaeological dig. Whatever his interests and the limitations prescribed by his professional activity, the geologist regards the sample at the time of his investigation as something for *him*, as a datum for his science, as an entity whose meaning is granted in the act of scientific classification. The mode of being of the rock sample is, more or less, what the geologist makes it. It is only at the narrow entrance of analysis that the density, sedimentation, and chemical properties of the rock become significant. The rock *becomes* in virtue of the geologist's activity. At the other extreme, the sociologist turns to a "sample" whose prime characteristic is that it has already "become," is already in a state of "becoming" before the social scientist looks into or at it. The human being investigated by the sociologist has a reality which not only permits the scientist to look "into" it but which enables the "subject" to look "out" or "into" his observer. Perhaps this is not all that distant from the lower animals. There is a legendary story in psychology of a well-known researcher into the behavior of apes who devised a complex experiment for one of his animals. He set up the materials in the ape's cell, a room purposely cut off from view by a wooden door. As soon as everything was ready, he placed the chimpanzee in the cell, closed the door, and immediately kneeled at the keyhole to observe. As he peered in, his glance was met by a large brown eye peering out. When the sociologist picks up his subject (his object, perhaps one should say), that being is already situated in a world of his choices, his particular biographical specificity, and, as important as anything else, his ongoing projects. The scientist enters the scene after the performance has already started. He comes in at mid-act. The implications of such interruption for sociology are informative.

Given the history and temporality of the interpretive life of the subject, the sociologist is confronted with a difficult choice. If he tries to secure rigorous results, he may, wittingly or not, be tempted to ignore those elements of the subject's experience which do not lend themselves to strict description and measurement. If he does turn to the full weight of the subject's lived reality, the sociologist may lose his perspective as observer and respond not only unrigorously but "unscientifically." How is it possible to resolve or

escape from these difficulties? An immediate reply, if not an answer, is to
suggest that the sociologist is really not concerned with concrete individuals
but with types, that he turns to the person only as a jumping-off point for
the analysis of the typical. This is an important but not an altogether
satisfactory response. It is true that the science of sociology is not built out
of the observation or analysis of specific individuals, but neither is mundane
existence. We have seen enough in our study of sociality to realize that everyday existence is highly typified in character, that the knowledge which the
individual has of the Other is richly constructive, and that social action is
composed of intended meaning which goes beyond the idiosyncratic character
of the actor. We have, then, two orders of constructs or typifications: those
made by men in social action within mundane existence and those created by
scientists within the methodology of their discipline. The first are naive
(though complex in structure) and immanent to social life; the second are
sophisticated and explicitly formulated in the theoretical apparatus of the
science. Some of the confusions, impasses, and genuine disagreements about
the philosophical grounding of contemporary social science may now be
stated in partisan fashion:

1 Between the "objectivists" and the "subjectivists" in sociology—
between those who believe in and aspire to practice a science of society and
those who look to a qualitatively different model for social-scientific inquiry—
there is a profound epistemological alienation. Objectivists are untroubled
by the givenness of mundane social life; for them, human reality is already
societally formed, men are *of course* in action in familiar form, and life goes
on at a pace and in a current which are unquestioned and, in a sense, un-
questionable. There "it" all is before us: the social world; and here we are:
men in that world. The epistemological evidentness of such givens is so
absolute that not only are no basic questions raised about the *phenomena* of
social reality but it is difficult to see the relevance of such questioning.
Philosophers may worry about whether the world is real or what it means to
say it is real, but the sociologist as objectivist has other business at hand,
more pressing concerns.

2 For the subjectivist, epistemology is inescapably relevant to his sociological work, for to ask about the nature of reality in social action, to turn to
the *phenomena* of social reality, is to shape the course of the inquiry and,
indeed, to alter and affect that which the inquiry is about. This point must
be made as forcefully as possible. The sociologist seriously interested in
understanding Man in the social world must find him first of all in the everyday existence which is taken for granted in its epistemological status by *both*

men in daily life and the sociologist himself. To turn to that taken-for-grantedness is to transcend, to some extent, the naive orientation of mundane existence and to raise the problem of philosophy and its relationship to social science. There is, of course, a difference between being conceptually aware that "common sense" and "daily life" are terms describing aspects of the world and turning to the immediacy of that world as expressed in common-sense terms. Philosophy demands something more from sociology than the notation of types.

3   Phenomenology transcends both "objectivistic" and "subjectivistic" approaches to social phenomena because it refuses to accept the duality of "exterior"-"interior" spheres of reality and action. It is not the surface of the Other which appears to me in the midst of social action but *the Other*, a fellow-man. And when I find myself confronted by the Other, it is not some "deep down inside" feeling or some private room in the house of consciousness which I attend to, but myself in-the-world, facing the person next to me, responding to what he says in the continuing flow of interpretive understanding. Essentially, the initial response of self to world establishes the matrix within which social action occurs. The history of that action is the power of the world to shake me, interrupt me, goad me, and persuade me. Self and world are facets of a single order of reality which is both pre-given to each individual and constituted by him in the interpretive recognition his life gives to the world.

We have come to the bridge between self and science. From the standpoint of the individual, typification is the fundamental means by which the social world is grasped; from the standpoint of the social scientist, the construction of models ("ideal types," in the language of social science) is the procedural means through which both actors and action are comprehended. Both involvements utilize typification. In the case of mundane reality, the construction of types is the naive activity which makes it possible for the individual not only to act in face-to-face situations but to confront a world which often is not available for direct perception—the world of the past and the future, and the remote contemporaneity of those who share our world only in obscure ways, by hearsay, as it were. In social science, model-building is a cardinal way of taking note of common-sense constructs, of seeing them in their concatenated form, that is, in relationship and discontinuity with each other. Two large obligations present themselves to the scientist proceeding in this way: first, in order to grasp the mundane constructs, he must see them in their relevance for the actors who are responsible for them; second, in order to see how the subjectively interpreted constructs coalesce and come to form a social order, the scientists must build a conceptual scheme—a theory—which brings together and places in relief the philosophical grounding of the models. He must arrange a rendezvous between the system of typifications of mundane reality and the principles of typification disclosed by science. I will leave aside the question of whether the party responsible for arranging that ultimate meeting is philosophy or social science; let me say instead that in functioning as a bridge between self and science, typification, in a generic sense, lends itself most properly to the work of a philosophical sociology whose method is essentially phenomenological. This is meant as a recommendation, not a pronouncement. It can best be justified by recognizing the *as-if* or fictive quality of typification.

In social action, as we have now come to understand, the particular, the specific is treated under the aegis of the universal and the general. The individual is translated in accordance with the formulas and rules which establish the patterns of typification. Not only roles but *things* are handled in typified terms. In fact, they are initially apperceived in the form of constructs. Tools, for example, are seen as functional: this hammer is perceived as graspable and as manipulable in certain ways. To be sure, we have all watched carpenters, craftsmen, and around-the-house repairers using hammers, pounding in nails. The type-aspect of the tool, however, is given its *content*, its particular history, through the background of learning. The *form* of the type involves the larger issue of the tool's being apprehended *as* utilizable. It is not primarily the great and distant themes of Man and World which are seized in typified terms by the individual, but the trivial, slight units of the daily world. Objects of the same kind—cans of soup, packs of cigarettes, quarters and dimes, umbrellas and pencils, guppies and elephants— the endless list and array of things and creatures—are, more or less, substitutable for each other without any difference to the purchaser, the user, or the viewer. This is more true of guppies than of elephants, but the distinction merely reinforces the underlying point. In the midst of day-to-day existence, we use, depend on, and consume exemplars of types, not, for the most part unique entities. Any cigarette in the pack will do. To tap one out, light up, inhale, is to treat that slender cylinder of tobacco in "as-if" terms: you smoke it as if it were a typical cigarette. What was said earlier about the adumbrative character of perception helps to explain the enormous reliance of interpretive awareness on typified features of experience. Reaching for the pack, extracting it from a pocket by the same few fingers of your right hand, tipping the rectangle over to permit the cigarette to pop out, and going through all the other small acts leading to smoking are habitual, almost automatic movements for the heavy smoker. They constitute a tiny ritual of body and object in which the concrete characteristics of the objects involved and the events in question are set aside by the force of typification. The as-if course of activity which ensues becomes the means through which objects are appropriated by the individual who seeks their surface aspect and their elemental properties. The range of the as-if goes from the trivial to the tremendous. Its disruption leads to curious results. For example:

For some time I've felt weighted down, almost smothered by routine existence. Not just work—not even primarily work, for I rather enjoy my job—but the up and down of days, the over and over again of the entire setup of living: after one, two, three it's always four, five, six. Something starts rotting inside and you have the feeling a machine has taken over that "Heart for Rent" space and a dibble-dabble computer is socking away in the cranium. You still feel but it gets harder and harder to distinguish between intake and output: it amounts to the same gross individual product. How much can a man intake? I've decided to make a change, split out to new fields, live again, as they say in the operas. So I've decided to *do* something about me: I've gotten an interview with the Sensitivity Foundation people, an outfit that specializes in what it calls "small group thera-dynamics." You've got to pass some sort of test to get in; they don't admit just anybody.

The interview took place in a downtown office building, in a loft-like room furnished only with straw mats. Before you enter you are required to change into a kimono. To tell the truth, what bothered me all the time I was undressing was what would happen to my wallet. There was no place for it in the kimono and I would look silly holding it in my hand. Since I happened to have quite a bit of cash in it as well as credit cards, I wasn't too happy about leaving it with the receptionist, an unsmiling and incommunicative soul who might have been a deaf-mute for all I got out of her. But you have to risk something (maybe everything) to start anew (to be born again, they used to say in church), so I decided to stop worrying and enjoy the prospect.

The interviewer was a man in his early fifties, heavy set, with bushy eyebrows and a receding hairline. His hands were extremely thick and stubby; across his middle was a black sash, dividing a denim-like shirt-and-trouser set. He was wearing sneakers. I wondered whether the belt meant he was a karate expert. His hands looked as if he could chop oak boards in two with a slice and a shriek. I decided to play the waiting game: the first move was up to him.

"Dial me!" he said.

I was dumbfounded and couldn't, for the life of me, think of a response.

"If you haven't got my number, call information!"

"Is this some game?" I asked. I had heard that they had some pretty unusual gimmicks at the SF.

"Look, baby, do I have to do it for you?"

He grabbed my wrist with those wrestler's hands and yanked my index finger straight. I thought he'd pulled it out of its socket. Then he made dialing motions, using his chest as the face of the telephone.

"O.K., you've got your party, now talk!"

I thought to myself, Well you've got to go along with it, you're here of your own volition. Give it a chance.

"Whoever this is," I said to the chest phone, "I need some help."

"You've got the wrong number," said the interviewer. "This isn't the AA."

And he slammed his lightly clenched fist down on my forearm. A red welt started exploding at the edge of the kimono.

"Look," I said, "that's my arm, not a drain pipe. Take it easy."

"Dial again," he said.

"Go to hell," I replied. "I didn't come here to play telephone and I didn't come here to get my arm broken."

With that a great beam turned his face into warmth and shelter, a smile which lifted me out of irritation and guided me to acceptance, as though a berth were being prepared for me after stormy seas. Perhaps that's the meaning of "rebirth," I thought : drydock. "You're admitted to the Intermediate class in body communication," he said. "Wednesdays and Fridays, early evening, no specific hours. You'll find us in session when you come and leave us still in session when you go. Fees are contingent on progress, a sliding scale."

"I'm not sure I understand . . ." I started, but was interrupted by the entrance of the receptionist, bringing me my bundle.

"Where can I change?" I asked.

"Wherever you are," she replied.

I've been at the Foundation now for three months and am undecided : some hypotheses but no conclusions thus far. Although I'm happy with the Intermediate group, I've got reservations about some of the principles. The main thing is that Wednesdays and Fridays follow each other like ducks. And what they call the "dramadetergent," the replaying of our sessions on the "human recorder"—all that tends to get repetitive. I know every square inch of my "group body"—another bit of SF jargon—but am, so far, none the body-wiser. Of course, I was never given promises but I did believe in a qualitative change, a development of self. Every time I try to talk about that in session, I'm hushed up, as though we were conducting Quaker services. "Communicate with your eyes and thighs," I'm told. The trouble is they don't say anything. It's getting to be a bit of a drag, frankly, and after ten or twelve sessions, you can't tell them apart. Perhaps I'm ready for the Advanced class. I've heard good things about that. If something doesn't give soon, though, I may have to quit. It's simply too much of the same. I can't stick it.

The social scientist too is concerned with the as-if of experience, though his placement of the problem and means of handling it are at some variance from common-sense procedures. Again, it is in typification that the clue to the fictive aspect of experience is to be found. In dealing with types, the sociologist may turn to a particular instance or example of a group or an institution only to set it aside for methodological purposes, that is, start with the instance and then vary it both quantitatively and qualitatively to determine its limits and to extrapolate beyond them. It is also possible, of course, to commence analysis with a purely fictive model and then introduce the specific, actual example into its machinery. In either case, the concrete instance is devalued, transformed, or placed in parentheses so that its larger meaning—that which the instance intended—can be determined and utilized. To emphasize the fact that the social scientist deals with types and not individuals is to say that he comprehends the individual in terms of the typifications which his models create. The individual stands to the model as the pattern of individually intended meaning stands to a phenomenology of intention. The most startling feature of typification, whether from the side of mundane experience or social science, is the quality of the fictive. It is not immediately evident that the as-if is fictive, not in the sense of being unreal but of possessing a mode of reality defined by possibility instead of actuality. When we say that the ordinary individual depends on recipes or formulas of interpretation and action, we mean that the anonymity, the very generality of such schemes makes it possible for them to legislate for all contingencies. The fictive, then, is an ontological mode, it is a way of all being as well as a means by which the individual is able to join in and with the world. We must also remember that if the scientific observer's job is to comprehend the subjective meaning the actor bestows on his own act, then it is through the construction of fictive reality—the reality of types—that the as-if of subjective interpretation is apprehended. Conversely, it is through the appreciation of the types posited by the observer that the individual actor is able to comprehend much of his own action, his life as he thinks it appears to the Other and to Society.

To put the problem of the relationship between science and mundanity forthrightly, the question is, "How can the objective outlook of science be true to the subjective reality of the mundane world?" Our answer so far has been this: Both realms utilize types, both realms presuppose typification, and so both the objective and the subjective are joined by the same meaning-creating activity of mind. The emphasis on the fictive quality of typification is a further support to the claim that the models of the social scientist are concerned with an everyday reality which is already the product of construction by men in daily life. So far, of course, we have avoided polemics. Not all social scientists stress the importance of mundane existence in the way we have; not all sociologists agree that the primary sphere of social reality is that of the subjective interpretation of meaning. Indeed, there are those who would insist that social science is science to the extent that its methods succeed in reaching conclusions which are intersubjectively verifiable in accordance with the canons of all science, that the "subjective" interpretation of participants in the social scene is either reducible to empirical results or inadmissible to the corpus of science, and that the epistemological problems of social science are not a proper part of the scientist's concern. If this is not the "old" guard, it is not altogether unrepresentative of the entrenched guard, an establishment which includes those who are wary of philosophical meddling in social-scientific affairs and fear that the hard work of three generations of, say, sociological research will be contaminated by grandiloquent talk of "social reality" At the same time, the last few years have seen the rise of a bold band of young social scientists who have not only challenged old attitudes but have insisted on locating their professional activity in the midst of mundane reality and on finding clues for their work in whatever quarter seems lively and likely, philosophy included. It is not possible to say either that "objectivists" and "subjectivists" are fighting the same battle fought by those at the beginning of this century who argued over the logic of the "natural" versus the "cultural" sciences (though some of the same ammunition has been used and some of the same wounds have reappeared) or that theirs is the only struggle going on in contemporary methodology. It is the case, though, that through the prism of this set of problems the entire spectrum of issues in the philosophy of social science can be viewed. This approach also enables us to move on to questions concerning the relationship between social and natural science.

If our concern were the logic of science, we would have to retrace our course and enter into a variety of qualifying remarks, for in both the natural and the social sciences, individual disciplines often vary from each other in significant methodological ways. Speaking of "natural science" tends to make it appear as if everything that can be said about physics can equally well be said of zoology, and talk of the "social sciences" lends itself readily to a lumping of economics and social psychology together. Anyone working in these fields has a right to be irritated and to argue that the differences between disciplines usually herded into one shed cannot be understood, let alone resolved, by methodological indifference to their separate needs and demands. Indeed, it may well be that certain aspects of economics are closer to the natural than to the social sciences; conversely, it may be suggested that the biological specialty of ecology may, in important respects, be understood as a social science. Besides, there are intellectual studies such as history which balk at the either-or of such classifications as the "social sciences," even though it is true that they cannot be considered "natural sciences." At this point in the discussion it is usually suggested that the term "humanities" needs redefinition. Fortunately, we need not involve ourselves in these disputes. Our problem is not the logic of science; it is the history of the ego. But in tracing that history, we may find something of value in the sphere of scientific inquiry if we manage to locate the individual at a proper intersection between the movement of social and natural science. What is needed is a science which is rooted in the domain of Nature but which studies Man. There are several candidates; we shall choose psychiatry. It qualifies both as a discipline grounded in medicine and as a profession eminently interested in human beings. At the same time, it offers a fresh terrain for our continuing examination of typification, role, and the subjective interpretation of meaning.

The psychiatrist treats someone like himself. A sick fellow-man is still a fellow-man. Pathology does not disrupt the fundamental identity of the patient as a being *like us*, those who are not diseased. In a way, we already know about some of the sharp and dramatic differences between a psychotic and a normal person. Let us, to start with, center on some of the similarities. Most basic to our awareness of the ill man is that he is a being whose history is evidence of the continuity of an interior or personal world. He *was* once well; he *is* sick; he *will*, we hope, recover. The movement, superficially at

least, is from a troubled present to a renewal of the past. Underlying that
hope, as I have said, is the assumption that a world defined by the individual
can be regained and continued. The illness is then an interruption in the
midst of mundane existence. These reflections are not, strictly speaking, a
part of the psychiatrist's analysis of his patient; they are presupposed by that
analysis. The recognition that a world has been displaced by the patient's
disease is an insight which belongs to common sense. I notice that my friend
has been acting strange of late, that he is "not himself," that something
seems to be wrong. Without any psychiatric training or medical credentials, I
have every reason to be concerned. Obviously, there is a qualitative difference
between observing unusual behavior and recognizing pathological change.
Few of us are always "ourselves" at all times, in all moments of our lives. And
even when we can discover no reason for odd or even peculiar behavior, we
assume—typically predicate—that there must be some explanation and that,
in the course of events, things will "straighten out." Upset, alteration, and
distress are features of normal existence; it is that "spacing" in the life of the
individual which permits us to say that the Other is going through a time of
trouble, unhappiness, or perplexity. When the Other does not respond as we
expect him to, we wait in confidence that he soon will, that he will "be
himself" again. There are no schedules or deadlines for such anticipations.
If, in a particular instance, the person seems to be drawing further into his
anxiety, if the instances of partial reassurance to his friends grow fewer and
fewer, and if we sense—intuit, if you like—that something is truly and radically wrong with *him*, then we urge him to seek professional help, to see a
psychiatrist. All of these recognitions and assessments are made in common-
sense life and in accordance with the unformulated criteria of mundane logic.
At this level, the response to mental illness is naively instigated within the
bounds of a quite nonprofessional comprehension of the person and his world.

   If we have stressed the insight of common sense into psychiatric disturbance, it is not because ordinary daily life is gifted with remarkable
powers. Nor should it be overlooked that the signs of serious pathology are,
at critical stages, unavoidably evident. Very simply, we see that something is
wrong with the Other when he can't function in his job, when he can't move
in the circles of the public world of buyers and sellers, of pedestrians and
window-shoppers, of travelers and repairmen without trouble which erupts
into scenes of violence or scandal. Whatever can be contained at home, in the
private lives of families, cannot, if it is profound enough, be secured or re-
pressed in the realms of work and the traffic of society. To say that pathology
is recognized in mundane life before it comes to the psychiatrist's office or to
the clinic is therefore to grant men in daily life a kind of insight which should
not be confused with psychiatric judgment. It is also humbling to admit that
in a great may instances—very often tragically consequential ones—fellow-

men fail to recognize pathology until it is too late, until it erupts irrevocably. What is being suggested, then, has its limits. Nevertheless, it remains importantly true that the psychiatrist's work is anticipated by the acknowledgment in nonprofessional terms that something is wrong with an individual, wrong to and for common-sense men. I believe that such recognition is circumscribed in a special way, for the actions of the sick person may in their surface presentation or manifestation indicate nothing abnormal. Rage, violence, emotional upheaval or melancholy, ennui, *tristesse* do not in themselves indicate pathology. Nor is the decision limited to "spacing" alone. The old theory of "humors" is still serviceable to common sense. "He's always like that" may mean that what would be considered abnormality in one person is merely a style of being in another. What is vital to the recognition of pathology is that, whatever the cast of the individual's temperament, something has affected the center of his being, affected *him*, so that the manifestation is judged in essential correlation to the self. It may well be, on this account, that calling a man mentally ill may be based on a set of behavioral characteristics which, for another person or even for most people, are normal ways of acting. The surface appearance, then, must be judged in relation to the core of the person's being, the individuation principle which is at the center of *his* world. It is no mean accomplishment that fellow-men who may be otherwise quite unsophisticated are capable of discerning a transformation in the *world* of the Other.

The insight of common sense is not altogether lost or completely transcended in the professional activity of the psychiatrist. Just as the sick man remains a man, so the psychiatrist continues also to be a man as he functions in his professional role. The relationship between role and individual is worth attending to here because the psychiatrist is a therapist as well as a scientific observer; he participates in social interaction with his patient in ways which call his personal being into question. It is, in fact, the interplay between profession and person which gives the case of the psychiatrist such interest. As an individual, the psychiatrist shares a very large segment of the mundane world with his patient. Like him, he is incarnate in a world, centered in a body which is always "here" for him and which cannot be discarded or exchanged. In addition to a bodily "here," there is a "now" which renews itself constantly in the temporal life of the psychiatrist as a man among fellow-men. In fact, all of the "constants" we described earlier must be called in as witnesses to the mundane complicity of the psychiatrist: like his patient he is born into a world, born of parents unique to him, born into a historico-cultural milieu, born into a language community, and born into the sociality sustained by fellow-men. In this world he must work and he must die. What every man shares with every other man is then a significant portion of what there is, a pervasive fraction of human reality. Essentially the same conditions and limitations reflect themselves, in varying ways, throughout the entire range of the psychiatrist-patient relationship. The "50-minute hour," the space of the office, the events of the week in the personal sphere of both persons, the "outside" world privately borne by each and publicly shared by both are all bits of a large pattern shaped in and by mundane reality. At what point, then, does the psychiatrist assume his role, soar out of the atmosphere of everyday life, and become scientifically disengaged?

Very simply, there is no borderline clearly demarcating person and role. Instead, there is a plethora of signs recognized by individuals more nearly as gesture is understood than as language is grasped. It is through a welter of sometimes half-formed and only partially formulated clues that the Other no less than the individual himself is able to express his intent and, indeed, discover his intent. We are speaking, of course, in the context of therapy, a peculiar and specialized sphere. Nevertheless, the implications of the rather special relationship between psychiatrist and patient have relevance for a vast domain of social action. In the taken-for-granted world of everyday life there is also a matrix of intent, a conversation of attitude carried on at a proto-linguistic level with a sliding base of meaning and role.

To get some picture of what such a web of communication looks like, we may start with a more nearly physicalistic model. Take the case of the surgeon and imagine, now, a great medical amphitheater in which a very large electronic screen covers one wall—something like a scoreboard at a sports park. The legends that flash on the screen during the operation are a commentary of a sort on what is happening to the patient. For example, when the surgeon makes his initial incision, a computerized set of indications flashes on the board: anatomical and physiological possibilities directly related to the kind of operation being performed. When a blood vessel is tied off, alternative circulatory routes appear on the screen (it might also be possible to announce the chief surgeon's record on this operation, how many patients he has lost, which hospitals he has operated in, and so on). The blinking lights correspond to the surgeon's medical awareness and may be understood as a continuing series of if-then chains of anticipatory reasoning and response to sudden developments. Thus, a surgeon knows that a tonsillectomy done on a child is a common but not unhazardous operation. On the basis of his training and experience, he anticipates a certain course of development in a particular patient but he is prepared for all sorts of contingencies. He plans for the ordinary but is prepared for the unusual. How? Look at the screen; it displays the tangled order of possibilities and alternatives at every step. If one procedure fails, another is adopted. If something unexpected arises, a standard medical maneuver may be altered or adapted to meet the new circumstance. The screen has no room for "I don't know what to do next." If all alternatives fail, if the surgeon's procedural permutations dwindle to an unsatisfactory minimum, then "nothing more can be done" for the patient, a benediction which will sooner or later be followed by death.

It is necessary to realize that one takes for granted the surgeon's training—we have a good doctor operating—and the richness of the if-thens which accompany his professional activity. Suppose an otherwise splendid man in general surgery were in the midst of doing an abdominal operation and, pointing to an organ in the cavity, asked an assistant, "What's that?" Unless the question is directed to some subtle or unusual feature of the organ in question, the assistant could have no proper answer. "Are you being serious?" is hardly an adequate response; laughter or ribaldry would be more appropriate: "Looks like the bottom of a monkey's cage!" "No," the surgeon persists, "I'm serious, what is that thing? I've never seen one before." "Why doctor, that's the liver." "Oh, that! You know I never got around to liver in med school; I always seemed to be absent when it was being discussed. So that's the liver, is it? Slimy customer!" This conversation cannot take place in any reputable hospital. It would be even more difficult to imagine it occurring in a disreputable institution. Good surgeons know about the liver and bad ones do not advertise their ignorance. If you do not know about the liver you are not a good surgeon; in fact, you are not a doctor at all, whatever your specialty. It's a matter of medical literacy, bread and butter. But the scope and richness of the flashing screen do vary from practitioner to practitioner. And it is here that we find a continuity between the surgeon and the psychiatrist. Some medical specialties are more patient-oriented than others and demand a sensitivity to human beings which both enlarges and intensifies the if-then screen. In the case of the psychiatrist, the depth and complexity of the possibilities of interpretation and response are overwhelming.

What does the psychiatric screen look like? It charts, in outline form, the entire range of common-sense constructs. It is a directory to the typifications of mundanity. In a sense, such a screen is available to every man; what makes the psychiatrist's version rather special is that he must utilize it as the medium through which he responds to his patient, for to assume and play his role properly, the psychiatrist cannot present himself in his uniqueness as a person; such privacy must be disguised in its appearance in the mundane world. Such notions as "distance" are, of course, familiar features of all professional relationships. The teacher may be friendly with his student; he risks a breach in their formal relationship if he is familiar with him. So the psychiatrist may be passionately concerned with the being and welfare of his patient. He knows, however, that he hurts his chances of therapeutic success if he involves himself as a person in the affairs of his patient. The screen of constructs helps to establish and maintain a suitable equilibrium between the sensitivity of the psychiatrist as a human being and the cunning he possesses as a physician. Unlike the surgeon's system of if-thens, the psychiatrist's screen is geared to a principle of self-correction. That is, the psychiatrist's own activity, his initiative, his interpretation of the situation alters and, in turn, corrects the readings which show up. The anesthetized patient responds physiologically to what the surgeon does; the psychiatric patient creates a response in his doctor which in turn leads to a change or transition in his own condition. The lights of the screen bound back and forth, gambol in the electronic field, and lead finally to the recognition that self-revelation requires self-protection. We have reached the limits of our metaphor and must set it aside in favor of new questions.

For whom is the psychiatrist responsible? What aspects of himself are involved in therapy? And is it altogether satisfactory to say that psychiatric practice presupposes distance between practitioner and patient? In what sense does the therapist remain an observer as he treats and cares for his fellow-man? And, to return to the initial point of departure, how does the psychiatrist function as a bond between the natural and the social scientist? Some answers may be suggested by recent developments in psychiatric theory which have been inspired and nursed by phenomenological and existential philosophy. In discussing what has come to be called "existential psychiatry," most questioners are eager to find out what new methods and techniques in the treatment of mentally ill people are offered by existentially oriented therapy. "What is it that an existential psychiatrist does which his more traditionally trained colleague does not do?" Posing the issue in this way ignores the fundamental conceptual distance which separates positions and their representatives. The first consideration must be a philosophical evaluation of the reality which concerns the psychiatrist. The existentialist starts by turning to the phenomena he confronts in mundane existence and interrogating their epistemological status and roots. Accompanying that investigation is a concomitant interest in the reality of the investigator —himself—and his connection with the object of analysis, a troubled fellow-man. The circle of inquiry is then enlarged from the outset to include the *situation* within which a rather uncanny ritual is celebrated: the effort of one man to cure another. If the existential analyst starts with the problematic status of the phenomena of mundanity, he ends by including himself in the catalog of the uncertain.

The situation of existential analysis and therapy is beset with its own paradox, for it is an embarrassment to the persons involved that roles remain and that the freedom of therapist and patient is not assured by the terms of encounter. It is rather the case that the meaning of role and meeting between doctor and patient must be chosen. Choice emerges as the central category, just as participation replaces observation in the narrower sense of scientific disengagement. But if roles remain in the context of existential encounter, embarrassment quickly gives way to the realization that roles may liberate and that the act of choice has definitive value for what occurs in the therapeutic relationship. To glance ahead at the conclusion to which we are moving, let us say that it is in virtue of the individual's presentation to the Other through role possibilities that the identity of the person is revealed. In existential encounter, such possibilities are exposed and supported by the participant-activity of the therapist-observer. In a way, his service is to make of a personal act a transcendent force, to show the universal meaning hidden in an individual performance. To do that, he must risk himself and continually confront his own identity in the course of his professional engagement. Before we can see how this is so, we must turn to some of the qualities of existential relationship.

All along we have contrasted anonymity and identity, role and person. Methodologically, we have turned to phenomenology for a way of understanding the structure of social action and to existentialism for an appreciation of some of the categories relevant to the terrific current of human reality in its historical unfolding. Clearly, these philosophies are taken to be integral to the purposes of our development both as individuals and as reflective beings trying to comprehend ourselves in the world. It has not been possible, however, to pursue one without alerting the other, to utilize structural analysis without pointing to the concrete reality which structure undergirds. Rather than merely complement each other, phenomenology and existentialism reflect different dimensions of an integral reality, that of Man-in-the-world. Turning to the existential aspect of psychiatric experience, then, is one way of viewing the grounding of role-playing and interpretive action in the perceptual life of Man. If it be objected that existential thought is concerned not with "Man" but with individual men, with you or with me, then it must be said that the truth of that assertion can be grasped only in the concrete subjectivity of the actor—reality's agent—who chooses to speak, that is, who communicates, however indirectly, instead of electing silence and refusal. The act of speech is a commitment to sociality and implies a rhetoric of intersubjectivity, a recognition that existential identity is not insular but cohesive. It is here that we find the significance of choice as an existential category. The mundane reality of the individual is weighted with connections and relevancies. The taken-for-granted recipes of daily life, the means for *doing*, coping in the world, are replete with intentions, arrows of implication, which say, in effect, "Follow this course if you choose to enter the world in a recognizable and efficacious manner." And with the considerable subtlety of everyday decisions—a tracing out on mundane screens of the intricate as-ifs of common-sense affairs—there goes the recognition or the possibility of recognizing that small events have complex structure, that individual action has universal character, that choice liberates role no less than self.

Now we can review the situation of existential encounter. The psychiatrist no less than the patient can choose to play hide and seek by presenting himself in formal disguises. More importantly, retreats from identity and commitment on both sides can take place if they elect to stage fraudulent intimacies and deceitful revelations. The individual who plays at honesty is erecting barricades behind which to retreat or hide from the problems which bring him to the doctor's office. The doctor who does so may be using strategies or may, in fact, be used by his techniques. The "face" the psychiatrist presents to the patient may be that of the classical silent mirror, an aloof scientist-observer, or that of a reasonably accessible, rational, fair-minded expert, or that of a warm, amiable, empathic, responsive participant. The "real" nature of the doctor remains enigmatic to the patient and may indeed prove to be problematic to himself. If the initial meeting or the early meetings indicate the necessity, the doctor may suddenly plunge through the politeness and expected order of discussion and devastate the patient with obscene language, with a fierce turn to sex which undercuts the defenses and facades of the individual and of the situation by its bluntness and its unexpectedness. The shock may be sufficient to get the patient in action, to dump the droning and introduce the vital focus of what is disturbing and upsetting. If the psychiatrist's maneuver is controlled and efficacious, it may succeed in permitting him to present himself in a new way to his patient, no longer as a superhuman man of science, above all failure and weakness, able to order and dominate the destinies of less fortunate people, but as a man among men, in the world much as the rest of us are. In existential terms, however, there are risks to all technique, risks having less to do with therapeutic efficacy than with the reality constituted by the doctor and his patient and the freedom and responsibility each finds within its bounds. Technique has something of the ring of phoniness to it in this context, a turning on and off which reveals the manipulator, not the person. If the doctor's effort is to cut through the disguises of the patient, what about his own masks? What justifies lies when they become enmeshed with truth? The concept of the "noble lie" survives in psychiatry because, whether consciously or not, both practitioner and patient recognize that as *persons* they can establish a relationship with each other only through roles, and that the discipline, the therapeutic direction and adequacy of their professional association, demands the principle of control provided through the observer. Even in the existentially fulfilled situation, the psychiatrist as participant must be reflexively restrained. To transcend the limits of such restraint is to risk hurting the patient by denying him the possibilities of his role under the name of personal freedom.

The therapeutic situation is larger than the confines of examining rooms. To a slight but not trivial extent, all men practice therapy in mundane experience insofar as they attempt to keep the public order of affairs, the continuity of everyday life, viable. There are typical ways of handling irritations, misunderstandings, quarrels, arguments, fights, displays of bad temper, outrage, and violence which are directed toward restoring a calm *status quo ante* or returning the participant to a more agreeable and publicly acceptable mode of behavior, or which at least help to avoid the persistence or intensification of the trouble. Reasoning, cajoling, pleading, sympathizing, threatening, distracting, and disengaging are all common-sense techniques for diminishing unacceptable behavior or displacing it with surrogates which can be dealt with by unembarrassing means. Once again, the art of daily life displays its sophistication. And therapy shows itself in professions otherwise distinct from medicine such as teaching, where student and professor are players of awkward but impressively strong roles. College students may turn to their teacher as a figure of omniscience if not omnipotence, or as a mentor in a paternal or avuncular sense, or as an ally in a rebellious underground, or as a confessor, screened by the regalia of academic circumstance. Younger instructors, not that much older than upperclassmen, may be regarded as "buddies," contemporaries who speak the same language and who can communicate in immediate terms, in a shorthand which allows for instant recognition, an argot of the times which is sensitive to what it is like to be alive in a certain situation at a certain point in history. In all of these cases, the underlying, thematic problem is the nature and meaning of personal identity seeking to express itself through formal roles. I would suggest that the example of psychiatry offers some instructive comment and advice to the other realms of human involvement in which normal people love and torment each other. The moral can be expressed in this way: existential subjectivity transcends mundanity only by honoring it. Social roles are the necessary condition for the emergence of the identity of the ego and remain essential to its expression as a being within a world. Concrete existence cannot be cut out of mundanity and preserved hermetically, for the meaning of concreteness and identity is woven into the fabric of sociality. The same interpretive consciousness which builds its world through typification discovers in its performances that identity whose uniqueness science must acknowledge and whose universality common sense must celebrate.

chapter
five

history

Before moving ahead it is time to glance back. Our journey so far has taken us from the alone ego to the recognition of other human beings, to the social existence that fellow-men share, and to the creation of a science of Man. The problem now is not to summarize our findings or recapitulate the argument but to take stock of our individual achievements in the intellectual venture we have been pursuing. Vast themes loom ahead: History, Art, Religion. Before turning to them, it is prudent to ask what gains we have made in the initial stages of the development of our analysis. Where is the concrete individual at this point in the proceedings? It might seem as if we left the reader in an egological trap set in the first chapter—that experiment in solitude. It might be helpful to go back for a moment to that effort of the self to suspend its ordinary assumptions and locate an ego-original world. As you recall, it was not the world we doubted in that early philosophical episode but our belief in it. In egological terms, my believing in the world was rendered thematic, made an explicit object of investigation. The point was to get beneath the fundamental assumptions of daily life, to see our taken-for-granted attitudes toward experience as well as ourselves from a vantage point which did not presuppose the very object of our concern. By placing in methodological suspension the basic *believing-in* the world, it was possible for the individual to locate a primordial sphere of his own existence, to disclose to himself the terrain of an existence regained in its "originary" quality. In a way, such discovery is like removing a series of overpaintings from a canvas and getting back to the original. But the phenomenological recovery of the initial force of experience carried with it certain existential implications. Centered within the solitude of the ego is the recognition of aloneness as well as loneliness. Stripped of the protective coloring of self-illusion, the individual confronts a double obligation: to look directly at himself apart from the stamp which experience and history have placed upon his being and to rejoin the experiential world suspended in the course of inquiry. Whatever claims phenomenology and existentialism may make, common sense suggests that there is something artificial and strained in the claim that any experimenter can really rid himself, even temporarily, of the marks his culture and his personal history have made upon him. It would seem that no methodological sleight of hand can bring off the experiential innocence called for by our venture, that each of us is caught irretrievably in the web of language, home, and history. Was the claim to egological autonomy false? How far are the suspicions of common sense to be trusted, especially when they are directed to matters of vested interest?

We have already observed that suspension does not mean getting "rid" of attitudes or assumptions in the sense of extirpating them or somehow erasing them from consciousness. Rather, methodological suspension is a radical procedure designed to render presuppositions and epistemological commitments explicit by making available and evident to consciousness its own activity, and to pursue the analysis in terms rigorous enough to merit the trust of unromantic but not insulated minds. The phenomenologist is not gifted with magical powers: he does not cease to have a name, an address, and responsibilities when he works at his job; he does not take leave of his body or his fellow-men; he remains in the world of social action and continues to thrive and suffer in its confines. In short, phenomenology is not a denial of reality, and most certainly it respects common sense. It is out of that respect that this book is written, for its message is that the taken-for-granted reality of ordinary daily life—what we have called mundanity—is worthy of the most diligent philosophical scrutiny and reflection. Indeed, what emerges from the phenomenological procedure is a respect for the obvious and a realization that it is too important to be left to its own devices. Mundanity requires a proper spokesman, one whose first loyalty is to self-examination. It is in this spirit that the experimenter in the egological sphere must confront the special difficulties of his position and the ambiguous aspects of his placement in a situation which at once seems to abandon him and yet swallow him up in the maw of history. The focal point is this: within the egological sphere the self undercuts the assumptions of mundane existence and yet must account for them. We are asked to reconstruct history from a history-free base. Outrageous as the request may appear to be, is it possible to satisfy? How can the alone ego build a world?

The answer to the puzzle of subjectivity lies in the character of its content. The solitary ego is able to achieve the coherence of a world because its cardinal feature, intentional consciousness, is transpersonal and non-idiosyncratic. What the ego discovers in its aloneness is its universal nature. The individuated "my" and "mine" emerge from the ego's reflective dimension; they do not antedate consciousness. Similarly, the existential insight which gives the ego knowledge of its identity is not "added" to consciousness but is a moment of its unfolding. To put matters bluntly, common sense is profoundly misled (and misleading) in its assumption that the "content" of the self is individually defined by each person and so varies from one privacy to another. If the phenomenological interpretation of consciousness has succeeded at all in establishing its fundamental claim, it should be clear that the *meaning* of subject-bound acts of intentional awareness is independent of the psychological event in which it takes place. In the "beginning," then, is the universal; the particular emerges as the vehicle for its expression. Understood in alternative terms, the egological sphere is the general matrix out of which individual consciousness arises and in which the person remains structurally embedded. Consciousness is "individual" only in the sense of having a distinctive career in its historical unfolding in the biography of one person. There what is involved is not consciousness in its underlying intentional character but rather the particularizations of the psychological development of the individual. Two careers move in tandem here: the history of intentional consciousness and that of the individual in his actual, biographical existence. In a way, we have returned to the problem of the relationship between the universal and the particular which has, in other forms, been shadowing our movements all along. The dualism of thought and life is one variant, that of role and person another. In whatever shape the polarities appear, the essential theme remains constant: the paradox of anonymity and identity expresses itself historically in the ego's movement from solitude to sociality.

Moving ahead at this stage on our journey, then, will mean recovering the sources which made the progression possible. The impetus is not a motive external to or causally prior to the consequence; the advance of the self is liberated by the reflective moment chosen by the individual who acknowledges the general pattern, the type, in the particular experience, the event. Nor is the triggering force an initial cause from which follow, sequentially, chains of effects. It is a series of implosions in the perceptual life of the person which give him the recurring possibility of recognizing the transcendent aspects of concrete experiences. Ignoring or denying those aspects is a mode of what we earlier called "Bad Faith":

I've lived a decent, a respectable life. No complaints. You get as much as you're willing to give in this world. I understood that early on and have no bitterness about lost opportunities. What if I didn't get all the breaks? Does anyone? And if I made my share of mistakes ? Who hasn't ? But let's be clear and honest with each other : A bankrupt is a man who used to have friends. Sure, they still speak to me. Any one of dozens would give me a loan, a stake maybe. I don't deny the offers of partnerships : my brains and their cash. Not relatives either ; business associates who know I've got what it takes to get ahead, even if I haven't. Whoever said success was a forever and always thing ? Also, I've kept my friends, and I've got a loyal family at home. You couldn't ask for more. The thing is that you hesitate to risk another's good will. His money I'd take in a minute, but his good will—that's something else. Although I'm not a religious man, I've got scruples. As soon as you commit yourself to somebody else in my situation you've given up a certain free will, if you know what I mean. It's not even-steven as long as you're down at the start when they're up. I'm at a psychological disadvantage. Everyone keeps after me about pride. Garbage! I don't give a damn about pride; it's psychology that keeps me bargaining, psychology that won't give me a break. "You're your own worst enemy," they tell me. It may be true, but not in the way they mean it. They think it's a question of em-barrassment, of having failed, of having to borrow. I know better. How can I explain what it is to know that something went wrong and that after all these years it stays there in me like bile, ready to come up, a stench. It's *in* me! Take apart my bones and nerves and it will drip out of their ends like pus. How can you get something like that out? It's not a boil that can be lanced; it's not a sore that's festering. It's *me*; *I'm* the rotten heart of it; *I'm* the bankrupt, and all your talk about a new life doesn't pay attention to *that*. Don't argue with me! I've had enough.

Bad Faith can harden or stultify not only the ego but the perceptual order created by the individual at various stages in his career. And there is even the possibility of what might be called retarded negation, a refusal at some later point in the life of the person when he repudiates something done earlier or refuses to honor some prior time in his history. Just as there are some individuals who seem fixed in their twenties forever, so there are others who seem never to have been children. Facial lines harden, and the earnest look of a young man of achievement begins to permeate the eyes and the jaw. There might be a curious circularity between the expression and the person, a variant of a theory of the emotions; paraphrased, this would read: I am dignified because that is the way my face looks. Temporal fixation can also mean an emphasis on a certain period in one's life at the cost of deriding other times or stages. The memory—real or exaggerated—of a "golden childhood" can be seized and staked out by the "owner," rendered a preserve for recol-lections to live in without fear of destruction or contamination from the "outside" world. Bad Faith amounts to the freezing of temporality, the denial of the openness and flexibility of the present as a basis for the reconstruction of the past no less than as a foundation for assessing and selecting lines for advance to the future. The temporality of the individ-ual in Bad Faith is sealed in and abandoned to fixation, a permanent image, settled and secure, with all danger of vitality gutted out. Here is an illustra-tive conversation. It takes place on a bus from San Francisco to Santa Cruz:

A "This seat taken?"

B "No, sit down, glad to have some company . . . makes the time go faster, you know?"

A "You live in Santa Cruz?"

B "Yeah, I moved down 14 years ago—from San Jose, where I used to work—and been there since."

A "You like it there? I hear it's real nice, beaches, ocean."

B "It's all right. We get along, you know. Got a pension keeps me pretty good. Uncle Sam sends me a little something every month too. All in all, I ain't complaining, not like some. Yeah, in comparison, I'm pretty good. For an old man I ain't doin' bad."

A "What'ya mean, an old man? I bet you ain't a day over sixty, maybe sixty-two, three at the most."

B "Seventy-four this September. I keep busy, do some gardening. I got pretty good health, bettern' most. But I don't feel so good, actually."

A "Something wrong?"

B "No, healthwise, I'm all right, got no complaints, like I say, but I'm lonely you know, same thing all the time: do some gardening, drink a beer, watch some TV . . . That can't take up the whole day, there's gotta be more, so I go up on the bus once in a while, but it don't change things."

A "What's this we're coming to? I thought we stayed on the freeway all the way down to Los Gatos."

B "Naw, he goes to Saratoga, this one . . . this driver got his own ideas. I know him from before."

A "Well I guess I'll get a little shut-eye, take a few winks."

B "I suppose you don't want to talk any more, huh? Old people's troubles . . ."

A "Say, you're all wrong. I just thought I'd take a nap for a few minutes, but sure I'd like to talk. It's not every day I get the chance to hear another point of view, you know."

B "Well, like I say, we get along. Uncle Sammy delivers the mail every month, and I got that pension besides."

A "So you're doing pretty good then?"

B "That's it, you see, there's nothing to do . . . the same thing all the time. I don't know what to do with myself."

A "Gee, I hate to hear you say that! What's wrong? The world's full of beauty. What'ya mean there's nothing to do? Get up at dawn and see the sky! Go down to the beach and see the birds. There's beauty! Read a good book; the library's full of them!"

B "I ain't much for reading."

A "Then listen to some good music . . . Take an interest in things."

B "Yeah, I tried that, but it don't work for me. Like I say, I do some gardening . . . but it gets lonely."

A "We coming into Santa Cruz now?"

B "Yeah, my brother-in-law's supposed to meet me."

A "It's nice having some family near you, should give you some joy."

B "I got no cause for complaint, you know. There's plenty got it worse."

A "Well, good luck to you."

B "It's been nice talking to you . . . makes the time go, don't it?"

The binding of time in Bad Faith is a way of denying the possibilities of the self, of stripping the individual of his involvement in history. It should be clear from what has been suggested so far that the concept of history has a double placement: in addition to history in the usual sense of the term—the story of the past, of what is significant or worth recording of Man's thought and action—there is the microcosm of the self's movement in the world, the more nearly biographical account of the concrete individual's interpretation of what he finds in mundane existence. Our concern is with history in its individuated manifestation, with the career of men in daily life. Obviously, no judgment of the value of macrocosmic history is made or intended by this choice; it is simply a matter of consistency. All along, we have been tracing out an account of the typified structure of the ego and its becoming in the social world. Far from turning to history as an afterthought or as an appendix to other, more important issues, we have been engaged from the outset in a form of historical investigation: the recovery of the person. The two notions of history are, of course, related to each other, but the connection is a curious one. It is possible, for example, to do a macrocosmic history of daily life. We already have studies available on *Daily Life in the Time of Homer*, *Daily Life in the Time of Jesus*, *Daily Life in Ancient Rome*, and *Daily Living in the Twelfth Century*. But such works are a part of the "history" of daily life in a specially limited way, for they do not and cannot purport to be accounts of the lives of individual people; they are concerned with types of men. Unlike traditional histories of ancient Greece and Rome, the time of Jesus and the twelfth century, they are without heroes, real men and women whose concrete lives are reconstructed and examined. A typical wine merchant in Jerusalem in the first century, A.D. may be described in a "Daily Life" book and his style of existence illuminated. We may learn about his home life, his manner of conducting business, his involvement in the affairs of his day, his attitudes and responses to social, economic, political, and religious affairs. In this way we may come to know him and his world in an extremely informative and satisfying way, but we shall never find out who he was; we shall never locate him in his concrete, actually lived existence. Nor do we expect to. The author of a "Daily Life" study has done his job well if he gives us the merchant as an "ideal type," as a construction built out of hundreds of descriptions, reports, documents, letters, diaries, and indirectly, out of a much larger and more profound study of the macrocosmic history of the times, including its literature, its art, its science and technology, and its philosophical and religious foundations. Knowing the merchant is learning what it must have been like to be alive in that period. But it would be as idle to search for the actual historical existence of the individual who exemplifies the ideal type as it would be to look in the streets for a character in a novel. Men *like* that can be located; the man himself is a methodological phantom.

A macrocosmic history of daily life, then, is necessarily concerned with a highly typified account of what happened at a certain period of our past. The story can at best utilize what may be known about actual persons; it cannot transcend the limits of hypothesis. And this is because daily life has no heroes.

When men worth remembering appear, they enter macrocosmic history. If not, they are lost to us. It is inconsequential to readers of history whether a foot soldier at Waterloo serving under Napoleon was named Jean or Paul, was a member of a large family or an only child, was well-tempered or choleric. It is not even necessary to know whether he was a good soldier, fought courageously, followed orders, and helped his cause. It is enough to be able to characterize the behavior of Napoleon's foot soldiers in that battle or perhaps to be able to describe accurately the military character of a particular division or segment of that army. Types dominate individuals; the performances of groups obscure the deeds of persons. To pursue the course of the macrocosmic historian is to settle for just such results. When we turn to microcosmic history, the situation is both remarkably similar and strikingly disparate. It must be understood at once that microcosmic history is not written at all; it has no historian. We are speaking of the life of the individual in the mundane world, and the "we" speaking is the participant himself, each of us who lives reflectively in the midst of the social world and seeks to transcend the limits of Bad Faith. Within the microcosm of daily life, the individual confronts his own history in the sense of his biography. And here identity, *for him*, is crucial. It is *his* career in the world which is at the center of the history of mundanity. To say that he is prejudiced or naive is to miss the point, for what is at issue is precisely mundane existence as it is lived by common-sense participants, not disengaged observers. Action, not description, is the operative category here. The *analysis* of microcosmic history in this sense is the task of the kind of phenomenological inquiry we have been attempting here. In terms of disciplines, it might be said that philosophical sociology concerns itself with such matters. The historian, it would appear, is oddly if not badly treated. No disrespect is meant. Let us apologize by saying that the history of mundane experience as it is lived by the concrete individual may be studied from *within*, that is, by way of the experiential reality of that individual—you or me—rather than from the zero point marking the coordinates of a detached observer. The "history" which emerges is then an egological or "first-person" report of the becoming of the person. If the "history" of each one of us were nothing more than the story of what befell us, we would be left with the simple meaning of autobiography. Why confuse that with history? What distinguishes microcosmic history from autobiography is that the typifications of ordinary existence which the individual lives through and defines are constitutive of an intersubjective matrix of mundane reality, the public world which transcends autobiography. The history of the individual is then caught up inevitably in the history of sociality, a structure which phenomenologists have called the "life-world."

Our discussion of common-sense constructs, typification, and mundanity together with our study of the subjective interpretation of meaning has prepared us for an understanding of the life-world; in fact, without appealing to the term, we have already started an investigation of some of its problems and features. By the "life-world" is meant the naively experienced, immediately perceived reality of everyday life as grasped and understood by men in the midst of their ordinary activities. Within the life-world, for example, the panorama of colors seen by the unassisted eye is appreciated and responded to quite apart from any scientific understanding of the theory of vision, the principles of optics, or the physiology of perception. In fact, it is the distinctive character of naive experience that its basis and framework for interpreting experience remain outside the realm of technical theory. Most common-sense men live and die without the vaguest knowledge of the anatomy and function of the retina, yet they manage to find their way in the hectic richness of visual reality. Very often it is a matter of chance that brings to their attention the nature of the complex organization of their bodies: accidents, emergencies, the unexpected moment which introduces them to a new vocabulary and a new domain of problems. In the common run of events, however, the ground for understanding the workings of the world is not the apparatus of science but models of quite modest character, typical of the mundane sphere. Yet the scope of such models is vast, including aspects of science itself which the ordinary man comprehends in only the most distant and generalized way. A glance at the terrain of typical constructs of the life-world shows a series of concentric rings moving out from what the individual knows best and most thoroughly to, ultimately, that of which he is not only totally ignorant but of which he knows merely "that it is" and that there are Others—specialists in the field—whose job it is to know about "such things." Thus, Miss Gloria Monday, computer programming technician, is trained to prepare work for a machine whose insides she will never see and whose electronic welfare is guarded by men from another office. And although she may be well trained and very competent at her job, she may know little about communications theory, cybernetics, and other esoterica whose rationale is deeply relevant to computers. But it would be a mistake to think that our theme is limited to science and technology. The problem goes much further.

Within the orbit of work—"doing one's job," in the generally understood sense of that phrase—the individual is "wise" to the ins and outs of his "line"; he knows not only how things are done in the used car trade or the life insurance business but how to "get around" rules and regulations, how to oil the machinery of procedure, how to get one's way or at least operate realistically within the limits imposed by the situation. The used car operator may be completely uninformed—a sucker—when it comes to life insurance, and the insurance man may fall for the world's worst lemon in the car trade. Outside the sphere of his own expertise, a person may be anything from extremely knowledgeable to utterly ingenuous. Yet each of us manages, more or less, to make his way in the world and to survive in sectors of its operation which are totally alien to our backgrounds, education, and proclivities. The capability of common sense to deal with the complexity of experience is rooted in one of its own typifications. We may call it the principle of restrictive transformation: Whatever isn't known can be accommodated for through what is known in normal experience. Thus, I may not know about automobiles but I know about getting gypped; I'm ignorant of life insurance but I'm wary of a door-to-door salesman trying to sell me a policy; I am not an expert on politics but I distrust some of the promises politicians make around election time; I may have limited knowledge of the history and culture of much of the rest of the world but I know that it is better for me to start with what I have, with what I do know first-hand, than to rely on haphazard opinions or reports of other people whose assurance may be self-authorized and whose claim to authority may have no substance. Of course, I can and very often must turn to others for expert advice. At such times, there are ways of making sure that the person appealed to is indeed in a position to know and to advise responsibly. It must be noted, however, that decisions to resort to experts in any sphere are made by common-sense men *within* common-sense terms. Here the principle of restrictive transformation operates in a vital way. If I need detailed as well as expert assistance on a federal income tax problem, I have to decide whether to consult a well-established firm of lawyers who specialize in such matters, a lawyer who has had some experience in the field but is not a specialist in it, a neighbor-friend who is an accountant who moonlights by taking in a little tax-work on the side, or a "guy I know" who hangs around with some of the boys at the Federal building in town and who might get some inside tips for me. If I decide to seek advice on whom to consult, I'm simply back in a similar circle of choice: should I call up a lawyer, a friend, or what? If decisions of this sort were permitted to percolate in consciousness for an extended period, they would simply boil away into ineffectiveness. At *some* point in reflection, the individual decides that one line of action is appropriate, and he "makes up his mind." Whatever the nature of the problem, whether it concerns fiscal, medical, or moral issues, it is in the region of common sense that the "decision to decide" is made. Advice, the appeal to authorities, the persuasive force of fellow-men—all outside factors inevitably present themselves, like process-servers, to the individual who must acknowledge them and make his choice in *mundane* terms.

It might appear that the life-world, as described so far, is a rather hit-or-miss arrangement in which the individual can founder as well as resolve his problems. No doubt, the element of chance—that stump of luck—must be credited with having its place in the scheme of mundane experience, but it would be a misreading of our analysis to think that common sense is being given a second-rate status in the hierarchy of knowledge. To the contrary, I am arguing for the recognition of the autonomy of mundane experience and its fundamental irreducibility to scientific subservience. The life-world is not a cheap or inferior copy of some more splendid original, nor is it a confused welter awaiting the organizational and promotional services of the scientist. The outstanding fact is that mundane experience not only has a logic proper to its complexity but is the experiential basis and grounding for the sophisticated disciplines commonly thought of as having long ago advanced far beyond the confines of mundanity. The life-world, then, has a double significance: it is, as we hope to show, the locus for Man's construction of reality and the point of access to his comprehension of all knowledge, that given to us by the social and natural sciences included. An earlier example may make clear the grounding character of the life-world. When we said that ordinary men know very little or nothing of the theory of vision, we meant that the knowledge they do have is adequate for ordinary purposes and sufficient for dealing with most situations. But now it must be added that when atypical or unusual circumstances arise, it is on the basis of mundane visual experience that the patient is able to understand the explanation of the ophthalmologist. The most complicated medical account of a disease of the eye is subject to simplification or translation of some sort. And even in disciplines such as mathematics and physics, where it is extremely difficult to explain a complex equation or formula in easily accessible terms, it is possible to give the statement an explanatory context, to indicate the general problem, and even to state a kind of subjunctive equivalent in language that the nonspecialist can follow. The entire range of perceptual experience may be understood as a threshold to the translation or reformulation of scientific concepts and language. Translation works both ways here: it enables the scientist to move from the resources of a natural language—the language he learned from his parents and associates—to a freedom from subject, place, and culture-bound determinations; at the same time, the man who still lives in the atmosphere of ordinary language—of the English or German he speaks at home—is able to grasp the significance or at least begin to understand the constructions of science *as* constructions, as models of a reality or a province of meaning which is otherwise closed to most of us. The content of the theory of quantum mechanics is opaque to most men; what is available to them is the knowledge (presented in the appropriate typifications of common sense) that a certain domain of contemporary physics exists, mastered by experts in the field, which is relevant to the scientific enterprise and which, in uncertain but consequential ways, affects our lives. We can all be blown up by what we don't understand; we do understand *that*! In the milieu of common-sense constructs, in the compass of the life-world, the uncomprehended and the incomprehensible achieve their interpretive equipoise.

As a point of access to knowledge, the life-world has distinctive implications for the meaning of microcosmic history. It is within the life-world that the significant events of the public world are understood by that great outdoorsman, the "man in the street." History, for him, is what he makes of what he hears and reads about important events in the public domain. Judging them to be important means either that they already have acknowledged status in the general mind—what an American child studies in his school books about the Revolutionary War, the Civil War, heroes such as Washington, Jefferson, and Lincoln, and the extension of these events and figures to the still larger scene of world history: the French Revolution, the Russian Revolution, Napoleon, Frederick the Great, and, as they say about the movies, a cast of thousands—or that they are defined as having major importance by the individual. That he may be mistaken is of course a real possibility; that he may be misguided in his judgment is equally obvious. What the individual takes or defines as being an event of world-history-shaking significance may be nothing but a trivial irruption on the local scene, not a cataclysm but a pimple. For the person who lives within the bounds of the interpretation he makes, however, the sense of history is dominant and efficacious. A small band of chiliasts, awaiting the coming of the Messiah, may be judged to be anything from dreamers to crackpots by outsiders; they may be treated as harmless, marginal figures or as fanatics or lunatics. What shall we make of a man who takes as true the twentieth chapter of the Revelation of St. John the Divine, who believes the angel shall chain the serpent, and who knows that on this scriptural foundation the millennium is assured? Whatever our opinion of him, that opinion is received and screened through the interpretive schemas of his commitments and outlook. If we despise him, he may say that contempt is hardly a measure of truth, that religious groups have traditionally suffered for their faith and have very often been considered and treated as troublemaking madmen. If our attitude is that of patronizing sufferance, we may be told that arrogance and pride are false ground for response to serious matters. And if we are indifferent, we are warned that history remembers its hots and colds, not its lukewarms. There is a certain logic to such responses, and perhaps it is because of the sustaining force of such an inner coherence that protagonists of difficult causes are able to keep going. It is in the immediacy of their own interpretation of history that the justification of their lives is located. It is that immediacy which the life-world embodies.

It is necessary to examine the point of access of the life-world to history more closely and to see something of its structure and operation. Three topics —really shorthand terms for more complex problems—present themselves for consideration: relevance, situation, and choice.

1   Relevance.   That which *matters* to me is relevant to me. It is not a question of whether what matters is "really" vital or important to my welfare and interests. If I *take* X as relevant, X *is* relevant. The word "really" is troublesome; it seems to presuppose a court of higher judgment or at least an observer detached from the fray and gifted with superior understanding and judgment. *He* knows what is *really* important; *I* may not. Of course, we are not speaking of eternal values, unchanging truths which are transcendentally relevant, forever *really* essential to the individual's existence. When I say something *matters* to me, I am pointing to a map of my world and indicating, in effect, where some theme finds its accommodation in the hierarchy of my priorities. We are not interested in *why* the map comes to be formed as it is. The phenomenological issue is the *what* of relevance, the makeup of values, their interconnection, and the functional unity they express. What matters to me forms part of a network of "all that matters," including the history of my past commitments, what "used to matter." Relevance is then a changing phenomenon, with horizons which extend in all temporal directions.

Perhaps a notion so great in its purview is in danger of encompassing too much. What if defining relevance in terms of what matters is a dormant redundancy, a fat tautology? After all, it might seem rather empty to attach so much importance to the claim that "if I *take* X as relevant, X *is* relevant." Perhaps that is merely a disguised way of saying that what I consider relevant is considered relevant by me—surely no remarkable discovery! The distinction intended between that which is *taken* as relevant and that which *is* relevant amounts to this: the "taken" is that which becomes part of an interpretive context and is alive in the individual's conception of and action in the world; the "is" of relevance points to the person's insertion in an intersubjective reality in which Others understand him to the extent that they recognize the equation between interpretation and being. To misgauge the equation is to say, in effect, "Sure he *thinks* it's vital to him, but it's not; there are much more important things than *that*." Or to misapproach a situation completely, one might say, "This is what is of commanding importance in a problem of this sort; this is what must be attended to." Such observations come from the center of the observer's reality, not that of the actor's. It may be that the two occasionally coincide and that what the Other takes as relevant for his alter ego *is* in fact relevant. The larger danger is that the observer may impose his own criteria for relevance on his fellow-man and assume that since those criteria hold good for most individuals or for most individuals of a certain type or in a certain situation, they are reliable indexes to the particular instance or occasion.

What we have here, in fact, is the construction of typifications of the Other, of typical situations, and of typical systems of relevance. A crucial consideration in both the individual's and the social scientist's articulation of types is that relevance in an individual case may not follow a general pattern. It may be true that middle-class male teenagers in a fairly affluent suburban town are deeply interested in girls, cars, sports, and fun. Individuals in that group may nevertheless define their reality in terms of black power, the art of mime, the study of the Talmud, or conscientious objection to war. For the political scientist, the concern of nationalities or distinctive cultural sub-groups within a nation with their own language, its preservation and official use, its place in education, and the respect paid it, must be given the most serious weight. It would be professionally imprudent for the student of Asian politics to assert that the demand of certain Indian groups for the maintenance of their own language is mere provincialism or for the European specialist to ignore the significance of those concerned with the preservation of Gaelic or Welsh. To the general question, "Well, after all, what relevance does Gaelic or Welsh have for modern life in Ireland or Wales; aren't these dying languages?" the answer, quite unsentimentally stated, is: "If you wish to understand the reality of these nations, their people, and their culture in terms of how they define themselves, then you must attend to what *they* take as significant; otherwise you will end up with an analysis of surfaces or a fabric of description whose design reflects the observer, the designer, not the reality observed." To comprehend what is relevant to the actor means to enter his situation and describe it from his perspective. To show how that is possible it is necessary to understand what is meant by the concept of "situation."

2   Situation.   The bare, primal ego we started off with in the early stage of our inquiry was located in the midst of an historically *thick* reality, not in a phenomenological incubator. We began this book with a reasonable appeal, a call to reflection of a stringent yet strange sort directed to the reader, an individual assumed to be *in* the world. It was an appeal to the adult character of experience which was really at issue. No one can reasonably expect a three-year-old child to understand the meaning of political involvement, nor is it likely that a high-school freshman will have the maturity to comprehend the emotional problems of the aged. The audience I am addressing—my reader— is already thrust into a world of adult responsibilities and has a history of responsibilities. That granted, each of us already has a preanalytic grasp of the meaning of "situation," for it is basically an appreciation of the totality of limiting conditions of existence matched with the projects of the person. What we earlier called the "constants" of human reality—being born into a world already inhabited by and defined by Others, having to work for a living, having to grow older and die—are the cardinal features of the limiting world. Within those necessities, the more concrete and variable possibilities of existence are formed.

My situation, then, involves having been born in the twentieth century of white European parents in the United States, and in a certain cultural, economic, and religious milieu. To this must be added the fact that I am male, possessed of a certain order of intelligence, and oriented toward certain goals. My home life, my education, and a variety of circumstances related to the places I've lived and the people I've come into touch with are all parts of my total situation. The failing of listings of this sort is that as they build up, category after category carted in, they tend to take on a vaguely familiar and lacklustre quality. It's as though we were asked to draw up a list of all the people we've known, the cities we've visited, the schools we've attended, the books we've read. After a while, a drowsiness seeps into the procedure and we begin to punch the keys without looking at them—an adding machine exercise. I mean to suggest something quite different: a sense of placement in the world as defined by what the concrete individual *makes* of the traditional labels of family and friends, of school and neighborhood. Those classifications are shot through with temporal and circumstantial individuality. Having had *these* parents, having grown up in *this* part of the country at *this* time are facts no less significant than those of the more general kind. Indeed, the meaning of situation begins to manifest itself only when the formal classifications are specified by the interpretation already given them by the concrete circumstances of an individual's career. But the nexus between what is "given" and what is "defined" is more than a simple interaction between general and specific features of situation; it is an active and dialectical one, for what is inherited as the general condition of being alive in the world (having to live with Others, work, die) is itself defined by the individual. It is misleading to set apart the large constants of human experience and then attempt to bring them into contact with the concrete person living his life in specific situations. I come to understand and act in a reality whose limiting features have themselves been defined by me. I cannot legislate history, language, intersubjectivity, or death out of existence by my decisions, but I can respond to them in such a way that they are, for purposes of my own life, negated, severely modified, or seriously qualified and transposed.

Again, it might seem as if a circle is being drawn: objectivities are said to be defined by subjective interpretation which arises within the limits of the objective. But all circles are not vicious, and it is helpful to be able to trace some of the elements of the problem of situation which explain the particular character of the circularity in question. As a limiting constant, the color of a person might be thought of as, in paradigm cases, an unalterable, objectively given absolute. However a distinctively *black* Negro may think of himself racially, it would seem that he cannot change the fact of his color. In physiological terms, he is a *black* man. In situational terms, the matter is far more complicated. It has been said that there are no Negroes in Africa. I recall

reading somewhere that in the forties, a visitor to the United States from that
continent seeking a hotel room in the South was advised by the desk clerk
that Negroes were not permitted as guests. "I am not a Negro," he replied;
"I am a black man from Africa." He was given a room and deferred to as a
distinguished foreign emissary. Indeed, in recent times there has arisen an
ethnorhetoric of color: distinctions very seriously drawn between the terms
"Negro," "colored," "black," "Afro-American," and "African-American."
It is now part of the situation of the black man in the United States that color
is debatable. Nor can the discussion be reduced to semantic distinctions
which somehow dwindle away into: "well, whatever word you use, it's
still . . . ." Which word you use defines you today as a "militant," a "liberal,"
an "Uncle Tom." Even the epithet "nigger" is utilized by aggressive black
men addressing white audiences and capitalizing on the language of abuse in
a reversal of assumptions: you don't expect the man you're insulting or
deriding to accept the name you give him and make a weapon of it. It may
be that the next step in this linguistic upheaval is the acceptance and control
of the word "racist." One thing is clear: race in some color-wheel sense has
little to do with the reality of being black, white, or anything else in the
present world. It is in the *situation* of the individual that race categories have
significance, and that means that the definition of the situation by the actor
on the social scene establishes the meaning which "objectivity" and the
constants have for social reality. Definition in this sense is a modality of
choice.

3 Choice. The dialectical relationship between what is "objectively" given
and "subjectively" defined requires further exploration. There are two
"moments" in the logic of the development: first, something pre-given as
somehow irrevocably, irretrievably, and universally binding; second, the
attitude on the part of the individual to what is pre-given. Ordinarily, we
would be inclined to say that the first is independent of the second, however
it may be understood in the course of individual translation. Thus, it is onto-
logically inescapable that the Second World War took place in the initial half
of the twentieth century, that it was preceded by the First World War, and
that the United States was militarily involved in both wars. Whatever interpretation an individual may give to those facts, however he responds to them
intellectually or emotionally, they remain unalterably the case. Refusing to
read or hear about war does not dissolve the reality of what occurred, nor does
the wildest reading of contemporary history change the primitive events
at issue. The wars may have been warranted or not, noble or treacherous,
"really" won by this side or that despite what the books or other people say;
still, they happened. Their stark but ineluctable historical weight remains
and haunts any discussion of the past. In what sense is it meaningful to

suggest that such primal reality can be "defined" by the individual or be affected by his choice of history? Unless we are willing to commit the historical past to a subjunctive mode of interpretive being (if you had been in or witnessed the Battle of the Marne or the Battle of the Bulge, if you had been present at the Somme, at Dunkirk, or at Normandy in certain years and at certain times, then you would have seen for yourself, experienced in full immediacy the reality of war), we are led to say, it would appear, that what happened, *happened*; that iterative insistence has its root in common sense, and it represents a refusal either to deny the past or to open it up to the disintegrative acids of private interpretations. It is the interpretations which differ, not the historical reality they seek to describe and understand. Our emphasis on the contribution of consciousness, of the defining force of individual interpretation, might seem to stand opposed to the facticity of the past. If "what happened" in its bone-hard actuality is inescapable, it is because it is recognized by us as constrainingly true; there is a "requiredness" we must acknowledge in dealing with it. Five thousand years from now what we call "Western civilization" may be as mysterious and inaccessible to historians as Etruscan civilization is to us now. Whether there were world wars in the twentieth century may be a debating point between rival schools of historical theory and methodology. For us, alive in the century of those disasters, the truth is inescapable.

But "requiredness" and "inescapability" refer to the agents who interpret experience no less than to the events described. If there is no discernible advantage to avoiding the force of the past, neither is there any profit in trying to separate what happened from the schemas of understanding in which the past is placed so that it can be examined. The raw, brutal facts of there having been war—bullets, bombs, blood, bodies—are not bits of historical grit, secure and self-defined entities, but the meaning of events to which they are bound and without which they would be reduced to ahistorical elements: lead, powder, fluid, limbs. Being blown up in a mining accident is utterly different from being blown up by a grenade thrown by an enemy intent on killing, even if the physical damage is identical in both cases. The meaning of the event cannot be stripped away in order to reveal some independent, forever factual core. To say that history is grasped through schemas of interpretation means that the agent in historical inquiry is in dialectical contact with the reality he investigates. What we have called "choice" may now be made clear. It is the engagement of the individual in the interpretation of reality. Rather than restricting the notion to questions of selection between alternatives—the more usual use of the term—we are following a tradition which attempts to give a broader placement to choice by understanding it at the level of all interpretation. In brief, to interpret is to choose. At the historical focus, choice signifies the commitment of the individual to various options:

to attend to the past, to study it and think about it, to relate the present to "what happened," to anticipate the future in terms of the horizon of the past, or to deny, ignore, negate, refuse, or attempt to eliminate what happened, whether that is done self-consciously, in the framework of Bad Faith, or in the sullenness of a conceptual nihilism. In any of these attitudes, a choice is made and its consequences are felt throughout mundane existence. Choice becomes the epistemological axis on which the historical world turns.

The discussion of relevance, situation, and choice was offered as an attempt to display some of the features of the individual's point of access in mundane life to historical reality. Some of the problems which appeared, such as the meaning of the ontological status of the past, are profound irritants to any methodology of historical scholarship and formidable difficulties for any philosophy of history. However, our interest in them is not from the standpoint of the practicing historian or the philosopher of history; rather, we are concerned with history as a dimension of mundane experience, history as grasped by men in common-sense terms. Once again, it is microcosmic history which engages our attention and commands our philosophical loyalty at this point. The issue is this: how are we to understand the placement of the individual in history—history as lived by mundane beings in the midst of their everyday lives. Enough has been said to permit the beginnings of an answer. First, the historical domain is one of several spheres of mundane involvement. Access to it is initially by way of our awareness of those who lived before we were born, whether their lives were noteworthy, pedestrian, or even anonymous. We are oriented to the historical past because much of our present is, in effect, analogous to its quality of distance and inaccessibility. That I could as an ordinary person meet the heads of state is a rather comfortless possibility and hardly enough to make a real difference between being isolated from persons of world power alive now and royal or magisterial personages who are dead. A cat may be able to look at a king and an insignificant person may be able to murder a president, but that hardly changes the condition of anonymity which marks the connection between the small and the great. But *awareness* of powers by mundane men is a forceful fact of their concrete lives, and it is in that interpretive matrix of daily life, in the typifications through which common sense is able to create an orderly world, that history arises. Second, there is a continuity to mundane life which is made possible by individual memory but also reinforced and enlivened by the collective memories of Others, public records in newspapers, journals, and books, and, perhaps most important of all, inscribed subtly in art and religion. The situation of the person who understands the past in common-sense terms has sedimented in it the interpretive record of his age and his tradition. What he chooses to fix upon, utilize, or celebrate in that communal totality depends on the criteria of relevance which govern his existence and give an edge to his situation. It would be a mistake to think that mundanity implies shallowness and provincialism. The failures of common sense are not built into its machinery; they are the results of refusals to appropriate the heritage of ordinary life, its historical continuity, its linguistic achievements, its aesthetic performances, and its philosophical victories. These are not *part* of common sense; they are open to common sense, available to its interpretive reality.

Third, there is in microcosmic history an internal analogy between the course of the concrete person's career and the developmental continuity of macrocosmic history. In a way, the life of the individual mirrors the course of civilization. It is not necessary, nor would it be justified, to claim that world history and individual history are basically alike; the only point at which the analogy is intended to be useful is the zero-point marking the center of the Here and Now coordinates of the person's existence. The historian, like the social scientist, is methodologically free of involvement in the reality he studies; the actor, immersed in microcosmic history, has a very definite place, and it is from the point of his involvement that the analogy becomes significant. The movement of the self from the alone ego to the historically-bound and committed individual is, we may say, the basis for the advance from common-sense to the scientific knowledge of historical reality.

The analogy between microcosmic and macrocosmic history needs closer examination. What is it that the individual is able to discover in the becoming of his own life which is fundamentally similar to the development evident in history? The answer is to be found in the universal sedimented in the particular, the type hidden in the individual. As an "ordinary" man, I find that there are things possible to "ordinary men," that the ordinary is a universal which not only invites the participation of the particular but which makes such involvement inevitable. What is not inevitable is the recognition which the actor may achieve of the universal significance of his concrete performances. There is a "pre-predicative" involvement of the self in the world which is structurally and even, in some respects, psychologically prior to our distinction between the universal and the particular. Within the naive standpoint of daily life, in the natural attitude of mundanity, the actor distinguishes between neither the general and the unique nor the public and the private. Instead, the milieu of involvement is intensely free of analysis in the course of its evolving. In this sense, daily life is most concentrated in nonreflective, utterly actualized participation by the self in the world. Such "actualization" is the meaning of the "taken-for-grantedness" we have referred to all along. At no point in the midst of the ongoing believing-in the world which characterizes mundanity is there a question raised about the status of that believing-in, or about the presuppositions of intersubjectivity. The self is "naive" to the extent that it moves in the world free of any questions about such movement. All the higher-level problems are built upon the assumption that acting in the world is the natural capacity of any individual. Doing this or that may prove to be difficult or troublesome to a person, but *doing* as such is truly a problem only for those who are primordially disturbed. Thus, in the center of human action there is a continuous flow of intention which precedes reflective analysis and which may be understood as the basis for all abstraction. Out of that stream of intending there arises the hierarchy of typification which we have described in various ways and which is also at work in the domain of historical consciousness. The analogy between personal and world history stems from that same intentive source.

How, then, does the universal sedimented in the particular leap out of its investiture in mundane experience and announce itself? The release comes by way of the construction of types as the intimate possibility of man's action in the social world. If the initial, pre-predicative stratum of the ego's involvement is antecedent to the universal-particular distinction, it is still the case that the typical features of objects and events present themselves to the individual. At the primordial level of perception, the reflective moment in which the typical is grasped *as* typical does not present itself immediately. It is only with the passage of time that the ego is able to reflect upon its experience, to turn upon itself and come to comprehend its own meaningful nature. In the language we appealed to earlier, the "I" is remembered in a "me." Of course, the "I" remains as a dialectical feature of the process of the self's continuing action and development, but its spontaneity is always seized in the reflective moment which follows its expression. Similarly, the embodiment of the self in mundanity at its pre-predicative level is recognized by a "me" which, to some extent, has rendered its own action an object for inquiry. The typical, caught by naive consciousness as the aspect of what is perceived, comes to self-conscious clarity in the experience of the individual who reflects on the moments of his involvement in the social world and comes to understand them as representatives of types. *This* experience, then, comes to clarity as one of *this type*, and with that movement there comes about the qualitative advance we are concerned with understanding from the typical pre-predicatively grasped in mundane experience to the typical self-reflectively appreciated as a model of action and in turn as a means of interpreting the action of Others. The psychological history of the evolution of the recognition of the universal and its connection with the individual, the place of repetition, conditioning, and habit in the process, are topics relevant to another book; here we are concerned solely with the phenomenological genesis of the universal, with the qualitative and not the causal elements of the process of recognition. Accordingly, the dominant clue to the release of the universal from the particular is the schema or model which characterizes the typical. To move from the aspect to the type is to understand reflectively that the aspect has an immanent structure whose outlines are filled in by the recipes and formulas of mundane experience. Typification is the process through which the individual is able to actualize the content of his experience. Understood in this way, the universal is the lucidity of the particular.

In recognizing the integrity of the universal in the particular, the person is able to grasp his own historical placement, for the patterns of his own life are the guides to the formation of the typical features of macrocosmic history. Time, efficacy, power, submission, connivance, deliverance, evil, and death are some of the essential categories whose significance for the person is relevant for world history. The translation of power from micro- to macrocosmic terms presupposes the individual's insight into the limits of the private: the knowledge that "my" power is an exemplar of the "individual's" power, that appreciating the domain of the personal is discovering the force of sociality. It is easy to misunderstand the claim to analogy that has been made. I hold that the ground for the comprehension of the macrocosmic is the individual's discovery within the life-world that the constructions of mundane experience which make the being of the common-sense world possible are also the means the individual has for locating order—history—in the world of predecessors, contemporaries, and successors which transcends both his immediacy and his life. There is no formal progression from "I find order in my life-world" to "I find History in the world." Prior to any movement from what I know intimately to what I appreciate indirectly, there is the question of how such progression is possible. The analogy between individual and world history arises out of the confrontation between mundane men and transmundane meaning. Earlier, we posed and explored the duality of Life and Thought and tried to portray some of the features characteristic of the existentially concrete and the phenomenologically essential. The historical theme we have pursued is an extension, transposed to a new key, of the same issue; at the same time, it is an avenue of penetration to a still deeper dimension of the self, for history offers the possibility of seeing the transcendent qualities of the life-world, those elements of mundanity whose genesis and destiny go beyond the person or, perhaps, carry the person beyond the sphere of his egological immediacy, beyond the domain of social reality, to the truth of Art and Religion. The instrument which mediates between the constructs of common-sense experience and the force of Transcendence is the symbol. I trust it will prove to be the vehicle that will carry us in two directions: back to the meaning of the typifications which connect sociality and history and forward to the significance of the constructions which intervene between history and transcendence. The final stages in our journey can be negotiated only by a procedure powerful enough to illuminate the past with the transformations of the present alive in the symbolic forms of creativity and religiosity.

chapter
six

art

The transcendencies of history which manifest themselves in the life-world have a certain ontological weight: they point back not only to events in the past but to a "finished and done" sense of what has happened. To be sure, the historical past is interpreted and, as we have seen, reconstructed in the present by way of the typifications of common sense. Yet despite the "typed" aspect of the past, there remains for the individual a quality of finality and distance experienced as a subtle but pervasive feature of the world of predecessors. The "re-membering" of the past is at best an effort to put together pieces and elements inherited from Others and inaccessible to us in their original immediacy. Perspective has its advantages, of course, and it may well be that an individual in the twentieth century can get back to the life of a nineteenth-century figure with a force and richness his contemporaries missed or lacked precisely because they took him and their time for granted. Yet there remains an aspect of what happened, what occurred, which haunts the present by its inaccessibility. Our present is not unique in being tainted with the lostness of the past; that sense is essentially possible or potential to every present, for each historical "Now" is destined to vanish in terms of its particular content and remain, be renewed in its formal aspect. What haunts us about the past, then, is that its transcendence is given to us by way of the familiar: we, in our present, sense the weight of what is gone through a balance which is itself inevitably marked to follow suit. We become the instrument, then, through which not only the transcendence of the past but our own future transcendence (what we will become for those who will be born after we die) is intelligible and imaginable. At this point type gives way to symbol, a sign which points either backward or forward to transcendencies whose constant form cloaks an irretrievable or unobtainable content. The progression we have traced from mundanity to history can itself be viewed as a grounding of the symbolic, a preparation by which the self is able to transcend its origin.

The irruption of symbols of transcendence in the sphere of the mundane is the announcement of art. The twin valences of the historical past and the uncertain, far future exert their most impressive force when the individual recognizes that both modes of transcendence are experienceable in the present, indeed, can be explored and illuminated by the entrance of the self into the symbolic. The *arts*, as distinguished from art, become the means through which the symbols that express transcendence are formulable, but *art*, as we are trying to approach it here, is the generic recognition of the present as the medium through which history and future sociality are joined. Recognition first comes to the individual in the encounter he has with art works, and it arises at the moment when he sees that there is a strangeness about the art work, that it cannot be "taken" as other objects of perception are grasped, that it is fugitive to straightforward viewing. It is necessary to remind ourselves that "first" in this discussion does not mean chronologically number one, nor does it refer to the biography of the person in the sense of saying, "At the age of seven I was taken to the Metropolitan Museum of Art, and there I first saw . . . ." "First" in the history of discovery means first in the order of recovery. What we are seeking is a coherent account of the place of the transcendentally symbolic in the life of consciousness. What comes "first" in that account is what will help to provide a basis for the individual's experience of art and the significance of that experience in the totality of his existence. The seven-year-old who is warned by the museum guard "not to touch" the sculpture or paintings may well have had his "first" encounter with art, whatever else may have already occurred in his introduction to the world of art. "Don't touch" may well have been preceded by a subtly instilled version of "Don't see." To those gifted with a fine teacher in childhood, one who made art into nothing but its own fresh power and who refused to sully consciousness with prissy instructions, what follows can only be understood as a warning; to others, it may bring back some old terrors:

1 "What did I tell you? Didn't I warn you? Don't look with your hands! Keep your rotten little fingers to yourself. If you can't enjoy, don't destroy. Do you remember I wrote that on the board? The Museum gave us special permission to come here; now you give the entire school—not just the class but the *entire* school—a bad name. You know what they'll remember us for? For *you*, that's what! Stop whimpering and blow your nose. Here. Now for the rest of the afternoon you can keep your hands in your pockets. I don't want to see those hands, understand? *Inside* the pockets, mister."

2   A is for art, furtive reminder,
        Pocketed offenders, left to dark roaming,
        Banished purveyors, flexing their sweat,
        Groping for the hot-shamed center of the afternoon.

The art work cannot be taken directly; its way of being requires the individual to set aside—to place in abeyance, once again—his ordinary mode of seeing. Of course, the painting can be handled as an object with certain dimensions, can be transported, packed, shipped as any other object, can even be cleaned and repaired in certain special ways. But then we are not concerned with it as an art work but as a physical entity, one on a par with a multitude of other entities which have to be manipulated and arranged in the world. In its distinctive aesthetic station, though, the art work stands forth as unlike other objects we perceive. What does that unlikeness consist of? Most simply, the art work is an "object" we cannot change, possess, or utilize. There are some obvious senses in which these qualities *can* be attributed to art; I'm interested now in presenting a less evident conception of the status and function of the art work. Of course, the words in a poem can be changed; of course, that Picasso may be mine; and of course, art functions in architecture. But we mean to speak of these qualities in a different way:

1 An "object" we cannot change. In contradistinction to the physical object, the aesthetic object is a unity of meanings, brought to focus by the individual who regards the art work—intends it—*as* itself, self-generated, irreducible to physical components or even structural elements. It is not simply the object which is different; it is the attitude in which the object is regarded or taken that is qualitatively remarkable. The viewer, then, the aesthetic participant, takes up a certain attitude toward the art work. This may sound rather formal and even patronizing, as though anyone interested in looking at a painting had to view it through an aesthetic monocle. What I am suggesting is far more open and far less democratic than it may first seem. There is an aesthetic mode of consciousness which allows the aesthetic object to appear, come into view. In the world of museums, concerts, and galleries, the individual knows that he is coming to a show of a sort. Even if he has never been to the theater before, he expects something rather special, unusual, out of the run of his daily experience. He is willing to try to look or to listen to what is there in an "aesthetically" attentive way. This willingness may trip him up, for the very formality of the occasion may give the individual the sense that his attitude toward "Art" must match his best suit, must be in line with his Sunday-visiting demeanor, must be stiffly appropriate. In sum, the art-viewer may not trust himself, and that embarrassment may lead him to artificiality and posing, not so much to impress others as to prepare himself for something different. Those more at home in art, familiar with its history and possibilities, turn to art works in a more relaxed yet willful stance. To concentrate properly on the art work requires a turning to it, an affectionate conceiving, which consciousness as a perceptual totality deliberately allows.

Through this acknowledgement, the art work appears; what is *there* springs into appreciative view. At the same time, the "independence" of the art work is acknowledged, for the viewer has merely allowed himself and the "object" to stand forth aesthetically. With the liberation of the art work the yielding of the physical object is achieved. The view of Toledo which El Greco presents can never be touched; the city cannot be entered, its clouded aspect will never clear; Toledo remains at a distance. The canvas and frame, the painted surface of that remarkable object we call a "painting," are put out of play, become unreal, in aesthetic experience. Whatever appreciation we have of the art work, then, hinges on the central fact that its meaning is given to us in an appreciative act which cannot alter it but can merely permit it. The full meaning of that unchangeability will emerge as we go on.

2   An "object" we cannot possess.   We have already distinguished between ownership and possession. In some cases we can both own and possess; in art, we can hold legal ownership of the art work and we can possess it, but when we speak in this way we are referring to the physical object, not the aesthetic unity. Possession signifies a certain privacy: I can show you my possessions and I can even give them to you, making them yours, but I cannot share them without entering into an intimate or special relationship with you. It makes quick sense to say that *we* share our furniture in this family, but it would be odd to say that we share the aesthetic response we have to our sculpture. Each of us has an aesthetic response to some art work and we may have the "same" response, but we do not share that response. What we "share" is the aesthetic object. It is possible to introduce a larger term, "aesthetic experience," to mediate between the individuality of response and the universality of the object responded to, but having the experience of listening together to a Beethoven quartet or going to a Bergman movie together does not affect the distinction just drawn between response and object. Experience may be shared without changing the object being experienced into a private content of consciousness. On the contrary, shared experience points to the autonomy of the object, its independence, and its refusal to be reduced to the status of a possession. The aesthetic object may be appreciated, then, but not conquered; it retains its own ontological valor.

However, it might be thought that the artist, rather than his audience, can possess the aesthetic object, that in virtue of his creative authorship he indeed succeeds in commanding it utterly and uniquely. There are a number of reasons for not accepting this view. First, the artist stands in his own temporal and developmental relationship to his work. What a particular creation meant to him while it was being done, what it was on completion, how he re-views it now, how it stands in relation to other works of the same period and other periods in his career, what others have made of that work, how the world itself has changed and the artist as well—all these features make it difficult to speak of *the* meaning a work has for its creator. Second, though the artist is responsible for his work, he is not its permanent master nor even the chief authority on its interpretation. He may be puzzled by what he has done or lose the sense, the intentive control, he perhaps had at some stage in its development. Indeed, he may lose interest in the work, refuse it, become estranged from it. If he is interested in the "meaning" of his work—and many artists would run from such discussions—he may turn to his fellow-men for aid in bringing to the conceptual surface the aesthetic qualities which live in other regions of meaning. Finally, even if we were to affirm the artist's perfect possession of his work, we must face the reality of his death and of his possession's dying with him. *We*, his audience, are inevitably left to our own resources. We may turn to Van Gogh's letters in search of his possession, but we are confronted with the insurmountable phenomenon of our own need to analyze those documents, breathe back interpretive life into them, try to resurrect the man from his remains. Fortunately, we have recourse to his art, and that means we must return to ourselves.

3   An "object" we cannot use.   If art has its "uses" it is because we are able to move from the aesthetic response to the social scene in which that response is transposed or transformed into a means for alternative purposes or ends. I may "use" a Faulkner novel in a university course on the history of the South; Handel's "Messiah" is "used" in church at Easter time; a piece of sculpture by Henry Moore has been "used" in the construction of the Lincoln Center. Such "use" demands that the art work be pressed into service in a larger or at least different framework than its own unity includes. Certainly, some art works are created in order to move masses of people to political action, to religious fervor, or to a sense of the totality of a time and a place, but the functional force of such works requires a context which lies outside the art work and to which that work is a signal, a clue, or a guide. Seen in its contextual unity, the art work serves a use; taken in its aesthetic unity, appreciated as an aesthetic object, the same work has no exteriority, no further resultant to which it points, no instrumental aspect. The "unuse" of the art work rests on its status as an aesthetic object, a unity of meaning which may be appreciated by us but which cannot be manipulated because it escapes any effort to bind it to the response of the individual. The aesthetic object is perceived by way of the response but is not contained in the response. Contextual utilization of the art work is possible because the response to art can be managed, influenced, and transposed. The aesthetic object remains sovereign.

It would be hard to avoid the charge or at least the caution that the term "use" is many-valued. Perhaps one way of acknowledging the ambiguity is to compare using art with using people. In the nonpejorative sense of the expression, we may say that "individuals may be used in a variety of ways." We mean that they have skills and talents which will serve certain needs, produce certain results, operate in ways which are deemed desirable. "I'm going to use Hackman on that job" means that the gentleman in question is right for supervising this particular piece of construction. But "I'm going to use Hackman" by itself is either a shorthand for a fuller statement or a threat to punish the man. "Use," in this sense, signifies "to make use of"; otherwise we enter the domain of personal domination, to which the retort would be: "You're just using me." We cannot use people without requiring them to function in some way, but then we are making use of their abilities, directing those abilities toward certain goals. *Persons*, individuals in their existential identity, cannot be used; they simply *are*. At this point, persons and aesthetic objects are alike. The essential quality which defines them is a nonfunctional and irreducible independence. We may appreciate them; we cannot package them. We may honor them; we cannot manipulate them. To treat either persons or aesthetic objects as means is, in the end, to degrade them.

If the art work, understood as the aesthetic object, cannot be changed, possessed, or used, what then are we to "make" of it? Language itself is rather odd here, for "making" would seem to be precisely what our considerations have ruled out. Perhaps it is possible to turn the oddness to our advantage and locate a point of connection between "making" as construing and interpreting and "making" as building and creating. As it stands, the art work has a presence in the world which can be accommodated neither to the pragmatic business of daily life nor to the pure realm of ideas. The uneasiness of that "neither-nor" reflects itself in the individual's recognition that the art work calls upon him in a special way, that it stands in his world in an "asking" manner, and that trying to understand it or interpret it ("making" something of it) involves a profound element of self-disclosure ("making" something of oneself). We are suggesting that the art work is bothersome, irritating, unsettling, and suggestively troublesome. To be sure, art can be ignored in mundane existence, tepidly tolerated, or ridiculed. We are not concerned with establishing a generalization nor with an empirical inquiry into how people in fact respond to particular works of art. Our effort moves toward the center of the reality which art in essence is capable of yielding and human beings are capable of achieving. Understood in this way, the manifestation of the art work in mundane reality poses a problem for the individual which can be seen as existentially directed: each of us is confronted with the puzzle and the disturbance of art in the midst of everyday reality.

What puzzles and disturbs us is the anchorage of the art work: its physical embodiment or vehicle is part of the physical world yet its meaning transcends nature. Further, the art work combines disparate qualities, for it is at once *this* particular, concrete unity and yet something unbounded and illimitable. Nor is this a matter of distinguishing between the art work as physical and as aesthetic object. The paradox of the art work as a presence to us in the world is its power to liberate a universal significance at the same time that it remains itself, given here and now in concrete form. Some analysis of the relationship between the universal and particular in art may help to clarify the nature of the art work as well as what we "make" of it.

Let us start with the literary work of art as an example, and more specifically, the novel. We have before us, then, an art work which is rather commonplace. In fact, it might seem that a novel, because of the very familiarity of the genre, can hardly serve as a striking instance of the irruption of art in mundane existence, But familiarity, as we have perhaps noticed, has its own oblique ways of nudging us toward the experientially perilous. I believe it will serve its purpose now. The initial observation should be that the very taken-for-grantedness of the novel—most of us read them without any vast fanfare—is based on the immanent assumption that its status and coherence as an art work are simply given: there the novel is; pick it up and read it. There might be some doubt about whether a particular book is fiction, but there is no doubt about what constitutes fiction, at least in everyday terms. Questions about the very nature of the novel, its constitutive structure, are reserved for theorists of literature, aestheticians, or epistemologists who stray into the province of art. But it is those questions which are relevant to our analysis; they pose the issues which must be faced if we are to understand the art work. A summary sketch of what might be called an epistemology of the novel is in order. First, in the novel the reader is presented with a *world*, a structured reality in which time, space, and a host of categorial elements of relationship and possibility are at work. That a world can be given at all, that a human creation of words can yield a microcosm, is the philosophically outrageous fact embedded in the apparent evidentness of the novel. Second, the world of the novel is peopled with individuals, characters, who have histories, fields of action, and styles of being. They are like us in the obvious sense of participating in a social reality, but that such activity can be presented in a reality other than ours is immensely remarkable. Finally, the novel invites us to witness events which are both free and determined, sustained and executed by beings who are both "real" and yet fictions. The way in which action takes place in the novel is hauntingly ambiguous. Characters choose, decide, agree, and abstain without any prompting or interference from the reader; yet the reader supports the fictive reality in which the novel moves by building up, as he attends to the work, a concatenated system of interpretation, information, attitude, and even commitment. He assumes responsibility for a world he cannot enter, whose action he cannot affect, and yet whose reality depends on his attention and complicity. The sense of entering the fictive world needs illustration:

I'm still looking for my reader. In fact, I'm still in search of my audience. Three novels, two collections of stories, the slim volume, the anthology—all that done, but no certain feeling that I'm talking to anybody. Or perhaps it's too large an audience I'm addressing, too many, much too much. They say I have a following, a readership. Lords and serfs, fiefs and vassals, hear the castle news! I'm setting out to survey my Readership: let the drummer announce my coming, let flower-bearing children strew my path, let maidens be provided . . . Later we'll cut joints from a brown-seared ox and drain flagons of lighter-brown ale. It had better be there; the mail doesn't show it, and my bankbook has leukemia, a lingering death. Every so often I do get something from a reader. The last one was an offer to be partners ("go halfies," was the way he put it) in building a boat. Why me? I've never sailed, never written a line about the water, yet my reader *knows* I'm the man for the sea he wants to sail. Another letter-sender wants to know the "secret of the craft" (another boat builder?); he thinks it's a matter of codes, signs, Freemasonry. I'll have to answer sometime, listing the books in my library: word-finders, dictionaries, lexicons, thesauri, grammars, rhetorics, vocabulary cards, verb wheels. All tools of the craft. When I sit down at my desk, my typewriter handy in case of emergency, I sort through my collection of old print. The printer's devil I was led me to the Mephistopheles I am. My study is a storehouse of old words, in lead, in bronze, in papier-mâché. From time to time I riffle through them, tinker with them, spray them with antirust and anticoagulant essences. Colloidal monstrosities! Junkmen of language! Still another supplicant wants to know whether my last joy was a *roman à clef.* He thinks he's seen that padlock before and he yearns to give my combination lock the old one-two. Won't I let him in on the dirt? And there are small black hints of publicity in case I decline to release the cat. Also unsigned notes from intelligent people (smarter than I am, anyway) to say they liked or didn't my last or that they thought this or that was good or didn't or that I was doing something valid and valuable (as one put it) and should ignore the reviewers. Finally, one communicant says he wants to write but can't begin. What do I prescribe? I'm answering that one because of my herbal persuasion. Yes, there's a tea for every organ, a root for every bane, Here's what I'm telling:

Beginning *is* the hardest moment, not because openers are all that scarce but because you're blowing into, cracking a universe. Where you enter, there you'll have to stay, no matter how far or fast you travel. Your choice in that moment of entrance is the world which you've called into being in that "real as you are" reality of may-being. Personally I never write opening sentences; I leave that to my editor, along with the blurb. Like a second-story specialist in housebreaking, I'm a second paragraph man myself. I'd really rather start with the last page, if I could manage it; and I sometimes do. The sad fact is, though, that the beginning is just as much a problem there, anywhere you start. *Each* sentence is the beginning. That's the calaminity of art, the Damoclean presence. Of course, a workman-like job can always be done by a pro, but that's not what I'm talking about. So we have to distinguish between the beginning and the start. You can start anywhere: from the last line back to the first. You can write hopscotch! Anything! The choice is yours. But *beginning* is another story. It's like breathing, something that's got to be done again and again, and each time is just as vital as the last. Then why speak about entrances and initial commitments? Why is beginning all that much? Because you and your reader as well are setting forth, establishing not only the route of the march but the smell of earth and the tension of mind that will pervade your world. You are asking your reader to give up his world for yours, to translate his space and time to fictive dimensions, and to risk his history for one he can appreciate but never appropriate. Beginnings such as these are as necessary to art as they are to love. Each *time* is an embarkation. Well, that's my message. I'll send it wrapped around a sachet of sassafras, one sniff guaranteed to initiate and regularize. Let no reader call me alienated.

Entrance into the world of the novel, then, is admission to a realm of particulars, each of which has its own essential horizon, its own universality. To discover a character in literature is to uncover a piece of a possible world, one whose universality depends on the reader's willingness to attend to that character as an aesthetic object, thereby transcending his "particularity." The combination of "this-ness" and "such-ness" (this one and one such as this) in the literary work may be understood in this way: The people we meet in novels and the events which surround and saturate their lives are, in one sense, abstract, unreal, imaginary, make-believe creatures. They seem to suck up particularity from the richness of the novelist's description, from his art, rather than from the power of concreteness in real life. At the same time, certain characters in fiction—those of whom we say that they are "fully realized"—are as "real" as some fellow-men, more real than some ghostly Others. The double pull of unreal-real has no point of resolution. It is simply the case that fictive beings are compellingly real in their imaginary existence and yet phantoms in reality. Moreover, they are real for each other in the world of the novel, a reality borne by a being who must remain outside the fictive reality he is responsible for sustaining. This is not a romantic view of literature. Rather, we are suggesting that the questions of how knowledge of a world is possible—questions simply presupposed in common-sense thinking—manifest themselves to the serious reader because their puzzling force pushes through the screen of the naive attitude and spontaneously irrupts in the center of mundane consciousness. How is it possible that a fiction can be so real? How is it possible that a fictive death can hurt us bitterly? How is it possible that we can return again and again to an unreal world and find there compelling reasons to reapproach and reevaluate ourselves and our human careers? The obvious answer that art represents or mirrors reality is of little help to us when what we are concerned with is a fundamental understanding of reality, when reality itself is placed in question. The nexus between art and life must be sought elsewhere, in a different region of questioning.

We have spoken of the art work as irrupting in the immediacy of mundane life. Now we may translate that implosion in terms of the relationship between the universal and the particular. The universal, understood as the aesthetic object, flares into presence in the mundane existence of the reader when corresponding elements of *his* world, understood as a set or pattern of possibilities, are rendered problematic and available for inspection. If the character in the novel is both *this* individual and yet also an individual of this sort, then it is equally possible for the reader to apprehend the same binding duality in himself, for he too is the concrete individual he is as well as someone of this sort. In the case of literature, the sheer possibilities the character is capable of actualizing have been delimited in the creation of the artist. The character he has given us can no longer be thought of as having been potentially different. In life, what each of us is, the character he possesses, is constantly expressed over and against the backdrop of possibilities, of our history, of our destiny. Paradoxically, the cardinal dimension of time in the novel is the future; in human existence it is the past. More properly, the quality of the present in both cases is the supreme temporal focus of reality, but the fictive present points forward, whereas the human present looks backward. Beyond the problem of temporal emphasis, however, is the persistent difficulty of how recognition takes place, how the reader comes to see that his life bears an interior connection with the realm of fictive possibility. The juxtaposition of universal and particular, the pointing to *this* one and one of this sort, might seem to imply a variant or an extension of the larger discussion of type and typification we have already pursued. It would seem that "sort" equals type, and that it is easiest to speak of literary characters as exemplifying types of men. In these terms, the universal element in fiction is merely the typical, or, more neutrally put, nothing more than the typical. With that, it would appear, some of the steam if not the mystery goes out of the search for the meaning of the art work. The line of analysis I propose to follow is based on a different conception of the place of type in art. Most simply, I hold that art is the moment in the career of the self when the typical gives way to the symbolic.

To set matters in their proper perspective at the outset, I am interested in the symbolic as a bearer of transcendence. Obviously, the word "symbol" can be used in contexts which are quite different, from symbols in the sense of special notation to systems of highly complex scientific meanings, and to mythic and culture-encompassing world views. The symbolic, as far as I am concerned here, is that which announces, presents (or "appresents") meaning whose elements are in the mundane world but whose qualitative unity and coherence are strange to common sense. The transcendent, in this approach, is not opposed to the mundane but penetrates it in such a way that the naive attitude of daily life is forced to the edge of its limits. Transcendence may be understood as the central implication of the metaphysical limitations—which earlier we called the constants—of human existence: birth, aging, intersubjectivity, and death. To say that each of us is necessarily born into a world of Others, that communication with fellow-men is a universal feature of man's history, that each of us is destined to grow older and to die, that the death of each man is followed by the birth of successors as the birth of each man follows the death of predecessors—to point to such constancies of man's social reality is to suggest as well that each universal indicates, implies most fundamentally, the transcendencies of birth, sociality, and death. Within the epistemological naiveté of mundane existence, the constants are commonplaces; within art they are elevated to the sphere of recognition, seen as powerful and upsetting, because the transcendencies they imply are possibilities of Man's being at the same time that access to that being comes by way of the concrete individual. To speak of concreteness at this point, however, is to move from mundane specificity to existential identity. It is that movement which cannot be accommodated within the sphere of typification. Indeed, it is by a qualitative leap that we are able to proceed from type to symbol. To see why this is so it is necessary to turn once again to the reality of everyday life, to the *world* of daily life, in order to account for its insulation from and yet its availability to transcendence.

Let us suppose for the sake of analysis, that concrete individuality is a typical feature of human existence, that existential subjectivity is universally to be found, and that each man, at some point in his life, questions himself radically about the meaning of his own identity. Perhaps such a generalization of the existentially unique (paradoxical as that might seem) is the meaning, or one of the meanings, of such concepts as "identity crisis." In psychological terms, then, each person goes through a searching of self, a fundamental bewilderment of personhood, at a certain time in his development. Typically, then, one may expect adolescents to manifest "crisis" behavior sometime in their late teens. Earlier or later signs of such changes may be understood as variables to which a composite picture of the history of the individual in question will give specific values. It would seem in these terms, that all of us undergo a typical set of changes when we are 17 or 19, that such alterations are often symptomatically announced by "philosophical-religious" questions: Who am I? What is the meaning of life? Why am I here? Is my everyday self my *real* self? Is there a pattern to the bits and pieces of existence? Do I have a mission to fulfill? In romantic form, such typical questions may find analogously typical responses: to build an ideal life in an ideal world, to bring love to the mundane, to do God's will, to be the secret answer to secret questions, to bring honor to a corrupted world. It would seem that what is supposedly existentially unique, supremely specific, is in fact everybody's possibility and every man's actuality. Existential identity would then vanish into the reaches of typification, there to live out its usefulness—a transitory prospect—in the same home to which all "stages" of the individual's development are committed upon retirement. That would indeed be rather a sad end, but before we mourn the existential dead

we should look for signs of life. *Is* it the case that individual existence in its existential subjectivity is one of the typifications of mundane
existence?

The *signs* of adolescence, or any other period in the life of the individual,
are observer reports in the present context. Our examination of the self and
its existential identity must come from an egological standpoint. Moreover,
the "same" signs, interpreted in their behavorial aspect, do not necessarily
point to the same source or indicate the same biographical reality. If we are
to recover the source along with the sign, we are compelled to start from some
theoretical foundation, and that, in turn, leads us back to questions of the
philosophical status of the basic terms of scientific discourse. In the end, we
are caught up in problems concerning the nature of the self which must be
approached from *some* philosophical vantage point. The existential approach
is one among them, and if that is so it becomes dubious at best to assert that
because there are typical patterns of genetic development in the individual,
existential identity (itself the creature of a philosophical attitude) is a piece
of the pattern. Apart from this early caution, however, there are other and
more serious objections to the "psychologizing" of personal identity. The
importance of the typical is compromised when it is put in the service of a
"nothing but" or an "it merely amounts to" way of accrediting sociality.
Typification, as we have tried to present it, is not reductionistic; it is an
accomplishment of cognition and a victory of affective intelligence. In part,
its power stems from the alternative side of man's existence, his history as a
being born at one moment in time and bound to live his life in the concreteness of the world of his contemporaries and the particular interpretations and
expectations he holds with respect to his predecessors and successors. From
the egological vantage point, there is nothing at all "typical" about my life
in its once given actuality; all typifications which undergird and support my
being are limited by the very transcendencies *I* must face: *my* temporality,
my death. To say, "Oh, but death is a typical feature of every man's existence;
after all, we all have to die," is to miss the existential point. Within the unity
of a single life, typification, and even self-typification, cannot touch the
meaning of *my* subjectivity without stepping outside the egological standpoint, from whose perspective "my" subjectivity is automatically transposed
into subjectivity in general—any "my," any "I." For the individual to pass
beyond the circle of his existential subjectivity, it is imperative that he move
from type to symbol, from the familiar to the transcendent. Art provides the
vehicle for that progression.

It would be wrong, of course, to cordon off art from the mundane or to
view them as distinct stages in the development of the self. We have been
exploring a dynamic of consciousness which is structural rather than linear,
and whose "progression" therefore may be seen at any moment, *in* any

moment, of the history of the self. In any case, mundane life is never transcended in the sense of being overcome or left behind. Each of us remains in the common-sense world into which we are born as long as our claim to sociality survives, but being in daily life, immersed in its pattern of types and its web of constructs, hardly delegates us to a social dungeon. We are also, *must* also be, men of other worlds: dreamers, phantasiers, visionaries, and so, in a way, explorers in art. What guides traffic between worlds? How is it possible for the individual squarely rooted in daily life to enter the world of art? Posing the question in this way is not the same as asking how art manifests itself in mundanity. We have already suggested that art irrupts in daily life, that there is an immediate presence of art in everyday existence which announces itself vigorously. But to ask about the *possibility* of common-sense men's entering a domain which is experientially distant from the quotidian is to turn to the many "provinces of meaning" which compose human reality. In the course of the day, most men pass from world to world in their involvements in home, family, friends, work, professional relationships, and their connections with officials, bureaucrats, workers in various jobs, professional people in different fields, and a host of others who participate in the business of running the daily world. But much of that movement is comprehensible in terms of a fundamental "base," a point of departure and return. We have already analyzed the body as the epistemic center and the domain of common sense as the structural ground of man's placement in the world. Now it is helpful to note that he is able to move from one world to another, from that of business to that of art, while retaining a firm hold on common sense. One remains a citizen of daily life while visiting the provinces, while touring other lands. But if that is so, is the mundane world ever truly transcended, or do we carry it along with us, in whatever worlds we enter, as we cart along our bodies? Are all worlds part of one social body?

The possibility of "worldly" movement rests on the principle of social role. Just as the individual's placement in common-sense reality presupposes his capacity to take roles and so participate, *act* in social reality, so movement to other worlds is based on the potentiality of the self to become a being capable of responding to the presence of transcendent elements, among them the symbols of art. To become capable of responding, in this sense, is to set aside (place in abeyance, once again) the straightforward attitude the individual takes to mundane experience and instead allow a new and different facet of the self to appear. To "take a role" as art-appreciator is to move on two fronts: on one, the naive attitude of daily life must be bracketed (it is no longer possible to look, touch, and hear what is presented in the art work as long as sensing is pragmatically committed and bound to the realm of common-sense manipulation); on the other front, a refusal of a number of possible role-stances is necessary so that *one* of them may indeed be realized (the gallery-goer must decide whether his professional interest in the sociology of small groups is relevant to his aesthetic experience). It would be foolish to assume that taking a role is synonymous with fulfilling a role (in the sense of meeting its requirements). It is patent that there is as much role-failure as there is adequacy—more, most likely. However, it is easy to understand the dangers which surround the role-taker. To begin with, roles tend to get habitualized and so the joy is squeezed out of them and only the mechanisms of response remain, skeletal reminders of what were once flesh. Furthermore, a lack of response or a very partial response to art, for example, may be disguised under social pressure. Few people wish to appear uncouth. But there are also spirited individuals who indeed have a very strong response to art works despite the fact that they may fail to find or even refuse to find a means of expressing their opinions in socially approved terms. And, of course, there are some who disguise their aesthetical poverty with a flurry of activity, a seasonal phenomenon. The question involves not only the authenticity of the response to art but also the history, the becoming of that authenticity. Once again, we meet with the pathology of the typical, its stagnation in "Bad Faith."

"Presented" with an art work on formal occasions, the individual may muster his critical forces, unlock his cabinet of responses. Words, of course, most frequently become the means by which the art work is given its due: "great" or "ghastly," "puzzling" or "exciting," and, of course, the magisterial "interesting." The word, the phrase of valuation, becomes the surrogate for aesthetic response; instead of heralding a turn for the symbolic, the "word" stands between the viewer and his existential subjectivity. To speak of "Bad Faith" here means that the self has chosen both a temporal and a moral mode of being, has in effect decided to avoid transcension of mundanity by embracing the typical as a form of protection from the freedom which art demands. The quality of Bad Faith is subtle. Rather than turning to a mode of pretense or fraudulence, the individual who chooses Bad Faith elects to avoid a clear and evident option. He may, of course, decide to pretend to be interested in art without having the least concern with it; but that is not what is meant by Bad Faith. Deception, in its simple and most obvious form, involves a liar, self-consciously telling his lie. In Bad Faith, on the other hand, the liar and the one lied to are the same individual, nor is the liar "aware" that he is lying. In the moment of choice he enacts a ritual: supposed to be responsive to art, he becomes "one who so responds." Ritual replaces confrontation because the art work tangentially suggests the limits of the mundane attitude, the circumference of the taken-for-granted world. And in ritual fashion, words replace realities or may be said to become realities by way of incantation. After all, what is it that truly seizes the individual in his mundane existence? What strikes him at his living center? Is it love? Profession? Is it the hedonic beast pacing the ego's cage? And what external forces touch that ultimacy, excite the nerve of the person's passion? Rituals are preservers of secret places and guardians of their own intensity. I believe that the individual who, in Bad Faith, refuses art is denying the scope of his freedom by insulating himself from the role of the symbolic.

Bad Faith is not an either-or. There may be times when the individual is in Bad Faith and times when he is free. It should also be recognized that the achievement of freedom with respect to the symbolic is not a permanent acquisition, is not a "state" of being—that *would* be Bad Faith! Rather, achievement is a risking of the self and the achievements of the self in a life-lasting effort to face and continue to appreciate the reality of transcendence in the mundane. Art can stale for some, and it is by no means rare to find a "professional" art man who is bored with art but immersed in its activities. Nor is it always easy to return again and again in lectures, in classes, or in criticism to devastatingly powerful works of art (how can we regain the meaning of "great"?) and respond to them with the fervor and the exultance of the initial recognition. There are reasonable explanations for the accommodation of art to mundanity, but they should not be a replacement for the underlying truth that the symbolic cuts a gash in common sense and draws its hot blood. In its positive aspect, common-sense life comes to terms with the irruption of art in its midst by liberating that aspect of the self capable of responding penetratingly to its demands, capable of recognizing its authority. Confronted with the art work, common-sense man is set searching for a role he can take which is resonant with, equal to, the symbolic. Let us call that proper role and the individual who succeeds in attaining it the "symbolic self." It might be characterized egologically in this way: In the paradigm presence of art, mediated by the great work of art, I am aware of the transcendencies of birth, sociality, and death (a triumvirate which may be taken as a short list of the more numerous metaphysical constants). Although I have knowledge of and a reasonable grasp of everyday life, I find the presentation of those themes in the art work primordially unlike all my acquaintance with individual births and deaths. Of course, the similarities are there, but they fade to nothing in comparison with the shattering quality of the art originals. In the art work I discover the origin of each man's birth and the finality of each man's destruction. It is proper to say, then, that the art work reveals sociality in its *originary* potency, in its capacity to display from the very start of a man's life the forces that are for and against him, that demand struggle and reconstruction, that implore a perpetual willingness to *agree* to undertake the having of a world. Within common sense our world is already begun, we are already en route. But in art the entire effort must be made all over again, and we are placed in the position of having to examine directly the essential history of the mundane creation. The "symbolic self" is capable of such scrutiny because it finds itself drawn to the groundless arena of art and is willing to construct its own foundations. It has literally nothing to bank on, no capital, no reserves, no collateral, and no credit. It must begin on its own, with its own truth, and so establish its own trust.

With this conception of the symbolic self it might appear that we have abandoned traditional conceptions of social role in favor of a metaphysics of creativity. I prefer to think that the considerations of social role involved in our movement from the alone ego to the present stage of analysis are unified expressions of the ways in which the individual is able to locate himself and Others in a common reality. Roles are means through which such communality is achieved, and they provide an entrance to social process. In speaking of "traditional conceptions" of social role, it is sensible to distinguish between theories which are predominantly genetic in their concern (those which take their central task to be providing an account of the origin and development of the self) and approaches which are more nearly descriptive efforts to survey the anatomy of role-takers and their roles. Although our phenomenology of the self has been structural, it has been deeply interested in the dialectical features of social role. The distinction, then, between "genetic" and "descriptive" is insufficient for our present purposes. Let us speak rather of a "genetic phenomenology" whose object is the descriptive uncovering and analysis of the meaning-structure of the self engaged in social roles. Very often, the sociology of roles begins with a typology of the self in its many-leveled involvements and then proceeds to elicit the network of obligations, prescriptions, rights, and expectations which go with different roles. The general result is an image of man as a unified ego capable of taking many standpoints, of assuming different attitudes, of accepting and living up to variant demands. But the status of "taking," "assuming," and "accepting" is not altogether clear. *What* is taken, assumed, and accepted is evident in terms of the role demands and prerogatives of a corporation executive, a union organizer, or a trial judge, but the conditions for the possibility of such action remain philosophically problematic. A "genetic phenomenology" is concerned with tracing out the history of the ego, its becoming, and with clarifying the relationship between the stages of its development and the concrete expression those stages take in the life of the individual. Such a viewing of the self precludes any translation of roles into mechanisms of social procedure. At the basis of the symbolic self is a vital impulse toward the fulfillment of the ego's journey.

The difficult relationship between the universal and the particular, which we have already discussed, may be reapproached through the symbolic self; in turn, the symbolic self may come into sharper focus. We know that the paradox of the particular is that class or type status may well be ascribed to it despite sharp objections. Very simply, it is somehow demeaning to be told that my critical and unique experience is part of a group of such experiences;

that robs and patronizes me. Yet it is also possible to view the matter in another way. Specificity, concreteness, and even uniqueness do not assure the quality of an experience. To delimit what is felt by saying that it is *mine* alone does not automatically insure the character or caliber of what is experienced. The claim to uniqueness may well receive the response: "Yes, it's *yours* and yours alone but it's second-rate and tawdry." Yet in reverse terms, it might be suggested that the particular is heightened when it is placed in the class of the typical and that it achieves a sense of the intersubjective continuity between the personal and the universal. Of course, such a mode of interpreting individual experience has its falsifying aspects, its own form of Bad Faith. "I went through the same thing when I was your age" may be a refusal to attend to the experience in its specificity. It may be perfectly true, as we have said, that many adolescents go through a psychological crisis involving problems of personal identity and even that such crises are endemic to the process of maturation, but to hold that *this* crisis falls into that classification is a judgment that comes either from a close examination of the individual involved or from a readiness to label the situation so that it then yields more easily to "analysis." What seems to emerge from these considerations is a "good" and a "bad" sense of the typical and the universal: good when a concrete reality is enriched by its universal implications and bad when the class or type is substituted for the original experience or when it blocks our turning to the concrete in its full weight. Matters are not that simple. Before we can speak of a "good" or "bad" sense of typicality, we shall have to probe the universal-particular relationship more closely. Our vantage point remains the concept of the symbolic self.

The transcendencies with which we have associated the symbolic self are universal constants, as we have noted, but they are also clues or directives which indicate the axial possibilities of the person. As guides to the illumination of the individual's being, birth, sociality, and death are existential symbols, that is, they are relevant only to the person whose freedom is risked in confronting them. But the risking of freedom is the most concrete and individual of all acts. It would seem that the symbolic self is the locus of both the universal and the particular. How is that possible? An answer may be found in the thematic nature of existential philosophy. In existential literature as well as philosophy, there are two almost archetypal motifs which characterize if they do not define the presence of man in the world. The first may be called abandonment, the second anguish. Although they are bound to each other intimately, I will consider them separately for our immediate purposes.

1   Abandonment.   As long as the individual is able to rely on the frame of his taken-for-granted world, on the causal efficacy of himself in action in that world, talk of "abandonment" will seem unreal or artificial. In ordinary terms, to be abandoned is to be left on one's own by Others upon whom one has depended. Abandonment, then, is isolation and implies that Others are guilty of dereliction. To be abandoned in circumstances of emergency would ease or erase charges against fellow-men but would then mean that the individual must suffer the consequences of having to go it alone. Existential abandonment arises when the common-sense frame of our lives is set aside in those moments or by those events which do not find accommodation in the categories or typifications of mundanity, when mundanity itself turns strange and becomes remote. Most easily but not most faithfully expressed, the individual has a *feeling* of being lost in the world, of all signs of familiarity gone or set awry, of becoming a stranger to himself. But to speak of a "feeling" of abandonment can help us to understand the existential problem only at the expense of misplacing its meaning. There is indeed a feeling of abandonment, but that is not what the existentialist is concerned with. Rather, we should say that the feeling is the emblem of a change in the person, in the reality of the self, which now experiences the world *through* a new categorial attitude. In the fundamental mood which the transformation establishes, the notions of origin and destiny are splintered into bits of "where I was raised" and "where I am tending." To be abandoned is for the self to be directionless in all but one very powerful way: it experiences its "here" as having been created by Others (whether persons or Gods) and then *left*. To be "here" in terms of abandonment is to be thrown or thrust into the world, cast into a reality one must become responsible for without having had a say in its creation or in the absurd event through which the predicament of the individual comes about. Finally, abandonment is the realization that placement in the world is unchangeable. Wherever the individual is, whatever relationships he establishes with fellow-men, however altered his affairs may become, the underlying recognition that he is on his own remains. The feeling of abandonment may be overcome, but what it signified is a perpetual presence. Each of us is *here*, in a world which offers signs and recommendations, but which cannot hide the obverse side of familiarity: estrangement and finitude.

2 Anguish. To find oneself alone in the world means that choice and decision are individual determinations, that neither Others nor the realms of authority can touch the interior freedom of the person. If abandonment brings each of us a recognition of his contingent "here," so anguish is the realization that no source other than the individual can provide an interpretation of reality or be responsible for what takes place in the world. Anguish is then twofold: it faces the world which lies beyond its dominion and it confronts itself in the recognition that within its own being must be found the resolution of its problems and the criteria for its choices. If self and world could be split apart, anguish would lose its purchase. In terms of self alone, the individual could conceivably make his decisions and come to terms with their consequences. Were it a matter of world alone, presumably the individual could find his way in consultation with Others. But this separation presupposes that all men have the *same* reality, that urgencies and problems are to be faced in the same way because they can be posed in general terms. But the meaning of existential anguish is based on the integrity of self and world, and this means that to speak of *each* man's situation is to recognize an absolute. Most directly, I am anguished precisely because I cannot confront or resolve an existential problem as "Others" might (however sagaciously and adequately they might do it), because the comprehension of *my* problem and the location of the solution true to *me* depend on the discovery of my own identity, and because each time I turn to a central term of my existence I meet the language of freedom. And last, the experience of anguish, like that of abandonment, is a discovery of limits. To the "here" found in abandonment must be added the "now" of anguish, seized in the recognition that choice is earth- and man-bound, that whether or not he is ultimately to be judged by History or God, it is the individual's responsibility to choose the meaning events have. Human reality, then, is given a temporal placement, and each man is responsible for himself and his time. Taken together, abandonment and anguish present a view of the individual as alone in a world thick with Others and as free in a harassed universe.

In existential discovery, the meaning of the universal and the particular unfolds in a series of choices through which the symbolic self encounters the typical and translates the transcendent. Abandonment is given its meaning in *this* situation in which I find myself at *this* moment—a "this" in both cases which merges with the anguish of "now" because its reality is inescapably my project. Paradoxically, perhaps, the existential experience which we have been exploring brings together the universal and the particular in such a way that both are transformed in the process. The universal is given a focus, an experiential content, in the immediacy of the individual's situation, and the particular is expanded, accelerated into an awareness of what we have called "possibility," that is, the form of expression the self is capable of achieving, the mode of being the individual is capable of realizing. At the same time, it must be understood that the interpenetration of the universal and the particular is not a simple merging or a borrowing. What is struck between them is an imbalance. In abandonment I can find no security in the knowledge that "all men" are abandoned; in anguish I can have no consolation in the realization that "my" lot is that shared by all men. Rather, we must say that the existential categories apply to human reality without familiar and acceptable facets of mundane existence. Similarly, the concrete moments in individual experience in which the existential is seized cannot be "explained" by saying that they belong to this or that category. In short, the quality of existential experience is such that it presents the person with an ongoing challenge: the universal features of his reality cannot be accommodated in mundanity; they remain strange to daily life, yet they call for recognition and some order of acceptance. In his typicality, common-sense man cannot make sense of the existential, but as a symbolic self, the individual is able to *become* the person capable of confronting the transcendent at the same time that he remains himself in the world.

With the symbolic self a vast entrance is found to the total order of transcendence. If the irruption of art in the mundane may be said to have initiated the arising of that aspect of the individual capable of becoming a free man, of liberating the "good" sense of the typical and the redeeming quality of role, then the goal to which the symbolic self is directed may be said to be the recovery and vindication not only of that initiating spark but of the entire range of development the self has gone through, from its solitary beginnings to its resplendent sociality. We shall understand the "total order of transcendence" to be the domain of religion. The history of the self that has been pursued so far has shown many characteristics of the transcendence-directed quality of mundane existence, but it is the decisive capacity of the symbolic self to assume the constructive task of coming to terms with art and, as we shall see, religion. By "constructive" I mean the more nearly literal sense of building, of what we have already spoken of as "making." It is the symbolic self which is charged with the responsibility not only of interpreting art but of rendering its interpretations microcosmic orders, cosmions of meaning. What we "make of art," then, is a function of whether and how the individual accepts the role of the symbolic self, that is, whether he acknowledges the transcendencies the art work presents, retaining their irreducible quality and holding them constantly in view in their independent givenness. In the crossing of art's transcendence with the person's existential engagement there comes into being the "concrete universal," the being who is at once "outside" himself and at the center of subjectivity. We are brought, finally, to the essence of the symbolic, to the source of art's irruption and the foundation of man's existential response: the ego's transcendence in religion.

chapter seven

religion

If art invades the mundane, religion reconstructs it. But before it is possible to speak of the ultimate transcendence which the symbolic self is capable of experiencing, we must turn to the more limited, more commonplace aspect of the individual's involvement in the everyday world. How does religion find its place in the typified reality of common sense? If we set aside its institutionalized dimension, religion is often thought of as a segment of the mundane which is discontinuous with the practical, the functional, the efficacious reality of politics and power. The more its "importance" is stressed, the more we tacitly admit that religion needs coaxing and coaching to show up in pragmatic costume. Proclaiming its urgency and ultimacy seems to be a way of hypnotizing ourselves into believing. For some, of course, religion is where they start from, the moral center of their placement in the world. Perhaps, for them, the null point of the body is superseded by the incarnation of the spirit, the Body of Man. It is neither possible nor appropriate here to attempt a survey of the place of religion in the lives of men. We must confine ourselves to the narrower and more restricted question of the way in which it is typified. To put matters bluntly, religion is the accommodation of the transcendent in the outskirts of what is deemed knowable. A certain negation presents itself here, for each determinate typification, it is being suggested, carries an open horizon of indeterminacy, a beyond which can be further specified but which is grasped initially as a fragment of a larger or extended totality which awaits presentation. In typified terms, then, religion is what does *not* show itself, does *not* reveal itself in what is known, yet which enters the mundane world by way of being intended as possible. Let us say that the transcendent is "appresented" beyond the typifications of common sense. We have seen appresentation at work before at other levels, in our discussion of our knowledge of objects and of Others; now we may transpose the analysis to a higher domain, where negation liberates the possible.

Before the meaning of negation can become clearer in the present context, it is necessary to take a closer look at the way in which *affirmation* functions in type and role. At the foundation of typification lie two expectancies, themselves both typified and typifying: we may call them "repeatability" and "continuity."

1 Repeatability. As a purchaser of tobacco, I typically expect that when my brand is in stock at the neighborhood store and I pay cash for my order, I will in turn receive the cigars I want. But the typicality involved is rooted in the assumption that what has typically worked in the past will continue to work in the future. If I were refused service one day at the tobacco counter, I would be justified in asking why. Imagine:

A "Morning. Abbot's Pleasure, please."
B "Sorry."
A "All out?"
B "No, as a matter of fact, a shipment just came in."
A "Not unpacked yet?"
B "Oh, we've got them out. They're right over there, to your right."
A "I don't understand."
B "It's the way things are now."
A "You mean my money's no good here? You don't want my business?"
B "I didn't say that."
A "Something wrong with me?"
B "Not at all."
A "What's up? Come on, what's going on here?"
B "Nothing at all, it's just the way it is now."
A "I can report you, you know."
B "As you please. Anything else this morning?"
A "You haven't heard the last of this."
B "I dare say."
A "I warn you, I'll be back."
B "Please call again, sir, a pleasure to serve you."
A "Abbot's Pleasure is exactly what you didn't serve me. I won't be mocked!"
B "No offense meant."
A "Well offense is taken. If you don't want my business, I know others who do."
B "I dare say."
A "I dare say!"
B "Will there be anything else?"
A "This is absurd."
B "As they say, the customer is always right."
A (leaving) "I can't sort this out."

B "Call again!"
A (to himself) "What's wrong with me?"
B (to himself) "I must remember to stock up on Abbot's Pleasure; that's the third customer I've had to turn down today."

The fantasied breakdown of the typical presupposes the essential repeatability of mundane experience. The most striking aspect of expectation in this regard is the assumption that a request or a question will meet with a response of some kind. The breakdown of the exchange principle in the realm of small purchases still takes for granted the principle of communication: that asking and answering imply each other. If repeatability were literally *uprooted*, torn out of the earth of intersubjective reality, what would be left would be an unstable fragmentation, a living in the moment which would no longer be capable of order or even definition. Typification is possible because repeatability is tacitly predicated of every perceptual act. More than that, however, each act is intended *as* repeatable, that is, as performable again and again in typically similar fashion. Both the object intended and the subject intending participate in the immanent claim to "again-ness," the assumption of renewal in perceptual life and in social action.

2 Continuity. A kind of *et cetera* shadows each typification. Not only do I expect to be able to do the same thing again and again, but I assume that whatever is done will move along an open horizon of further action, that the deed will take its place in a continuous unfolding of future experience. It is not *because* the past has proved to be continuous in its relationships and its resultants that I expect the present to move analogously into the future; rather, I perceive the world through the typifying agency of continuity. Its breakdown would return us to an obverse absurdity:

B "Hello! Good to see you again. The usual?"
A "Usual what?"
B "Abbot's Pleasure, your brand."
A "You're not making sense."
B "Well, then, what can I do for you today?"
A "That's a long story, one day; I haven't time for it."
B "Something wrong?"
A "Don't jump to conclusions; you might not make it, too much distance to cover."
B "If you'll excuse me, sir, I have some things to do. Perhaps I can serve you another time."
A "What other time? It will still be now. Now is when I want service."
B "Exactly how may I be of service? What would you like?"
A "It has got to be here and there, is that it? Something behind the counter to be handed over, back and forth, in and out, now it's hidden and now it's not. The old shell game."
B "I don't follow you."
A "Small wonder! I'm time's desperado : I leave no trail."

B "I would like to be helpful. Frankly, I think you need some help. Is there someone I can call?"
A "The only help I need is straight answers to straight questions."
B "Shoot!"
A "Violence everywhere. How can I take you seriously?"
B "We're simply not getting anywhere. Look, have an Abbot on the house. I'll light you up."
A "Vandal! Keep that Lucifer away from me!"
B "I'm going to the phone for just a minute. Will you promise to wait?"
A "You're supposed to wait on me."
B (starting to leave) "I'll only be a minute."
A (leaving) "Too long. Time's up and no one can bring it down. No more jawing: lockjaw."

The crackup of continuity would disallow the sequential intentionality of any act. It is not so much a matter of "nothing following" as of nothing conceivable as bound or related to a given unity of experience. Plenty could "follow" in the sense of there being new units, more givens. The point is that each unit would be on its own, itself, and therefore stripped of development, and that in turn would mean that the original units were sealed off from each other as well as from the world. Rather than making monads of them, such isolation would compel us to say that particulars were not typifiable, could never achieve "suchness" of any order, were destined to flicker into and out of being, consuming themselves utterly, leaving nothing behind and no trace for the future to recover. Each particular would have its own pyre and suffer its own immolation. We are spared that pathology by the affirmation of typicality which continuity assures. Whether or not experience proves to be quite as we expect it to be, it is taken as ongoing, as presenting a prospect, as bearing the momentum of futurity. Within that root-belief, experience unfolds as conceivable and familiar. Together with repeatability, continuity assures not only a recognizable and controllable world but one in which the individual can locate his fellow-men and communicate with them. At bottom, the affirmation of typicality is the refusal of finitude. With that we come to the meaning of negation.

In an obvious sense, we know that individual experience is repeatable and continuous only within the limits of a lifetime, that each life is, in its historical unfolding, unrepeatable and severed by death. Do the affirmations of typical expectancy hold, then, only within a tacitly agreed-upon limit? To the assumption that of course I can perform again and again in essentially the same way and that the flow of experience will accommodate renewed action in continuous fashion, it would appear that there is an accompanying legend which reads: "Of course, all of this holds good for a lifetime, but no more." Such a legend is hidden and ambiguous for a number of reasons.

First, is it really believed? Or is the notation more nearly like the signs in public buildings which tell us where to go in case of disaster? We know what they mean but we don't believe them. Second, it would seem that the limitation is somehow untrue. Granted that I will die, my actions nevertheless seem to have a universal character which my death cannot affect. Perhaps that universality is the meaning of typification. Finally, from whose standpoint is the recognition made? Is the truth of limitation necessarily an egological one or is it discoverable and attributable *in the same way* for the alter ego? Carried to its final implications, the analysis of limitation leads to a philosophy of death. Moving along the lesser or smaller phase of the theme, we will first be concerned with the ways in which the fundamental negation of the typical takes place in mundane experience. Later, the interpretation of negation as appresenting religious transcendence will be discussed.

Within the essentially naive attitude of man in daily life (returning to our early description of mundanity), the ongoing character of experience is straightforwardly taken to be not only continuable but seamlessly continuous. At the same time, it is perfectly well known that the individual's career is finite, that his experience is destined to suffer permanent disruption and cessation. How can mundanity tolerate both the assumption of continuity and the recognition of fracture? Most simply, by dissipating and disguising the force of negation with a mode of Bad Faith, the refusal of death. Recognition must mean more than formal acknowledgment; it must spring from and yet remain grounded in the temporality of the person. It is exactly the loss of temporality which expresses itself in the typifications of mundane existence, for their repeatability and continuity hold in *time*, in public chronology, and are only secondarily recovered by the concrete individual. That recovery, however, poses the problem of negation, for the individual who "knows" that he will die will also be confronted with the reality of his finitude in that moment when the quotation marks which guard "knowing" no longer function as protectors, when they are thrown into spasm. We may, then, speak of negation in two ways: as the "not" of formal denial and as the nihilation of experiential positing. As a mundane man, rooted in common sense, alive to the sorrows of the adult world, I know that my plans for tomorrow may be interrupted by my death; but I do not believe it will happen. Just as I live in my faith that the world will continue as it has in the past, so I place in abeyance the most hurtful possibility of all, my death, and live in the faith that it will not occur. Rather, it is something for the future, for some other time. However, when my death becomes an imminent possibility, when I no longer think of "perhaps" but of "when", the status of typification changes in a radical way; I find that "tomorrow" or "next year" are charged with a temporal puzzlement which is inseparable from my own presence in the world. The negation of my being able to act again and again and of the world's continuing to absorb my action in an orderly fashion is no longer understandable through the phrase "it may not be so" but is expressed in the intention of a more primordial "no," the destruction of temporality in the loss of a world. All typification—all experiencing, it would not be unfair to say—carries an interior horizon of negation through which what is presented is grasped as limitable. The difference between reflective awareness of that limitability and Bad Faith with regard to its meaning is the measure of the individual's comprehension of death. If typification merely points back to the self as an anonymous agent, a typifier, then negation means little more than a surface acceptance of the word "not." If, however, the typical is transcended by the symbolic and the agent replaced by the symbolic self, then negation is seized in its existential aspect and the individual is in the presence of a temporal world. The movement from formal to experiential negation is the condition for the experience of religious transcendence. Though it is not in itself sufficient to assure transcendence, it is necessary as a condition for the advance of the self to its ultimate fulfillment. In different terms, we are interested in the connection between death as a mundane typification and death as an existential reality. To explore that connection it is necessary to retrace the "stages along death's way" by returning to the central moments of the self's development. However, we shall proceed in reverse order, moving from art back to the solitary ego. That return trip will, in a way, show us where we now are.

1   Art.   The arising of the symbolic self in the recognition of the transcendencies of birth, sociality, and death may be understood as a response to the possibilities of experiential reconstruction. In domains other than art, it is possible to alter and even transform what exists within the context of the ongoing world, within the horizon of historical continuity. In art, however, the ground of experience itself is examined and interpreted without the support of the traditional props. Indeed, the fundamental act of the artist is a rebuilding, *from nothing*, of the human world, the reconstruction of mundanity. The fundamental negation which is involved here directs itself to the preinterpreted world, seeks to shatter its monumental embeddedness in the taken-for-granted attitudes and conceptions common-sense men share, and turns from that conceptual rubble to the stone-by-stone reordering of human existence. It is the symbolic self which is able to undertake such reordering because its role is made possible and effective through existential commitment. A resonance exists between the negation of the mundane and the abandonment of the self in a world it must interpret for itself. What emerges from this line of analysis is the idea that negation is not only the recognition—even the existential recognition—that everything given in human experience is limited and that the individual is a finite creature, but that what has been experienced, what has already been absorbed in the self's encounters, can (and, for the purposes of art, must) be broken down into its primal elements or even razed to unrecognizable bits in order to rebuild a world. In a way, the validation of repeatability and continuity must be preceded by the artist's vindication of the constitutive givens which make the unity of his life comprehensible. Those givens must be stripped to nothing, spoiled, and reclaimed for art. In these terms, death becomes a negation of life productive of new life, a negation of beginnings.

2   History.   If the point of access to macrocosmic history is the life-world of the actor on the social scene, then microcosmic history is founded on a mode of negation: predecessors and successors are "present" to contemporaries as *not* being experienceable in face-to-face relationships. Furthermore, death becomes the essential barrier between the history of the macrocosmic world and the social action taking place in contemporary life. It is because they died before we were born that Others in the past are our predecessors; it is because we will die before they are born that Others in the future are our successors. Nor is this a matter of definition or stipulation. For the individual engaged in present action, the historicity of his activity is encountered in the very means, the instrumentalities, through which he chooses his goals and projects his efforts. In everything from language to technology, the actor encounters the activity of his predecessors. Not only did they live out their lives before he was born, but they interpreted their world and so made it into history, created the order which the actor now alive inherits as the horizon of his efforts to create and sustain a coherent existence. The historical past, then, is renewed, enlivened, and reconstituted in the negation which separates every contemporary from his predecessors. So too with the future: those who will be born after we die are intended by us as bearers of what historical order there now is. What we mean, of course, is that our present will be similar to the past we have, that each of us is capable of assuming the role of predecessor because we are able to be successors. However, we can "take" the role of predecessor only by negation; we must die to fulfill our historical possibilities. We perhaps can understand now, in this retrospective movement, how the symbols which art liberates are foreshadowed in the historical realm: there too one meets the fundamental negation which makes the universal possible.

3   Science.   The shift, in science, from the role of actor to that of observer may be understood as an aspect of the theme of negation. To take the formal role of scientific observer is, as we have seen, to set aside the biographical situation as well as the concrete placement of the individual in favor of the role-demands of science. But why should such methodological neutralization be understood as any kind of negation? In fact, it would appear that such an interpretation would contradict the entire conception of bracketing which phenomenology employs. Hitherto, we have expressly warned that placing in abeyance does *not* mean denying or negating. The difficulty is only an apparent one, for I am not suggesting that the element of negation in question in moving from the individual to the scientific domain means a denial of the concrete existence of the observer. Rather, no use will be made of that rich specificity. The negation becomes clearer when we turn to the new role which the scientist assumes. As a formal observer, bound to the methodological rigor of the larger enterprise of which he is a part, the scientist negates any link to his "private" life, or at least he attempts to stay clear of such entanglements. The ideal result is a freedom of the work from the man, the achievement of "results" which will stand, fall, or be superseded in terms of their own validity. What is negated, then, is the person acting in the role of observer; he has *become* his role. The reality of the person as an individual remains, though it has been set off to the side. In the history of science we are witnesses to a methodological death which, far from interfering with the glory of individual scientists, hardly affects the lives of astronomers, physicists, or anatomists. We speak of Copernicus and Newton and Harvey when we wish to speak most directly of their work. However, in separating scientist from science, we are, strictly speaking, negating the historical actuality of the person acting as scientist in order to understand his professional accomplishment. Once that separation has been made, we cannot keep apart the scientist *qua* scientist from science. The eclipse of the individual makes possible the fulfillment of the role.

4 Sociality. If the "We" relationship is basic to sociality, then the being of man with his fellow-man is threatened persistently by the negation of both formal and existential aspects of typification. Certain aspects of social action are made possible—the formal We is assured—by facets of individual involvement through role-playing. The fact that the existential identity of the person is *not* involved makes possible a host of relationships in the public world whose importance is not to be dismissed casually yet whose level of commitment (on the part of the actors involved) is necessarily shallow. Seriousness, urgency, fervor are negated in the role-demands of much of the activity of daily life, yet they are not eliminated or destroyed as potential forces in the action of men. The negation is a temporary settlement of sorts, a procedural compromise. However, the risk of all role activity is that the agreement will not be honored or that it will be partially denied. Interestingly enough, denial can come from two sources: a minimally demanding role can be refused altogether, that is, reduced even further, or at the other extreme, a complex and honored role can be "overdone," worked beyond its proper boundaries and so transformed into something it is not intrinsically capable of handling. When such negations occur, the We-relationship the roles are intended to support suffers a reversal. In the case of existentially committed individuals who create the We of friendship and love, the threat of negation is an interior possibility for the world they share. If love transcends role, it still demands some structure of affection, some order for expression. In this sense, it is possible to speak of the negation of love finding its manifestation in the social relationship sustained by those who love each other rather than in a private, individual sphere. The death of love, then, is a phenomenon of sociality rather than an egological event. With its despair goes as well the loss of those features of potential development which otherwise would lead to the fulfillment of the symbolic self. The shattering of the We reverberates throughout the social world.

5 Other selves. It is, of course, always the Other who dies, and so the fundamental negation of experience derives from an event which demands the individual's direct and immediate prehension, yet which transcends his awareness. It is not I but you who die. With that recognition, the ego is assured of its own permanence and affirms its perspective on the world: the self is the everlastingly authentic point of access to the world because all Others are moribund. Truth and time seem to greet each other in the apparent strength of the individual, in the fact that death holds for everyone but him. Of course, the individual "knows" that he, too, will die, but that knowledge is typified and, most often, is diluted in Bad Faith. And even with respect to Others, it is not "you" who will die, but "they," Others known by way of pure types or merely glimpsed in societal encounters. The specification of the "you" as a concrete individual makes it much more difficult to say with honesty and insight, "I know that you will die." What is intended instead is something closer to, "You are one of those who will die." When the "you" is intimately known, related, and loved, when the Other is addressed as "Thou" (in the familiar form in those languages which allow it and as "you" in English), it is as difficult to say "I know that you will die" as it is to say of oneself, "I know that I will die." *As* difficult, but no more. The language, of course, is no obstacle, nor is it especially problematic to announce the fact of mortality—one's own or that of fellow-men—in ordinary terms. What is elusive is the comprehension of the reality of death, that blue negation, in egological terms or in relation to a concrete Other to whom one is bound intimately. It will remain true that the Other whom I love will die, but that death may shock me into self-appraisal and may compel me to recognize in the Other an irreplaceable presence. The negation of the Other seized in the experience of the death of a "Thou" may force the individual to self-recognition.

6 The self. Within the egological sphere, it would seem that death is a possibility hidden to the self, a secret that will be disclosed only in the progression to sociality. Somewhat differently put, it might be suggested that death *becomes* a possibility for the self when the ego has attained socialization; before that, in the purely egological aspect of its being, the self is "pre-finite." With sociality, however, the self is able to uncover its egological sources as they intend the development through the stages we have described. The fundamental distance to be covered is between the solitude of the ego and the formation of the symbolic self. In terms of negation, the ego discovers its symbolic capacity in its initial recognition that it is indeed finite and that what is true of the Other (grasped as "Thou") is true of the self. In this realization, negation ceases to be a formal operation, something "known" abstractly, and becomes an agency of transformation, a process of alteration, which establishes the claim to transcendence characteristic of the symbolic self. In straightforward terms, the individual who truly comprehends the fact that *he* will die becomes a being capable of understanding the transcendence of death as a thematic reality for all men. Of course, we have discovered the source of the symbolic self in the egological sphere only by reading back into it the sedimented history of its becoming in all the stages from Other Selves to Art. The primal negation, however, is rooted in the ego's capacity to move from what we have termed its "pre-finite" being to its grasp of transcendence by means of the symbolic self. The principle which gives life to that "capacity" of the ego is the power of typification as it expresses itself in social role. To recognize, in existential dread, that *I* in my concrete being will die is to know that I am *a* being who will die. Just as the force of the "I" can be dissimulated in Bad Faith, so the authentic power of the "a" can be negated in social role. The fulfillment of both demands the socialization of the "I" and the individualization of the "a." Both may be achieved in the symbolic self and affirmed in the role of transcendence. For the self, however, such resolution is not without its tensions:

ME "Perhaps we can summarize the major points which have been made thus far in the discussion."
I "You've been planning that, haven't you? Rehearsing?"
ME "Not at all, it's simply a matter of clarity. We should try to bring together some of the threads of the argument so that . . ."
I ". . . we can shed some light? There's a phrase for you."
ME "Are you quite done?"
I "How do you shed light, by the way? Like a skin? How about molting some light or sloughing it?"
ME "This is deliberate, isn't it? You're trying to avoid the truth that you can't do without me, so you scamper about with your tactic of deceit. In the end, we'll have to come to terms with each other. Why not let me proceed?"
I "Peace! You've converted me."

ME "What's that?"

I "I'm converted, proceed."

ME "Well, then, the essential point is that the self we share is capable of enlargement, of becoming profoundly aware of the transcendencies of . . ."

I "I'm the one responsible for that. Credit where credit is due!"

ME "For the sake of our symbolic self, will you please stop interrupting?"

I "Windy! That's your trouble, you've swallowed a mess of semicolons. Break them up, and spit up an occasional top part. Hath any periods in thee, shepherd?"

ME "You're incorrigible . . . All right, for the nth time: We are shareholders in one corporate body. Your vote represents change, new departures, expansion; my shares speak for continuity, tradition, retrenchment. Together we can build an empire; apart we will go into bankruptcy, receivership. Further . . ."

I "I won't go any further. In fact, I won't go this far. Now hear this, Wilbur: I'm not the Bourse! I won't be starched up and I won't be regulated. Campy as it may sound, I'm free."

ME "My dear fellow, don't panic; you're overreacting! My only concern was to emphasize cooperation, not to deprive you of anything, freedom least of all. After all, if you're wounded, I bleed."

I "Careful!"

ME "You see, we're both upset. Let me get back to the main thrust of the argument."

I "What are you, Yale Divinity?"

ME "Really!"

I "Let's get down to the rough : for all your chanting about equal partnership, when it comes down to it, I'm the one who feeds life into this mess; I'm the one who darts out and forages for what you need to survive. Without that you'd starve into a stupor. Admit that and we can have what you'd call a dialogue."

ME "Aren't you the tough! Are you all that sure of yourself? Have you ever been on your own? Answer me that one: Have you ever been on your own?"

I "Have you?"

ME "Evader! Who is the one claiming independence?"

I "I never said independence; I said freedom."

ME "Quibbling will get us nowhere. Can't you realize that we share a career and a destiny? If it isn't 50–50, let's call it 60–40 or 30–70—let it be in your favor—but the decisive truth is that neither your fraction nor mine can add up to the whole; we complete each other."

I "Have it your way, but that won't change the fact that when it comes to that symbolic self you've been trumpeting, I'm the one who breathes life into those stodgy types; I'm the one who climbs out over your roles and shakes fire out of darkness."

ME "Quite the dramatist, aren't you? But it seems to me I've heard those lines before. May one ask what happens to your old scripts? To whom is copyright assigned?"

I "Yes, I deliver my rummage to you; is that what you're angling for? And you're welcome to it! Receptacle!"

ME "To dispense with the pyrotechnics, the only point we were interested in eliciting was that in time your choicest morsel reappears as my hash. No complaints, sir, but fair is fair. The past of your freedom is my present, and that's what infuriates you. You can't look at me without seeing yourself."

I "How wearisome. I thought you were going to show how we cooperate in the creation of the symbolic self. All that talk about partnership—for nothing. All it comes down to is you need yeast, light, air, and in desperation you pat your paunch and warble about the delight of the original ingredients that went into it. Talk of corporations! In the end, you're nothing but Buster Brown. I'm Huck Finn."

ME "Well, like it or not, you're stuck with me."
I   "I'm yours till your thrust turns to rust."
ME "Till death do us part."
I   "Copacetic!"

The inner strain between stability and improvisation in the development of the symbolic self reflects the dualities we have been contrasting throughout our story: the universal and the particular, Thought and Life, phenomenology and existentialism; in each pair the Me and the I are embattled and allied, self-dividing and self-uniting. Unlike tensions which impair or cripple the individual, the forces which contend in the symbolic self are dialectically productive; they make it possible for the self to generate its own ascent from sociality to transcendence. It is now possible to examine the symbolic self more closely, to scrutinize its operation, and to understand the way in which it transforms social role into a principle of *order*. The problematic bond between type and instance may serve as a point of departure. We have already mentioned a number of examples and seen some illustrations at work. To be "a" something (mother, employer, soldier, housemaid) often means to be compromised in one's concrete identity, to have the "thisness" of one's being denied. Yet, as we have also seen, the universal can be liberating for the existential specificity of the person: through the "a" the unique "I" can arise. In art, the interconnection between the general and the particular was interpreted as a "concrete universal." In the domain of religion, the presence of the symbol which yields transcendence may be understood as the discovery in the universal of a horizon of meaning which carries the self beyond the "a" to what is required for the possibility of the "a" to represent an order of being instead of a functional type. The following elements are at work: the concrete individual, the role he may play, the symbolic self, and the transcendent role to be achieved. We may see them in operation in the case of "the student."

In the very nature of social organization, the individual student is always a junior or an upperclassman or an academic this or that. He is a member of the student body, part of the institutional anatomy. And, of course, he is also himself, bearer of his biographical situation, maneuverer within his skin-envelope, noisemaker to the world. So far we have the familiar "a" and "this." But to be a student may also be to recognize that such a role is possible within the total shape of social reality, to understand that *this* student may not only be *a* student but may participate in reality, in all that there is, through being a student. There is no reason to suggest that there is something in the nature of the role which requires such recognition (any more than there is in the fish-peddler's activity), and it is surely the case that masses of students will do no more than go about their role-business routinely. Yet there is something at issue in the life of the student which cannot be quickly dismissed, something which leads us to say that insight into the larger implications of role is not all that rare a phenomenon and also that being a student (unlike fish-peddling) carries a reflexive dimension to it which may well prove to be the student's entrance to transcendence. Apart from there being times when the student has a glimpse of himself as fulfilling an archetypal role, there are more crucial moments in which he encounters what I have called the principle of "order," that is, the transcendent force of the symbolic activity of being a student. What is announced in that encounter is the truth that the student as common-sense individual, as a mundane being, cannot respond to the implications, the demands of the transcendent role. As a man in daily life, the student can meet his obligations as a student; he may carry them off more or less in typical fashion. However, when, in effect, he is called upon to act as a fulfiller of a style of being, one whose action involves a claim to the entire range of humanity, he is involved in a role which says, "I bring to the world, for all time though only through this time, a mode of action which is that of the student: one who studies, one who prepares himself for a profession, one whose individual acts intend a meaning larger than they can bear." The recognition of the transcendent role calls forth the response of the symbolic self. In the measure of human possibilities, a recognition of transcendence calls for an agent capable of respecting order.

The mechanism through which the symbolic self is able to attend to its remarkable object is that of "appresentation," the phenomenological concept we have already employed but which now needs clarification. For a proper basis on which to build an explanation of appresentation, we will turn back to an earlier discussion of the body. Very simply, when I perceive the body of the Other his psyche is appresented to me. I do not see his body and infer that he is a psychophysical unity, a consciousness like me; rather, I have direct access to him in his distinctively human being. "Direct access" should not be misunderstood. I cannot *be* the Other. What I am capable of, however, is apprehending him *as* a fellow-man, as a being *like* me because, in my response to him, I am in the presence of his vital or sullen awareness. To be sure, it is possible to say that such awareness amounts only to perceiving his overt behavior, including his speech, his gestures, and his facial expression. But what is left out of such an account is the way in which speech, gesture, and expression are perceived. They, too, are grasped by way of an appresentative process in which the Other as *another* is apprehended. In being looked at by the Other, I find his "expression" not so much *on* his face as *through* my situation—in feeling admired, in sensing coolness, in apparent indifference, in being shamed or humiliated. Even the eyes of the Other, the instrument of his stare, are revealed through his glance, his looking at me, rather than in his head, a little above and on either side of his nose. Moreover, it is in my looking at him, in my glance, that his stare is revealed. In strict physiological terms, the eye has no stare, for its vision cannot, on its own, be differentiated into subject or object terms. The eye looking and the eye being looked at are one and the same anatomically. In the field of human expression, however, they are radically different. To speak of appresentation, then, is to honor the difference and, even more, to search for the perceptual reality of the Other in terms consonant with the direct experience which intersubjectivity allows.

For the symbolic self, appresentation functions as a deliverer of transcendence. To continue with our example, the student who recognizes his role in transcendent terms is able to move from the traditional role of student to what that role appresents: a way of the world's being organized, an order of being in which every individual has a potential share. The symbolic self arises to meet the need of the transcendency which has been gained; but another way of understanding the matter is to see in the symbolic self an analog to the transcendent. If the symbolic self makes possible the appresentation of the transcendent, it is no less the case that co-appresented in that transaction is the reality of the symbolic self. If we ask, "Appresented to *whom*?" we may answer: to the existential self. To go a step back, ordinary roles presuppose a typifying self, "a" self; but extraordinary roles, those which confront the transcendent, cannot be handled by "this" individual because he is bound to his biographical situation. The only movement out of that specificity is in the direction of anonymity, into the universal "a" which turns on the axis of typification. But the individual confronted with transcendence is not the typifying but the symbolizing self. All that can be made of the symbols of transcendence by typification is an inventory of traditional religious or cultural values; the existential self, on the other hand, is capable of responding to such symbols because of its sensitivity to and involvement in negation. In such structures as anguish and abandonment it finds a resonance with the transcendently appresented. If we recall that religious transcendence is *not* given directly, is *not* presented along with the typifications of mundane reality, then it is possible to understand the sympathy which relates the existential self to the transcendent. They are both possibilities of mundane being; both lie on the far side of common sense. At the same time, they are realized within the very mundanity they surpass. That realization which points to the transcendent and validates the symbolic self may be called religious response. It is the homeland of appresentation.

Response intends some object: it is always response *to*. In the case of religious response, let us say broadly that the response is to ultimacy, and understand by that, most simply, God. It will hardly be possible to explore that contention with appropriate seriousness, but it might be just as well to have it said. Hereafter, we shall not speak of God but of response. Whatever burden the reader carries forward from these pages, however, can hardly be free of that reference; how he manages it must remain his own choice. In response, though, we have a more nearly neutral starting point for the description of the religious. It is not necessary to make ontological claims about the status of the object of response; we may say that whatever the character of the object intended, such character can be examined without committing ourselves to its "existence" or "nonexistence," its "independence" or person-dependency. At the same time, we have, if not a universal, at least a widely recognized phenomenon: it is not difficult for most of us to locate an entire dimension of our lives which concerns itself with an "object" unlike all concrete givens in experience, an object which concerns us unconditionally. Of course, such response may be what Others may deem to be less than truly ultimate—to individuals, to special causes, to politics, to secret glories —but if the person takes them as absolute, we will attend to the intention which gives valence to that placement of value. The vantage point for analysis remains that of the actor rather than the observer. In egological terms, then, my religious response posits that which I take to have ultimacy. Granting the validity of my positing, I may still be misled on my own terms. Response has its history, even for the individual.

Let us say that I have given myself utterly to the cause of nationalism. In the course of events it may turn out that my cause conquers; my fervor and struggle are vindicated. After the flush of victory, however, my involvement in the cause necessarily changes, for the problems of transformation of a people into a nation are different from those of the development of that nation when its status has been recognized. The power of a will to freedom and identity gives way to the tenacity of purpose necessary for working out less dramatic but no less essential problems: the politics of freedom from oppression is replaced by the mechanics of sanitary engineering; sewers instead of saviors. And even at the level of policy and outlook, the disagreements between partisans which had been relatively easily suppressed in the common cause of the large struggle for dominion become divisive issues for the post-victorious nationalists. Allies in struggle become opponents in peace, and the pattern of the individual's involvement in both rarely achieves symmetry. What started as a total commitment, a response to ultimacy, may then change to a fierce loyalty and a continuing devotion but without the unique quality of absolute concern. In retrospect, for the individual who undergoes such an alteration, is it then appropriate to say that *while* the commitment was total, the response was absolute, but that when the situation changed from struggle to achievement, the ultimacy waned? If so, would a similar line of argument hold as well for all instances of fervent commitment, from an overriding passion for soccer to holy crusades? At a minimum, we can say that it is not uncommon for an individual to learn that what had indeed *seemed* at the time a total commitment to something later proved to be considerably less

than absolute. "At the time I believed, thought, felt . . ." but now "I know
. . ." That familiar transition of language points to the ambiguity of the original commitment. Granted that the individual's object of concern may
change, is it possible that his response, the quality of his commitment, may
alter? Or is it the case that if the response varies it cannot be justly termed
"absolute"? If there are no simple solutions to such questions, there are
some distinctions to be made.

The individual who changes in his response may in fact be involved in
his commitment with only a part of himself, that is, with a segment of his
being which relates to an analogous segment of the world: that aspect of the
self which acknowledges "social responsibility" and, accordingly, finds its
focus of action in the political sphere. Instead of speaking of "political man"
or "economic man," we might instead think of the "political self." In negative
terms, to speak of the political or economic self is to deny these structures
any centrality, to relegate them to peripheral positions (however important
they may be) for which the existential self is the decisive centrum. When
response comes from the person in his existentiality, there is no analogous
sphere in the world to which it is directed. Rather, response is to the transcendencies which lie beyond mundane experience; in turn, those transcendencies are recognized by the individual in his existential concern, as a symbolic
self. In religious response the transcendencies are most pointedly presented,
not as abstract possibilities of a theoretical ego, but as the life and death of
the being who is able to grasp his concreteness and identity in the symbols
of transcendent order. If the symbolic self finds no analogous sphere of
import in the mundane world, it is also the case that there are no formal or
traditional specifications which can regulate or guide its response to transcendence. As a being in the social world, the individual comes to learn about
his various roles and masters his playing of them. As a symbolic self, the
individual must create for himself the form and terms of his action. Unlike
the common-sense world whose typifications greet his involvement in society,
the transcendent order to which the symbolic self directs its response remains
fugitive to human appropriation. In religious response, the individual has
appresented to him an order he can comprehend but never enter. Paradoxically, the recognition of the transcendent in religious response helps to generate
a self which can find its resolution neither in the structure of daily life nor
in the realm of transcendence. But if appresentation cannot yield resolution,
it can provide a fundamental clue to the relationship between transcendence
and order.

The transcendencies appresented in religious response have their own
coherence and internal logic. Understood in their unity, they constitute the
realm of order. The symbolic self which appreciates and honors transcendence
is involved with the problematic character of the entire range of its intending

rather than with picked elements such as sociality or death. The range of transcendence, however, remains a creative mystery. There is no reason to be embarrassed about mystery or to shun its awkwardness. In some ways, the meaning of mystery in this context can be easily defined. We are confronted with mystery when our inquiry strikes itself, that is, when the inquirer meets his own image in the course of his inquiry. Mystery, in these terms, far from being something "unknown," is directly apprehended. Its peculiarity—a methodological uncanniness—consists in the fact that inquirer and inquiry at one and the same time intersect and astonish each other. In the case of transcendence, the symbolic self seizes its own apprehending in recognizing the complexity of the range it intends. Although it is not possible to make an inventory of all transcendencies, it is possible to know that their manifold company constitutes a unified domain, what I have called an *order*. That there is order is revealed in the interrelationships which hold between the symbols which appresent transcendence. Whether in art or in life, man moves between "death and the devil," gropes or fights his way in a world replete with dangers and temptations, advances through love to redemption. It is not reasonable to ignore the interrelatedness of such symbolic forces, nor is it convincing to suggest that in the plethora of their being the symbolic self confronts disorder and fragmentation. That which is *not* appresented in the realm of order is still intended as related to what is apprehended. Death but not resurrection may be appresented to an individual in religious response, but he may still recognize both to be *possible* aspects of a coherent unity. There is no compulsion here. The symbolic self is not driven to acknowledge the principle of order. Rather, I am suggesting that allowing for the possibility of the unity of transcendence is sufficient for our purposes. To ask for more would strip the symbolic self of its most fundamental choice: the acknowledgment of order. Co-given with the appresentation of transcendence is the mystery of order.

At this point, it might be thought that we have moved beyond phenomenology and relinquished the phenomena of experience for esoteric signs and hermeneutic portents. However that may be, I am concerned with a different problem: the status of the constructs we have been exploring. Whether or not our discussion of the symbolic self and its appresentational reality has led beyond the phenomena to a "trans-intentional" domain, it is true that transcendence has a rather "special" station. The immediate question is whether what is intended by the symbolic self is subject-dependent or whether transcendence and order have an ontological weight of their own, a reality which, if not "independent" of the self, is not merely a fabric devised by consciousness. Once again, it is necessary to move back in order to carry the discussion forward. We must return to the concept of intentionality. Consciousness, we said, is essentially directional in its nature, that is, it is always consciousness *of.* Rather than speaking of mind "inside" and the world "outside" the body or the individual, the phenomenologist maintains that there is an integral relationship between man and world, between consciousness and reality. In its dynamic, consciousness and its object are polarities of a unity, world-as-meant. From this standpoint, to be "real" is to be "meant-as-real." And the "really-real" is that which is intended as such. Here there is no denial of nature, of the "objectivity" of material things, or of the guts of history. Rather, every affirmation is an act of consciousness. Since man and world are united, the epistemological nightmare of philosophical idealism (common sense set cowering) need no longer trouble the citizenry. Instead, we are left with an alternative despair: what if the taken-for-granted constructs of mundanity are the only reality? If common sense is a tissue of constructs, it would seem that the solidity of naive belief—that granite of the natural attitude—contains a fissure, an internal negation which slashes its claim to truth. Intentionality is a way out of that impasse; better, a way which avoids the impasse. Intentionality spans the fateful distance between consciousness and world. The constructs of mundanity are as "real" as the creatures we call fellow-men. The intentional approach to what is presented in experience leads to a consideration of symbolic appresentation: the status of transcendence.

It would seem that, if not by definition, then almost by its very nature, transcendence is "beyond" mundane experience; yet it is appresented within the reality of the symbolic self. The "beyond" needs qualification, for transcendence is a pointing, an intentional arrow, which itself lies within experience but which intends an object (the transcendent) which does not. In appresentation, however, the transcendent is brought within the experiential reality of the individual, but the individual not as a mundane being but as a symbolic self. In alternative language, transcendence becomes immanence when man ascends the scale of his possibilities and responds to the constants of his being—birth, sociality, death—as a realized self, in explicit existential differentiation. For common sense, transcendence is a hypothetical construct, because it is the product of an anonymous typification. Death, as we saw, is known and treated as a public event, something which "sooner or later" comes to "all men" or to "every man." In these terms, the transcendence of death is denied rather than appresented. For the symbolic self, on the contrary, death is recognized (from its earlier anticipation in art to its fulfillment in the symbolic) as *my* negation in a transformation of reality in which my being is seized by the symbolic and lifted to a new level of expression. For my symbolic self, not only am I this being who will die but "my death" is itself a transcendency. Appresented in the symbolic is the existential identity of my being as well as the universal signification of death as the negation of that being. Transcendence understood in this way becomes a vital part of the life of the self. Rather than being pushed off into a realm of inaccessibility, transcendence reveals its proper status as a force *within* the human career, as forceful and as "present" as the startling immediacies of intersubjectivity: the appresented reality of the Other as a being like me. The paradoxical conclusion to these considerations is that common-sense typification creates that kind of transcendence whose elements are "beyond" mundane validation, whereas the transcendence appresented to the symbolic self is fleshed out in the transformation of the mundane into the symbolic. Consciousness, in its intentional operation, is indeed responsible for the "construction" of a world, but the development of the self from its solitary beginnings to its religious response makes possible the transmogrification of the typical and the taken-for-granted from their function as the variables of mundanity to their transcendent appresentation as symbols for a fulfilled self. The movement is from solitude to order.

With the advance of the self comes a change as well in the meaning of role. As we have already said, there are no specified or specifiable role-requirements or role-obligations for the symbolic self. The mundane self can treat death as a "sooner or later" phenomenon, but the symbolic self must build its own image and response to death from the resources of its own subjectivity. Accordingly, the role of the symbolic self demands existential choice, a continuing spiral of decision through which the concrete individual establishes his stance in mundane life by defining his relation to transcendence. Role itself, then, emerges finally as a dynamic of consciousness, a primordial means through which individuation is able to merge with the universal and come to terms with its own history. That history is the movement we have traced from the self to religion and may be understood as the liberation of the person through the fulfillment of the possibilities of social role. At the same time, our account produces its own internal challenge and a systematic criticism: isn't the ego as incapsulated in transcendence as it was in its root-beginning? Isn't the entire history of consciousness, as developed in our story, out of touch with praxis, with the hard and staunch realm of human action? Aren't we left at the end with the very transcendental solitude which enveloped the primal ego? Haven't we betrayed mundanity in the name of transcendence? And for all the talk of existential subjectivity, have we not bartered Life for Thought? At this point, the response to those essential questions must become the responsibility of the reader. We return at last to him, to you, for support or repudiation. It should be remembered that the content of each of the stages in the development of the self, as well as the dialectic of movement through them, presupposed the active participation of the reader. The "control" which can render our analysis veridical is that of experiential acknowledgment by the individual addressed in these pages. If he has lost touch with the phenomena being discussed or if he has found that his own experience permits no adequate principle of translation from his reality to ours, then no amount of defense or argument will substitute for that qualitative lack. It should be recognized, however, that comprehension and active participation are not synonymous with philosophical agreement. We must look for results in a different dimension of evaluation. A final glance is due the troublesome theme of participation: the relation of Life to Thought.

From the outset, our effort, our philosophical concern, has been to show the solidarity of consciousness and world. The early experiment we entertained, which attempted to suspend the naive believing in the public world that characterizes common sense, was an effort to penetrate the assumptions and presuppositions of mundanity to reach the bedrock of the ego. Instead of beginning with a world already structured in causal terms, instead of taking for granted the categories of history and science, let alone the fabled kingdom of familiarity, and instead of building the edifice of Man on the foundation of an opaque conception of intersubjectivity, we attempted to regain the world in its "originary" givenness, in its uninfected presence. That turn to consciousness, whatever its motives and whatever its results, will unfailingly elicit distrust and primitive suspicion. For some it represents a denial of the social, an attempt to compress the social into the confines of a single skull, to reduce reality to thought. For others, phenomenological suspension turns away from societal and historical struggle in favor of a transcendental quietism, a searching out of "conditions for the possibility of a world" while the ongoing world flames and plummets. For a few, finally, phenomenological procedure accepts the pleasures of "pure consciousness" at the expense of ignoring the historically consequential force of the undermined ego, the devastation of false consciousness. To these oppositions our reply consists in placing radical emphasis on the *constitutive* character of consciousness. At each level of the self's development we have examined, consciousness (understood as intentionality) has played a formative role. In fact, it is more than a play on phrases to say that movement from stage to stage in the history of the self is possible because consciousness enables roles to be played. The least we can do to avoid confusion is to repudiate a "cowboys and Indians" scenario of history in which the good guys are analysts of ideology armed with the straight-shooting irons of sociology of knowledge and the bad guys are methodologists of intentionality fitting self-directed arrows to solipsistic bows. Significant analysis is possible at all levels, but its relevance depends on the kinds of questions we are committed to raising and the obligations we assume in following our answers to their conceptual sources. We have turned to the genesis of sociality in the ego; accordingly, the story of the self from its transcendental beginnings to its encounter with transcendence is told from the vantage point of the participant. In *his* life, the life of history is celebrated.

What mode of action does participation imply? We must distinguish between the internal dialectic of ascent we have outlined and followed in moving from the self to religion and the dynamic of action proper to each level. The perpendicular rises through stages which have their own horizontals. It would be a misplaced confidence to look to intentional consciousness for an account of the career of Alexander the Great; it would be as severe a misgauging of history to speak of a "career" without accounting for the unity and continuity which, among other categorial elements, constitute the hero's "world." But a further distinction must be made. It is one thing to speak of participation with respect to the alter ego, another to comprehend the phenomenon in first-person terms. My—*your*—movement through the perpendicular of development has an "outside" *intended* as "the past," "history," "the pressure of events," the "requiredness of mores." At the horizontal of societal process, each of those structures may be viewed as discrete elements to be evaluated by the historian, the student of ideology, or the psychologist. The stance is then shifted to that of the observer, not the actor. The difference between the logic of ascent and the empirics of the individual stages is in the locus of the inquirer. From "outside" the immediacy of my career as a concrete being in the life-world I inhabit and define, that life is exchangeable and replaceable, for the most part, according to the interests of the Other as analyst or even as actor on the political-historical scene. From "inside" my life's terrain, I interpret not only the Other but all that there is in social reality *through* rather than from my participation in the stages we have explored. For the observer, the ascent is repeatable; for the actor, it is unique. What is universal is the essence of role, and that returns us to the principle of continuity we have found throughout the stages.

As a participant in mundane reality I am a taker of roles, able to see the world not only from my own place and through my own eyes but also from the standpoint of the Other, as he sees things. Through role-taking I am able to go beyond the restrictions of my biographical situation and understand variant cultural realities. Typification serves as the clue to the translation of that which is strange to me and that which otherwise escapes my style of life. Of course, typification hardly assures comprehension; it may yield Bad Faith or it may mean the refusal of improvisation. The self, as we have seen, is both enhanced and demonized by the polarities of the traditional and the spontaneous. But what emerges as vital to the progression of the person is his capacity to respond to the new possibilities of higher stages in his development. As a social being he masters the requirements of fairly limited roles in order to live and work in the world as a fellow-man. Later, however, he comes to respond to the more sophisticated demands of historical and scientific roles by setting aside aspects of his mundane involvements and participating in reality in trans-mundane as well as trans-individual terms. Finally, in the realms of art and religion, roles become larger and more bewildering burdens than the self can bear. The formulas of earlier stages cannot be repeated; the machinery of typification is inadequate to create the power needed to carry the individual to the station of transcendence. Here typification is transposed into appresentation, negation is encountered, and the symbolic self arises to respond to the ambiguous challenge of a role for which there are neither rules nor prescriptions. In religious response the existential solitude of the self is regained, and in assuming the role of transcendence, the individual participates in the reconciliation of Thought and Life. That reconciliation is the recognition of order; it is also journey's end.

conclusion

Philosophy no less than role has been our theme and it is time now to return to it explicitly. Some reflections on method will lead the way. The reader who has come this far will hardly be startled to learn that we do not intend to summarize, restate, or recapitulate the story. Instead, we shall use this Conclusion as a philosophical service entrance, a rushed and chaotic point of entry for the materials which supply the kitchens or the stores, the factories or the plants, of intellectual service and production. There is a rawness which characterizes the atmosphere of the back door: the pace is charged, not sedate; the language is tangy, not proper; and tempers which are quick to leap are also ready to loll in the late morning interval, a subtle time between preparation and operation. This is the place to speak of the procedures we have followed, whether by explicit design or oblique intention. The image has its counterparts, of course. The wings of the theater where the off-stage players move about are no less zones of incertitude and release. We are interested in inspecting ourselves, probing (or at least poking) our procedures, calling our techniques to account. If our examination of social role has been a philosophical enterprise, it has also been a meta-philosophical exercise, an inquiry into the province of philosophy. Results inevitably point back to method, and the philosopher has the responsibility for self-examination. Included in our history of the self are five major methodological categories which we have utilized, adapted, or sidestepped with varying degrees of insight, responsibility, and magic. Each will now be given its moment in court:

1 **Description.** There seems to be something cold-blooded about straight description; but what appears to be "straight" may be slanted by the moral stance of the critic. An inventory of events in a torture cell may be used by an author to shatter the complacency of his audience by the starkness of his report or may, on the contrary, reflect an amorality of consciousness: one can describe the details of brutality as an automotive guide shows the reader the components of a carburetor. Similarly, seemingly objective legal or economic or sociological reports usually include descriptive material. Accounts of warfare, riots, poverty, and disease can be fitted to a neutral harness. What, then, shall we say of barbarism? Isn't the reporter aware to begin with that what he is describing *is* uncivilized, inhumane, morally appalling? Is he dismayed by what he sees and is the reader to be upset by what he reads? "The pain is exquisite," the textbook in pathology reports of a certain condition. Is the student to race up the adjectival slope: intense, unbearable, excruciating? The gradient of "more than" or "less than" can easily be accommodated, but it would be a callous recorder of a patient's case history who would be content to note the degree of suffering with the same exactitude with which he would enter his temperature readings. To the question, "What about the need for clinical distance?" the counter-question is, "What about the need for therapeutic intent?" Who does the philosopher side with?

I have sought to describe for the sake of liberating the phenomena from their entrapment in pre-judgment and perceptual mediocrity. By that I mean that within the naiveté of common sense, both man and nature are pre-plastered with the Paris of familiarity; the living force of experience is entombed in molds. The descriptive act sets free what is *there* before we learn to bury it from ourselves. The virtue of description in this sense lies in its commitment to truth, to the release and regaining of the perceptual world in its *originary* givenness. There is also a forward horizon to descriptive procedure: it looks to projects and situations in which the phenomena are involved. Thus, a catalog of typifications and a listing of constructs are stages in the reconstruction of mundane reality rather than isolated artifacts of the methodologist's handicraft. Phenomenological description is an achievement because it strips from the phenomena that which conceals their immediacy: the root belief that they are realities *in* a real world, known and knowable by all of us as the same and in the same way. With description that belief itself comes into view, and with it the primal recognition of our mundane being.

2 **Analysis.** The clarification of the structural relationships between the elements located in description is the task of analysis. Actually, it is difficult to establish an absolute frontier between description and analysis, for describing is organizing and organization is a stage in analysis. The uncovering of the sedimentation of meaning which has been a dominant motif in our inquiry into the history of the self is a major example of phenomenological analysis. But more than delineating the components of meaning, analysis seeks to determine the principles underlying their development and transformation in the ascent from stage to stage. That phenomenology involves analysis is hardly surprising, for all philosophical work is analytic. In fact, it would be difficult to point to any example of serious and substantive philosophical activity of any school or representative of any position which does not pursue analysis. The question is not whether a philosophy is analytic but rather what kind of analysis it undertakes and what its distinctive procedures are for doing analysis. But just as description seems to lend itself to the charge of value-erraticism or insensitivity, so analysis sometimes draws criticism for its apparent surgical inclination. To cut something up into pieces, to take it apart, to break it down is, it would appear, to dishonor its vital principle: the act of cognitive dissection commits conceptual mayhem. In my high-school English class I was told about "constructive" and "destructive" criticism. As I recall, the former meant admiring the whale before hurling your harpoon. To write poetry was to live dangerously in those days. In our present focus, the defamation of analysis must be protested. Far from decomposing the unity of the given, analysis is an effort to strengthen its integrity by recognizing its formative nature and establishing the relevance of subjectivity for the environing world. Phenomena reconstructed by analysis emerge as resplendent in meaning and enriched in implication. In the simplest human terms, what worries common sense about analysis is that it endangers belief in the certitude of the taken-for-granted world of everyday life. The worry is not only genuine but well-taken, though not for reasons common sense itself would give. The fear is of philosophy: radical reflection on experience changes not only experience but the experiencer. Change means risk; mundanity prefers the security of its own style. But to say that analysis is suspect means that common sense has intuitively located an internal threat, for philosophy originates in the soil of the mundane. Analysis can be avoided only at the expense of Bad Faith. The real question is how serious, how urgent that analysis becomes. In its most decisive expression philosophical analysis is an act not of destruction but of generation. With description, it helps to rebuild a world.

3   Argument. The egological standpoint characteristic of our study gives a special placement to the function of argument in an essentially descriptive and analytic enterprise. What is at issue is the willingness of the individual within the naive attitude of everyday life to "give up" his standpoint by granting the methodological viability of fundamental alternatives to mundanity. As we have seen, "giving up" does not mean denying or destroying; it does involve a qualitative movement from straightforward acceptance of and reliance on the veridical character of common-sense experience to reflection on that acceptance. It is extremely difficult to say what leads the individual to effect such a transposition. The psychological and cultural motives for wonder vary in ways which do not even begin to touch the problem of philosophical motivation. The demarcation, however, is between internal and external factors. Arguments may attract the individual in the spirit of debate; argument will draw those who come to believe that the activity of philosophy is more important than the content of its concrete manifestations—arguments. If philosophy arises within the mundane world as one of its paradoxical possibilities, it is no less true that within philosophy there may come about a radical effort to search out beginnings and to scrutinize the very ground on which one stands. Argument, rather than being directed "against" something, is centered inward, concerned with its own demands. At the decisive moment, the individual becomes convinced of the truth of what is given when he first *sees*, recognizes the phenomenon in its originary presence. What we termed the irruption of art in the mundane is such a presence. Nor is it the case that the shock of the given manifests itself in esoteric domains. The recognition of the Other may be as powerful an experiential presentation. To have assumed the egological vantage point, then, is to have allowed for disruption and, in a strong sense, disagreement. Argument, I am suggesting, must arise within the reality of the thinker if it is to have relevance for the history of the self. Once again, we may recall the distinction between perpendicular and horizontal dimensions of that history. Nothing we have said about argument can be properly taken to deny the significance—indeed, the inescapability—of disputation. It would be hopeless to wave aside the discussion of such a problem as causation in, let us say, eighteenth-century philosophy with the claim that to be valid such discussion must somehow irrupt in the existential living room. The horizontal has its own dialectics. I have *argued* that the perpendicular of ascent in the genesis of the self has its own logic and must be understood on its own terms. Far from imprisoning the philosopher, the egological discipline we have recommended hurls him into confrontation with Others, including other philosophers.

4 Proof. Seeing *that* something is the case comes, ultimately, to an egological act. The canons of proof in jurisprudence or in formal logic presuppose an agent capable of recognizing the elements of the law of evidence or the strategy of implication. Law and logic are not reduced to egology; neither is the primordial act of intuition dispensable. The structure of proof, the forms of proof, the rationale of proof—all these are independent of the psychological disposition of the individual; but the truly simple, the primitive, elements of proof demand recognition for the logical engine to turn over. In court, an attorney sometimes claims to have "proved beyond a reasonable doubt." When is a doubt reasonable? After the evidence is in and the pleas have been heard, is not the juror faced with an interior evaluation which must be settled by his own judgment? There must come a moment or a point in his delibera- tions when he *sees* that something is the case. Or at least, such a moment does not come and he is left uncertain and unable to decide one way or another. In that case, he may conclude that the lack of intuitive certainty must be counted as a sign of reasonable doubt. A more positive interpretation of reasonable doubt's having been "proved" would be the demonstration of alter- native explanations for conduct. Granted that the defendant purchased the revolver five days before the murder; granted that he had threatened the deceased; granted that he had sought him out just before killing him—is all that enough to establish premeditated murder? Is it not possible that the weapon was bought for another purpose, that the threats were no more than an emotional outburst, that the murderer had gone to the deceased to taunt but not to kill him? And how clear and distinct is "premeditation" anyway? Did the wish to see a man dead take the form of a plan in which, move by move, the accused used time to bring about destruction? Or did the murderer come to realize only after the crime that his deed had been prepared for? Is there postmeditated murder? The responsibility of decision here is as complex as it is enormous, but the burden of individual judgment cannot be shifted from the egological sphere, whatever advice or warnings are received from the court. Proof, then, comes back to the individual whose direct apprehen- sion of the elements of argument is an ineradicable mark of consciousness. Getting him to *see* is the problem. It is true that seeing is the privileged responsibility of the individual, one which cannot be transferred. But seeing is not necessarily exercised. I have tried in these pages to jostle the reader into a change of conceptual attitude so that he can *see* for himself in a new way. The result perhaps is an off-balance or decentered appeal for a re-viewing of the entire range of experience. We are giving back to "demonstration" something of its original force.

5 Persuasion.   The account of the self we have presented, even at its most descriptive level, is far from neutral. I'm pleased to affirm a partisan concep- tion of my responsibilities to the reader. The effort has been to persuade him to see things my way. And to that end I've resorted to subterfuge and stunts: diversions in language, imaginative altercations, short tours of the under- ground, aesthetic distractions, and excursions in the rhetoric of subjectivity. Philosophy requires some rudeness and I have not hesitated to hawk an occasional ware, slip past corseted sentries, and eavesdrop on solemn occa- sions. The world is neither tidy nor tedious; there is no excuse for stuffing its mouth with the mush of obedience. Instead, I have elected to understand persuasion as the effort to bring the alter ego to his own freedom by insisting on the radicality of philosophical reflection. An implicit appeal has followed every suggestion: Turn to your own experience! Confront your own reality! But that request is received in Bad Faith if it is taken to mean: Pick up bits of common sense and store them in the old hiding places.

The difference between subterfuge and deceit in methodology is the willingness of the persuader to stand by and honor the efforts of the one he seeks to persuade. The philosopher's techniques, the methods which inform his maneuvers, are not sacrosanct; neither can they be kept hidden from the discussion. In this sense, the persuader must risk himself through inquiry. The nature of philosophical commitment, then, involves persuasion as a temporal venture, for the philosopher's activity, as I have conceived of it here, is addressed to the Other as a being whose life is an unrepeatable unit. "This is where we start" can only be a shorthand for announcing the site for a picnic. As I have tried hard to show, where one *begins* in philosophy is not a convenience but a choice. Moreover, it is a choice which must constantly be renewed or abandoned, validated or negated. Nor can the individual's choice legislate for his fellow-man. That philosophy which seeks to dominate men denies its own office. Instead of persuasion it commends manipulation. Whatever techniques it uses are contaminated with trickery and evil. I am inveighing against timidity in the name of a more lasting honesty. In the warren of objectivity qualifiers multiply like rabbits: in the main and for the most part, other things being equal, on the one side and on the other, in the long run, and in the overview. The danger in these seemingly mild locutions is that they arouse in us an insular security. After all, if you've balanced out matters, the conclusion must be reasonable; if you've looked in all directions, it must be safe to cross the street. What I hope emerges from these deliberations is a respect for philosophical persuasion and a gladness that partisanship has been exploited in the cause of candor.

If this romp through categories leads anywhere, it is to the conclusion that philosophical argument is futile without philosophical experience. And philosophical experience is achieved by the action of the individual; it cannot be secured by demand, like information, or inherited from Others, like china or silver. Yet the individual attains illumination in a social world. What can the Other give him philosophically? Our answer has already been presented. As Other, the philosopher seeks to bring his alter ego to his own truth, and he makes the effort in many ways: by writing and lecturing, by discussing and teaching. In all those activities, however, the trick is to bring the individual addressed to see for himself, to come to stand in that relationship to experience which acknowledges and respects the temporality of a concrete life. Once again, the secret concern of philosophy is to resolve the imbalance between the universal and the concrete. But it would be wrong to think of the philosopher in academic terms. His methods are manifold: to persuade may be to dazzle, to hector, to shame, to irritate, or to bedevil. The individual must be *moved*, and the interesting ambiguity of that term is reflected in philosophical activity, for all dialectic is a mode of indirection. The existential question the philosopher raises is: How do I stand in the world? Each of us must not only ask that question but must come to be able to discover it for himself, in his own way. To help the Other to express his questions is the point of teaching, and to bring the Other to recognize himself in his questions is the point of philosophy.

It might appear as if we are overloading the function of interrogation. What about answers? Is the search everything or has philosophy relinquished its traditional role? Is the love of wisdom idyllic or is that love consummated? Some direct answers to *these* questions at least can be given. The traditional view of philosophy as the love of wisdom has suffered an eclipse in the present scene; few believe in philosophy's having to do with wisdom, and those few are often viewed with professional patronization or hostility. Their appeal, it would seem, is to an audience outside the academy. Presumably, common-sense men have become the recipients of the concerns of an older Academy. If both answers and questions have become puzzlements, it must also be remembered that answerers and questioners can be the same. Wisdom may be the love of wisdom.

I prefer to end with a last glimpse of the mundane world from which and with which we began. If philosophy seems a stranger in that world, it is because common sense is on guard; indeed, it has much to guard, most of all its intransigent faith in the reality of its involvement and the communality of its perceptual experience. To challenge animal faith—even to examine it —is to raise the hackles of mundanity. To common sense, there is something about the philosopher which smacks of the confidence man, the charlatan, the swindler, the grafter, the mountebank. Yet everyday life is well acquainted with the trickster and is the first to admit, in private at least, that you must keep a sharp eye out to survive in this world. Why the suspicion of philosophy then? Perhaps the reason comes to this: In turning its critical glance to the fundamental assumptions and presuppositions underlying mundane experience, philosophy threatens to leave the individual unprotected, exposed to the elements; in a strange way, it threatens his life. It is, after all, profoundly unsettling to be forced to examine one's oldest and deepest beliefs. How can we be sure that what will follow analysis will be a fair exchange for what we had before? And what assurance is there that philosophy will bring satisfaction or contentment? In the recesses of his mother wit, mundane man clings to what he knows in fear of what he does not know. At the same time, daily life is aware of the realms of politics and history, of art and religion. Living within the province of everyday life does not make common-sense man a provincial. He knows and is involved in manifold ways in the large commerce of reality. It is the limits of uncertainty which threaten him, and it is those limits which the philosopher probes. Thus, mundanity and philosophy complement each other in disturbing ways and reinforce each other through tension and opposition. Out of the conflict between them arises the unity of the self, and a fable:

The Lizard and the Hummingbird

On a flat rock, deep in the forest, a lizard was sunning himself in a narrow shaft of light. A hummingbird trembled overhead.

"Do I disturb you, Master Lizard?" she asked.

"Not until now," he replied.

"A thousand pardons, then, I'll be gone."

"Wait," said the lizard, "why are you so solicitous about my welfare? You've never troubled to ask before."

"Ah, so you noticed me," sang the hummingbird.

"It's my business to notice everything in the forest," replied the lizard.

"And are you pleased with me? Do I delight you?"

"Not especially. You're you and I'm me. Do I delight you?"

"I hover and you crawl," said the bird. "We'd never make a pair."

"That wouldn't prevent our being friends, if we're so inclined."

"What do we have in common?" she asked.

"The forest," he replied.

"Oh, but even our enemies share that."

"Then why bother with me?" snapped the lizard.

Said the hummingbird, "Most creatures admire me."

"Scales and warts for me. But you didn't answer my question."

"I led you to ask it," said the hummingbird. "That's my gift."

"Yours or mine?"

"Ours."

"Where does this leave us?" asked the lizard.

"This doesn't leave us," shrilled the hummingbird in flight. "This is where we leave each other."

notes

The following pages contain references, quotations, bibliography, and occasional comments or addenda relating to the text. The procedure is intended to acknowledge my sources, display something of the relevant literature, and encourage the reader to go on to his own explorations. Not all of the titles I list or the quotations I give support my position or argument, nor have I tried to survey the problems treated in this book with bibliographical impartiality. My first loyalty has been to what is lively and likely to interest the reader rather than to balance and proportion. However, I have tried to lead the reader to as wide a range of pertinent titles as I could manage. Wherever a book includes a bibliography which is especially helpful, informative, or simply worth looking into, I have made a parenthetical notation: (bibliography). All titles mentioned in these notes are listed in the final bibliography, where full citations will be found.

Preface

Although I will be turning to many of the works of Edmund Husserl, Jean-Paul Sartre, and Alfred Schutz in the notes devoted to the main chapters of the book, it might be well to present, at the outset, a fairly detailed list of the primary and secondary sources. With minor exceptions, we will be concerned here (and throughout these notes) with works in English. Among the bibliographies cited are some which will aid the reader interested in the foreign literature. For books by Husserl, see: *Ideas, Cartesian Meditations, The Idea of Phenomenology, The Paris Lectures, Phenomenology and the Crisis of Philosophy, The Phenomenology of Internal Time Consciousness*. For essays by Husserl, see: "Phenomenology" and

"Phenomenology and Anthropology" (the important essay on "Philosophy as Rigorous Science"—not a bad place at which to begin reading Husserl—is included in *Phenomenology and the Crisis of Philosophy*). Works on Husserl include: Farber, *The Foundation of Phenomenology*; Spiegelberg, *The Phenomenological Movement*, Vol. 1 (bibliography); Ricoeur, *Husserl*. A more detailed survey of the literature on phenomenology will be reserved for notes on the Introduction. We turn now to books by Sartre. *Existentialism and Humanism* is the simplest but not the most reliable or the fairest text with which to begin; a larger and more representative sample will be found in *The Philosophy of Jean-Paul Sartre* (edited by Cumming), *Being and Nothingness* (huge and complex but essential to the understanding of Sartre), *The Emotions, Imagination, The Psychology of Imagination, Situations, The Transcendence of the Ego, Literary and Philosophical Essays*. Secondary works on Sartre are: Manser, *Sartre* (bibliography); Thody, *Jean-Paul Sartre* (bibliography); Murdoch, *Sartre*; Cranston, *Sartre*; Desan, *The Tragic Finale* (bibliography); Natanson, *A Critique of Jean-Paul Sartre's Ontology* (bibliography); Fell, *Emotion in the Thought of Sartre* (bibliography); Jameson, *Sartre*. A detailed bibliography of both primary and secondary literature is included in Biemel, *Sartre*. Schutz's writings can be found in his *The Phenomenology of the Social World* and the three volumes of his *Collected Papers*. For studies of his work, see (in addition to the Introductions to his books): Natanson, "Alfred Schutz" and "The Phenomenology of Alfred Schutz"; Stonier and Bode, "A New Approach to the Methodology of the Social Sciences"; Zaner, "Theory of Intersubjectivity: Alfred Schutz." Related works will be mentioned elsewhere.

Introduction

For introductions to philosophy with which our approach is more or less consonant, see: Ortega y Gasset, *What Is Philosophy?*; Wahl, *The Philosopher's Way* (bibliography); Marías, *Reason and Life*. Those who prefer to follow alternative routes may turn to Russell, *The Problems of Philosophy* or, among recent textbooks: Scriven, *Primary Philosophy*; Olson, *A Short Introduction to Philosophy*; Hospers, *An Introduction to Philosophical Analysis*. *What Is Philosophy?*, edited by Johnstone, is a useful anthology of answers to the title question by philosophers of different schools. Also worthwhile is Waismann, "How I See Philosophy." For a survey of various philosophical methods, see Bocheński, *The Methods of Contemporary Thought*. For a general guide to the literature of philosophy, a valuable work is Varet, *Manuel de bibliographie philosophique*. Anthologies of writings by the major philosophers are: Smith and Grene (Editors), *Philosophers Speak for Themselves*; Edwards and Pap (Editors), *A Modern Introduction to Philosophy*; Mandelbaum, Gramlich, Anderson, and Schneewind (Editors), *Philosophic Problems*; Margolis (Editor), *An Introduction to Philosophical Inquiry*; Barrett and Aiken (Editors), *Philosophy in the Twentieth Century*. Among encyclopedias, two recent works are noteworthy: Edwards (Editor), *The Encyclopedia of Philosophy* in eight volumes and Sills (Editor), *International*

Encyclopedia of the Social Sciences in seventeen volumes. Both have extensive bibliographies. Among the many histories of philosophy are: Copleston, *A History of Philosophy* in eight volumes (bibliographies); Bréhier, *The History of Philosophy* in six volumes to date; Randall, *The Career of Philosophy* in two volumes to date. One-volume compendiums include: Lamprecht, *Our Philosophical Traditions*; Thilly and Wood, *A History of Philosophy*; Collins, *A History of Modern European Philosophy* (bibliographies). Russell's *A History of Western Philosophy* is a spirited account. For a very concise but reliable study, read Webb, *A History of Philosophy*. Finally, among other surveys of the history of philosophy which the reader might find useful, I include: Passmore, *A Hundred Years of Philosophy*; O'Connor (Editor), *A Critical History of Western Philosophy* (bibliographies); and Klibansky (Editor), *Philosophy in the Mid-Century* in four volumes (bibliographies).

Works on phenomenology: The articles on "Phenomenology" by Farber and Cairns are expert but brief introductions to Husserl's thought. For a longer essay, see Thévenaz, *What Is Phenomenology?* Collections include: Lawrence and O'Connor (Editors), *Readings in Existential Phenomenology* (bibliography); Natanson (Editor), *Essays in Phenomenology* (bibliography); and Kockelmans (Editor), *Phenomenology*. Spiegelberg's *The Phenomenological Movement* should be mentioned again. Also, the reader may be interested in Schmitt's account of "Phenomenology" in the *Encyclopedia of Philosophy*, Farber's *The Aims of Phenomenology*, and the volume of *Philosophical Essays in Memory of Edmund Husserl*, which Farber edited. Among other important works concerned with phenomenology are: Gurwitsch, *The Field of Consciousness* and *Studies in Phenomenology and Psychology*; Merleau-Ponty, *Phenomenology of Perception* (bibliography) and "Phenomenology and the Sciences of Man" in his *The Primacy of Perception*; Chapman, *Sensations and Phenomenology*; and Strasser, *Phenomenology and the Human Sciences* (with a bibliography strong in German and French titles). Also see Lee and Mandelbaum (Editors), *Phenomenology and Existentialism*, and Schrader (Editor), *Existential Philosophers*.

There are a great many introductions to and surveys of existentialism. Among the better studies are Collins, *The Existentialists* (bibliography), and Kuhn, *Encounter with Nothingness*. Also see: Harper, *Existentialism*; Grene, *Introduction to Existentialism;* Wild, *The Challenge of Existentialism*; Barrett, *Irrational Man* and *What Is Existentialism?*; Blackham, *Six Existentialist Thinkers*; Reinhardt, *The Existentialist Revolt* (bibliography). There are also several anthologies available: Wilde and Kimmel (Editors), *The Search for Being*; Spanos (Editor), *A Casebook on Existentialism*; Kaufmann (Editor), *Existentialism from Dostoevsky to Sartre*; and Friedman (Editor), *The Worlds of Existentialism*. Also see: Clive, *The Romantic Enlightenment*; Cohn, *Existentialism and Legal Science*; Schrag, *Existence and Freedom*.

Among the general introductions to the theory of social role are: Sarbin and Allen, "Role Theory," in *The Handbook of Social Psychology* (bibliography), and Sarbin, "Role: Psychological Aspects," in *International Encyclopedia of the Social Sciences*, which also includes an article on "Role: Sociological Aspects" by Turner. Also see: Biddle and Thomas (Editors), *Role Theory* (with an extremely thorough bibliography); Preiss and Ehrlich, *An Examination of Role Theory* (detailed bibliography); Gross, Mason, and McEachern, *Explorations in Role Analysis*; Rocheblave-Spenlé, *La Notion de rôle en psychologie sociale* (comprehensive bibliography); Znaniecki, *Social Relations and Social Roles*; Banton, *Roles* (bibliography); Strauss, *Mirrors and Masks*; Nadel, *The Theory of Social Structure*; Dreitzel, *Die gesellschaftlichen Leiden und das Leiden an der Gesellschaft* (extensive bibliography). The most readable study of social role is Goffman, *The Presentation of Self in Everyday Life*. His *Encounters* is also an appealing work. In philosophy, the key work is Mead, *Mind, Self, and Society*. Further bibliography will be found in the notes to the text of the Introduction, which now follow. The page number for each reference is given in the margin.

---

1   **. . . a distance between the reality of . . . individual experience and the texts of the classroom.**

Stephen Spender writes in his autobiography, *World Within World*: "I do not know whether it is usual to teach philosophy as I was taught it. In the first lesson we were told that J. S. Mill's *Utilitarianism* meant the greatest happiness of the greatest number and that, for Mill, happiness was the criterion of moral value. In the next tutorial we were told that Mill was wrong because he had forced himself into the position where, according to his criterion, a very happy pig might be considered morally better than a moderately happy human being. Obviously this was outrageous. Mill himself realized that it was unthinkable; accordingly he introduced standards of higher and lower kinds of happiness into his philosophy. Here he was caught out because, if you talk of a higher happiness, your criterion which qualifies happiness is not happiness but something else. Next please. The next philosopher is Locke. We were told what he thought and then why he was wrong. Next please. Hume. Hume was also wrong. Then Kant. Kant was wrong, but he was also so difficult to understand that one could not be so sure of catching him out. This might be described as the Obstacle Race way of teaching philosophy. The whole field of human thought is set out with logical obstructions and the students watch the philosophers race around it. Some of them get further than others but they fall sooner or later into the traps which language sets for them. It soon occurred to me that it was useless to enter a field where such distinguished contestants had failed."[1]   William James writes of the other end of the spectrum: "Philosophy, beginning in wonder, as Plato and Aristotle said, is able to fancy everything different from what it is. It sees the familiar as if it were strange, and the strange as if it were familiar. It can take things up and lay them down again. Its mind is full of air that plays round every subject. It rouses us from our native dogmatic slumber and breaks up our caked prejudices. Historically it has always been a sort of fecundation of four different human

---

[1]   From Stephen Spender, *World Within World*, New York: Harcourt, Brace, 1948, p. 36. Copyright 1948, 1949, 1951 by Stephen Spender. Reprinted by permission of Harold Matson Company, Inc.

interests, science, poetry, religion, and logic, by one another. It has sought by hard reasoning for results emotionally valuable. To have some contact with it, to catch its influence, is thus good for both literary and scientific students. By its poetry it appeals to literary minds; but its logic stiffens them up and remedies their softness. By its logic it appeals to the scientific; but softens them by its other aspects, and saves them from too dry a technicality. Both types of student ought to get from philosophy a livelier spirit, more air, more mental background. 'Hast any philosophy in thee, Shepherd?'—this question of Touchstone's is the one with which men should always meet one another. A man with no philosophy in him is the most inauspicious and unprofitable of all possible social mates" (*The Writings of William James*, p. 475).

Within the career of day-to-day, common-sense existence, each of us goes about his business without philosophical worries. 2

In Husserl's formulation: "I am aware of a world, spread out in space endlessly, and in time becoming and become, without end. I am aware of it, that means, first of all, I discover it immediately, intuitively, I experience it. Through sight, touch, hearing, etc., in the different ways of sensory perception, corporeal things somehow spatially distributed are *for me simply there*, in verbal or figurative sense 'present', whether or not I pay them special attention by busying myself with them, considering, thinking, feeling, willing. Animal beings also, perhaps men, are immediately there for me; I look up, I see them, I hear them coming towards me, I grasp them by the hand; speaking with them, I understand immediately what they are sensing and thinking, the feelings that stir them, what they wish or will. They too are present as realities in my field of intuition, even when I pay them no attention. But it is not necessary that they and other objects likewise should be present precisely in my *field of perception*. For me real objects are there, definite, more or less familiar, agreeing with what is actually perceived without being themselves perceived or even intuitively present. I can let my attention wander from the writing-table I have just seen and observed, through the unseen portions of the room behind my back to the verandah, into the garden, to the children in the summer-house, and so forth, to all the objects concerning which I precisely 'know' that they are there and yonder in my immediate co-perceived surroundings—a knowledge which has nothing of conceptual thinking in it, and first changes into clear intuiting with the bestowing of attention, and even then only partially and for the most part very imperfectly."[2] For a basic analysis of "common-sense existence," to which this book is deeply indebted, see Schutz's *Collected Papers*, Volume I, Chapter 1, "Common-Sense and Scientific Interpretation of Human Action."

---

[2]   From Edmund Husserl, *Ideas: General Introduction to Pure Phenomenology*, translated by W. R. Boyce Gibson, New York: Macmillan, 1931, pp. 101–102. Copyright 1931 by The Macmillan Company, Inc. Foreign rights held by George Allen and Unwin, Ltd., London. Reprinted by permission.

2   Consciousness . . . will refer to all of perceptual experience . . .

Husserl writes: "In unreflective consciousness we are 'directed' upon objects, we 'intend' them; and reflection reveals this to be an immanent process characteristic of all experience, though infinitely varied in form. To be conscious of something is no empty having of that something in consciousness. Each phenomenon has its own intentional structure, which analysis shows to be an ever-widening system of individually intentional and intentionally related components. The perception of a cube, for example, reveals a multiple and synthesized intention: a continuous variety in the 'appearance' of the cube, according to differences in the points of view from which it is seen, and corresponding differences in 'perspective,' and all the difference between the 'front side' actually seen at the moment and the 'backside' which is not seen, and which remains, therefore, relatively 'indeterminate,' and yet is supposed equally to be existent. Observation of this 'stream' of 'appearance-aspects' and of the manner of their synthesis, shows that every phase and interval is already in itself a 'consciousness-of' something, yet in such a way that with the constant entry of new phases the total consciousness, at any moment, lacks not synthetic unity, and is, in fact, a consciousness of one and the same object. The intentional structure of the train of a perception must conform to a certain type, if any physical object is to be perceived as there! And if the same object be intuited in other modes, if it be imagined, or remembered, or copied, all its intentional forms recur, though modified in character from what they were in perception, to correspond to their new modes. The same is true of every kind of physical experience. Judgment, valuation, pursuit, these also are no empty experiences having in consciousness of judgments, values, goals and means, but are likewise experiences compounded of an intentional stream, each conforming to its own fast type."[3] For a study of consciousness in a larger context, see Ey, *La Conscience* (bibliography).

---

3   I "confront" the Other as a being among other beings . . .

Schutz writes: ". . . the social world is experienced from the outset as a meaningful one. The Other's body is not experienced as an organism but as a fellow-man, its overt behavior not as an occurrence in the space-time of the outer world, but as our fellow-man's action. We normally 'know' what the Other does, for what reason he does it, why he does it at this particular time and in these particular circumstances. That means that we experience our fellow-man's action in terms of his motives and goals."[4]

---

[3]   From Edmund Husserl, "Phenomenology," translated by C. V. Salmon, *Encyclopaedia Britannica*, 14th edition, 1927, Vol. XVII, p. 700. Reprinted by permission of Encyclopaedia Britannica, Chicago.

[4]   From Alfred Schutz, *Collected Papers*: Vol. I, *The Problem of Social Reality*, edited by Maurice Natanson, The Hague: Martinus Nijhoff, 1962, pp. 55–56. Reprinted by permission of the publisher.

By 'engagement' is meant the involvement of the individual in his world, his action   3
in it as distinguished from his observation of it.

My use of the term "engagement" derives from but is not synonymous with
Sartre's notion of commitment (*engagement*). See his *What Is Literature?* In
Existentialism and Humanism, he writes: "What is at the very heart and center
of existentialism, is the absolute character of the free commitment, by which
every man realizes himself in realizing a type of humanity—a commitment
always understandable, to no matter whom in no matter what epoch—and its
bearing upon the relativity of the cultural pattern which may result from such
absolute commitment" (p. 47). The concept of "action" we are concerned with in
speaking of "engagement" derives from Max Weber. He writes: "In 'action' is
included all human behaviour when and in so far as the acting individual attaches
a subjective meaning to it. Action in this sense may be either overt or purely
inward or subjective; it may consist of positive intervention in a situation, or of
deliberately refraining from such intervention or passively acquiescing in the
situation. Action is social in so far as, by virtue of the subjective meaning
attached to it by the acting individual (or individuals), it takes account of the
behaviour of others and is thereby oriented in its course."[5] Compare Schutz, *The
Phenomenology of the Social World*, pp. 144 ff. Also see Parsons, *The Structure
of Social Action*.

. . . in an ingenuous yet remarkably penetrating sense, each of us is aware of him-   3
self as a being in the world, a self for which experience is coherent and possible.

The world of each individual involves not only a style but a concrete texture. In
the language of Lavater, each person has his own *physiognomy*. Expanding on
this notion, Goethe writes: "The study of physiognomy 'deduces the inner from
the outer' but what is the 'outer' in Man? Surely not just his naked form, his
unintended gestures which denote the forces within him and their interplay? A
host of things modifies and shrouds him: his social status, his habits, his possessions
and his clothes! It would seem extremely difficult, if not impossible, to penetrate all
these different layers into his innermost self, even find some fixed point among all
these unknown quantities. But we need not despair . . . he is not only affected by
all that envelops him; he too takes effect on all this and so on himself and, as he is
modified, so he modifies all that is around him. Clothes and furniture help us to
deduce a man's character. Nature forms man, man naturally transforms himself.
Set in the vast universe, he builds his own small world within it, makes his own
fences and walls, and furnishes everything after his own image. His social status
and circumstances may well determine his surroundings but the way in which he
lets himself be determined is of the greatest significance. He may furnish his world
indifferently, as others of his kind, because this is how he finds it. Indifference

---

[5]   From Max Weber, *The Theory of Social and Economic Organization*, translated by
A. M. Henderson and Talcott Parsons, edited by Talcott Parsons, New York: Oxford
University Press, 1947, p. 88. Reprinted by permission.

may grow into neglect. But he may also show eagerness and energy, he may go on to higher levels or (which is not so common) take a step back. It will not be held against me, I hope, that I try in this way to enlarge the field of physiognomic study."[6] Among "physiognomic" essays, I would recommend: Agee and Evans, *Let Us Now Praise Famous Men; Evans, Three Men;* Williams, *The Speakers;* and Wain, *Sprightly Running,* for its wonderful portrait of E. H. W. Meyerstein.

---

4   **. . . fragments of total exposure and unities of partial expression.**

See *The Sociology of Georg Simmel:* "In the interest of interaction and social cohesion, the individual *must* know certain things about the other person. Nor does the other have the right to oppose this knowledge from a moral standpoint, by demanding the discretion of the first: he cannot claim the entirely undisturbed possession of his own being and consciousness, since this discretion might harm the interests of his society. The businessman who contracts long-range obligations with another; the master who employs a servant (but also the servant before entering the service); the superior who advances a subordinate; the housewife who accepts a new member into her social circle: all these must have the right to learn or infer those aspects of the other's past and present, temperament, and moral quality on the basis of which they can act rationally in regard to him, or reject him. These are very crude instances of the case where the duty of discretion—to renounce the knowledge of all that the other does not voluntarily show us—recedes before practical requirements. But even in subtler and less unambiguous forms, in fragmentary beginnings and unexpressed notions, all of human intercourse rests on the fact that everybody knows somewhat more about the other than the other voluntarily reveals to him; and those things he knows are frequently matters whose knowledge the other person (were he aware of it) would find undesirable."[7]

---

4   **. . . the image of Man which is projected is that of a being whose presence in the world is a unitary reality . . .**

See Heidegger, who hyphenates the central phrase, commenting: "The compound expression 'Being-in-the-world' indicates in the very way we have coined it, that it stands for a *unitary* phenomenon. This primary datum must be seen as a whole" (*Being and Time,* p. 78). Compare Merleau-Ponty, *Phenomenology of Perception,* Part Three, and Binswanger, *Being-in-the-World.*

---

[6]   Quoted in Karl Jaspers, *General Psychopathology,* translated by J. Hoenig and Marian W. Hamilton, Chicago: University of Chicago Press, 1963, p. 275. Reprinted by permission. For the original, see Goethe, "Beiträge zu Lavaters Physiognomischen Fragmenten," pp. 20–21.

[7]   From Georg Simmel, *The Sociology of Georg Simmel,* translated and edited by Kurt H. Wolff, Glencoe, Ill.: Free Press, 1950, p. 323. Copyright © 1950 by The Free Press. Reprinted by permission.

... it is the sciences of geology and archaeology which come closest to providing a   5
clue to what we are about.

Spiegelberg writes: ". . . Husserl would have liked to call philosophy 'archaeology,' had this term still been available to philosophers" (*The Phenomenological Movement*, p. 82).

... the rubric of "social role," . . .   6

Some traditional definitions of role might prove helpful. Sarbin and Allen write: "A *role* is a patterned sequence of learned *actions* or deeds performed by a person in an interaction situation" ("Role Theory," p. 225). Linton distinguishes between status and role: "A status, as distinct from the individual who may occupy it, is simply a collection of rights and duties. . . . A *role* represents the dynamic aspect of a status. The individual is socially assigned to a status and occupies it with relation to other statuses. When he puts the rights and duties which constitute the status into effect, he is performing a role" (*The Study of Man*, pp. 113–114). Banton writes: "Every member of a social unit, be it a ship, a football team, or a nation, has one or more parts to play. He has tasks to perform and is entitled to receive services from other people in recognition of his contributions. These clusters of rights and obligations constitute roles" (*Roles*, p. 2). Daniel J. Levinson says: "There are at least three specific senses in which the term 'role' has been used, explicitly or implicitly, by different writers or by the same writer on different occasions. (a) Role may be defined as the *structurally given demands* (norms, expectations, taboos, responsibilities, and the like) associated with a given social position. Role is, in this sense, something outside the given individual, a set of pressures and facilitations that channel, guide, impede, support his functioning in the organization. (b) Role may be defined as the member's *orientation* or *conception* of the part he is to play in the organization. It is, so to say, his inner definition of what someone in his social position is supposed to think and do about it. . . . (c) Role is commonly defined as the *actions* of the individual members . . . actions seen in terms of their relevance for the social structure (that is, seen in relation to the prevailing norms). In this sense, role refers to the ways in which members of a position act (with or without conscious intention) *in accord with or in violation of a given set of organizational norms*. Here, as in (b), role is defined as a characteristic of the actor rather than of his normative environment."[8] Last, short, and most revealing, Berger writes: "A role . . . may be defined as a typified response to a typified expectation" (*Invitation to Sociology*, p. 95).

---

[8]   From Daniel J. Levinson, "Role, Personality, and Social Structure," in *Sociological Theory: A Book of Readings* (edited by Lewis A. Coser and Bernard Rosenberg), 2nd edition, New York: Macmillan, 1964, pp. 284–285. Copyright © 1957, 1964 by The Macmillan Company, Inc. Reprinted by permission.

Chapter One: The Self

For studies of the self, including the concept of the person and the problem of identity, see: the classical statement in Hume's *A Treatise of Human Nature*; Hocking, *The Self*; Laird, *Problems of the Self*; Taylor, *Elements of Metaphysics*; Wilson, *The Self and Its World*; Shaw, *The Ego and Its Place in the World*; Parker, *The Self and Nature*; Symonds, *The Ego and the Self*; Hyde, *I who Am*; Frondizi, *The Nature of the Self*; Ryle, *The Concept of Mind*; Hampshire, *Thought and Action*; Shoemaker, *Self-Knowledge and Self-Identity*; Jones, "Self-Knowledge" and "The Self in Sensory Cognition"—replied to by Flew, "Selves," with a rejoinder by Jones, "Selves: A Reply to Mr. Flew"; Penelhum, " Personal Identity" in *The Encyclopedia of Philosophy* (bibliography); Paton, *In Defense of Reason* (chapter on "Self-Identity"); Castell, *The Self in Philosophy* (bibliography). On "persons" see: Strawson, *Individuals*; Ayer, *The Concept of a Person*; Laguna, *On Existence and the Human World*, especially Chapter 4, "The Person," and Chapter 6, "The Freedom of the Person"; Stearns, "The Person"; Johnstone, "Persons and Selves"; Tillman, "On Perceiving Persons"; Clarke, "The Self as Source of Meaning in Metaphysics." Related works: Macmurray, *The Self as Agent* and *Persons in Relation*; Emmet, *Rules, Roles, and Relations*; Mukerji, *The Nature of the Self*; Raju, *Indian Idealism and Modern Challenges*; Ducasse, *Nature, Mind, and Death*; Strasser, *The Soul in Metaphysical and Empirical Psychology* (bibliography, largely in German and French); Minkus, *Philosophy of the Person*; Werkmeister, *The Basis and Structure of Knowledge*, Chapter III, "The World About Us"; Campbell, *On Selfhood and Godhood*. Among titles in the literature of psychology are: Rogers, *On Becoming a Person*; Allport, *Personality*; Freud, *The Ego and the Id*. Finally, the reader will profit from Camus, *The Myth of Sisyphus*. Additional references follow, in conjunction with the notes for Chapter One.

---

8   **We begin with an experiment.**

The experiment is an exercise in what Husserl called "phenomenological reduction" and utilizes his notion of "epoché" (which might be translated as "suspension" or "restraint"). He writes: "The General Thesis according to which the real world about me is at all times known not merely in a general way as something apprehended, but as a fact-world *that has its being out there*, does *not* consist of course *in an act proper*, in an articulated judgment *about* existence. It is and remains something all the time the standpoint is adopted, that is, it endures persistently during the whole course of our life of natural endeavour. . . . *We do not abandon the thesis we have adopted, we make no change in our conviction*, which remains in itself what it is so long as we do not introduce new motives of judgment, which we precisely refrain from doing. And yet the thesis undergoes a modification—whilst remaining in itself what it is, *we set it as it were 'out of action,'* we *'disconnect it,' 'bracket it.'* It still remains there like the bracketed in the bracket, like the disconnected outside the connexional system. . . . *We put out of action the general thesis which belongs to the essence of the natural standpoint*, we place in brackets whatever it includes respecting the Nature of being: *this entire natural world therefore* which is continually 'there for us,' 'present to our hand,' and will ever remain there, is a 'fact-world' of which we continue to be conscious, even though it pleases us to put it in brackets. If I do this, as I am fully free to do, I do *not* then *deny* this 'world,' as though I were a sophist, *I do not doubt that it is there* as though I were a sceptic; but I use the 'phenomenological' *epoché*, which *completely bars* me *from using any judgment that concerns* spatio-temporal existence."[9] The theme of phenomenological reduction is crucial to the meaning and nature of phenomenology, and it is important at this stage, therefore, to present it as fully as possible. Gurwitsch writes: "Instead of abiding by the natural attitude, we are free to subject the general existential [to be understood in this context as referring to the existence of a real world, etc.] belief to the *phenomenological reduction*. The existential belief is 'put out of action,' no 'use is made of it,' it is 'bracketed,' 'suspended.' It is not as though the existence of the world and of mundane existents were denied or doubted or, instead of being admitted as certain, were held as merely probable, etc. That would be modalization rather than suspension of the existential belief. Strictly speaking, the phenomenological reduction does not concern the existential belief itself or the existential character exhibited by the things perceived and the perceptual world at large. Instead, it concerns the role which the existential belief is permitted to play within the context of phenomenology. In this sense, the phenomenological reduction may be considered as a methodological device resorted to for the sake of arriving at radical and radically justified philosophical knowledge. Every perceived thing which in the natural attitude counts as a real existent continues so to count under the phenomenological reduction. The same holds for the perceptual world as a whole, which continues to present itself as existing and as the real world. However, whereas, in the natural attitude, the existential belief is simply accepted, implicitly and unreflectingly as a rule, acceptance of the belief is withheld under the phenomenological reduction, which for this reason proves to be an *epoché*, i.e., suspension or withholding of assent. Though reduced, because no longer accepted as a basis upon which to proceed, the existential belief continues to be experienced. Therefore, it is misleading to speak of the existential belief as being disregarded, set aside, suppressed, eliminated, and the like. In truth, the existential belief and, correspondingly, the existential character of real things are so far from being disregarded that, on the contrary, that character is explicitly disengaged and, along with other characters exhibited by those things, subjected to radical reflection and analysis. It is one of the most important tasks of phenomenology to provide an ultimate clarification of the very existence of perceptual things and the perceptual world at large."[10]

---

[9]   Husserl, *Ideas*, pp. 107–111. Reprinted by permission.
[10] From Aron Gurwitsch, *Studies in Phenomenology and Psychology*, Evanston, Ill.: Northwestern University Press, 1966, pp. 92–93. Reprinted by permission of the publisher.

8   **Geared into mundane action . . .**

In Schutz's formulation (*Collected Papers*, Volume I, p. 20): ". . . gearing into the outer world . . ."

---

8   **Ordinary, matter-of-course believing in the reality of the world . . . is a fundamental presupposition of mundanity . . .**

Husserl refers to such primordial believing as "The General Thesis of the Natural Standpoint" (see his *Ideas*, pp. 105 ff.). Santayana terms it "animal faith" (see his *Scepticism and Animal Faith*), and calls it "a living dart" (in a letter cited in Cory's *Santayana*, p. 192).

---

9   **. . . the act of trying to take a fresh look at something . . .**

See Parmenter, *The Awakened Eye*, for an off-beat account of "seeing." A bibliography is included.

---

9   **In some professions, a "distancing" of the self from its involvement with Others is essential to the success of a relationship.**

Jaspers writes: "The psychotherapist as a person cannot help but play a decisive part in the psychic processes of the patient. What has to be done is to combine this *personal function* with *impassible distance* so that objectivity is preserved and in the course of the unavoidable, unique indiscretion of the revelations of depth-psychology personal factors in the psychotherapist are successfully excluded. Within the personal factor something impersonal must be operative. Even social contact between psychotherapist and patient is already a mistake, and what relationship there is must be limited to the psychotherapeutic contact. But if this distance cannot be achieved, the risks are obvious. Once an element of desire and mutual private attachment enters into the ordinary respect for the person who carries out psychic counsel and cure, in principle the situation is ruined."[11]

Psychotherapy and teaching are not altogether unrelated; a special relationship is necessary with the pupil no less than the patient. As Sidney Hook writes: ". . . the teacher should not essay the role of amateur psychiatrist or nurse. His sympathy must be primarily directed to his students as growing intellectual organisms in a growing intellectual community, in the faith that they will become integrated persons capable of responsible choice. He cannot cope with all their emotional needs or assume the responsibilities of family and society, priest or judge. He must be friendly without becoming a friend, although he may pave the way for later friendship, for friendship is a mark of preference and expresses itself in indulgence, favors and distinctions that unconsciously find an invidious form. There is a certain distance between teacher and student, compatible with sympathy, which should not be broken down—for the sake of the student. A

---

[11]   Jaspers, *General Psychopathology*, p. 822. Reprinted by permission.

teacher who becomes 'just one of the boys,' who courts popularity, who builds up personal loyalties in exchange for indulgent treatment, has missed his vocation. He should leave the classroom for professional politics."[12]

There are odd moments in our lives when . . . we are aware of ourselves as attending a lecture, . . . witnessing an event.   10

Occasionally, what manifests itself in those moments is the representative character of the event. For example, Virginia Woolf writes in *To the Lighthouse*: "So that is marriage, Lily thought, a man and a woman looking at a girl throwing a ball. That is what Mrs. Ramsay tried to tell me the other night, she thought. For Mrs. Ramsay was wearing a green shawl, and they were standing close together watching Prue and Jasper throwing catches. And suddenly the meaning which, for no reason at all, as perhaps they are stepping out of the Tube or ringing a doorbell, descends on people, making them symbolical, making them representative, came upon them, and made them in the dusk standing, looking, the symbols of marriage, husband and wife. Then, after an instant, the symbolical outline which transcended the real figures sank down again, and they became, as they met them, Mr. and Mrs. Ramsay watching the children throwing catches."[13]

Instead of "time," we can say "temporality" . . .   11

For discussions of temporality, see: Bergson, *An Introduction to Metaphysics*; Husserl, *The Phenomenology of Internal Time-Consciousness*; Brock, "An Account of 'Being and Time,'" in Heidegger, *Existence and Being*; Merlan, "Time Consciousness in Husserl and Heidegger"; Langer, *Feeling and Form*, Chapter 7, "The Image of Time"; Minkowski, *Le Temps vécu*. A momentous statement of the problem is to be found in the eleventh book of St. Augustine's *Confessions*.

. . . instead of space, "spatiality."   12

On "spatiality," see: Merleau-Ponty, *Phenomenology of Perception*, Part Two; Bergson, *Time and Free Will*; Straus, *Phenomenological Psychology*, Chapter 1, "The Forms of Spatiality"; Bollnow, "Lived-Space"; Bachelard, *The Poetics of Space*; Cassirer, *The Philosophy of Symbolic Forms*, Volume III, pp. 142 ff.; Lewin, *Field Theory in Social Science*. Compare Langer, *Feeling and Form*, Chapter V, "Virtual Space," and Sheets, *The Phenomenology of Dance*.

Over and against my Here I discover what is There . . .   12

See the fifth of Husserl's *Cartesian Meditations*. Following Husserl, Schutz writes: "The sector of the world within my actual reach is centered around my Here, and

---

[12]   From Sidney Hook, *Education for Modern Man*, New York: Dial Press, 1946, p. 189. Reprinted by permission of the author.
[13]   From Virginia Woolf, *To the Lighthouse*, New York: Harcourt, Brace and World (Harvest Book), 1955, pp. 110–111. Reprinted by permission.

the center of the world within the actual reach of my fellow-man around his, which is, seen from my Here, a There. Both sectors may partially overlap, and some of the objects, facts, and events in the outer world may be in mine as well as my fellow-man's actual reach, and even within his and my manipulatory zone. Nevertheless, such an object, fact, or event will have a different appearance as to direction, distance, perspective, adumbration, etc., seen from the center of my coordinates, called Here, than from his, called There. Now it is a basic axiom of any interpretation of the common world and its objects that these various co-existing systems of coordinates can be transformed one into the other; I take it for granted, and I assume my fellow-man does the same, that I and my fellow-man would have typically the same experiences of the common world if we changed places, thus transforming my Here into his, and his—now to me a There—into mine."[14]

---

12 **It means the location of my physical body . . . as *mine*.**

See: Sartre, *Being and Nothingness*, pp. 303 ff.; Merleau-Ponty, *Phenomenology of Perception*, Part I; Marcel, *The Mystery of Being*, Volume I, Chapters V and VI. Compare Zaner, *The Problem of Embodiment*. Also see de Waelhens, "The Phenomenology of the Body."

---

12 *I am my body.*

The formulation is Sartrean. See *Being and Nothingness*, p. 326.

---

13 **What is mine is mine alone.**

Ortega y Gasset writes: "I can repeat mechanically that two and two make four, without knowing what I am saying, simply because I have heard it countless times; but really to think it on my own account—that is, to acquire the clear certainty that 'two and two veritably make four and not three or five'—*that* I have to do for myself, by myself, I alone—or, what is the same thing, I in my solitude. And as the same is true of my decisions, volitions, feelings, it follows that since human life in the strict sense is untransferable, it is essentially *solitude, radical solitude*."[15]

---

13 **. . . the *originary* status of the ego . . .**

The Husserlian term "originary" may give some trouble. The word "original" will not do because the immediate force of what is given to consciousness is understood phenomenologically in a presentative rather than a chronological sense.

---

[14]   Schutz, *Collected Papers*, Vol. I, pp. 315–316. Reprinted by permission of the publisher.
[15]   From José Ortega y Gasset, *Man and People*, translated by Willard R. Trask, New York: W. W. Norton, 1957, p. 46. Foreign rights held by George Allen and Unwin, Ltd., London. Reprinted by permission.

The childhood experience of being lost . . . 13

Henry Roth presents a penetrating description in *Call it Sleep*:

"Eagerly, he scanned the streets ahead of him. Which one was it. Which? Which one was—Long street. Long street, lot of wooden houses. On this side. Yes. Go through the other side. Then other corner . . . Right away, right away. Be home right away . . . This one? . . . Didn't look like . . . Next one bet . . . Giddyap, giddyap, giddyap. . . . One little house . . . two little house . . . three little house. . . . Corner coming, corner coming, corner—Here?

—Here? This one? Yes. Looked different. No. Same one. Wooden houses. Yes.

He turned the corner, hastened toward the opposite one.

—Same one. But looked a little teenchy weenchy bit different. Same one though.

But at the end of the block, uncertainty would not be dispelled. Though he conned every house on either side of the crossing, no single landmark stirred his memory. They were all alike—wooden houses and narrow sidewalks to his right and left. A shiver of dismay ran through him.

—Thought this—? No. Maybe went two. Then, when he ran. Wasn't looking and went two. Next one. That would be it. Find it now. Mama is waiting. Next one. Quick. And then turn. That was. He'd see. Has to be.

He broke into a tired jog.

—Yes, the next one. That big yellow house on the corner. He'd see it. He'd see it. Yea! How he'd holler when he saw it. There it is! There's my street! But if—if it wasn't there. Must be! Must be!

He ran faster, sensing beside him the soft pad of easy-loping fear. That next corner would be haven or bay, and as he neared it, he burst into the anguished spring of a flagging quarry—

—Where! Where was it?

His eyes, veering in every direction, implored the stubborn street for an answer it would not yield. And suddenly terror pounced.

'Mama!' The desolate wail split from his lips. 'Mama!' The aloof houses rebuffed his woe. 'Mama!' his voice trailed off in anguished abandonment. And as if they had been waiting for a signal, the streets through his tear-blurred sight began stealthily to wheel. He could feel them turning under his feet, though never a house changed place—backward to forward, side to side—a sly, inexorable carousel.

'Mama! Mama!' he whimpered, running blindly through a street now bleak and vast as nightmare.

A man turned the corner ahead of him and walked briskly away on clicking heels. For a tense, delirious instant, he seemed no other than his own father; he was as tall. But then the film snapped open. It was someone else. His coat was greyer, he swung his arms and he walked erect. His father always hunched forward, arms bound to his side.

But with the last of his waning strength, he spurted after him. Maybe he would know. Maybe he could tell him.

'Mister!' he gasped for breath, 'Mister!'

The man slackened his pace and glanced over his shoulder. At the sight of the pursuing David, he stopped and turned about in quizzical surprise. Under a long, heavy nose, he had a pointed moustache, the waxed blonde of horn.

'What's the matter, sonny,' he asked in loud good humor. 'What're you up to?'

'I'm losted.' David sobbed."[16]

---

15   **The awareness of being truly an ego "on its own" is the experience of anguish.**

Sartre writes: "But it can happen that consciousness suddenly produces itself on the pure reflective level. Perhaps not without the ego, yet as escaping from the ego on all sides, as dominating the ego and maintaining the ego outside the consciousness by a continued creation. On this level, there is no distinction between the possible and the real, since the appearance is the absolute. There are no more barriers, no more limits, nothing to hide consciousness from itself. Then consciousness, noting what could be called the fatality of its spontaneity, is suddenly anguished . . . ."[17]

---

16   **. . . death as a typified event.**

Heidegger writes: "In the publicness with which we are with one another in our everyday manner, death is 'known' as a mishap which is constantly occurring—as a 'case of death.' Someone or other 'dies,' be he neighbour or stranger. . . . People who are no acquaintances of ours are 'dying' daily and hourly. 'Death' is encountered as a well-known event occurring within-the-world. As such it remains in the inconspicuousness characteristic of what is encountered in an everyday fashion."[18] Also see Tolstoy's story, *The Death of Ivan Ilych.*

---

16   **. . . philosophy . . . is not an evolutional or "additive" phenomenon . . .**

Nor is the history of philosophy "additive"; Tatarkiewicz writes: "The difficulty of philosophical problems explains why their solutions, unlike those in other fields of learning, are never satisfactory or universally approved. But, thanks to this, their recent solutions do not render earlier ones obsolete. This disadvantage

---

[16]   From Henry Roth, *Call It Sleep*, New York: Avon Books, 1964, pp. 96–97. Published in hardback by Cooper Square Publishers, New York, 1960. Reprinted by permission of Cooper Square Publishers, Inc.

[17]   From Jean-Paul Sartre, *The Transcendence of the Ego: An Existentialist Theory of Consciousness*, translated by Forrest Williams and Robert Kirkpatrick, New York: Noonday Press, 1957, pp. 101–102. Reprinted by permission of Farrar, Straus and Giroux, Inc., New York, and Librairie A. Hatier, Paris.

[18]   From Martin Heidegger, *Being and Time*, translated by John Macquarrie and Edward Robinson, New York: Harper, 1962, pp. 296–297. Reprinted by permission of the publisher.

for philosophical science constitutes an advantage for its history. In other sciences, earlier solutions, the previous stages of development, are merely a part of history and have no actuality. In philosophy, on the contrary, they preserve their characteristic of actuality; if not all the solutions, at least some of them remain valid, despite the fact that the evolution of philosophy has progressed, sometimes even in other directions."[19] Merleau-Ponty suggests a related line of analysis: "Between an 'objective' history of philosophy (which would rob the great philosophers of what they have given others to think about) and a meditation disguised as a dialogue (in which we would ask the questions and give the answers) there must be a middle-ground on which the philosopher we are speaking about and the philosopher who is speaking are present together, although it is not possible even in principle to decide at any given moment just what belongs to each."[20] Compare Passmore, "The Idea of a History of Philosophy." For studies of Merleau-Ponty, see: Bannan, *The Philosophy of Merleau-Ponty*; Langan, *Merleau-Ponty's Critique of Reason*; and Rabil, *Merleau-Ponty* (bibliography).

. . . basic components of the self which have been termed the "me" and the "I."   18

The classic discussion of the self was given by George H. Mead: "It is because of the 'I' that we say that we are never fully aware of what we are, that we surprise ourselves by our own action. It is as we act that we are aware of ourselves. It is in memory that the 'I' is constantly present in experience. We can go back directly a few moments in our experience, and then we are dependent upon memory images for the rest. So that the 'I' in memory is there as the spokesman of the self of the second, or minute, or day ago. As given, it is a 'me,' but it is a 'me' which was the 'I' at the earlier time. If you ask, then, where directly in your own experience the 'I' comes in, the answer is that it comes in as a historical figure. It is what you were a second ago that is the 'I' of the 'me.' It is another 'me' that has to take that role. You cannot get the immediate response of the 'I' in the process. The 'I' is in a certain sense that with which we do identify ourselves. The getting of it into experience constitutes one of the problems of most of our conscious experience; it is not directly given in experience. The 'I' is the response of the organism to the attitudes of others; the 'me' is the organized set of attitudes of others which one himself assumes. The attitudes of the others constitute the organized 'me,' and then one reacts toward that as an 'I.' . . . The 'I', then, in this relation of the 'I' and the 'me,' is something that is, so to speak, responding to a social situation which is within the experience of the individual. It is the answer which the individual makes to the attitude which others take toward him when he assumes an attitude toward them. Now, the attitudes he is

---

[19]   From Ladislas Tatarkiewicz, "The History of Philosophy and the Art of Writing It," translated by Elaine P. Halperin, *Diogenes*, No. 20, 1957, p. 66. Reprinted by permission.

[20]   From Maurice Merleau-Ponty, *Signs*, translated by Richard C. McCleary, Evanston, Ill.: Northwestern University Press, 1964, p. 159.

taking toward them are present in his own experience, but his response to them will contain a novel element. The 'I' gives the sense of freedom, of initiative. The situation is there for us to act in a self-conscious fashion. We are aware of ourselves, and of what the situation is, but exactly how we will act never gets into experience until after the action takes place. Such is the basis for the fact that the 'I' does not appear in the same sense in experience as does the 'me.' The 'me' represents a definite organization of the community there in our own attitudes, and calling for a response, but the response that takes place is something that just happens. There is no certainty in regard to it. There is a moral necessity but no mechanical necessity for the act. When it does take place then we find what has been done. The above account gives us, I think, the relative position of the 'I' and 'me' in the situation, and the grounds for the separation of the two in behavior. The two are separated in the process but they belong together in the sense of being parts of a whole. They are separated and yet they belong together. The separation of the 'I' and 'me' is not fictitious. They are not identical, for, as I have said, the 'I' is something that is never entirely calculable. The 'me' does call for a certain sort of an 'I' in so far as we meet the obligations that are given in conduct itself, but the 'I' is always something different from what the situation itself calls for. So there is always that distinction, if you like, between the 'I' and the 'me.' The 'I' both calls out the 'me' and responds to it. Taken together they constitute a personality as it appears in social experience. The self is essentially a social process going on with these two distinguishable phases. If it did not have these two phases there could not be conscious responsibility, and there would be nothing novel in experience."[21] For examinations of Mead's thought, see: Natanson, *The Social Dynamics of George H. Mead* (bibliography); Pfuetze, *Self, Society, Existence* (also discusses Martin Buber; bibliography); Lee, *George Herbert Mead*; Clayton, *Emergent Mind and Education*; Victoroff, *G. H. Mead* (bibliography). The reader should also turn to William James, *Principles of Psychology*, Volume I, Chapter X, "The Consciousness of Self." Cooley's *Human Nature and the Social Order* is highly relevant.

---

18   **. . . the *deed* is sprung by the I.**

Compare James's notion of the "fiat" in *Principles of Psychology*, Volume II, Chapter XXVI, "Will." For a phenomenological approach to James's philosophy in general, see: Linschoten, *On the Way toward a Phenomenological Psychology*; Schutz, *Collected Papers*, Volume III, "William James's Concept of the Stream of Thought Phenomenologically Interpreted"; Gurwitsch, *The Field of Consciousness*; Edie, "Notes on the Philosophical Anthropology of William James."

---

[21]   From George H. Mead, *Mind, Self, and Society: From the Standpoint of a Social Behaviorist*, edited by Charles W. Morris, Chicago: University of Chicago Press, 1934, pp. 174–178. Reprinted by permission.

. . . the types and typifications of mundane reality.   18

The entire discussion of typification in this book derives from Schutz's analysis of the problem, an analysis which in turn is rooted in Husserl's thought. Schutz writes: "The factual world of our experience . . . is experienced from the outset as a typical one. Objects are experienced as trees, animals, and the like, and more specifically as oaks, firs, maples, or rattlesnakes, sparrows, dogs. This table I am now perceiving is characterized as something recognized, as something foreknown and, nevertheless, novel. What is newly experienced is already known in the sense that it recalls similar or equal things formerly perceived. But what has been grasped once in its typicality carries with it a horizon of possible experience with corresponding references to familiarity, that is, a series of typical characteristics still not actually experienced but expected to be potentially experienced. If we see a dog, that is, if we recognize an object as being an animal and more precisely a dog, we anticipate a certain behavior on the part of this dog, a typical (not individual) way of eating, of running, of playing, of jumping, and so on. Actually we do not see his teeth, but having experienced before what a dog's teeth typically look like, we may expect that the teeth of the dog before us will show the same typical features though with individual modifications. In other words, what has been experienced in the actual perception of one object is apperceptively transferred to any other similar object, perceived merely as to its type. Actual experience will or will not confirm our anticipation of the typical conformity of these other objects. If confirmed, the content of the anticipated type will be enlarged; at the same time, the type will be split up into subtypes. On the other hand, the concrete real object will prove to have its individual characteristics which, nevertheless, have a form of typicality. Now, and this seems to be of special importance, we *may* take the typically apperceived object as an example of a general type and allow ourselves to be led to the general concept of the type, but we do not *need* by any means to think of the concrete dog thematically as an exemplar of the general concept 'dog.' 'In general,' this dog here is a dog like any other dog and will show all the characteristics which the type 'dog,' according to our previous experience, implies; nevertheless, this known type carries along a horizon of still unknown typical characteristics pertaining not only to this or that individual dog but to dogs in general. Every empirical idea of the general has the character of an open concept to be rectified or corroborated by supervening experience."[22] Also see Schutz's *Collected Papers*, Volume III, "Type and Eidos in Husserl's Late Philosophy."

. . . patterns of action, largely evident in common-sense experience, which are   18
known as formulas or recipes for practical affairs . . .

Schutz writes: "What is supposed to be known in common by everyone who shares our system of relevances is the way of life considered to be the natural, the

---

[22]   Schutz, *Collected Papers*, Vol. I, pp. 281–282. Reprinted by permission of the publisher.

good, the right one by the members of the 'in-group'; as such, it is at the origin
of the many recipes for handling things and men in order to come to terms with
typified situations, of the folkways and mores, of 'traditional behavior,' in Max
Weber's sense, of the 'of-course statements' [in Robert S. Lynd's sense] believed
to be valid by the in-group in spite of their inconsistencies, briefly, of the 'relative
natural aspect of the world' [in Max Scheler's sense]. All these terms refer to
constructs of a typified knowledge of a highly socialized structure which supersede
the thought objects of my and my fellow-man's private knowledge of the world
as taken for granted."[23] Schutz directs us to Weber, *The Theory of Social and
Economic Organization*, pp. 115 ff.; Parsons, *The Structure of Social Action*,
Chapter XVI; Lynd, *Middletown in Transition*, Chapter XII, and *Knowledge for
What?*, pp. 38–63; Scheler, *Die Wissensformen und die Gesellschaft*, pp. 58 ff.;
Becker and Dahlke, "Max Scheler's Sociology of Knowledge." The conception
of the "world as taken for granted," as in the case of typification, involves the
theme of "familiarity." That which is most familiar is precisely that which is
most fundamentally taken for granted. Changes in "how things are done,"
indeed, in what things may be done, are sources of profound individual un-
settlement. So, for example, Sir Thomas Phillipps, the eminent manuscript
collector and bibliophile, wrote in 1864: "England is going mad.... People *begin*
their letters on the last Page—They are cutting London to Pieces—They are
turning the Dead out of the Churchyards—In lettering Books the author's name
is put at the bottom instead of the top—Tradesmen now ask for their Money
before the Goods are received by their Customers."[24] The changes in what is
taken for granted from one era to another are reflected in small no less than
dramatic ways. John Andrew Rice reminds us in *I Came Out of the Eighteenth
Century*: "I was born into a spitting world. Everybody, except ladies and as-
pirants to that title, spat. No public place was without its receptacle. In hotels
and local trains one still sees survivals of those days in the cuspidors—'spittoons'
to us—squat and dumpy in the trains, tall and shining brass in hotel lobbies and
legislative halls. (They cost the state two hundred and fifty dollars apiece during
Reconstruction.) Most homes had them also—'bring paw his spittoon' was a
familiar command—and in any case it was a wise precaution to have one handy, for
the use of a spitting guest."[25] Finally, familiarity and taken-for-grantedness have
cultural and linguistic as well as temporal dimensions. Translation from one
mundane sphere to another may be hampered by differences which are buried in
the linguistic roots of a people. The translator encounters this problem not in-
frequently. So, for example, Keene writes: "The problems of translating Japanese
are not confined to works of the distant past. Some modern short stories cannot

[23]   *Ibid.*, p. 13. Reprinted by permission of the publisher.
[24]   Quoted from A. N. L. Munby, *Portrait of an Obsession: The Life of Sir Thomas
Phillipps, the World's Greatest Book Collector*, adapted by Nicolas Barker from the five
volumes of *Phillipps Studies*, New York: G. P. Putnam's Sons, 1967, p. 237. Copyright
© 1967 by A. N. L. Munby. Reprinted by permission.
[25]   From John Andrew Rice, *I Came Out of the Eighteenth Century*, New York: Harper,
1942, p. 64. Reprinted by permission.

be translated effectively because they depend on the instant recognition of the associations of an article of clothing or food or architecture unfamiliar to Western readers. The falling of a camellia blossom, for example, immediately suggests a beheading to a Japanese, but how to convey this eerie quality to a Western reader except by tedious explanation?"[26]

The concept of role is familiarly known in mundane experience through the model   21
of theatrical performance.

See and compare: Diderot, *The Paradox of Acting* (published in one volume with Archer's *Masks or Faces?*); Barrault, *Le Phénomène théâtral*; Hethmon (Editor), *Strasberg at the Actor's Studio*; Funke and Booth, *Actors Talk about Acting*; Natanson, "Man as an Actor" (with comments by James M. Edie); Willett (Editor), *Brecht on Theatre*; Stanislavski, *An Actor Prepares*; Simmel, *Fragmente und Aufsätze*, Chapter VI, "Zur Philosophie des Schauspielers"; Baumann, "George H. Mead and Luigi Pirandello."

. . . the span of action in which the individual expresses the meaning of his own act.   22

The span of action has a distinctive time structure, as Schutz points out: "I have to visualize the state of affairs to be brought about by my future action before I can draft the single steps of my future acting from which this state of affairs will result. Metaphorically speaking, I have to have some idea of the structure to be erected before I can draft the blueprints. In order to project my future action as it will roll on I have to place myself in my phantasy at a future time when this action *will* already *have been* accomplished, when the resulting act *will* already *have been* materialized. Only then may I reconstruct the single steps which will have brought forth this future act."[27]

We may understand the loneliness of the ego . . .   23

The following conjoined passage and part of a poem were brought to my attention a number of years ago by a student whose face I can still see but whose name I have forgotten.

"When making certain of the transcendental ego, we are standing at an altogether dangerous point, even if at first we leave out of consideration the difficult question of apodicticity . . . it is as though we were on the brink of a precipice, where advancing calmly and surely is a matter of philosophical life and death."[28]

---

[26]   From Donald Keene, "Confessions of a Specialist," *The New York Times Book Review*, June 30, 1968, p. 2. Copyright © 1968 by The New York Times Company. Reprinted by permission.
[27]   Schutz, *Collected Papers*, Vol. I, pp. 68–69. Reprinted by permission of the publisher.
[28]   From Edmund Husserl, *Cartesian Meditations: An Introduction to Phenomenology*, translated by Dorion Cairns, The Hague: Martinus Nijhoff, 1960, p. 23. Reprinted by permission of the publisher.

"A man goes far to find out what he is—
Death of the self, in a long tearless night,
All natural shapes blazing unnatural light.
Dark, dark my light, and darker my desire.
My soul, like some heat-maddened summer fly,
Keeps buzzing at the sill. Which I is *I*?"[29]

---

24   **. . . persons are selves whose identities have achieved expression.**

Compare Gabriel Marcel: ". . . I tend to establish myself as a person in so far as I assume responsibility for my acts and so behave as a real being (rather than a dreamer who reserves the strange power of modifying his dreams, without having to trouble whether this modification has any repercussions in the hypothetical outside world in which everybody else dwells). From the same point of view we might also say that I establish myself as a person in so far as I really believe in the existence of others and allow this belief to influence my conduct. What is the actual meaning of *believing* here? It means to realize or acknowledge their existence in itself, and not only through those points of intersection which bring it into relation with my own."[30]

---

24   **The person is not an "essence" precontained in the self, nor is the self a blank slate as far as identity and character are concerned.**

For phenomenology, "essences" are not mysterious entities but rather intended meanings—*irrealities*—appreciated in their unmediated givenness. Santayana, an acute though critical reader of Husserl, remarks in *Realms of Being*: "Husserl . . . is an analytic psychologist of the most conscientious systematic kind, never forsaking the plane of reflective autobiography; and to boot he is a convinced transcendental idealist, always remembering the activity of thought involved in the contemplation or definition of any object; so that his theory is like those early maps of the known world in which the geographer, proud of his young art, placed in the foreground a representation of the compass, sextant, and telescope, which had served him in his construction; while in another part, to fill in some large tract of *terra incognita*, he might show us the gallant ship in which he made his voyages of discovery, or a group of the naked savages found at the antipodes. Such marginal decoration is not without its charm; and the modern reader, accustomed to

---

[29]   From Theodore Roethke, "In a Dark Time," *Collected Poems of Theodore Roethke*, New York: Doubleday, 1966. Copyright © 1960 by Beatrice Roethke as Administratrix to the Estate of Theodore Roethke. British rights held by Faber and Faber, Ltd., London. Reprinted by permission of Doubleday and Company, Inc. and Faber and Faber, Ltd.

[30]   From Gabriel Marcel, *Homo Viator: Introduction to a Metaphysic of Hope*, translated by Emma Craufurd, New York: Harper Torchbooks, 1962, p. 22. Reprinted by permission of Éditions Montaigne, Paris.

romanticism even in philosophers, may be more willing to look on essence if he is told at the same time that he is looking at it, and how the vision has been achieved. Autobiography may be enlightening even in logic: it reminds us that our map is a map; but it is also grotesque, since it is not the map's business to describe cartography; and thought turns towards essence for the sake of essence, not for the sake of thought. Yet there are advantages in this circumspection or contortion; it is not so easy in learned Germany as in England or America for the gay philosopher to ignore transcendental criticism and psychological fact simply because they were known to some past generation, or because they annoy him and he is interested in something else."[31] It is scandalous, by the way, that *Realms of Being*, Santayana's major work, is out of print.

In a sense, the brain has nothing to do with consciousness.   24

This may strike the reader as outrageous. I am, however, concerned with consciousness as intentionality, not as a neurophysiological or a distinctively psychological reality. For a general discussion of brain-consciousness-mind, see: Smythies (Editor), *Brain and Mind*; Hayek, *The Sensory Order*; Adrian, *The Physical Background of Perception*; Eccles, *The Neurophysiological Basis of Mind* (includes a highly technical bibliography); Sherrington, *Man on His Nature*.

The power of typification is precisely its capacity to create anonymous reality. 25

See Schutz, *Collected Papers*, Volume II, pp. 48 ff. Compare Natanson, "Anonymity and Recognition."

Chapter Two: Other Selves

In the more nearly Continental approach to problems of intersubjectivity, the following works are available: Sartre, *Being and Nothingness*, Part Three, "Being-for-Others"—compare Schutz, *Collected Papers*, Volume I, "Sartre's Theory of the Alter Ego"; Merleau-Ponty, *Phenomenology of Perception*, pp. 346 ff.; Scheler, *The Nature of Sympathy*. The central statement by Husserl on other selves is found in the fifth of his *Cartesian Meditations*. Compare Schutz, *Collected Papers*, Volume III, "The Problem of Transcendental Intersubjectivity in Husserl," and Ricoeur, *Husserl*, "Husserl's Fifth Cartesian Meditation." Also see: Ortega y Gasset, *Man and People*; Marcel, *The Mystery of Being*, Volume I; Toulemont, *L'Essence de la société selon Husserl*, Chapter II, "L'Expérience d'autrui"; Löwith, *Das Individuum in der Rolle des Mitmenschen*; Chastaing, *L'Existence d'autrui*

---

[31] From George Santayana, *Realms of Being*, Vol. XIV of the Triton Edition of the *Works of George Santayana*, New York: Charles Scribner's Sons, 1937, pp. 167–168. Canadian and British rights held by Constable and Company, Ltd., London. Reprinted by permission.

(contains an extremely thorough bibliography); Theunissen, *Der Andere* (bibliography in German and French).

Studies in the Anglo-American tradition are: Price, "Our Knowledge of Other Minds" and "Our Evidence for the Existence of Other Minds"; Aaron, "Our Knowledge of One Another"; Jones, "Our Knowledge of Other Persons"; Hampshire, "The Analogy of Feeling"; Malcolm, *Knowledge and Certainty*, "Knowledge of Other Minds"; Austin, *Philosophical Papers*, Chapter 3, "Other Minds"; Wisdom, *Other Minds*; Strawson, *Individuals*; Coval, *Scepticism and the First Person*; Shorter, "Other Minds," in *The Encyclopedia of Philosophy* (bibliography); Wittgenstein, *Philosophical Investigations*; Ayer, *Language, Truth, and Logic*, Chapter VII, "The Self and the Common World"; Locke, *Myself and Others*. For a study which considers both Continental and Anglo-American theories, see Chatterjee, *Our Knowledge of Other Selves*. Also to be noted: Webb, *Our Knowledge of One Another*; Tagiuri and Petrullo (Editors), *Person Perception and Interpersonal Behavior*; Brown, *Kierkegaard, Heidegger, Buber, and Barth*. Further references follow in the notes.

---

28   **The "egocentric predicament" . . .**

The phrase comes from Ralph Barton Perry, "The Ego-Centric Predicament," in *The Development of American Philosophy* (edited by Muelder, Sears, and Schlabach); the book includes bibliographies following the introductions to each part.

---

28   **For common-sense men in daily life, each individual is in touch or may come into relationship with his fellow-men.**

The Other, of course, must first—and this is immanent to the entire theme of intersubjectivity—be recognized as a human being. There are limiting cases in which the very humanity of the Other is in question. Ruesch and Bateson write: "The late Doctor Stutterheim, Government Archeologist in Java, used to tell the following story: Somewhat before the advent of the white man, there was a storm on the Javanese coast in the neighborhood of one of the capitals. After the storm the people went down to the beach and found, washed up by the waves and almost dead, a large white monkey of unknown species. The religious experts explained that this monkey had been a member of the court of Beroena, the God of the Sea, and that for some offense the monkey had been cast out by the god whose anger was expressed in the storm. The Rajah gave orders that the white monkey from the sea should be kept alive, chained to a certain stone. This was done. Doctor Stutterheim told me that he had seen the stone and that, roughly scratched on it in Latin, Dutch, and English were the name of the man and a statement of his shipwreck. Apparently this trilingual sailor never established verbal communication with his captors. He was surely unaware of the premises in their minds which labeled him as a white monkey and therefore not a potential recipient of verbal messages: it probably never occurred to him that they could doubt his humanity. He may have doubted theirs."[32] Whatever one may think of that story, a somewhat different but historically grounded report of fundamental failure to recognize the Other as human is given by Prescott in his *History of the Conquest of Mexico*: "The approach of Cortés had been greatly retarded by the broken nature of the ground. When he came up, the Indians were so hotly engaged that he was upon them before they observed his approach. He ordered his men to direct their lances at the faces of their opponents, who, terrified at the monstrous apparition,—for they supposed the rider and the horse, which they had never before seen, to be one and the same,—were seized with a panic. Ordaz availed himself of it to command a general charge along the line, and the Indians, many of them throwing away their arms, fled without attempting further resistance" (pp. 352–354).

. . . solipsism, the view that only the self is real.   29

For discussions of solipsism, see: Stace, *The Theory of Knowledge and Existence*, Chapter V, "The World of the Solitary Mind"; Bradley, *Appearance and Reality*, Chapter XXI, "Solipsism"; Santayana, *Scepticism and Animal Faith*, Chapter III, "Wayward Scepticism"; Wittgenstein, *Tractatus Logico-Philosophicus* (and compare Black, *A Companion to Wittgenstein's 'Tractatus'*, pp. 308 ff.); Rollins, "Solipsism," in *The Encyclopedia of Philosophy* (bibliography). Finally, see Russell's *Human Knowledge*, Part three, Chapter II, "Solipsism"; it is there he quips, "I once received a letter from an eminent logician, Mrs. Christine Ladd Franklin, saying that she was a solipsist, and was surprised that there were no others" (p. 180).

Knowledge of fellow-men is possible because knowledge is socially grounded . . .   30

George H. Mead is representative of this view. He writes: ". . . the social individual is already in a perspective which belongs to the community within which his self has arisen. He has become a self by responding to himself in the attitudes of other selves . . . the appearance of the self is antedated by the tendencies to take the attitudes of the others, so that the existence of the others is not a reflection of his self-experience into other individuals. The others are not relative to his self, but his self and the others are relative to the perspective of his social organism. Whatever metaphysical difficulties the conception may present, it is one which we constantly use in biography and history. The individual and the society are selectively and causally determinative of the environment, and this determines the individual or the society—neither can be explained in terms of the other except as the other is determined by it. The attempt to proceed otherwise leads

---

[32] From Jurgen Ruesch and Gregory Bateson, *Communication: The Social Matrix of Psychiatry*, New York: W. W. Norton, 1968, pp. 204–205 (footnote). Reprinted by permission of the publisher.

to an impossible solipsism or to an equally impossible determinism."[33] And John Dewey warns in *The Public and Its Problems*: "The problem of the relation of individuals to associations—sometimes posed as the relation of *the* individual to society—is a meaningless one. We might as well make a problem out of the relation of the letters of an alphabet to the alphabet. An alphabet *is* letters, and 'society' is individuals in their connections with one another" (p. 69).

---

31   **The solution of the problem of other selves demands a rigorous proof.**

Husserl attempted such a proof in the fifth of his *Cartesian Meditations*. A very valuable summary exposition is given by Schutz, *Collected Papers*, Volume I, pp. 124 ff.

---

32   **. . . the phenomenologist argues that, within the suspension, the Other is *presented* as an incarnate being . . .**

Husserl writes: "Experience is original consciousness; and in fact we generally say, in the case of experiencing a man: the other is himself there before us 'in person.' On the other hand, this being there in person does not keep us from admitting forthwith that, properly speaking, neither the other Ego himself, nor his subjective processes or his appearances themselves, nor anything else belonging to his own essence, becomes given in our experience originally. If it were, if what belongs to the other's own essence were directly accessible, it would be merely a moment of my own essence, and ultimately he himself and I myself would be the same. The situation would be similar as regards his animate organism, if the latter were nothing else but the 'body' that is a unity constituted purely in my actual and possible experiences, a unity belonging—as a product of *my* 'sensuousness' exclusively—in my primordial sphere. *A certain mediacy of intentionality* must be present here, going out from the substratum, 'primordial world,' (which in any case is the incessantly underlying basis) and making present to consciousness a 'there too,' which nevertheless is not itself there and can never become an 'itself-there.' We have here, accordingly, a kind of *making 'co-present,'* a kind of '*ap-presentation.*'"[34] Strictly speaking, the Other is not *presented* but *appresented*; it is his body which is presented to me. Compare Ricoeur, *Husserl*, p. 125.

---

32   **. . . the position is not without some substantial difficulties . . .**

See Schutz, *Collected Papers*, Volume III, "The Problem of Transcendental Intersubjectivity in Husserl." For a different line of criticism, see Ortega y Gasset, *Man and People*, Chapter VI.

---

[33]   From George H. Mead, *The Philosophy of the Act*, edited by Charles W. Morris in collaboration with John M. Brewster, Albert M. Dunham, and David L. Miller, Chicago: University of Chicago Press, 1938, pp. 152–153. Reprinted by permission.
[34]   Husserl, *Cartesian Meditations*, pp. 108–109. Reprinted by permission of the publisher.

... the location of the ground of intersubjectivity in pure consciousness involves   32
a "transcendental ego" ...

By the "transcendental ego" Husserl means the ultimate grounding of the life of
consciousness in the pure source of intentionality. The ego can always be understood from two standpoints: empirically as a concrete and actualized reality or
transcendentally as a possible structure of a subjectivity of which "my" life is
merely one exemplar. Both standpoints may be investigated phenomenologically
and the results of such investigations mirror each other. Husserl writes: "Transcendental self-experience may, at any moment, merely by a change of attitude,
be turned back into psychological self-experience. Passing, thus, from one to the
other attitude, we notice a certain 'identity' about the ego. What I saw under the
psychological reflection as 'my' objectification, I see under the transcendental
reflection as self-objectifying, or, as we may also say, as objectified by the transcendental 'I'. We have only to recognize that what makes the psychological and
transcendental spheres of experience parallel is an 'identity' in their significance,
and that what differentiates them is merely a change of attitude, to realize that
the psychological and transcendental phenomenologies will also be parallel."[35]

... whether the ego's knowledge of and relation to his alter is not *experienced*   32
rather than known.

The direct "manifestation" of the Other is, in its primal form, an aspect of the
"naive realism" of common sense. By a sophisticated reversal, however, it has
been suggested that any proof for the existence of the alter ego is, in principle, a
failure. Instead of proving the existence of the Other, he *manifests* himself in
experiential immediacy. As Sartre puts it, "the Other is on principle the *one who
looks at me*" (*Being and Nothingness*, p. 257).

... the self comes into awareness of the Other by taking his role ...   33

The classical and still fundamental discussion of "taking the role of the Other" is
to be found in Mead, *Mind, Self, and Society*. Also compare Cooley, *Human Nature
and the Social Order*.

... "dialogue" stands for all elements of address and response between man and   35
fellow-man.

See Buber, *Between Man and Man*, "Dialogue." There are important distinctions
to be drawn between "dialogue," "conversation," "talk," and "chatter." Friedman points out in *Martin Buber*: "By far the largest part of what is called conversation today would be more correctly described as talk. In general, people do
not really speak to one another. Each turns to the other, to be sure, but he speaks

---

[35] Husserl, "Phenomenology," p. 702. Reprinted by permission of Encyclopaedia
Britannica.

in reality to a fictitious audience which exists only to listen to him. The understanding of true conversation is so rare in our time that one imagines that one can
arrange a genuine dialogue before a public of interested spectators with the assistance of proper publicity. But a public debate, on no matter how high a level, can
neither be spontaneous, direct, nor unreserved. Such public discussion is un-
bridgeably separate from genuine dialogue."[36]   Friedman's book includes a
bibliography of the primary and secondary literature on Buber.   Compare
Heidegger's analysis of "idle talk" in *Being and Time*, pp. 211 ff., and Dufrenne
Language and Philosophy, p. 99.

---

35   . . . a vast range of communicatory awareness which antecedes speech (the responsive smile the infant gives its mother) and which accompanies all subsequent
human expression.

Schutz speaks of the primordial ground of communication as a "tuning-in" relationship. See his *Collected Papers*, Volume II, "Making Music Together." On
the smile of the infant, see Kurt Goldstein, "The Smiling of the Infant and the
Problem of Understanding the 'Other.'"

---

36   . . . the accessibility of the Other is proved, for common-sense purposes, when I
speak to him.

Compare Gusdorf, *Speaking*, and note Ortega's warning against any simplistic
equation of speaking and communicating. He writes: "I am persuaded that
speech, like almost everything that man does, is far more illusory than is commonly
supposed. We define language as the means of revealing our thoughts. But any
definition—this one included—if not indeed misleading, is ironic; it implies tacit
reservations, and if not so interpreted may be exceedingly harmful. It is not so
much that language serves also to hide our thoughts, to lie; lying would be impossible if original and normal speech were not sincere. Like the counterfeit coin, which
is carried in circulation by real money, lying is in the last analysis nothing but the
humble parasite of truth. No, the real danger lies not in the definition itself, but
in the optimism with which we fill it out. For if it does not go so far as to say that
language will reveal all our thought with some degree of accuracy, neither does
it tell the strict truth: that it is impossible for men to truly understand one another,
that they are condemned to profound loneliness and waste themselves in efforts
to reach their fellow beings. Of these efforts it is language that at times comes
nearest to expressing a little of what goes on within us: nothing more."[37]

---

[36]   From Maurice S. Friedman, *Martin Buber: The Life of Dialogue*, Chicago: University of Chicago Press, 1955, p. 124. Reprinted by permission.
[37]   From José Ortega y Gasset, *Toward a Philosophy of History*, translated by Helene
Weyl, New York: W. W. Norton, 1941, pp. 44–45. Republished in 1961 as *History as a
System*. Quotation reprinted by permission of the publisher.

Analogy. 36

For discussions of "analogy," see: Joseph, *An Introduction to Logic*, Chapter XXIV, "Of Induction by Simple Enumeration and the Argument from Analogy"; Emmet, *The Nature of Metaphysical Thinking*; Macdonald, "The Philosopher's Use of Analogy." Compare Stevens, *The Necessary Angel*, Chapter V, "Effects of Analogy." Also see Black, "Metaphor."

Activity, in the broadest sense, which presents itself to the Other may be called 37 behavior.

Compare Schutz, *The Phenomenology of the Social World*, pp. 53 ff.

Put together, this means that consciousness is translated into behavior. 37

See Blanshard and Skinner, "The Problem of Consciousness—A Debate," and Wann (Editor), *Behaviorism and Phenomenology* (individual chapters have bibliographies).

. . . the raised fist is the anger . . . 38

Sartre writes: "These frowns, this redness, this stammering, this slight trembling of the hands, these downcast looks which seem at once timid and threatening— these do not *express* anger; they *are* the anger. But this point must be clearly understood. In itself a clenched fist is nothing and means nothing. But also we never perceive a *clenched fist*. We perceive a man who in a certain situation clenches his fist. This meaningful act considered in connection with the past and with possibles and understood in terms of the synthetic totality 'body in situation' *is* the anger."[38]

Interpretation. 39

On "interpretation," see among the literature on *Verstehen* (interpretive under-standing): Weber, *The Theory of Social and Economic Organization*, pp. 87 ff.; Jaspers, *General Psychopathology*, pp. 301 ff.; Don Martindale, "Verstehen," in *International Encyclopedia of the Social Sciences* (bibliography); Natanson (Editor), *Philosophy of the Social Sciences*; Becker, "Interpretive Sociology and Constructive Typology."

By itself . . . the hand says nothing . . . clenched in a fist it may mean friendly 39 greetings.

Firth writes: ". . . if the anthropologist is travelling in the Plateau of Northern Nigeria . . . he may meet men from the Bi Rom and other pagan tribes living there.

---

[38] From Jean-Paul Sartre, *Being and Nothingness: An Essay on Phenomenological Ontology*, translated by Hazel E. Barnes, New York: Philosophical Library, 1956, pp. 346–347. Reprinted by permission of the publisher.

They will probably shake their clenched fists in the air as he approaches. According to his fears or his politics, he may interpret this as a symbol of anger or of solidarity among fellow-workers. In time he will find it is merely the normal greeting"[39] (quoted by Leon J. Goldstein, "The Phenomenological and Naturalistic Approaches to the Social").

---

40   To discover the Other is to be a subject for which the Other is object.

See Sartre, *Being and Nothingness*, Part III.

---

41   . . . action as centered in the Here and Now as well as in the biography and projects of the individual.

See Schutz, *Collected Papers*, Volume I, "Choosing Among Projects of Action" and, in the same volume, "Common-Sense and Scientific Interpretation of Human Action," where he writes: "Man finds himself at any moment of his daily life in a biographically determined situation, that is, in a physical and socio-cultural environment as defined by him, within which he has his position, not merely his position in terms of physical space and outer time or of his status and role within the social system but also his moral and ideological position. To say that this definition of the situation is biographically determined is to say that it has its history; it is the sedimentation of all man's previous experiences, organized in the habitual possessions of his stock of knowledge at hand, and as such his unique possession, given to him and to him alone."[40]

---

42   . . . the Other is severed from his subjectivity insofar as his being-for-me is reduced to the presentation of his body to my gaze.

"To you," says a character in a recent story by Phillip Roth, "I'm just another *her* . . ." ("Civilization and its Discontents," p. 51).

---

42   The familiar examples of master and slave have been used in classical accounts . . .

The paradigm account, of course, is offered by Hegel in his *Phenomenology of Mind*, pp. 229 ff. on "Lordship and Bondage." On Hegel, see: Loewenberg, *Hegel's Phénomenology*; Mure, *The Philosophy of Hegel*; and Findlay, *Hegel*.

---

43   I discover myself as object for the Other when his glance, his order, his decision constitute the field within which my presence irrupts.

See Sartre, *Being and Nothingness*, "The Look," pp. 252 ff.

---

[39]   From Raymond Firth, *Elements of Social Organization*, New York: Philosophical Library, 1951, p. 23. Reprinted by permission of the publisher.

[40]   Schutz, *Collected Papers*, Vol. I, p. 9. Reprinted by permission of the publisher.

. . . **even at the time of his complete dominance over the Other, the self may falter**   43
and relinquish its freedom.

Compare the discussion of sadism in Sartre, *Being and Nothingness*, pp. 399 ff.

That which threatens the self by fixing and desiccating the subject has been called   45
"Bad Faith."

Sartre writes: "We say indifferently of a person that he shows signs of bad faith
or that he lies to himself. We shall willingly grant that bad faith is a lie to oneself,
on condition that we distinguish the lie to oneself from lying in general. . . . To
be sure, the one who practices bad faith is hiding a displeasing truth or presenting
as truth a pleasing untruth. Bad faith then has in appearance the structure of
falsehood. Only what changes everything is the fact that in bad faith it is from
myself that I am hiding the truth. Thus the duality of the deceiver and the
deceived does not exist here. Bad faith on the contrary implies in essence
the unity of a *single* consciousness."[41] Sartre gives examples of bad faith in the
section on "Patterns of Bad Faith," which follows the passage just quoted. Compare this passage from Pirandello: ". . . while the sociologist describes social life
as it presents itself to external observation, the humorist, being a man of ex-
ceptional intuition, shows—nay, reveals—that appearances are one thing and the
consciousness of the people concerned, in its inner essence, another. And yet
people 'lie psychologically' even as they 'lie socially.' And this lying to ourselves—
living, as we do, on the surface and not in the depths of our being—is a result of
the social lying. The mind that gives back its own reflection is a solitary mind,
but our internal solitude is never so great that suggestions from the communal
life do not break in upon it with all the fictions and transferences which characterize them."[42]

Chapter Three: Sociality

For general introductions to the study of society, see MacIver and Page, *Society*,
and W. H. Sprott, *Sociology*. Those who abhor textbooks in general and sociology
textbooks in particular should read Berger's *Invitation to Sociology*. A number of
anthologies are available: Parsons, Shils, Naegele, and Pitts (Editors), *Theories
of Society* in two volumes (bibliography); Ruitenbeek (Editor), *Varieties of Classical Social Theory* and *Varieties of Modern Social Theory* (bibliographies in both
volumes); Coser and Rosenberg (Editors), *Sociological Theory*. On the history of
sociology and social thought: Becker and Barnes, *Social Thought* in three volumes

---

[41]   Sartre, *Being and Nothingness*, pp. 48–49. Reprinted by permission of the publisher.
[42]   Quoted by Eric Bentley in his Introduction to Luigi Pirandello, *Naked Masks:
Five Plays*, edited by Eric Bentley, New York: E. P. Dutton (Dutton Paperback
Edition), 1952, p. xiv. Reprinted by permission. For the original, see Pirandello, *Saggi*,
p. 163.

(bibliographies); Barnes (Editor), *An Introduction to the History of Sociology*; Aron, *Main Currents of Sociological Thought* in two volumes. A general bibliographical survey is given in Hoselitz (Editor), *A Reader's Guide to the Social Sciences*. On sociological theory: Timasheff, *Sociological Theory*; Llewellyn Gross (Editor), *Symposium on Sociological Theory*; Martindale, *The Nature and Types of Sociological Theory*; Loomis and Loomis, *Modern Social Theories*; Becker and Boskoff (Editors), *Modern Sociological Theory*. Among treatises: Sumner, *Folkways*; Cooley, *Social Organization*; Malinowski, *A Scientific Theory of Culture*; Znaniecki, *Cultural Sciences*. Also see: Merton, *Social Theory and Social Structure*; Parsons, *The Social System*; Levy, *The Structure of Society*; Murdock *Studies in the Science of Society*; Aron, *German Sociology*; Kelsen, *Society and Nature*; Homans, *The Human Group* and *Social Behavior*; Nadel, *The Foundations of Social Anthropology* (bibliography); Dufrenne, *La Personnalité de base* (with a bibliography in anthropology, social psychology, and sociology composed chiefly of titles in English); Berger and Luckmann, *The Social Construction of Reality*. Among other collections: White (Editor), *The State of the Social Sciences*; Lerner (Editor), *The Human Meaning of the Social Sciences*; Merton, Broom, and Cottrell (Editors), *Sociology Today*. And a final miscellany: Udy, "Social Structural Analysis," in *International Encyclopedia of the Social Sciences* (bibliography); Lévi-Strauss, *The Scope of Anthropology*; Berdyaev, *Solitude and Society*. Additional references can be found in the notes which follow.

---

47   **Sociality . . . is what happens *between* selves.**

Buber writes: "The fundamental fact of human existence is neither the individual as such nor the aggregate as such. Each, considered by itself, is a mighty abstraction. The individual is a fact of existence in so far as he steps into a living relation with other individuals. The aggregate is a fact of existence in so far as it is built up of living units of relation. The fundamental fact of human existence is man with man. What is peculiarly characteristic of the human world is above all that something takes place between one being and another the like of which can be found nowhere in nature. Language is only a sign and a means for it, all achievement of the spirit has been incited by it. Man is made man by it; but on its way it does not merely unfold, it also decays and withers away. It is rooted in one being turning to another as another, as this particular other being, in order to communicate with it in a sphere which is common to them but which reaches out beyond the special sphere of each. I call this sphere, which is established with the existence of man as man but which is conceptually uncomprehended, the sphere of 'between.' Though being realized in very different degrees, it is a primal category of human reality."[43]

---

[43]   From Martin Buber, *Between Man and Man*, translated by Ronald Gregor Smith, New York: Macmillan, 1965, p. 244. Copyright © 1965 by The Macmillan Company, Inc. Foreign rights held by Routledge and Kegan Paul, Ltd., London. Reprinted by permission.

We are, therefore I am.   47

Contrast Hocking, "Marcel and the Ground Issues of Metaphysics": ". . . without some subject-matter of thought and action neither a 'We are' nor an 'I am' could exist. For there is no 'I think' that is not thinking *something,*—an obvious consideration, which Descartes may have overlooked. Not only is there no attraction between empty minds, an empty mind is no mind at all. The 'We are' is simply an unfinished statement" (p. 452).

The most striking feature of the We is its taken-for-grantedness.   48

Schutz writes in *The Phenomenology of the Social World*: "The basic We-relationship is already given to me by the mere fact that I am born into the world of directly experienced social reality. From this basic relationship is derived the original validity of all my direct experiences of particular fellow men and also my knowledge that there is a larger world of my contemporaries whom I am not now experiencing directly" (p. 165). Compare the discussion of the "We" in Romero, *Theory of Man*, Chapter X, "Sociability." Also note Foster, " 'We' in Modern Philosophy."

. . . the broadest horizon being that of the sense of mundanity . . .   48

The term "horizon" is a technical one in phenomenology. Kuhn writes in "The Phenomenological Concept of 'Horizon' ": "Three elements of meaning may be pointed out, all three adumbrated by the pre-philosophical usage. (1) Horizon is the ultimate circumference within which all things, real and imaginable, are bound to appear. To explore the horizon means to move away from the ordinary foci of attention with a view to integrating the things at hand in a broader and ever broader context. The idea of horizon stands for the progressive drive inherent in experience. (2) While limiting the totality of given things, the horizon also frames it. The frame of a picture, though forming no part of it, helps to constitute its wholeness. Similarly, the horizon determines that which it frames. The fact that the object is framed by a horizon is relevant to its mode of appearance. Its way of being is essentially a 'being within.' Hence horizon as a guiding motion enables us to reveal shades of meaning cast on the object by its environment. It stands for the striving after intensification and concreteness. (3) By its very nature every horizon is 'open.' As we move from the center toward the circumference fresh horizons open up. We are constantly invited to transcend the boundary of our field of vision. This process is either infinite or limited. In the first case, no truth would be obtainable. We could make no statements but provisional ones. In the second case, the limitations would have to be provided by something outside all imaginable horizons, that is, by some non-empirical factor (analogous to the shape of the globe, which limits the shifting from one 'horizon,' in the original sense of the word, to another). Thus the notion of horizon points to a basis of experience outside experience. It stands for the impetus of self-transcendence with which experience is animated."[44]

---

48   **The push and pull, the hefting and budging of lifting has its counterpart in the striving involved in all action . . .**

George H. Mead had remarkable insight into the problem of effort and resistance. He writes: "There is, of course, the critical difference between the pressure of hands against each other, and that of the stone against the hand: that in the case of the pressure of the hands against each other there is the sense of effort in each hand, while in the case of the stone there is only the sense of resistance in the stone against the pressing hand. However, the resistance remains an identical content of the two. Furthermore, the resistance of the hand arises only over against that of the stone. The stone defines the hand as necessarily as the hand the hand. It is a fundamental experience in which each object involves the other. . . . Out of the experience arise the physical thing and the organism. Neither is prior. They mutually bound each other. The illusions of contact are the exceptions that prove the rule. The critical difference of the sense of effort gives the hand an 'inside' which primarily belongs only to the hand. It is in the invitation to resistance when we put the shoulder to the wheel or grip the object to steady ourselves or heave it over that the object acquires an inside which is in a sense transferred from the organism to the object. As above indicated, the pressure of the two hands against each other offers the sort of experience from which this transfer is made, but the transfer calls for more than such an experience. The situation out of which this transfer arises is the co-operation of resistances offered by physical things to the organism and by the organism to physical things. Human posture in any position involves it. Manipulation of any sort is an expression of it. The floors and stairs of our buildings, the forms of our articles of furniture, and the handles of everything we handle are but elaborations of it. It is impossible to exaggerate the fundamental nature of this co-operation of the human animal with his contact environment or his dependence upon it. He rests upon it, demands and beseeches it in every position and at every step."[45] An earlier philosopher concerned with the nature of "effort" was Maine de Biran. See his *Essai sur les fondements de la psychologie* and, for a general study, Hallie, *Maine de Biran.*

---

48   **The primitive fact of man's "upright posture" presupposes a countervailing force to that of gravity to keep him standing.**

Straus writes: "Upright posture characterizes the human species. Nevertheless, each individual has to struggle in order to make it really his own. Man has to

---

[44]   From Helmut Kuhn, "The Phenomenological Concept of 'Horizon,'" in *Philosophical Essays in Memory of Edmund Husserl* (edited by Marvin Farber), Cambridge, Mass.: Harvard University Press, 1940, pp. 107–108. Reprinted by permission of the publisher.
[45]   Mead, *Philosophy of the Act,* pp. 186–187. Reprinted by permission.

become what he is. The acquisition does not make him an 'absentee landlord.' While the heart continues to beat from its fetal beginning to death without our active intervention and while breathing neither demands nor tolerates our voluntary interference beyond narrow limits, upright posture remains a task throughout our lives. Before reflection or self-reflection start, but as if they were a prelude to it, work makes its appearance within the realm of the elemental biological functions of man. In getting up, in reaching the upright posture, man must oppose the forces of gravity. It seems to be his nature to oppose nature in its impersonal, fundamental aspects with natural means. However, gravity is never fully overcome; upright posture always maintains its character of counteraction. It calls for our activity and attention."[46] Compare, Canetti, *Crowds and Power*, pp. 387 ff. (this book has a varied bibliography, rich in titles on myth, anthropology, and psychology) and the discussion of the "vertical" and the "horizontal" in Madariaga, *Portrait of a Man Standing*.

. . . the domain of sociality extends far beyond the perimeter of direct confrontation.   50

Our discussion of past, present, and future is indebted to Schutz, who distinguished between and analyzed the worlds of predecessors, contemporaries, consociates, and successors. See his *The Phenomenology of the Social World*, Chapter IV, and *Collected Papers*, Volume I, pp. 15 ff.

**The dead . . . continue to exert influence on me, in subtle and indirect ways, and   51
find their way, curiously, into the present.**

Jules Romains illustrates this beautifully in his *The Death of a Nobody*.

**It is an essential feature of transcendence that misinterpretation is a permanent   53
possibility for all reconstruction.**

This is true because the Other not only survives my death but, in virtue of that survival, becomes responsible for interpreting my life. Sartre writes: "So long as I live I can escape what I *am* for the Other by revealing to myself by my freely posited ends that I *am* nothing and that I make myself what I am; so long as I live, I can give the lie to what others discover in me, by projecting myself already toward other ends and in every instance by revealing that my dimension of being-for-myself is incommensurable with my dimension of being-for-others. Thus ceaselessly I escape my outside and ceaselessly I am reapprehended by the Other; and in this 'dubious battle' the definitive victory belongs to neither the one nor the other of these modes of being. But the *fact of death* without being precisely allied to either of the adversaries in this same combat gives the final victory to

---

[46]   From Erwin W. Straus, *Phenomenological Psychology: Selected Papers*, translated, in part, by Erling Eng, New York: Basic Books, 1966, p. 141. Reprinted by permission of the publisher.

the point of view of the Other by transferring the combat and the prize to another level—that is, by suddenly suppressing one of the combatants. In this sense to die is to be condemned no matter what ephemeral victory one has won over the Other; even if one has made use of the Other to 'sculpture one's own statue,' to die is to exist only through the Other, and to owe to him one's meaning and the very meaning of one's victory."[47]

---

54   **What would *not* qualify as action . . . ?**

Von Mises writes in *Human Action*: "The opposite of action is not *irrational behavior*, but a reactive response to stimuli on the part of the bodily organs and instincts which cannot be controlled by the volition of the person concerned" (p. 20).

---

54   **. . . the concern of the individual for the Other must be capable of being interiorized so that response is significant.**

See Mead's discussion of the "significant gesture" in *Mind, Self, and Society*.

---

55   **There is an entire domain of . . . negative or covert action which is essential to the career of mundane life.**

This was a point which Schutz emphasized. See his *Collected Papers*, Volume I, pp. 67 ff.

---

56   **. . . "subjective" is the antonym of "objective," . . .**

For a study of "subjective" and "objective" approaches to social reality, see Natanson (Editor), *Philosophy of the Social Sciences*.

---

58   **. . . what is "real" on the social scene is that which is defined as real by the individual.**

In W. I. Thomas's formulation of the "definition of the situation," "If men define situations as real they are real in their consequences" (Thomas and Thomas, *The Child in America*, p. 572). Compare Volkart (Editor), *Social Behavior and Personality*. Also see Schutz, *Collected Papers*, Volume I, pp. 9, 348-349; Volume II, p. 103.

---

59   **. . . when the typification on which sociality is founded is damaged, what is alienated is social reality itself . . .**

See Natanson, "Alienation and Social Role."

---

[47]   Sartre, *Being and Nothingness*, p. 544. Reprinted by permission of the publisher.

. . . it is through aspects or adumbrations that we come into touch with fellow-men.   59

I am utilizing Husserl's notion of "adumbration", but adapting it for persons rather than things. With respect to the latter, Husserl writes: "A certain *inadequacy* belongs . . . to the perception of things, and that too is an essential necessity. In principle a thing can be given only 'in one of its aspects,' and that not only means incompletely, in some sense or other imperfectly, but precisely that which presentation through perspectives prescribes" (*Ideas*, p. 137). Compare Gurwitsch, *The Field of Consciousness*, pp. 202 ff., and Bosanquet, *Implication and Linear Inference*, pp. 78 ff.

. . . there is both a *situation* and a *perspective* in terms of which the Other appears.   59

The concept of "situation" is a basic one in both existential and phenomenological thought and in sociology as well. See: Sartre, *Being and Nothingness*, pp. 481 ff.; Strasser, *Phenomenology and the Human Sciences*, pp. 42 ff.; Marcel, *Creative Fidelity*, Chapter IV, "Phenomenological Notes on Being in a Situation" (compare Gallagher, *The Philosophy of Gabriel Marcel*, Chapter II, "Being in a Situation"). Sartre writes: "For us, man is defined first of all as a being 'in a situation.' That means that he forms a synthetic whole with his situation—biological, economic, political, cultural, etc. He cannot be distinguished from his situation, for it forms him and decides his possibilities; but, inversely, it is he who gives it meaning by making his choices within it and by it. To be in a situation, as we see it, is *to choose oneself* in a situation, and men differ from one another in their situations and also in the choices they themselves make of themselves. What men have in common is not a 'nature' but a condition, that is, an ensemble of limits and restrictions: the inevitability of death, the necessity of working for a living, of living in a world already inhabited by other men. Fundamentally this condition is nothing more than the basic human situation, or, if you prefer, the ensemble of abstract characteristics common to all situations."[48] Compare Mead in *Mind, Self, and Society*: "We are individuals born into a certain nationality, located at a certain spot geographically, with such and such family relations, and such and such political relations. All of these represent a certain situation which constitutes the 'me'; but this necessarily involves a continued action of the organism toward the 'me' in the process within which that lies" (p. 182). We may understand "perspective" as the particular way in which the individual is inserted in a more general "situation." The terms imply each other and the distinctions shade into each other. Both perspective and situation involve the common history, experience, and assumptions of groups no less than individuals and are marked by what is *not* shared as much as by what is universally common in human reality. Sartre points out: "If I were to tell an audience of Americans about the German occupation, there would have to be a great deal of analysis and precaution. I

---

[48]   From Jean-Paul Sartre, *Anti-Semite and Jew*, translated by George J. Becker, New York: Schocken Books, 1948, pp. 59–60. Copyright © 1948 by Schocken Books, Inc. Reprinted by permission.

would waste twenty pages in dispelling preconceptions, prejudices, and legends. Afterward, I would have to be sure of my position at every step; I would have to look for images and symbols in American history which would enable them to understand ours; I would always have to keep in mind the difference between our old man's pessimism and their childlike optimism. If I were to write about the same subject for Frenchmen, we are 'entre nous.' For example, it would be enough to say: 'A concert of German military music in the band-stand of a public garden'; everything is there: a raw spring day, a park in the provinces, men with shaven skulls blowing away at their brasses, blind and deaf passers-by who quicken their steps, two or three sullen looking listeners under the trees, this useless serenade to France which drifts off into the sky, our shame and our anguish, our anger, and our pride too.''[49]

The situation of the Negro is nothing less than the history of American consciousness.

The bibliographical support for this statement could be selected from a vast literature, ranging from Baldwin's *The Fire Next Time* to Carmichael and Hamilton's *Black Power* and from Ellison's *Invisible Man* to Williams' *The Man Who Cried I Am*, but to balance what may seem like extravagant rhetoric, I will restrict myself to a small scene from Richard Wright's *Black Boy*:

"The most colorful of the Negro boys on the job was Shorty, the round, yellow, fat elevator operator. He had tiny, beady eyes that looked out between rolls of flesh with a hard but humorous stare. He had the complexion of a Chinese, a short forehead, and three chins. Psychologically he was the most amazing specimen of the southern Negro I had ever met. Hard-headed, sensible, a reader of magazines and books, he was proud of his race and indignant about its wrongs. But in the presence of whites he would play the role of a clown of the most debased and degraded type.

One day he needed twenty-five cents to buy his lunch.

'Just watch me get a quarter from the first white man I see,' he told me as I stood in the elevator that morning.

A white man who worked in the building stepped into the elevator and waited to be lifted to his floor. Shorty sang in a low mumble, smiling, rolling his eyes, looking at the white man roguishly.

'I'm hungry, Mister White Man. I need a quarter for lunch.' The white man ignored him. Shorty, his hands on the controls of the elevator, sang again:

'I ain't gonna move this damned old elevator till I get a quarter, Mister White Man.'

'The hell with you, Shorty,' the white man said, ignoring him and chewing on his black cigar.

---

[49]   From Jean-Paul Sartre, *What Is Literature?*, translated by Bernard Frechtman, New York: Philosophical Library, 1949, pp. 68–69. Reprinted by permission of the publisher.

'I'm hungry, Mister White Man. I'm dying for a quarter,' Shorty sang, drooling, drawling, humming his words.

'If you don't take me to my floor, you will die,' the white man said, smiling a little for the first time.

'But this black sonofabitch sure needs a quarter,' Shorty sang, grimacing, clowning, ignoring the white man's threat.

'Come on, you black bastard, I got to work,' the white man said, intrigued by the element of sadism involved, enjoying it.

'It'll cost you twenty-five cents, Mister White Man; just a quarter, just two bits,' Shorty moaned.

There was silence. Shorty threw the lever and the elevator went up and stopped about five feet shy of the floor upon which the white man worked.

'Can't go no more, Mister White Man, unless I get my quarter,' he said in a tone that sounded like crying.

'What would you do for a quarter?' the white man asked, still gazing off.

'I'll do anything for a quarter,' Shorty sang.

'What, for example?' the white man asked.

Shorty giggled, swung around, bent over, and poked out his broad, fleshy ass.

'You can kick me for a quarter,' he sang, looking impishly at the white man out of the corners of his eyes.

The white man laughed softly, jingled some coins in his pocket, took out one and thumped it to the floor. Shorty stooped to pick it up and the white man bared his teeth and swung his foot into Shorty's rump with all the strength of his body. Shorty let out a howling laugh that echoed up and down the elevator shaft.

'Now, open this door, you goddamn black sonofabitch,' the white man said, smiling with tight lips.

'Yeeeess, siiiiir,' Shorty sang; but first he picked up the quarter and put it into his mouth. 'This monkey's got the peanuts,' he chortled.

He opened the door and the white man stepped out and looked back at Shorty as he went toward his office.

'You're all right, Shorty, you sonofabitch,' he said.

'I know it!' Shorty screamed, then let his voice trail off in a gale of wild laughter.

I witnessed this scene or its variant at least a score of times and I felt no anger or hatred, only disgust and loathing. Once I asked him:

'How in God's name can you do that?'

'I needed a quarter and I got it,' he said soberly, proudly.

'But a quarter can't pay you for what he did to you,' I said.

'Listen, nigger,' he said to me, 'my ass is tough and quarters is scarce.'

I never discussed the subject with him after that."[50]

---

[50]   From Richard Wright, *Black Boy: A Record of Childhood and Youth*, New York: Harper and Row (Perennial Classic), 1966, pp. 248–250 (pp. 198–200 in hardcover edition). Copyright 1937 by Richard Wright; renewed 1965 by Ellen Wright. Reprinted by permission of the publisher.

60   "Stop calling us ghetto people . . ."

Quoted from Asbury, "Protesters Boo Shriver at Talk on 'Struggle for Urban Power.'"

---

63   . . . every person . . . is a partial expression both of his accomplishments and of his possibilities.

Simmel writes: "All of us are fragments, not only of general man, but also of ourselves" (*The Sociology of Georg Simmel*, p. 343).

---

64   Such "constants," as they have been called . . .

In his lectures, Alfred Schutz used to refer to Birth, Aging, and Death as "metaphysical constants."

---

64   . . . there is a *Thou* experienced which . . . has undeniable and irreducible force.

Schutz writes: ". . . the Thou-orientation is the pure mode in which I am aware of another human being as a person. I am already Thou-oriented from the moment that I recognize an entity which I directly experience as a fellow man (as a Thou), attributing life and consciousness to him. However, we must be quite clear that we are *not* here dealing with a conscious *judgment*. This is a prepredicative experience in which I become aware of a fellow human being *as a person*. The Thou-orientation can thus be defined as the intentionality of those Acts whereby the Ego grasps the existence of the other person in the mode of the original self. Every such external experience in the mode of the original self presupposes the actual presence of the other person and my perception of him as there."[51]

---

65   . . . the actual risk his partner in friendship must take in making himself utterly available as a person . . .

Marcel writes: ". . . the person who is at my disposal is the one who is capable of being with me with the whole of himself when I am in need; while the one who is not at my disposal seems merely to offer me a temporary loan raised on his resources. For the one I am a presence; for the other I am an object. Presence involves a reciprocity which is excluded from any relation of subject to object or of subject to subject-object. . . . Unavailability is invariably rooted in some measure of alienation. Say, for instance, that I am told of some misfortune with which I am asked to sympathise: I understand what I am told; I admit in theory that the sufferers deserve my sympathy; I see that it is a case where it would be logical and just for me to respond with sympathy; I even offer my sympathy,

---

[51]   From Alfred Schutz, *The Phenomenology of the Social World*, translated by George Walsh and Frederick Lehnert, Evanston, Ill.: Northwestern University Press, 1967, pp. 163–164. Reprinted by permission of the publisher.

but only with my mind; because, when all is said and done, I am obliged to admit that I feel absolutely nothing. Indeed, I am sorry that this should be so; the contradiction between the indifference which I feel in fact and the sympathy which I know I ought to feel is humiliating and annoying; it diminishes me in my own eyes. But it is of no use; what remains in me is the rather embarrassing awareness that, after all, these are people I do not know—if one had to be touched by every human misfortune life would not be possible, it would indeed be too short. The moment I think: After all, this is only a case, No. 75,627, it is no good, I can feel nothing."[52]

It would seem that these philosophies represent divergent standpoints rather than   66
complementary approaches to human reality.

On the relationship between phenomenology and existentialism see: Spiegelberg, "Husserl's Phenomenology and Existentialism"; Earle, "Phenomenology and Existentialism"; Natanson, *Literature, Philosophy, and the Social Sciences*, Chapter II, "Phenomenology and Existentialism"; Moore, "Existential Phenomenology" (with comments by Handy); Wild, "Contemporary Phenomenology and the Problem of Existence." Also see Shestov, who maintains that "There is a profound inner kinship between Husserl's teaching on the one hand, and that of Nietzsche and Kierkegaard on the other" ("In Memory of a Great Philosopher: Edmund Husserl," p. 266).

Chapter Four: Science

General studies in the philosophy and methodology of the social sciences include: Kaufmann, *Methodology of the Social Sciences*; Kaplan, *The Conduct of Inquiry*; McEwen, *The Problem of Social-Scientific Knowledge* (comprehensive bibliography); Rudner, *Philosophy of Social Science*; Winch, *The Idea of a Social Science*; Homans, *The Nature of a Social Science*. Among the anthologies are: Natanson, (Editor), *Philosophy of the Social Sciences* (detailed bibliography); Braybrooke (Editor), *Philosophical Problems of the Social Sciences*; Brodbeck (Editor), *Readings in the Philosophy of the Social Sciences* (bibliography). For studies of the nature of science in general, see: Nagel, *The Structure of Science*; Wartofsky, *Conceptual Foundations of Scientific Thought* (annotated bibliography); Werkmeister, *A Philosophy of Science*; Caws, *Philosophy of Science;* Margenau, *The Nature of Physical Reality*; Kemeny, *A Philosopher Looks at Science*. Anthologies concerned predominantly with the natural sciences: Feigl and Brodbeck (Editors), *Readings in the Philosophy of Science* (bibliography); Madden, *The Structure of Scientific Thought* (bibliography); Danto and Morganbesser (Editors), *Philosophy of Science* (bibliography). Also see: Burtt, *The Metaphysical Foundations of Modern Physical*

---

[52]   From Gabriel Marcel, *The Philosophy of Existentialism*, translated by Manya Harari, New York: Citadel Press, 1961, pp. 40–41. Reprinted by permission.

Science; Arber, The *Mind and the Eye*; Cohen and Nagel, *Introduction to Logic and Scientific Method*; Von Weizsäcker, *The History of Nature*; Lundberg, *Can Science Save Us?*; Tymieniecka, *Phenomenology and Science in Contemporary European Thought*; Von Uexküll, *Theoretical Biology*. Other references follow in conjunction with the notes.

---

69   ... the history of science is not that of a continuous accumulation ...

See: Kuhn, *The Structure of Scientific Revolutions*; Gillispie, *The Edge of Objectivity*; Hanson, *Patterns of Discovery*.

---

70   ... the resolution of the problems calls for a Saint Francis of philosophy.

It may be, however, that something more than Franciscan love is necessary. Sherrington writes: "The medieval view generally denied to brute kind any loftier status than that of terrestrial furniture provided for man's use during his probation here. The Cartesian lack of sympathy and understanding in this matter of creature-kind went further, an unaccountable trespass both against our fellow-creatures and against common-sense, Even supposing, and it is a questionable supposition, that St. Francis's 'brotherliness' with all that was animate, was, despite its phrasing, not a sympathy recognizing kinship but simply part of a love extended to everything created by God and essentially a worship of Him, even so such a view was venial blindness as contrasted with the ruthless Cartesian rupture of the traditional stair of life ranging upward step by step to man. Science since Descartes has repaired the stair and finds it more significant than before. It marks the way that man has climbed. And it is a stair of mind as well as of body, and it is without break, man's mind nothing more than the topmost rung continuous with related degrees below."[53]

---

70   ... a brilliance and patience of interpretive observation which was characteristic of Charles Darwin.

See his *The Expression of the Emotions in Man and Animals*. For different sorts of exactitude, see Thompson, *On Growth and Form*, and Stroud, *Stroud's Digest on the Diseases of Birds*.

---

71   ... the scientific observer is free of value commitments in his work.

There has, of course, been ferocious debate on the subject of "value-free" science. See, for example, Gouldner, "Anti-Minotaur: The Myth of a Value-Free Sociology," and Schoeck and Wiggins (Editors,) *Scientism and Values*.

---

[53]   From Charles Sherrington, *Man on His Nature*, 2nd edition, Cambridge: Cambridge University Press, 1963, pp. 155–156. Reprinted by permission of the publisher.

It would be simplistic to assume that . . . an antiseptic atmosphere obtains in all   71
scientific work. . .

For vivid evidence that it doesn't, see Watson, *The Double Helix.*

. . . those following the tradition of Comte maintained that the methods of physics   71
and mathematics could be applied with equally satisfactory results in . . . social
science.

It is important to note that those who would argue for the principle of the
qualitative continuity in methodology between the natural and the social sciences
are not thereby bound to the view that there are unified, generic laws which hold
good for all phenomena, social as well as natural. Nagel writes: ". . . in no area
of social inquiry has a body of general laws been established, comparable with
outstanding theories in the natural sciences in scope of explanatory power or
in capacity to yield precise and reliable predictions. It is of course true that, under
the inspiration of the impressive theoretical achievements of natural science,
comprehensive systems of 'social physics' have been repeatedly constructed,
purporting to account for the entire gamut of diverse institutional structures and
changes that have appeared throughout human history. However, these am-
bitious constructions are the products of doubtfully adequate notions of what
constitutes sound scientific procedure, and, though some of them continue to
have adherents, none of them stands up under careful scrutiny."[54] Compare
Beck, "The 'Natural Science Ideal' in the Social Sciences," in Manners and Kaplan
(Editors), *Theory in Anthropology* (bibliography).

. . . on one side the claim that the proper model for the methodology of the social   71
sciences is that of the natural sciences . . .

In different terms, it has been argued that there is a qualitative continuum of
inquiry between the methodologies of the natural and the social sciences. Dewey
writes: "In the degree in which what passes for social science is built upon the
notion of a gap between natural and social phenomena, that science is truncated,
arbitrary and insecure" (*Philosophy and Civilization*, p. 82).

The arguments, in transposed and more sophisticated form, are still going on.   72

See Natanson (Editor). *Philosophy of the Social Sciences.*

. . . "ideal types," . . .   74

Weber writes: "The ideal typical concept will help to develop our skill in impu-
tation in research: it *is* no 'hypothesis' but it offers guidance to the construction

---

[54]   From Ernest Nagel, *The Structure of Science: Problems in the Logic of Scientific
Explanation*, New York: Harcourt, Brace, 1961, pp. 447–448. British rights held by
Routledge and Kegan Paul, Ltd., London. Reprinted by permission.

of hypotheses. It is not a *description* of reality but it aims to give unambiguous means of expression to such a description. . . . An ideal type is formed by the one-sided *accentuation* of one or more points of view and by the synthesis of a great many diffuse, discrete, more or less present and occasionally absent *concrete individual* phenomena, which are arranged according to those one-sidedly emphasized viewpoints into a unified *analytical* construct. . . . In its conceptual purity, this mental construct . . . cannot be found empirically anywhere in reality. It is a *utopia*."[55] According to Jaspers, "In order to compare human contexts, I must subsume them under concepts which denote their meaning—either the meaning imputed to them by the participants, or their potential bearing on other developments, or an objective meaning. Reality is an endless fabric of meaningful and meaningless factors. In order to apprehend it, we require constructed concepts which, developed with an inner logic, serve only as standards of reality: we then proceed to inquire to what degree reality conforms to them. Weber calls these constructed concepts *ideal types*. To his mind they are not reality itself, but technical instruments of investigation by which to approach reality. They do not denote classes of phenomena, they are formal patterns, by means of which we measure reality, in order, in so far as it conforms to them, to gain a pregnant formulation of it, and in order to bring out clearly the elements that do not conform to them. They are not the goal of investigation, not the laws of process, but means by which to gain the clearest awareness of the specific characteristics of the human reality in question."[56] For general studies of Weber, see: Bendix, *Max Weber*; Freund, *The Sociology of Max Weber*; and Loewenstein, *Max Weber's Political Ideas in the Perspective of Our Time* (includes an Epilogue on "Personal Recollections of Max Weber").

---

75   **He must arrange a rendezvous between the system of typifications of mundane reality and the principles of typification disclosed by science.**

See Schutz, *Collected Papers*, Volume I, pp. 62 ff.

---

75   **Tools . . . are seen as functional . . .**

See Heidegger, *Being and Time*, pp. 96 ff.

---

78   **. . . the subjective meaning the actor bestows on his own act . . .**

The subjective interpretation of meaning is an axial theme in the methodology of Max Weber and the philosophy of Alfred Schutz. It should be understood that

---

[55]   From Max Weber, *On the Methodology of the Social Sciences*, translated and edited by Edward A. Shils and Henry A. Finch. Glencoe, Ill.: Free Press, 1949, p. 90. Copyright © 1949 by The Free Press. Reprinted by permission.

[56]   From Karl Jaspers, *Three Essays: Leonardo, Descartes, Max Weber*, translated by Ralph Manheim, New York: Harcourt, Brace and World, 1964, p. 240. Canadian and British rights held by Routledge and Kegan Paul, Ltd., London. Reprinted by permission.

the term "subjective" in this context refers to the fact that meaning is related to the experiencing individual, to the individual as a "subject" of experience, and not to any private or idiosyncratic translation of experience which is limited to the individual and which may vary from person to person. Schutz writes: "There will be hardly any issue among social scientists that the object of the social sciences is human behavior, its forms, its organization, and its products. There will be, however, different opinions about whether this behavior should be studied in the same manner in which the natural scientist studies his object or whether the goal of the social sciences is the explanation of the 'social reality' as experienced by man living his everyday life within the social world. . . . we take the position that the social sciences have to deal with human conduct and its common-sense interpretation in the social reality, involving the analysis of the whole system of projects and motives, of relevances and constructs. . . . Such an analysis refers by necessity to the subjective point of view, namely, to the interpretation of the action and its settings in the terms of the actor. Since this postulate of the subjective interpretation is . . . a general principle of constructing course-of-action types in common-sense experience, any social science aspiring to grasp 'social reality' has to adopt this principle also."[57] Compare Natanson, "Alfred Schutz on Social Reality and Social Science."

. . . there are those who would insist that social science is science to the extent that its methods succeed in reaching conclusions which are intersubjectively verifiable. . .   78

See Lundberg, *Foundations of Sociology.*

. . . the last few years have seen the rise of a bold band of young social scientists . . .   78

I must disappoint the reader who may have been led to think that the members of this group are associated with an older alliance, originating in Sicily. Actually, the "band" includes individuals who disagree strongly with each other, are not all that interested in each other, and are by now well into middle age. Representatives and some of their works are: Berger, *The Precarious Vision*; Stein and Vidich (Editors), *Sociology on Trial*; Garfinkel, *Studies in Ethnomethodology*; Polsky, *Hustlers, Beats, and Others*; Engler, "Social Science and Social Consciousness"; Bay, "The Cheerful Science of Dismal Politics." Compare Mills, *The Sociological Imagination.*

. . . it is . . . suggested that the term "humanities" needs redefinition. . . . we need not involve ourselves in these disputes.   79

Those interested in the problem should read Cassirer, *The Logic of the Humanities.*

. . . we shall choose psychiatry.   79

It may be helpful to list the general literature in psychiatry drawn upon or in the background for this discussion: Jaspers, *General Psychopathology*; May, Angel,

---

[57]   Schutz, *Collected Papers*, Vol. I, p. 34. Reprinted by permission of the publisher.

and Ellenberger (Editors), *Existence*; Straus, *Phenomenological Psychology* and *On Obsession*; Binswanger, *Being-in-the-World*; Minkowski, *Traité de psychopathologie* (bibliography in French and German); Mayer-Gross, Slater, and Roth, *Clinical Psychiatry*; Sonnemann, *Existence and Therapy* (bibliography); Van Den Berg, *The Phenomenological Approach to Psychiatry*; May (Editor), *Existential Psychology* (includes an annotated bibliography by Joseph Lyons); Gendlin, *Experiencing and the Creation of Meaning*; Fromm-Reichmann, *Principles of Intensive Psychotherapy* (bibliography); Rapaport (Editor), *Organization and Pathology of Thought* (extensive bibliography).

---

83   ... the psychiatrist cannot present himself in his uniqueness as a person ...

See Robertiello, Friedman, and Pollens, *The Analyst's Role.*

---

84   **In what sense does the therapist remain an observer as he treats and cares for his fellow-man?**

See Percy, "The Symbolic Structure of Interpersonal Process."

---

86   **The concept of the "noble lie" ...**

We are, of course, utilizing and adapting Plato's phrase (see Book III of *The Republic*). The common translation of "noble lie," by the way, has been challenged. Cornford refers to it, in a note to his translation, as "... a self-contradictory expression no more applicable to Plato's harmless allegory than to a New Testament parable or the Pilgrim's Progress, and liable to suggest that he would countenance the lies, for the most part ignoble, now called propaganda" (*The Republic*, p. 106 footnote). Compare Voegelin, *Order and History*, Volume III, p. 105 footnote.

Chapter Five: History

For general works on the philosophy and methodology of history written by historians, see: Bloch, *The Historian's Craft*; Carr, *What is History?*; Smith, *The Historian and History* (bibliography); Renier, *History*; Geyl, *Debates with Historians*. For works by philosophers, see: Collingwood, *The Idea of History*; Cohen, *The Meaning of Human History*; Hook, *The Hero in History*; Rotenstreich, *Between Past and Present*; Gallie, *Philosophy and the Historical Understanding*; White, *Foundations of Historical Knowledge*; Gardiner, *The Nature of Historical Explanation*; Dray, *Philosophy of History*. A brief conspectus of problems will be found in Walsh, *Philosophy of History*. For works concerned with existential and phenomenological issues, see: Ortega y Gasset, *Toward A Philosophy of History*; Jaspers, *The Origin and Goal of History*; Ricoeur, *History and Truth*; Fackenheim, *Metaphysics and Historicity*; Nota, *Phenomenology and History* (bibliography).

The first volume of Voegelin's *Order and History* is the foundation for a major philosophy of history. Other titles of interest: Bultmann, *History and Eschatology*; Case, *The Christian Philosophy of History*; Alfred Stern, *Philosophy of History and the Problem of Values*; Weiss, *History*; Aron, *Introduction to the Philosophy of History*; Mandelbaum, *The Problem of Historical Knowledge*; Löwith, *Meaning in History*. Berlin's *The Hedgehog and the Fox* is an exciting essay; also see his *Historical Inevitability*. There is an excellent article on "The Rhetoric of History" by Hexter, listed under "Historiography" in the *International Encyclopedia of the Social Sciences* (bibliography). For detailed listings, see the "Bibliography of Works in the Philosophy of History" compiled individually by Rule, Nowicki, and Wurgaft in the journal, *History and Theory*. Anthologies include: Meyerhoff (Editor), *The Philosophy of History in our Time*; Gardiner (Editor), *Theories of History* (bibliography); and Fritz Stern (Editor), *The Varieties of History*. Additional references follow.

What the ego discovers in its aloneness is its universal nature.   90

Merleau-Ponty writes: "Every intentional object refers to consciousness but to a consciousness which is not the incarnate individual that I am as a man, living at a certain moment in time and in a certain position in space. When I carry out the phenomenological reduction, I do not bring back information concerning an external world to a self that is regarded as a part of being, nor do I substitute an internal for an external perception. I attempt rather to reveal and to make explicit in me that pure source of all meanings which constitute the world around me and my empirical self."[58]

. . . the history of intentional consciousness and that of the individual in his actual   90
biographical existence.

Husserl writes: "That the being of the world 'transcends' consciousness . . . and that it necessarily remains transcendent, in no wise alters the fact that it is conscious life alone, wherein everything transcendent becomes constituted, as something inseparable from consciousness, and which specifically, as world-consciousness, bears within itself inseparably the sense: world—and indeed: 'this actually existing' world."[59]

There might be a curious circularity between the expression and the person . . .   91

Lavater's *Essays on Physiognomy* are still well worth perusal. Also see: Picard, *The Human Face*; Brophy, *The Human Face*; Piper, *The English Face*; Bell, *The*

---

[58] From Maurice Merleau-Ponty, "Phenomenology and the Sciences of Man," translated by John Wild, in Merleau-Ponty, *The Primacy of Perception, and Other Essays on Phenomenological Psychology, the Philosophy of Art, History, and Politics* (edited by James M. Edie), Evanston, Ill.: Northwestern University Press, 1964, p. 56. Reprinted by permission of the publisher.
[59] Husserl, *Cartesian Meditations*, p. 62. Reprinted by permission of the publisher.

Anatomy and Philosophy of Expression; Sartre, "Faces, Preceded by Official Portraits"; Simmel, "The Aesthetic Significance of the Face" in *Georg Simmel 1858-1918* (edited by Wolff); Goldscheider (Editor), *Five Hundred Self-Portraits*. Lichtenberg writes: "Once in Hanover my apartment was so located that my window opened onto a narrow street which connected two large ones. It was very pleasant to see how people's faces changed when they came into the small street where they thought they were less noticed, how one man was pissing while another one over there was tying his stocking, one was laughing up his sleeve and still another shook his head. Some girls thought smilingly of the past night and arranged their ribbons for conquests in the next large street. . . . To me the most entertaining surface on the earth is the human face. . . . I once saw in Stade such peacefulness combined with a furtive smile—in the face of a fellow who had succeeded in driving his swine into a bathing place which they usually disliked entering—as I have never seen since."[60] Finally, consider the illustrations of the sculpture of F. X. Messerschmidt and the essay devoted to him in Kris, *Psychoanalytic Explorations in Art*, Chapter IV, "A Psychotic Sculptor of the Eighteenth Century."

---

91   **The temporality of the individual in Bad Faith is sealed in and abandoned to fixation . . .**

See Sartre, *Being and Nothingness*, pp. 58 ff.

---

93   **. . . we have been engaged from the outset in a form of historical investigation: the recovery of the person.**

Compare Dardel: "We ourselves are in history. It is what happens to us and our reaction to events; it is what we do with our life. History is ourselves. Outside of time and history, no one can gain access to a bay window whence he could, without risk or emotion, survey the course of events, score the points, and referee the match. To write history is also to realize its existence, to 'historicize one's self.'"[61]

---

93   **We already have studies available on *Daily Life* . . .**

The authors of the "Daily Life" books are: Mireaux, Daniel-Rops, Carcopino, and Holmes.

---

94   **. . . a structure which phenomenologists have called the "life-world."**

The theme of the "life-world" is of enormous importance to a phenomenology of the social world. Husserl's discussion of the problem is found in his *Die Krisis der*

---

[60] From Georg Christoph Lichtenberg, *The Lichtenberg Reader: Selected Writings*, translated and edited by Franz H. Mautner and Henry Hatfield, Boston: Beacon Press, 1959, p. 23. Copyright © 1959 by Franz H. Mautner and Henry Hatfield. Reprinted by permission of the publisher.

[61] From Eric Dardel, "History and Our Times," translated by Elaine P. Halperin, *Diogenes*, No. 21, 1958, p. 13. Reprinted by permission.

europäischen Wissenschaften und die transzendentale Phänomenologie (soon to appear in English), an enlightening review of which is given by Gurwitsch, *Studies in Phenomenology and Psychology*, Chapter 18, "The Last Work of Edmund Husserl." Compare Marcuse, "On Science and Phenomenology" (with comments by Gurwitsch). For studies of the "life-world" see: Schutz, *Collected Papers*, Volume III, "Some Structures of the Life-World"; Farber, *Phenomenology and Existence*, Chapter VI, "The Life-World"; Wild, "Husserl's Life-World and the Lived Body" (with comments by De Boer); and Natanson, "The *Lebenswelt*" (with comments by Kuiper).

. . . decisions to resort to experts in any sphere are made by common-sense men   96
within common-sense terms.

Compare Schutz, *Collected Papers*, Volume II, "The Well-Informed Citizen."

The life-world is not a . . . confused welter awaiting the organizational and pro-   97
motional services of the scientist.

Gurwitsch writes: "Not only must the life-world be distinguished from the universe of science in the specific modern sense—the universe of science being constructed and not immediately experienced—but the experience of the life-world, which is perceptual experience, must be taken in its original immediacy, i.e., as we have it independently of, and prior to, conceptualization of any kind."[62] It must be understood that phenomenology is not "anti-scientific"; to the contrary, it may be understood, in one sense, as a return to the Leibnitzian dream of a universal science or, in another sense, as seeking the foundations for the grounding concepts of all sciences. See Husserl's "Philosophy as Rigorous Science" (in *Phenomenology and the Crisis of Philosophy*) and his article on "Phenomenology."

. . . the point of access of the life-world to history . . .   98

For rather technical analyses of the relationship of history to the life-world, see: Ricoeur, *Husserl*, Chapter VI, "Husserl and the Sense of History"; Hohl, *Lebenswelt und Geschichte* (bibliography); and Fritz Kaufmann, "The Phenomenological Approach to History."

Relevance.   99

See Schutz, *Collected Papers,* Volume I, pp. 227 ff., 283 ff.; Volume III, pp. 117 ff. Compare Gurwitsch, *The Field of Consciousness.*

---

[62]   Gurwitsch, *Studies in Phenomenology and Psychology*, pp. 120–121. Reprinted by permission of the publisher.

100 Situation.

We have already referred to the Sartrean conception of situation. The problem has been widely treated in existential and phenomenological thought. Jaspers writes: "Strictly speaking, only an individual can be said to be in a situation. By extension, we think of the situation of groups, States, mankind; of that of such institutions as the Church, the university, the theatre; of that of science, philosophy, art, literature. When the will of the individual espouses the cause of one of these things or institutions, his will and the cause he has espoused are in a situation. In some instances, situations are unconscious, and become effective without awareness on the part of the person concerned. In other instances, situations are concretely regarded from the outlook of the self-conscious will of one who can accept them, utilise them, and transform them. A situation of which the observer or participator is conscious demands purposive behaviour in relation thereto. The situation does not lead on automatically to something inevitable, but rather it indicates certain possibilities and the limits of what is possible. What happens as a result of it is partly determined by the person who is in the situation, and by what he thinks about it. The 'grasping' of a situation modifies it, insofar as the grasping of it renders possible the adoption of a definite attitude towards it and an appeal to the tribunal of action."[63] "Situation" and "milieu" are related concepts. See Spitzer, "*Milieu* and *Ambiance*."

---

102 . . . in recent times there has arisen an ethnorhetoric of color . . .

Carmichael and Hamilton write: "Black people must redefine themselves, and only *they* can do that. Throughout this country, vast segments of the black communities are beginning to recognize the need to assert their own definitions, to reclaim their history, their culture; to create their own sense of community and togetherness. There is a growing resentment of the word 'Negro,' for example, because this term is the invention of our oppressor; it is *his* image of us that he describes. Many blacks are now calling themselves African-Americans, Afro-Americans or black people because that is *our* image of ourselves. When we begin to define our own image, the stereotypes—that is, lies—that our oppressor has developed will begin in the white community and end there. The black community will have a positive image of itself that *it* has created. This means we will no longer call ourselves lazy, apathetic, dumb, good-timers, shiftless, etc. Those are words used by white America to define us. If we accept these adjectives, as some of us have in the past, then we see ourselves only in a negative way, precisely the way white America wants us to see ourselves. Our incentive is broken and our will to fight is surrendered. From now on we shall view ourselves as African-Americans and as black people who are in fact, energetic, determined, intelligent,

---

[63] From Karl Jaspers, *Man in the Modern Age*, translated by Eden and Cedar Paul, Garden City, N.Y.: Doubleday Anchor Books, 1957, pp. 23–24. Published in Britain by Routledge and Kegan Paul, Ltd., London. Reprinted by permission.

beautiful and peace-loving."[64] Nor is the repudiation of the word "Negro" limited to black power advocates. Brotz writes in *The Black Jews of Harlem*: "The Black Jews contend that the so-called Negroes in America are really Ethiopian Hebrews or Falashas who had been stripped of their knowledge of their name and religion during slavery. The term Negro, they further contend, is a word invented by the slavemasters and imposed upon the slaves together with the white man's religion in order to demoralize them; and they did this by instilling in the slaves the view that they had no gods, no ancestors, no principles of right and wrong—nothing worthwhile—of their own.[65]

Choice. 102

We come, of course, to a fundamental category of existential philosophy. As Sartre writes: ". . . for human reality, to be is to *choose oneself*; nothing comes to it either from the outside or from within which it can *receive* or *accept*" (*Being and Nothingness*, p. 440).

Their stark but ineluctable historical weight remains and haunts any discussion of 102
the past.

"Listen to a story," Elie Wiesel says. "Once I asked an American friend why he did nothing to save European Jewry. He answered: 'We did not know what was going on.' 'Impossible,' I said. 'In 1942–43 the whole world knew. After the Warsaw Ghetto uprising, a clear, full picture was offered to anyone who wanted to see and learn. Unimpeachable documents were available: photographs, figures, facts.' 'We did not believe they were true,' my friend remarked. Suddenly he turned towards me, looked me straight in the eye, and asked: 'You were there. Do you believe it now?' Well . . . I do not believe it. The event seems unreal, as if it occurred on a different planet."[66]

. . . there is a "requiredness" we must acknowledge . . . 103

Compare the notion of "requiredness" in Köhler, *The Place of Value in a World of Facts*.

[64] From Stokely Carmichael and Charles W. Hamilton, *Black Power: The Politics of Liberation in America*, New York: Vintage Books, 1967, pp. 37–38. Copyright © 1967 by Stokely Carmichael and Charles Hamilton. British rights held by Jonathan Cape, Ltd., London. Reprinted by permission.
[65] From Howard Brotz, *The Black Jews of Harlem: Negro Nationalism and the Dilemmas of Negro Leadership*, New York: Free Press of Glencoe, 1964, p. 15. Copyright © 1964 by The Free Press of Glencoe. Reprinted by permission.
[66] From Elie Wiesel, in "Jewish Values in the Post-Holocaust Future: A Symposium," *Judaism*, Vol. XVI, 1967, p. 284. Reprinted by permission of the publisher.

103   ... neither is there any profit in trying to separate what happened from the schemas
           of understanding in which the past is placed ...

Oakeshott writes: "... what is sundered from present experience is sundered
from experience altogether. A fixed and finished past, a past divorced from and
uninfluenced by the present, is a past divorced from evidence (for evidence is
always present) and is consequently nothing and unknowable. If the historical
past be knowable, it must belong to the present world of experience; if it be unknowable, history is worse than futile, it is impossible."[67] Mead writes: "It is
idle, at least for the purposes of experience, to have recourse to a 'real' past
within which we are making constant discoveries; for that past must be set over
against a present within which the emergent appears, and the past, which must
then be looked at from the standpoint of the emergent, becomes a different past.
The emergent when it appears is always found to follow from the past, but before
it appears it does not, by definition, follow from the past. It is idle to insist upon
universal or eternal characters by which past events may be identified irrespective
of any emergent, for these are either beyond our formulation or they become so
empty that they serve no purpose in identification."[68]

104   **Choice becomes the epistemological axis on which the historical world turns.**

Consider Kierkegaard's *Fear and Trembling* and his warning in *Philosophical
Fragments*: "With slipshod thoughts, with higgling and haggling, maintaining
a little here and conceding a little there, as if the individual might to a certain
extent owe something to another, but then again to a certain extent not; with
loose words that explain everything except what this 'to a certain extent' means—
with such makeshifts it is not possible to advance beyond Socrates, nor will one
reach the concept of a Revelation, but merely remain within the sphere of idle
chatter."[69] Also see Wyschogrod, *Kierkegaard and Heidegger* (bibliography), and
Schrag, *Existence and Freedom* (bibliography).

104   **The situation of the person who understands the past in common-sense terms has
           sedimented in it the interpretive record of his age and his tradition.**

The phenomenological theme of the "sedimentation" of meaning applies to
science and history no less than to the phenomena of the life-world. As Klein
writes, an "... interlacement of original production and 'sedimentation' of significance constitutes the true character of history. From that point of view there

---

[67]   From Michael Oakeshott, *Experience and Its Modes*, Cambridge: Cambridge
University Press, 1933, p. 107. Reprinted by permission of the publisher.
[68]   From George H. Mead, *The Philosophy of the Present*, edited by Arthur E. Murphy,
Chicago: Open Court, 1932, p. 2. Reprinted by permission of The Open Court Publishing
Company, La Salle, Illinois.
[69]   From Søren Kierkegaard, *Philosophical Fragments; or, A Fragment of Philosophy*,
translated by David F. Swenson, Princeton, N.J.: Princeton University Press, 1944,
p. 7. Reprinted by permission of the publisher.

is only *one* legitimate form of history: the history of human thought. And the main problem of any historical research is precisely the disentanglement of all these strata of 'sedimentation,' with the ultimate goal of reactivating the 'original foundations,' i.e., of descending to the true beginnings, to the 'roots,' of any science and, consequently, of all prescientific conceptions of mankind as well. Moreover, a history of this kind is the only legitimate form of epistemology. The generally accepted opposition between epistemology and history, between epistemological and historical origin, is untrue. More exactly, the problem of history cannot be restricted to the finding out of 'facts' and of their connection. They embrace all stages of the 'intentional history.' History, in this understanding, cannot be separated from philosophy."[70]

The historian, like the social scientist, is methodologically free of involvement in the reality he studies . . .   105

For a contrary view, see Staughton Lynd, "A Profession of History."

. . . the initial, pre-predicative stratum of the ego's involvement . . .   106

Schutz writes: "Phenomenological analysis shows . . . that there is a pre-predicative stratum of our experience, within which the intentional objects and their qualities are not at all well circumscribed; that we do not have original experiences of isolated things and qualities, but that there is rather a field of our experiences within which certain elements are selected by our mental activities as standing out against the background of their spatial and temporal surroundings; that within the through and through connectedness of our stream of consciousness all these selected elements keep their halos, their fringes, their horizons; that an analysis of the mechanism of predicative judgment is warranted only by recourse to the mental processes in which and by which pre-predicative experience has been constituted."[71]

. . . history offers the possibility of seeing the transcendent qualities of the life-world   107

The terms "transcendent" (as well as "transcendence") and "transcendental" should not be equated. The "transcendent" refers to that which lies "outside of" or "beyond" experience, though the signs which point to transcendence and also its recognition are immanent to experience. "Transcendental" signifies the structural (or *a priori*) conditions necessary for the very possibility of experience. Compare our note on the "transcendental ego," p. 185.

---

[70] From Jacob Klein, "Phenomenology and the History of Science," in *Philosophical Essays in Memory of Edmund Husserl* (edited by Marvin Farber), Cambridge, Mass.: Harvard University Press, 1940, p. 156. Reprinted by permission of the publisher.
[71]   Schutz, *Collected Papers*, Vol. I, p. 112. Reprinted by permission of the publisher.

Chapter Six: Art

Concise introductions to the philosophy of art include Carritt, *An Introduction to Aesthetics*, and Aldrich, *Philosophy of Art*. Among larger and more far-ranging studies are: Langer, *Philosophy in a New Key* and *Feeling and Form* (both have bibliographies); Collingwood, *The Principles of Art*; Hofstadter, *Truth and Art*; Anderson, *The Realm of Art*; Kallen, *Art and Freedom*. A few modern classics: Tolstoy, *What is Art?*; Santayana, *The Sense of Beauty*; Dewey, *Art as Experience*. Anthologies: Rader (Editor), *A Modern Book of Aesthetics* (bibliography); Weitz (Editor), *Problems in Aesthetics*; Hofstadter and Kuhns (Editors), *Philosophies of Art and Beauty*; Philipson (Editor), *Aesthetics Today* (bibliography); Margolis (Editor), *Philosophy Looks at the Arts*; Vivas and Krieger (Editors), *The Problems of Aesthetics*; Levich (Editor), *Aesthetics and the Philosophy of Criticism*. Stolnitz (Editor), *Aesthetics* is a small collection. Some other titles are: Panofsky, *Meaning in the Visual Arts*; Gilson, *Painting and Reality*; Auerbach, *Mimesis*; Pepper, *The Work of Art* and *The Basis of Criticism in the Arts*; Caudwell, *Illusion and Reality* (with a variegated bibliography); Fischer, *The Necessity of Art*; Weiss, *The World of Art*; Kris, *Psychoanalytic Explorations in Art* (extensive bibliography); Rank, *Art and Artist*; Phillips (Editor), *Art and Psychoanalysis*. Two articles of importance: Heidegger, "The Origin of the Work of Art," in *Philosophies of Art and Beauty* (edited by Hofstadter and Kuhns), and Merleau-Ponty, "Eye and Mind," in his *The Primacy of Perception*. Two histories of aesthetics: Bosanquet, *A History of Aesthetic*, and Gilbert and Kuhn, *A History of Esthetics*. Among the textbooks are: Beardsley, *Aesthetics*; Stolnitz, *Aesthetics and Philosophy of Art Criticism*; Tejera, *Art and Human Intelligence*. For an antidote to texts and compendiums, see Aub, *Jusep Torres Campalans*. A final miscellany: Lipman, *What Happens in Art* (bibliography); Ducasse, *The Philosophy of Art*; Tomas (Editor), *Creativity in the Arts*; Fallico, *Art and Existentialism*; Harries, *The Meaning of Modern Art*; Langer, *Problems of Art*; and the article on "Problems of Aesthetics" by John Hospers in *The Encyclopedia of Philosophy* (bibliography). Lucas, *Art Books* is a useful bibliographical guide. The notes include other titles.

---

108   **The "re-membering" of the past is at best an effort to put together pieces and elements inherited from Others . . .**

Mead writes: "And yet the character of irrevocability is never lost. That which has happened is gone beyond recall and, whatever it was, its slipping into the past seems to take it beyond the influence of emergent events in our own conduct or in nature. It is the 'what it was' that changes, and this seemingly empty title of irrevocability attaches to it whatever it may come to be. The importance of its being irrevocable attaches to the 'what it was,' and the 'what it was' is what is not irrevocable. There is a finality that goes with the passing of every event. To every account of that event this finality is added, but the whole import of this finality belongs to the same world in experience to which this account belongs."[72]

---

[72]   Mead, *Philosophy of the Present*, p. 3. Reprinted by permission of the publisher.

At this point type gives way to symbol . . . 108

For studies of symbolism, see: Langer, *Philosophy in a New Key*; Cassirer, *An Essay on Man* and *The Philosophy of Symbolic Forms*; Wheelwright, *The Burning Fountain*; Morris, *Signs, Language, and Behavior*; Whitehead, *Symbolism*; Kahler, *Out of the Labyrinth* ("The Nature of the Symbol" in Part Two); Schutz, *Collected Papers*, Volume I, "Symbol, Reality, and Society"; Foss, *Symbol and Metaphor in Human Experience*.

. . . there is a strangeness about the art work . . . it cannot be "taken" as other 109
objects of perception are grasped . . .

Susanne Langer writes: "Every real work of art has a tendency to appear . . . dissociated from its mundane environment. The most immediate impression it creates is one of 'otherness' from reality—the impression of an illusion enfolding the thing, action, statement, or flow of sound that constitutes the work. Even where the element of representation is absent, where nothing is imitated or feigned in a lovely textile, a pot, a building, a sonata—this air of illusion, of being a sheer image, exists as forcibly as in the most deceptive picture or the most plausible narrative. Where an expert in the particular art in question perceives immediately a 'rightness and necessity' of forms, the unversed but sensitive spectator perceives only a peculiar air of 'otherness,' which has been variously described as 'strangeness,' 'semblance,' 'illusion,' 'transparency,' 'autonomy,' or 'self-sufficiency.'"[73]

The art work cannot be taken directly . . . 110

Compare Husserl's discussion of "neutrality-modification" in his *Ideas*, pp. 309 ff.

In its distinctive aesthetic station . . . the art work stands forth as unlike other 110
objects we perceive.

On the nature of the "aesthetic object," see: Pepper, *The Work of Art*; Ritchie, "The Formal Structure of the Aesthetic Object"; Wellek and Warren, *Theory of Literature*, Chapter XII, "The Mode of Existence of a Literary Work of Art."

. . . though the artist is responsible for his work, he is not its permanent master nor 112
even the chief authority on its interpretation.

Compare: Goldwater and Treves (Editors), *Artists on Art*; Rodman, *Conversations with Artists*; Friedenthal (Editor), *Letters of the Great Artists*; *The Complete Letters of Vincent Van Gogh*; Lord, *A Giacometti Portrait*; and, most emphatically, Shahn, *The Shape of Content*.

---

[73] From Susanne K. Langer, *Feeling and Form: A Theory of Art*, New York: Charles Scribner's Sons, 1953, pp. 45–46. British rights held by Routledge and Kegan Paul, Ltd., London. Reprinted by permission.

113   . . . the individual's recognition that the art work calls upon him in a special way . . .
       Compare Lipman, *What Happens in Art*, Chapter VII, "The Problem of Self."

---

114   **What puzzles and disturbs us is the anchorage of the art work . . .**
       Compare Pepper, *The Work of Art*, Chapter I, "What is a Work of Art?"

---

114   . . . **in the novel the reader is presented with a *world* . . .**
       On the general concept of "world" see Landgrebe, "The World as a Phenomeno-
       logical Problem," and Werkmeister, "On 'Describing a World.'" On "world" in
       literature, see Natanson, *Literature, Philosophy, and the Social Sciences*, Chapter
       VIII, "Phenomenology and the Theory of Literature." Implicit in the philo-
       sophical analysis of "world" in literature is the tension between philosophy and
       literature. Simone de Beauvoir writes: "I read a good deal when I was eighteen:
       I read as few people do except at that age, with naiveté and passion. When I
       opened a novel I really entered a new world—a concrete, temporal world full of
       strange figures and events; and a philosophical treatise carried me beyond earthly
       appearances into the serenity of an intemporal sky. In both cases, I remember
       the dizzy surprise that overcame me the moment I closed the book. After having
       thought the universe through Spinoza or Kant, I asked myself: 'How can anyone
       be so frivolous as to write novels?' But when I left Julian Sorel or Tess of the
       D'Urbervilles, it seemed to me a waste of time to devise philosophical systems.
       Where did the truth reside? On earth or in eternity? It seemed to me that I was
       being pulled apart."[74]

---

115   . . . **in that "real as you are" reality of may-being.**
       I was led to the coinage "may-being" by the language of Charles Sanders Peirce:
       ". . . there is a possible, or potential, point-place wherever a point might be placed;
       but that which only *may be* is necessarily thereby *indefinite*, and as such, it is not
       subject to the principle of contradiction, just as the negation of a may-be, which
       is of course a *must-be*, (I mean that if 'S *may be* P' is untrue, then '*S must be* non-P'
       is true), in those respects in which it is such, is not subject to the principle of
       excluded middle. This renders may-be's and must-be's very delicate objects for
       thought to handle, and propositions concerning them that sound absurd some-

---

[74]   From Simone de Beauvoir, "Two Essays: 'Literature and Metaphysics' and 'Freedom
       and Liberation,'" translated by Ralph Manheim, in *Art and Action: Twice A Year—
       1938–1948*, 10th Anniversary Issue, New York: Twice A Year Press, 1948, p. 86.
       Reprinted by permission.

times express plain facts. This, however, is a matter that I cannot pretend to have got to the bottom of; and logic here seems to touch metaphysics."[75]

**. . . certain characters in fiction . . . are as "real" as some fellow-men, more real   116
than some ghosty Others.**

Hospers writes: "Becky Sharp never existed in the flesh, yet the world is full of Becky Sharps, and probably Thackeray's heroine is a truer, more convincing picture of Becky Sharps everywhere than any of the particular historical members of the class ever have been or will be. Nor did anyone in history probably have quite the set of experiences related by Thackeray; yet they give expression to the character more fully and convincingly, probably, than any that the historical Becky Sharps ever went through. This, I think, is approximately what is meant when it is said that characters in great literature are *universal*."[76] Compare the dying and death of Little Nell in Dickens's *The Old Curiosity Shop*, which in the original serialization produced a dramatic response in letters from readers, who pleaded with the author not to let Little Nell die and who later mourned her passionately. G. K. Chesterton writes in his article on Dickens in the *Encyclo-paedia Britannica*: "He was flattered because silly people wrote him letters imploring him not to let Little Nell die; and forgot how many sensible people there were, only hoping that the Marchioness would live for ever. Little Nell was better dead, but she was an unconscionable long time dying . . ." (14th edition, Volume VII, p. 333).

**The symbolic . . . is that which announces, presents . . . meaning whose elements are   117
in the mundane world . . .**

Croce warns that ". . . the *symbol* has sometimes been given as the essence of art. Now, if the symbol be conceived as inseparable from the artistic intuition, it is a synonym for the intuition itself, which always has an ideal character. There is no double bottom to art, but one only; in art all is symbolical, because all is ideal. But if the symbol be conceived as separable—if the symbol can be on one side, and on the other the thing symbolized, we fall back again into the intellectualist error: the so-called symbol is the exposition of an abstract concept, an *allegory*; it is science, or art aping science."[77]

---

[75]   From Charles Sanders Peirce, *Collected Papers:* Vol. VI, *Scientific Metaphysics*, edited by Charles Hartshorne and Paul Weiss, Cambridge, Mass.: The Belknap Press of Harvard University Press, 1960, pp. 128–129. Reprinted by permission of the publisher. (It is usual, by the way, to refer to Peirce's writings by paragraph number rather than by page—something the curious reader may keep in mind if he goes to this volume and consults its index—but there is little point in doing that here.)

[76]   From John Hospers, *Meaning and Truth in the Arts*, Chapel Hill: University of North Carolina Press, 1946, p. 167. Reprinted by permission of the publisher.

[77]   From Benedetto Croce, *Aesthetic: As Science of Expression and General Linguistic*, translated by Douglas Ainslie, New York: Noonday Press, 1960, p. 34. Reprinted by permission of Farrar, Straus and Giroux, Inc., New York, and Vision Press, Ltd., London.

118   ... such concepts as "identity crisis."

See Erikson, *Identity and the Life Cycle*, Chapter III, "The Problem of Ego Identity."

---

120   ... the many "provinces of meaning" which compose human reality.

See James, *The Principles of Psychology*, Volume II, Chapter XXI, "The Perception of Reality," and Schutz, *Collected Papers*, Volume I, "On Multiple Realities."

---

120   ... comprehensible in terms of a fundamental "base," a point of departure and return.

For Schutz, that "base" is the paramount reality of the world of working. He writes: "The world of working as a whole stands out as paramount over against the many other sub-universes of reality. It is the world of physical things, including my body; it is the realm of my locomotions and bodily operations; it offers resistances which require effort to overcome; it places tasks before me, permits me to carry through my plans, and enables me to succeed or to fail in my attempt to attain my purposes. By my working acts I gear into the outer world, I change it; and these changes, although provoked by my working, can be experienced and tested both by myself and others, as occurrences within this world independently of my working acts in which they originated. I share this world and its objects with Others; with Others, I have ends and means in common; I work with them in manifold social acts and relationships, checking the Others and checked by them. And the world of working is the reality within which communication and the interplay of mutual motivation becomes effective."[78]

---

120   ... the naive attitude of daily life must be bracketed ...

Contrast Dewey, who writes: "The enemies of the aesthetic are neither the practical nor the intellectual. They are the humdrum; slackness of loose ends; submission to convention in practice and intellectual procedure. Rigid abstinence, coerced submission, tightness on one side and dissipation, incoherence and aimless indulgence on the other, are deviations in opposite directions from the unity of an experience."[79]

---

123   Let us speak ... of a "genetic phenomenology" whose object is ... descriptive uncovering and analysis ...

"Genetic phenomenology" is concerned with tracing out the intentional history of phenomena, in contrast to the genetic method in psychology, which is concerned,

---

[78]   Schutz, *Collected Papers*, Vol. I, pp. 226–227. Reprinted by permission of the publisher.

[79]   From John Dewey, *Art as Experience*, New York: Minton, Balch, 1934, p. 40. Copyright, 1934, by John Dewey. Reprinted by permission of G. P. Putnam's Sons.

generally, with the causal history of events. The two methods are radically different yet not totally unrelated. Farber comments: "The phenomenological 'genetic' method has meaning within the framework of the phenomenological philosophy. Its difference from the ordinary genetic method is to be traced to the difference between the natural and the pure reflective attitudes, although *qua* descriptive methods they have features in common. Each type of method has its range of achievement. If one of them is able to bear forests on its back, it also turns out that it cannot crack a nut."[80]

A "genetic phenomenology" is concerned with tracing out the history of the ego . . .   123

And that has been our concern in this book.

To be "here" in terms of abandonment is to be thrown or thrust into the world . . .   125

See Heidegger, *Being and Time*, pp. 172 ff.

To find oneself alone in the world means that choice and decision are individual determinations . . .   125

Sartre writes: "The existentialist frankly states that man is in anguish. His meaning is as follows—When a man commits himself to anything, fully realizing that he is not only choosing what he will be, but is thereby at the same time a legislator deciding for the whole of mankind—in such a moment a man cannot escape from the sense of complete and profound responsibility."[81]

. . . to speak of *each* man's situation is to recognise an absolute.   126

Compare Vassar Miller, "The Common Core":

"Each man's sorrow is an absolute
Each man's pain is a norm
No one can prove and no one refute.
Which is the blacker, coal or soot?
Which blows fiercer, gale or storm?
Each man's sorrow is an absolute.

---

[80] From Marvin Farber, "Phenomenology," in *Twentieth Century Philosophy: Living Schools of Thought* (edited by Dagobert D. Runes), New York: Philosophical Library, 1943, p. 367. Reprinted by permission of the publisher.

[81] From Jean-Paul Sartre, "Existentialism and Humanism," translated by Philip Mairet, in *Existentialism from Dostoevsky to Sartre* (edited by Walter Kaufmann), New York: Meridian Books, 1956, p. 292. Also available as a book, *Existentialism and Humanism*, London: Methuen, 1948. Reprinted by permission of Methuen and Co., Ltd., and the Philosophical Library.

No man's sickness has a synonym,
No man's disease has a double.
You weep for your love, I for my limbs—
Who mourns for reason? who over whims?
For, self-defined as a pebble,
No man's sickness has a synonym.

Gangrene is fire and cancer is burning.
Which one's deadlier? Toss
A coin to decide; past your discerning
Touch the heart's center, still and unturning,
That common core of the Cross;
You die of fire and I die of burning."[82]

---

126   **. . . each man is responsible for himself and his time.**

Sartre writes: ". . . man being condemned to be free carries the weight of the whole world on his shoulders; he is responsible for the world and for himself as a way of being" (*Being and Nothingness*, p. 553).

---

127   **. . . the responsibility not only of interpreting art but of rendering its interpretations microcosmic orders, cosmions of meaning.**

The problem of symbolic interpretation has implications for spheres other than art. See the discussion of "representation" in Voegelin's *The New Science of Politics*.

---

127   **In the crossing of art's transcendence with the person's existential engagement there comes into being the "concrete universal," . . .**

We are utilizing but also adapting Hegel's "concrete universal." See *The Logic of Hegel*.

Chapter Seven: Religion

For brief introductions to the philosophy of religion, see Frank, *Philosophical Understanding and Religious Truth*, and Hick, *Philosophy of Religion*. Among other surveys are: Ducasse, *A Philosophical Scrutiny of Religion;* Hutchison, *Faith, Reason, and Existence*; Wells, *God, Man, and the Thinker* (bibliography). Anthologies include: Hick (Editor), *The Existence of God* and *Classical and Contemporary Readings in the Philosophy of Religion* (the Appendix to this work

---

[82] Vassar Miller, "The Common Core," in *Wage War on Silence: A Book of Poems*, Middletown, Conn.: Wesleyan University Press, 1960. Copyright © 1957 by Vassar Miller. Reprinted by permission of the publisher.

includes a bibliography); Alston (Editor), *Religious Belief and Philosophical Thought*; Hartshorne and Reese (Editors), *Philosophers Speak of God.* Some psychological studies are: Freud, *The Future of an Illusion*; Jung, *Psychology and Religion*; Fromm, *Psychoanalysis and Religion.* For books concerned with existential problems, see: Tillich, *Dynamics of Faith*; Bonhoeffer, *The Cost of Discipleship* and *Letters and Papers from Prison*; Weil, *Waiting for God*; Earle, Edie, and Wild, *Christianity and Existentialism.* In the phenomenological tradition, see: Van Der Leeuw, *Religion in Essence and Manifestation*; Otto, *The Idea of the Holy*; Scheler, *On the Eternal in Man* and *Man's Place in Nature*; Duméry, *The Problem of God.* For a more nearly analytic approach: Martin, *Religious Belief*; Flew and MacIntyre (Editors), *New Essays in Philosophical Theology*; and compare Paton, *The Modern Predicament.* A last batch: Pike (Editor), *God and Evil*; Cogley (Editor), *Religion in America*; Wild, *Human Freedom and Social Order*; Guttmann, *Philosophies of Judaism* (bibliography). Additional citations follow.

. . . a survey of the place of religion in the lives of men.   128

See James, *The Varieties of Religious Experience,* and Van Der Leeuw, *Religion in Essence and Manifestation.*

Let us say that the transcendent is "appresented" beyond the typifications of common sense.   128

See Schutz, *Collected Papers*, Volume I, "Symbol, Reality, and Society."

Repeatability.   129

See Husserl, *Cartesian Meditations*, p. 60. Schutz writes: ". . . all projecting involves a particular idealization, called by Husserl the idealization of 'I-can-do-it-again,' i.e., the assumption that I may under typically similar circumstances act in a way typically similar to that in which I acted before in order to bring about a typically similar state of affairs" (*Collected Papers*, Volume I, p. 20).

Continuity. A kind of *et cetera* shadows each typification.   130

Schutz writes: ". . . the idealization of 'and so forth and so on' . . . implies the assumption, *valid until counter-evidence appears*, that what has been proved to be adequate knowledge so far will also in the future stand the test" (*Collected Papers*, Volume II, pp. 285–286). The idealizations of "I can do it again" and "and so forth and so on" are corollaries. Compare Jonas: "In viewing an object there is the situation of a 'vis-à-vis,' which discloses the object as the terminal of a dimension leading from me toward it, and this dimension lies open before me. The facing across a distance thus discloses the distance itself as something I am free to traverse; it is an invitation to forward motion, putting the intervening space at my disposal. The dynamics of perspective depth connects me with the projected terminus. The terminus itself is arbitrary in each given case, and my glance even if focused on it includes as a background the open field of other presences behind it, just as it includes, as a corona fading toward the edges, the manifold co-present in the plane. This indefinite 'and so on' with which the visual perception is imbued, an ever-ready potential for realization, and especially the 'and so on' in depth, is the birthplace of the idea of *infinity*, to which no other sense could supply the experiential basis."[83]

---

131   **. . . each life is, in its historical unfolding, unrepeatable and severed by death.**

It may be helpful at this point to present some of the literature concerning philosophical problems of death. Choron's *Modern Man and Mortality* (comprehensive bibliography) and *Death and Western Thought* are very useful surveys. Feifel (Editor), *The Meaning of Death* includes essays by psychologists, psychiatrists, and philosophers. Also see: Unamuno, *The Tragic Sense of Life*; Ferrater Mora, *Being and Death*; Boros, *The Mystery of Death*; Fulton (Editor), *Death and Identity* (detailed bibliography, chiefly of psychological literature); Eissler, *The Psychiatrist and the Dying Patient* (bibliography); Scott (Editor), *The Modern Vision of Death*. Among memoirs: Gunther, *Death Be Not Proud*; Wertenbaker, *Death of a Man*; Beauvoir, *A Very Easy Death*. Two shorter works deserve special mention: Dolci, "What Does It Mean, to Die?" and Landsberg, "The Experience of Death." In literature, Tolstoy's "The Death of Ivan Ilych" may be mentioned again and Agee's *A Death in the Family* added. For a diversion, see Richardson and Toynbee, *Thanatos*.

---

132   **. . . I place in abeyance the most hurtful possibility of all, my death, and live in the faith that it will not occur.**

As Freud writes: ". . . at bottom no one believes in his own death . . ." ("Thoughts for the Times on War and Death," p. 223).

---

133   **. . . stages along death's way" . . .**

Our paraphrastic theft is from Kierkegaard.

---

134   **. . . what has been experienced . . . must . . . be broken down into its primal elements . . . in order to rebuild a world.**

This is the procedure followed in some of the plays of Samuel Beckett.

---

134   **. . . we must die to fulfill our historical possibilities.**

Compare Koestler, *Darkness at Noon*, and Camus, *The Rebel*.

---

[83] From Hans Jonas, *The Phenomenon of Life: Toward a Philosophical Biology*, New York: Harper and Row, 1966, p. 150. Reprinted by permission of the publisher.

The shattering of the We reverberates throughout the social world.   136

And the work of man is, as Buber says, "to make the broken world whole" (quoted
in Friedman, *Martin Buber*, p. 101).

... it is not "you" who will die, but "they," ...   136

Heidegger writes: "*The 'they' does not permit us the courage for anxiety in the face
of death.* The dominance of the manner in which things have been publicly interpreted by the 'they,' has already decided what state-of-mind is to determine
our attitude towards death" (*Being and Time*, p. 298). Note: for a small book on
Heidegger see Grene, *Martin Heidegger*; for a big one, see Richardson, *Heidegger*
(bibliography). Also see Mehta, *The Philosophy of Martin Heidegger* (bibliography).

... death is a possibility hidden to the self, a secret that will be disclosed only in the   137
progression to sociality.

This theme is subtly presented in Agee's *A Death in the Family*.

... the individual student ... is also himself, bearer of his biographical situation,   139
maneuverer within his skin-envelope, noisemaker to the world.

Meeting that student on the far side of individuality may lead to the paradox of
madness and morality suggested in Trilling's story, "Of This Time, Of That Place."

In the case of religious response, let us say broadly that the response is to ultimacy ...   141

We are using the word "ultimacy" in Tillich's sense. See, for example, his *Dynamics of Faith*, pp. 9 ff. On page 11 he writes: "In terms like ultimate, uncon-
ditional, infinite, absolute, the difference between subjectivity and objectivity is
overcome. The ultimate of the act of faith and the ultimate that is meant in the
act of faith are one and the same."

It is not necessary to make ontological claims about the status of the object of   142
response ...

Compare Duméry, *The Problem of God*.

The range of transcendence ... remains a creative mystery.   144

We are using the term "mystery" in Marcel's sense. He distinguishes between a
"problem" and a "mystery": "A problem is something which I meet, which I
find complete before me, but which I can therefore lay siege to and reduce. But
a mystery is something in which I am myself involved, and it can therefore only
be thought of as a sphere where the distinction between what is in me and what

is before me loses its meaning and its initial validity. A genuine problem is subject to an appropriate technique by the exercise of which it is defined: whereas a mystery, by definition, transcends every conceivable technique. It is, no doubt, always possible (logically and psychologically) to degrade a mystery so as to turn it into a problem. But this is a fundamentally vicious proceeding, whose springs might perhaps be discovered in a kind of corruption of the intelligence."[84] And in *The Philosophy of Existence*, Marcel writes: "A mystery is a problem which encroaches upon its own data, invading them, as it were, and thereby transcending itself as a simple problem" (p. 8). Compare his *The Mystery of Being*, Volume I. There Marcel warns: "The opposition between the problem and the mystery is always in danger of being exploited in a tiresomely 'literary' way by writers without a proper philosophic grounding, who lose sight of the technical relevance of the distinction. The sort of philosophy that I have been trying to present to you in this volume makes a very special appeal to the eloquent amateur, and that, in fact, is one of its most disquieting features . . . ."[85]

---

145   **. . . to be "real" is to be "meant-as-real."**

Compare Spiegelberg, "The 'Reality-Phenomenon' and Reality."

---

146   **Isn't the entire history of consciousness, as developed in our story, out of touch with praxis . . . ?**

On "praxis" see Sartre, *Search for a Method*. For another approach, see Rudich, "The Dialectics of Poesis."

---

147   **For some . . . phenomenological suspension turns away from societal and historical struggle in favor of a transcendental quietism . . .**

For others, however, as Sartre points out in *The Transcendence of the Ego*, "The phenomenologists have plunged man back into the world; they have given full measure to man's agonies and sufferings, and also to his rebellions" (p. 105).

---

147   **. . . the historically consequential force of the undermined ego, the devastation of false consciousness.**

See Mannheim, *Ideology and Utopia*, pp. 62 ff., and Marcuse, *One-Dimensional Man*, Chapter VIII, "The Historical Commitment of Philosophy."

---

[84]   From Gabriel Marcel, *Being and Having: An Existentialist Diary*, translated by Katherine Farrer, New York: Harper Torchbooks, 1965, p. 117. Published in Britain by Dacre Press, A. and C. Black, Ltd., London. Reprinted by permission.

[85]   From Gabriel Marcel, *The Mystery of Being*, translated by G. S. Fraser, Chicago: Henry Regnery (Gateway Edition), 1960, Vol. I, p. 261. Reprinted by permission of the publisher.

... to repudiate a "cowboys and Indians" scenario of history in which the good   147
guys are analysts ...

Collingwood writes: "... philosophical controversies are not to be settled by a
kind of police-regulation governing people's choice of words, and ... a school of
thought (to dignify it by that name) which depends for its existence on enforcing
a particular jargon is a school which I neither respect nor fear" (*The Principles of
Art*, p. 255). On the other hand, it might be said that there is philosophical
safety in schools. Philosophy has a Victorian penchant for never throwing anything away. As Philip Blair Rice says, "The history of philosophy is capacious
and tolerant: it preserves not only the great rigorous system-builders and the
great lucid destroyers but also some of the muddleheads, the eccentrics, and even
the stinkers, provided they can suggest possible styles of life or possible perspectives on reality" ("Existentialism and the Self," p. 216).

Conclusion

The literature which reflects on philosophy, its nature and its methods, is relevant
here: Collingwood, *An Essay on Philosophical Method*; Bocheński, *The Methods
of Contemporary Thought*; Hall, *Philosophical Systems*; Kaiser, *An Essay on
Method*; Radnitzky, *Contemporary Schools of Metascience* (bibliography); Buchler,
The Concept of Method. Related references follow.

... what appears to be "straight" may be slanted by the moral stance of the critic.   151

Compare Ross, *Portrait of Hemingway*, and Meyerhoff, "'The New Yorker' in
Hollywood."

Isn't the reporter aware to begin with that what he is describing is uncivilized,   151
inhumane, morally appalling?

So Leo Strauss asks, "Is it not the plain duty of the social scientist truthfully and
faithfully to present social phenomena? How can we give a causal explanation
of a social phenomenon if we do not first see it as what it is? Do we not know
petrifaction or spiritual emptiness when we see it? And if someone is incapable
of seeing phenomena of this kind, is he not disqualified by this very fact from
being a social scientist, just as much as a blind man is disqualified from being an
analyst of painting?"[86]

"What about the need for therapeutic intent?"   151

I have borrowed the phrase "therapeutic intent" from Zilboorg. See his *Mind,
Medicine, and Man*.

---

[86]   From Leo Strauss, *Natural Right and History*, Chicago: University of Chicago Press,
1953, pp. 49–50. Reprinted by permission.

151   . . . it is difficult to establish an absolute frontier between description and analysis . . .

See Brown, *Explanation in Social Science*, Chapter II, "Social Description."

---

152   **To cut something up into pieces, to take it apart, to break it down is, it would appear, to dishonor its vital principle . . .**

It might also be argued that a corollary of conceptual dissection is methodological dispersal, the proliferation of disciplines each of which studies a disembodied fragment. Riezler writes: "We have discarded eternal man and cut mutable man into pieces to be inquired into by different sciences, each of which claims autonomy. The pieces fit into one another less and less. A relatively immutable remnant, called human nature, is left to the care of a biology that speaks the language of physics and chemistry. In this language the mammal we call Man is meaningless to himself."[87]

---

152   **The fear is of philosophy: radical reflection on experience changes not only experience but the experiencer.**

It might be asked how this is evidenced in the lives of philosophers. Here is a scattered sampling of philosophical autobiography, biography, letters, and memoirs: Saint Augustine, *Confessions*; Rousseau, *Confessions*; *The Autobiography of Michel de Montaigne* (edited by Lowenthal); Maimon, *Autobiography*; Mill, *Autobiography*; Russell, *Autobiography*; section on "Personal Depression and Recovery" in *The Writings of William James* (edited by McDermott); Santayana, *Persons and Places*; Collingwood, *Autobiography*; Marcel, *The Existential Background of Human Dignity*; Moore, " An Autobiography" in *The Philosophy of G. E. Moore* (edited by Schilpp); Cohen, *A Dreamer's Journey*; Sartre, *The Words*; Berdyaev, *Dream and Reality*; Feibleman, *Philosophers Lead Sheltered Lives*; *The Correspondence of Spinoza* (edited by Wolf); *The Journals of Søren Kierkegaard* (edited by Dru); *The Letters of George Santayana* (edited by Cory); Engelmann, *Letters from Ludwig Wittgenstein*; Marcel, *Metaphysical Journal*; Bugbee, *The Inward Morning*; Chesterton, *St. Thomas Aquinas*; McGill, *Schopenhauer*; Lowrie, *Kierkegaard*; Zweig, *Master Builders* (section on Nietzsche); Hollingdale, *Nietzsche*; Allen, *William James*; Cory, *Santayana*; Shestov, "In Memory of a Great Philosopher: Edmund Husserl"; Staude, *Max Scheler*; Hook, *John Dewey*; Dickinson J. McT. E. McTaggart; Farquharson, "Memoir," in John Cook Wilson, *Statement and Inference*, Volume I; Glatzer, *Franz Rosenzweig*; Edmund Wilson, *Europe without Baedeker* (the fragment on Norman Kemp Smith in Chapter XVI "Homecoming: Final Reflections"); Malcolm, *Ludwig Wittgenstein*; Beauvoir *Prime of Life* and *Force of Circumstance*; Sartre, *Situations* (section on Merleau Ponty); and finally, *Dialogues of Alfred North Whitehead* (recorded by Price).

---

[87]   From Kurt Riezler, *Man, Mutable and Immutable: The Fundamental Structure of Social Life*, Chicago: Henry Regnery, 1950, p. vii. Reprinted by permission of the publisher.

**It is extremely difficult to say what leads the individual to effect such a   153
transposition.**

Waismann writes: "It is notorious that a philosophy is not made, it grows. You
don't choose a puzzle, you are shocked into it" ("How I See Philosophy," p. 379).

**Argument . . . must arise within the reality of the thinker if it is to have relevance   153
for the history of the self.**

See Natanson and Johnstone (Editors), *Philosophy, Rhetoric, and Argumentation*
(bibliography), and Johnstone, *Philosophy and Argument*.

When is a doubt reasonable?   154

This question proved to be troublesome to jurors in the trials of Alger Hiss. See
Cooke, *A Generation on Trial*. Referring to Judge Goddard's charge to the jury
in the second trial, Cooke writes: "The Government was not required to prove . . .
'beyond all possible doubt. For if that were the rule, very few people would ever
be convicted.' It must be done 'beyond a reasonable doubt,' which he—coming
after Mr. Stryker, Mr. Murphy, Judge Kaufman, and Mr. Cross—was the fifth
man to redefine. To Judge Goddard it did not mean 'a doubt arbitrarily or
capriciously asserted' to avoid an unpleasant task, nor 'a possible doubt or a
fanciful doubt,' nor a doubt 'arising from the natural sympathy which we all
have for others.' It was 'a doubt which a reasonable person has after carefully
weighing all the testimony.' They should be governed by 'the convincing force
of the testimony.'"[88]

**There must come a moment or a point in his deliberations when he *sees* that   154
something is the case.**

Compare Gass, "The Case of the Obliging Stranger."

I have tried . . . to jostle the reader into a change of conceptual attitude . . .   154

Style and method are integral, though there are, of course, other styles and other
methods. See Bouwsma's *Philosophical Essays*, of which Anne Lloyd Thomas
writes in a review: "Bouwsma's style is important; the wit, anecdote and drama-
ization with which the papers are packed are not incidental but are crucial to
his treatment of problems. Any attempt to restate his theses stripped of this
wealth of elaborative and illustrative material does not just render them duller and
less original in tone; it does, I believe, destroy something essential to Bouwsma's

---

[8]   From Alistair Cooke, *A Generation on Trial: U.S.A. v. Alger Hiss*, New York:
Alfred A. Knopf, 1952, p. 324. Copyright 1950, 1952 by Alistair Cooke. Reprinted by
permission.

approach. This is not to say that his theses can only be stated metaphorically, but it should indicate the kind of complexity which they possess . . ."[89] Compare Blanshard, *On Philosophical Style*.

---

155   . . . the persuader must risk himself through inquiry.

Again, see Natanson and Johnstone (Editors), *Philosophy, Rhetoric, and Argumentation*, especially pp. 11 ff.

---

155   . . . philosophical experience is achieved by the action of the individual . . .

In Husserl's words, ". . . anyone who seriously intends to become a philosopher must 'once in his life' withdraw into himself and attempt, within himself, to overthrow and build anew all the sciences that, up to then, he has been accepting. Philosophy—wisdom . . .—is the philosophizer's quite personal affair. It must arise as *his* wisdom, as his self-acquired knowledge tending toward universality, a knowledge for which he can answer from the beginning, and at each step, by virtue of his own absolute insights."[90]

---

156   . . . the secret concern of philosophy is to resolve the imbalance between the universal and the concrete.

Simmel writes: "Philosophical thinking objectifies the personal and personalizes the objective. For philosophy expresses the most profound and ultimate aspect of a personal attitude toward the world in the language of an image of the world. And just because of this, it depicts an image of the world according to certain directional lines and a certain total significance. Choosing among these will always be a matter of the differences among essential human traits and types."[91]

---

156   . . . all dialectic is a mode of indirection.

See Kierkegaard's discussion of "indirect communication" in his *Training in Christianity*, pp. 132 ff.

---

156   . . . philosophy threatens to leave the individual unprotected . . .

Ortega y Gasset says it this way: "Philosophy, then, is not a science but, if you like, an indecency, since it consists in baring things and oneself, stripping them to stark nakedness—to what they are and I am—and that is all" (*Man and People*, p. 99).

---

[89]   From Anne Lloyd Thomas, Review of *Philosophical Essays* by O. K. Bouwsma, *Mind*, Vol. LXXVI, 1967, p. 606. Reprinted by permission.

[90]   Husserl, *Cartesian Meditations*, p. 2. Reprinted by permission of the publisher.

[91]   Simmel, *Sociology of Georg Simmel*, p. 298. Reprinted by permission of the publisher

bibliography*

Aaron, R. I., "Our Knowledge of One Another," *Philosophy*, Vol. XIX, 1944, pp. 63–75.

Adrian, E. D., *The Physical Background of Perception*, Oxford: Clarendon Press, 1947.

Agee, James, *A Death in the Family*, New York: McDowell, Obolensky, 1957.

————, and Walker Evans, *Let Us Now Praise Famous Men: Three Tenant Families*, New York: Ballantine Books, 1966.

Aldrich, Virgil C., *Philosophy of Art*, Englewood Cliffs, N.J.: Prentice-Hall, 1963.

Allen, Gay Wilson, *William James: A Biography*, New York: Viking Press, 1967.

Allport, Gordon W., *Personality: A Psychological Interpretation*, New York: Henry Holt, 1937.

Alston, William P. (Editor), *Religious Belief and Philosophical Thought: Readings in the Philosophy of Religion*, New York: Harcourt, Brace and World, 1963.

Anderson, John M., *The Realm of Art*, University Park: Pennsylvania State University Press, 1967.

Arber, Agnes, *The Mind and the Eye: A Study of the Biologist's Standpoint*, Cambridge: Cambridge University Press, 1964.

Aron, Raymond, *German Sociology*, translated by Mary and Thomas Bottomore, New York: Free Press of Glencoe, 1964.

---

* This list is restricted to titles mentioned in the book. Reprint editions are often cited, and so the date given is not always that of original publication.

————, *Introduction to the Philosophy of History: An Essay on the Limits of Historical Objectivity*, translated by George J. Irwin, Boston: Beacon Press, 1961.

————, *Main Currents of Sociological Thought*, translated by Richard Howard and Helen Weaver, New York: Basic Books. Vol. I: *Montesquieu, Comte, Marx, Tocqueville: The Sociologists and the Revolution of 1848*, 1965; Vol. II: *Durkheim, Pareto, Weber*, 1967.

Asbury, Edith Evans, "Protestors Boo Shriver at Talk on 'Struggle for Urban Power,'" *The New York Times*, March 3, 1968, p. 50.

Aub, Max, *Jusep Torres Campalans*, translated by Herbert Weinstock, Garden City, N.Y.: Doubleday, 1962.

Auerbach, Erich, *Mimesis: The Representation of Reality in Western Literature*, translated by Willard Trask, Garden City, N.Y.: Doubleday Anchor Books, 1957.

Augustine, Saint, *The Confessions*, translated by Edward B. Pusey with an Introduction by Fulton J. Sheen, New York: Modern Library, 1949.

Austin, J. L., *Philosophical Papers*, Oxford: Clarendon Press, 1961.

Ayer, Alfred Jules, *The Concept of a Person, and Other Essays*, New York: St. Martin's Press, 1963.

————, *Language, Truth, and Logic*, New York: Dover, 1946.

Bachelard, Gaston, *The Poetics of Space*, translated by Maria Jolas, New York: Orion Press, 1964.

Baldwin, James, *The Fire Next Time*, New York: Dell, 1967.

Bannan, John F., *The Philosophy of Merleau-Ponty*, New York: Harcourt, Brace and World, 1967.

Banton, Michael, *Roles: An Introduction to the Study of Social Relations*, New York: Basic Books, 1965.

Barnes, Harry Elmer (Editor), *An Introduction to the History of Sociology*, Chicago: University of Chicago Press, 1948.

Barrault, Jean-Louis, *Le Phénomène théâtral*, Oxford: Clarendon Press, 1961.

Barrett, William, *Irrational Man: A Study in Existential Philosophy*, Garden City, N.Y.: Doubleday Anchor Books, 1962.

————, *What Is Existentialism?*, New York: Grove Press, 1964.

————, and Henry D. Aiken (Editors), *Philosophy in the Twentieth Century: An Anthology*, 2 volumes, New York: Random House, 1962.

Baumann, Bedřich, "George H. Mead and Luigi Pirandello: Some Parallels between the Theoretical and Artistic Presentation of the Social Role Concept," *Social Research*, Vol. XXXIV, 1967, pp. 563–607.

Bay, Christian, "The Cheerful Science of Dismal Politics," in *The Dissenting Academy* (edited by Theodore Roszak), New York: Pantheon Books, 1967, pp. 208–230.

Beardsley, Monroe C., *Aesthetics: Problems in the Philosophy of Criticism*, New York: Harcourt, Brace, 1958.

Beauvoir, Simone de, *Force of Circumstance*, translated by Richard Howard, New York: G. P. Putnam's Sons, 1964.

———, *Prime of Life*, translated by Peter Green, New York: World, 1962.

———, "Two Essays: 'Literature and Metaphysics' and 'Freedom and Liberation,'" translated by Ralph Manheim, in *Art and Action: Twice A Year—1938-1948*, 10th Anniversary Issue, New York: Twice A Year Press, 1948, pp. 86-114.

———, *A Very Easy Death*, translated by Patrick O'Brian, New York: G. P. Putnam's Sons, 1966.

Beck, Lewis White, "The 'Natural Science Ideal' in the Social Sciences," in *Theory in Anthropology: A Source Book* (edited by Robert A. Manners and David Kaplan), Chicago: Aldine, 1968, pp. 80-89.

Becker, Howard, "Interpretive Sociology and Constructive Typology," in *Twentieth Century Sociology* (edited by Georges Gurvitch and Wilbert E. Moore), New York: Philosophical Library, 1945, pp. 70-95.

———, and Harry Elmer Barnes, with the assistance of Émile Benoît-Smullyan, *Social Thought: From Lore to Science*, 3 volumes, 3rd edition, New York: Dover, 1961.

———, and Alvin Boskoff (Editors), *Modern Sociological Theory: In Continuity and Change*, New York: Dryden Press, 1957.

———, and Helmut Otto Dahlke, "Max Scheler's Sociology of Knowledge," *Philosophy and Phenomenological Research*, Vol. II, 1942, pp. 310-322.

Bell, Charles, *The Anatomy and Philosophy of Expression*, 7th edition, London: George Bell, 1877.

Bendix, Reinhard, *Max Weber: An Intellectual Portrait*, Garden City, N.Y.: Doubleday Anchor Books, 1962.

Berdyaev, Nikolai, *Dream and Reality: An Essay in Autobiography*, translated by Katharine Lampert, New York: Collier Books, 1962.

———, *Solitude and Society*, translated by George Reavey, New York: Charles Scribner's Sons, 1938.

Berger, Peter L., *Invitation to Sociology: A Humanistic Perspective*, Garden City, N.Y.: Doubleday Anchor Books, 1963.

———, *The Precarious Vision: A Sociologist Looks at Social Fictions and Christian Faith*, Garden City, N.Y.: Doubleday, 1961.

———, and Thomas Luckmann, *The Social Construction of Reality: A Treatise in the Sociology of Knowledge*, Garden City, N.Y.: Doubleday, 1966.

Bergson, Henri, *An Introduction to Metaphysics*, translated by T. E. Hulme with an Introduction by Thomas A. Goudge, New York: Liberal Arts Press, 1955.

———, *Time and Free Will: An Essay on the Immediate Data of Consciousness*, translated by F. L. Pogson, London: George Allen and Unwin, 1921.

Berlin, Isaiah, *The Hedgehog and the Fox: An Essay on Tolstoy's View of History*, New York: Simon and Schuster, 1966.

————, *Historical Inevitability*, London: Oxford University Press, 1954.

Biddle, Bruce J., and Edwin J. Thomas (Editors), *Role Theory: Concepts and Research*, New York: John Wiley and Sons, 1966.

Biemel, Walter, *Jean-Paul Sartre: In Selbstzeugnissen und Bilddokumenten*, Hamburg: Rowohlt, 1964.

Binswanger, Ludwig, *Being-in-the-World: Selected Papers*, translated with an Introduction and Preface by Jacob Needleman, New York: Harper Torchbooks, 1967.

Black, Max, *A Companion to Wittgenstein's 'Tractatus,'* Ithaca, N.Y.: Cornell University Press, 1964.

————, "Metaphor," in *Art and Philosophy: Readings in Aesthetics* (edited by W. E. Kennick), New York: St. Martin's Press, 1964, pp. 449–465.

Blackham, H. J., *Six Existentialist Thinkers*, New York: Harper Torchbooks, 1959.

Blanshard, Brand, *On Philosophical Style*, Bloomington: Indiana University Press, 1967.

————, and B. F. Skinner, "The Problem of Consciousness—A Debate," *Philosophy and Phenomenological Research*, Vol. XXVII, 1967, pp. 317–337.

Bloch, Marc, *The Historian's Craft*, translated by Peter Putnam with an Introduction by Joseph R. Strayer, New York: Vintage Books, 1964.

Bocheński, J. M., *The Methods of Contemporary Thought*, translated by Peter Caws, New York: Harper Torchbooks, 1968.

Bollnow, O. F., "Lived-Space," in *Readings in Existential Phenomenology* (edited by Nathaniel Lawrence and Daniel O'Connor), Englewood Cliffs, N.J.: Prentice-Hall, 1967, pp. 178–186.

Bonhoeffer, Dietrich, *The Cost of Discipleship*, revised edition, translated by R. H. Fuller with some revision by Irmgard Booth, New York: Macmillan, 1959.

————, *Letters and Papers from Prison*, translated by Reginald H. Fuller and edited by Eberhard Bethge, New York: Macmillan, 1962 (originally published as *Prisoner for God*).

Boros, Ladislaus, *The Mystery of Death*, New York: Herder and Herder, 1965.

Bosanquet, Bernard, *A History of Aesthetic*, 2nd edition, London: George Allen and Unwin, 1949.

————, *Implication and Linear Inference*, London: Macmillan, 1920.

Bouwsma, O. K., *Philosophical Essays*, Lincoln: University of Nebraska Press, 1965.

Bradley, F. H., *Appearance and Reality: A Metaphysical Essay*, 2nd edition, New York: Macmillan, 1897.

Braybrooke, David (Editor), *Philosophical Problems of the Social Sciences*, New York: Macmillan, 1965.

Bréhier, Émile, *The History of Philosophy*, translated by Joseph Thomas and by Wade Baskin, 6 volumes, Chicago: University of Chicago Press, 1963–1968.

Brock, Werner, "An Account of 'Being and Time,'" in *Existence and Being* by Martin Heidegger, Chicago: Henry Regnery, 1949, pp. 11–116.

Brodbeck, May (Editor), *Readings in the Philosophy of the Social Sciences*, New York: Macmillan, 1968.

Brophy, John, *The Human Face*, London: Harrap, 1945.

Brotz, Howard, *The Black Jews of Harlem: Negro Nationalism and the Dilemmas of Negro Leadership*, New York: Free Press of Glencoe, 1964.

Brown, James, *Kierkegaard, Heidegger, Buber, and Barth: A Study of Subjectivity and Objectivity in Existentialist Thought*, New York: Collier, 1962 (originally published as *Subject and Object in Modern Theology*).

Brown, Robert, *Explanation in Social Science*, Chicago: Aldine, 1963.

Buber, Martin, *Between Man and Man*, translated with an Introduction by Ronald Gregor Smith, New York: Macmillan, 1965.

Buchler, Justus, *The Concept of Method*, New York: Columbia University Press, 1961.

Bugbee, Henry G., Jr., *The Inward Morning: A Philosophical Exploration in Journal Form*, with an Introduction by Gabriel Marcel, New York: Collier, 1961.

Bultmann, Rudolf, *History and Eschatology*, Edinburgh: Edinburgh University Press, 1957.

Burtt, Edwin Arthur, *The Metaphysical Foundations of Modern Physical Science*, revised edition, Garden City, N.Y.: Doubleday Anchor Books, 1954.

Cairns, Dorion, "Phenomenology," in *A History of Philosophical Systems* (edited by Vergilius Ferm), New York: Philosophical Library, 1950, pp. 353–364.

Campbell, C. A., *On Selfhood and Godhood*, New York: Macmillan, 1957.

Camus, Albert, *The Myth of Sisyphus, and Other Essays*, translated by Justin O'Brien, New York: Alfred A. Knopf, 1964.

——, *The Rebel: An Essay on Man in Revolt*, translated by Anthony Bower with a Foreword by Herbert Read, New York: Vintage Books, 1956.

Canetti, Elias, *Crowds and Power*, translated by Carol Stewart, New York: Viking Press, 1962.

Carcopino, Jérôme, *Daily Life in Ancient Rome*, translated by E. O. Lorimer and edited by Henry T. Rowell, New Haven: Yale University Press, 1960.

Carmichael, Stokeley, and Charles W. Hamilton, *Black Power: The Politics of Liberation in America*, New York: Vintage Books, 1967.

Carr, Edward Hallett, *What Is History?*, New York: Alfred A. Knopf, 1962.

Carritt, E. F., *An Introduction to Aesthetics*, London: Hutchinson's University Library, 1949.

Case, Shirley Jackson, *The Christian Philosophy of History*, Chicago: University of Chicago Press, 1943.

Cassirer, Ernst, *An Essay on Man: An Introduction to a Philosophy of Human Culture*, New Haven: Yale University Press, 1944.

————, *The Logic of the Humanities*, translated by Clarence Smith Howe, New Haven: Yale University Press, 1960.

————, *The Philosophy of Symbolic Forms*, translated by Ralph Manheim with a Preface and Introduction by Charles W. Hendel, New Haven: Yale University Press. Vol. I, *Language*, 1953; Vol. II, *Mythical Thought*, 1955; Vol. III, *The Phenomenology of Knowledge*, 1957.

Castell, Alburey, *The Self in Philosophy*, New York: Macmillan, 1965.

Caudwell, Christopher, *Illusion and Reality: A Study of the Sources of Poetry*, New York: International Publishers, 1947.

Caws, Peter, *Philosophy of Science: A Systematic Account*, Princeton, N.J.: D. Van Nostrand, 1965.

Chapman, Harmon M., *Sensations and Phenomenology*, Bloomington: Indiana University Press, 1966.

Chastaing, Maxime, *L'Existence d'autrui*, Paris: Presses Universitaires de France, 1951.

Chatterjee, Margaret, *Our Knowledge of Other Selves*, London: Asia Publishing House, 1963.

Chesterton, G. K., "Charles Dickens," *Encyclopaedia Britannica*, 14th edition, 1929, Volume VII, pp. 331–336.

————, *St. Thomas Aquinas*, London: Hodder and Stoughton, 1943.

Choron, Jacques, *Death and Western Thought*, New York: Collier Books, 1963.

————, *Modern Man and Mortality*, New York: Macmillan, 1964.

Clarke, W. Norris, "The Self as Source of Meaning in Metaphysics," *Review of Metaphysics*, Vol. XXI, 1968, pp. 597–614.

Clayton, Alfred Stafford, *Emergent Mind and Education: A Study of George H. Mead's Bio-Social Behaviorism from an Educational Point of View*, New York: Teachers College, Columbia University Contributions to Education, No. 867, 1943.

Clive, Geoffrey, *The Romantic Enlightenment*, New York: Meridian Books, 1960.

Cogley, John (Editor), *Religion in America: Original Essays on Religion in a Free Society*, New York: Meridian Books, 1958.

Cohen, Morris R., *A Dreamer's Journey: The Autobiography of Morris Raphael Cohen*, Boston: Beacon Press, 1949.

————, *The Meaning of Human History*, La Salle, Ill.: Open Court, 1947.

————, and Ernest Nagel, *Introduction to Logic and Scientific Method*, New York: Harcourt, Brace, 1934.

Cohn, Georg, *Existentialism and Legal Science*, translated by George H. Kendal, Dobbs Ferry, N.Y.: Oceana Publications, 1967.

Collingwood, R. G., *An Autobiography*, London: Oxford University Press, 1959.

————, *An Essay on Philosophical Method*, Oxford: Clarendon Press, 1933.

————, *The Idea of History*, New York: Oxford University Press (Galaxy Book), 1956.

————, *The Principles of Art*, Oxford: Clarendon Press, 1945.

Collins, James, *The Existentialists: A Critical Study*, Chicago: Henry Regnery, 1952.

————, *A History of Modern European Philosophy*, Milwaukee: Bruce, 1954.

Cooke, Alistair, *A Generation on Trial: U.S.A. v. Alger Hiss*, New York: Alfred A. Knopf, 1952.

Cooley, Charles Horton, *Human Nature and the Social Order*, with an Introduction by Philip Rieff and a Foreword by George Herbert Mead, New York: Schocken Books, 1964.

————, *Social Organization: A Study of the Larger Mind*, with an Introduction by Philip Rieff, New York: Schocken Books, 1962.

Copleston, Frederick, *A History of Philosophy*, 8 volumes, new revised edition, Westminster, Md.: Newman Press, 1960–1966.

Cory, Daniel, *Santayana: The Later Years, a Portrait with Letters*, New York: George Braziller, 1963.

Coser, Lewis A., and Bernard Rosenberg (Editors), *Sociological Theory: A Book of Readings*, 2nd edition, New York: Macmillan, 1964.

Coval, S., *Scepticism and the First Person*, London: Methuen, 1966.

Cranston, Maurice, *Sartre*, London: Oliver and Boyd, 1962.

Croce, Benedetto, *Aesthetic: As Science of Expression and General Linguistic*, translated by Douglas Ainslie, New York: Noonday Press, 1960.

Daniel-Rops, Henri, *Daily Life in the Time of Jesus*, translated by Patrick O'Brian, New York: Hawthorn Books, 1962.

Danto, Arthur, and Sidney Morgenbesser (Editors), *Philosophy of Science: Readings*, New York: Meridian Books, 1961.

Dardel, Eric, "History and Our Times," translated by Elaine P. Halperin, *Diogenes*, No. 21, 1958, pp. 11–25.

Darwin, Charles, *The Expression of the Emotions in Man and Animals*, with a Preface by Konrad Lorenz, Chicago: University of Chicago Press, 1965.

Desan, Wilfrid, *The Tragic Finale: An Essay on the Philosophy of Jean-Paul Sartre*, New York: Harper Torchbooks, 1960.

Dewey, John, *Art as Experience*, New York: Minton, Balch, 1934.

————, *Philosophy and Civilization*, New York: Minton, Balch, 1934.

————, *The Public and Its Problems: An Essay in Political Inquiry*, Chicago: Gateway Books, 1946.

Dickens, Charles, *The Old Curiosity Shop*, New York: Oxford University Press, 1951.

Dickinson, G. Lowes, *J. McT. E. McTaggart*, with chapters by Basil Williams and S. V. Keeling, Cambridge: Cambridge University Press, 1931.

Diderot, Denis, *The Paradox of Acting* (together with *Masks or Faces?* by William Archer), with an Introduction by Lee Strasberg, New York: Hill and Wang, 1957.

Dolci, Danilo, "What Does It Mean, to Die?", translated by Adrienne Foulke, *Hudson Review*, Vol. XVII, 1964, pp. 167–186.

Dray, William H., *Philosophy of History*, Englewood Cliffs, N.J.: Prentice-Hall, 1964.

Dreitzel, Hans Peter, *Die gesellschaftlichen Leiden und das Leiden an der Gesellschaft: Vorstudien zu einer Pathologie des Rollenverhaltens*, Stuttgart: Ferdinand Enke, 1968.

Ducasse, C. J., *Nature, Mind, and Death*, La Salle, Ill.: Open Court, 1951.

————, *A Philosophical Scrutiny of Religion*, New York: Ronald Press, 1953.

————, *The Philosophy of Art*, New York: Dover, 1966.

Dufrenne, Mikel, *Language and Philosophy*, translated by Henry B. Veatch with a Foreword by Paul Henle, Bloomington: Indiana University Press, 1963.

————, *La Personalité de base: un concept sociologique*, 2nd edition, Paris: Presses Universitaires de France, 1966.

Duméry, Henry, *The Problem of God: In Philosophy of Religion*, translated with an Introduction by Charles Courtney, Evanston, Ill.: Northwestern University Press, 1964.

Earle, William, "Phenomenology and Existentialism," *Journal of Philosophy*, Vol. LVII, 1960, pp. 75–84.

————, James M. Edie, and John Wild, *Christianity and Existentialism*, Evanston, Ill.: Northwestern University Press, 1963.

Eccles, John Carew, *The Neurophysiological Basis of Mind: The Principles of Neurophysiology*, Oxford: Clarendon Press, 1953.

Edie, James M., "Notes on the Philosophical Anthropology of William James," in *An Invitation to Phenomenology: Studies in the Philosophy of Experience* (edited by James M. Edie), Chicago: Quadrangle Books, 1965, pp. 110–132.

Edwards, Paul (Editor), *The Encyclopedia of Philosophy*, 8 volumes, New York: Macmillan and Free Press, 1967.

————, and Arthur Pap (Editors), *A Modern Introduction to Philosophy: Readings from Classical and Contemporary Sources*, revised edition, New York: Free Press, 1965.

Eissler, K. R., *The Psychiatrist and the Dying Patient*, New York: International Universities Press, 1955.

Ellison, Ralph, *Invisible Man*, New York: New American Library (Signet Book), 1952.

Emmet, Dorothy M., *The Nature of Metaphysical Thinking*, London: Macmillan, 1949.

————, *Rules, Roles, and Relations*, New York: St. Martin's Press, 1966.

Engelmann, Paul, *Letters from Ludwig Wittgenstein, with a Memoir*, translated by L. Furtmüller and edited by B. F. McGuiness, with a Preface by Joseph Schächter, New York: Horizon Press, 1968.

Engler, Robert, "Social Science and Social Consciousness: The Shame of the Universities," in *The Dissenting Academy* (edited by Theodore Roszak), New York: Pantheon Books, 1967, pp. 182–207.

Erikson, Erik H., *Identity and the Life Cycle: Selected Papers*, with a Historical Introduction by David Rapaport, Psychological Issues, Vol. I, Monograph 1, New York: International Universities Press, 1959.

Evans, Jean, *Three Men: An Experiment in the Biography of Emotions*, with an Introduction by Gordon W. Allport, New York: Alfred A. Knopf, 1954.

Ey, Henri, *La Conscience*, Paris: Presses Universitaires de France, 1963.

Fackenheim, Emil L., *Metaphysics and Historicity*, Milwaukee: Marquette University Press, 1961.

Fallico, Arturo B., *Art and Existentialism*, Englewood Cliffs, N.J.: Prentice-Hall, 1962.

Farber, Marvin, *The Aims of Phenomenology: The Motives, Methods, and Impact of Husserl's Thought*, New York: Harper Torchbooks, 1966.

————, *The Foundation of Phenomenology: Edmund Husserl and the Quest for a Rigorous Science of Philosophy*, 3rd edition, Albany: State University of New York Press, 1967.

————, "Phenomenology," in *Twentieth Century Philosophy: Living Schools of Thought* (edited by Dagobert D. Runes), New York: Philosophical Library, 1943, pp. 345–370 (also available under the title, *Living Schools of Philosophy*).

————, *Phenomenology and Existence: Toward a Philosophy within Nature*, New York: Harper Torchbooks, 1967.

———— (Editor), *Philosophical Essays in Memory of Edmund Husserl*, Cambridge, Mass.: Harvard University Press, 1940.

Farquharson, A. S. L., "Memoir," in John Cook Wilson, *Statement and Inference, with Other Philosophical Papers* (edited by A. S. L. Farquharson), Vol. I, Oxford: Clarendon Press, 1926, pp. xii–lxiv.

Feibleman, James K., *Philosophers Lead Sheltered Lives: A First Volume of Memoirs*, London: George Allen and Unwin, 1952.

Feifel, Herman (Editor), *The Meaning of Death*, New York: McGraw-Hill, 1959.

Feigl, Herbert, and May Brodbeck (Editors), *Readings in the Philosophy of Science*, New York: Appleton-Century-Crofts, 1953.

Fell, Joseph P., III, *Emotion in the Thought of Sartre*, New York: Columbia University Press, 1965.

Ferrater Mora, José, *Being and Death: An Outline of Integrationist Philosophy*, Berkeley: University of California Press, 1965.

Findlay, J. N., *Hegel: A Re-examination*, New York: Collier Books, 1962.

Firth, Raymond, *Elements of Social Organization*, New York: Philosophical Library, 1951.

Fischer, Ernst, *The Necessity of Art: A Marxist Approach*, translated by Anna Bostock, Baltimore: Penguin Books, 1963.

Flew, Antony, "Selves," *Mind*, Vol. LVIII, 1949, pp. 355–358.

——, and Alasdair MacIntyre (Editors), *New Essays in Philosophical Theology*, London: SCM Press, 1955.

Foss, Martin, *Symbol and Metaphor in Human Experience*, Lincoln: University of Nebraska Press, 1964.

Foster, M. B., " 'We' in Modern Philosophy," in *Faith and Logic: Oxford Essays in Philosophical Theology* (edited by Basil Mitchell), London: George Allen and Unwin, 1957, pp. 194-220.

Frank, Erich, *Philosophical Understanding and Religious Truth*, New York: Oxford University Press (Galaxy Book), 1966.

Freud, Sigmund, *The Ego and The Id*, translated by James Strachey, New York: W. W. Norton, 1961.

——, *The Future of an Illusion*, translated by W. D. Robson-Scott, Garden City, N. Y.: Doubleday Anchor Books, 1957.

——, "Thoughts for the Times on War and Death," translated by E. Colburn Mayne, in *On Creativity and the Unconscious: Papers on the Psychology of Art, Literature, Love, Religion* (Introduced and Annotated by Benjamin Nelson), New York: Harper Torchbooks, 1958, pp. 206–235.

Freund, Julien, *The Sociology of Max Weber*, translated by Mary Ilford, New York: Pantheon Books, 1968.

Friedenthal, Richard (Editor), *Letters of the Great Artists: From Ghiberti to Gainsborough*, 2 volumes, New York: Random House, 1963.

Friedman, Maurice S., *Martin Buber: The Life of Dialogue*, Chicago: University of Chicago Press, 1955.

—— (Editor), *The Worlds of Existentialism: A Critical Reader*, New York: Random House, 1964.

Fromm, Erich, *Psychoanalysis and Religion*, New Haven: Yale University Press, 1950.

Fromm-Reichmann, Frieda, *Principles of Intensive Psychotherapy*, Chicago: University of Chicago Press (Phoenix Books), 1950.

Frondizi, Risieri, *The Nature of the Self: A Functional Interpretation*, New Haven: Yale University Press, 1953.

Fulton, Robert (Editor), *Death and Identity*, New York: John Wiley and Sons, 1965.

Funke, Lewis, and John E. Booth, *Actors Talk about Acting: Fourteen Interviews with Stars of the Theatre*, New York: Random House, 1961.

Gallagher, Kenneth T., *The Philosophy of Gabriel Marcel*, with a Foreword by Gabriel Marcel, New York: Fordham University Press, 1962.

Gallie, W. B., *Philosophy and the Historical Understanding*, London: Chatto and Windus, 1964.

Gardiner, Patrick, *The Nature of Historical Explanation*, London: Oxford University Press, 1955.

―――― (Editor), *Theories of History: Readings from Classical and Contemporary Sources*, Glencoe, Ill.: Free Press, 1959.

Garfinkel, Harold, *Studies in Ethnomethodology*, Englewood Cliffs, N.J.: Prentice-Hall, 1967.

Gass, William, "The Case of the Obliging Stranger," in *Philosophic Problems: An Introductory Book of Readings* (edited by Maurice Mandelbaum, Francis W. Gramlich, Alan Ross Anderson, and Jerome B. Schneewind), 2nd edition, New York: Macmillan, 1967, pp. 525–531.

Gendlin, Eugene T., *Experiencing and the Creation of Meaning: A Philosophical Approach to the Subjective*, New York: Free Press of Glencoe, 1962.

Geyl, Pieter, *Debates with Historians*, New York: Meridian Books, 1958.

Gilbert, Katharine Everett, and Helmut Kuhn, *A History of Esthetics*, revised edition, Bloomington: Indiana University Press, 1954.

Gillispie, Charles Coulston, *The Edge of Objectivity: An Essay in the History of Scientific Ideas*, Princeton, N.J.: Princeton University Press, 1960.

Gilson, Etienne, *Painting and Reality*, New York: Pantheon Books, 1957.

Glatzer, Nahum N., *Franz Rosenzweig: His Life and Thought*, 2nd revised edition, New York: Schocken Books, 1961.

Goethe, Johann Wolfgang von, "Beiträge zu Lavaters Physiognomischen Fragmenten," in *Goethes Sämtliche Werke*, Jubiläums-Ausgabe (herausgegeben von Eduard von der Hellen), Vol. XXXIII, Stuttgart: J. G. Cotta, 1902 ff.

Goffman, Erving, *Encounters: Two Studies in the Sociology of Interaction*, Indianapolis: Bobbs-Merrill, 1961.

―――― , *The Presentation of Self in Everyday Life*, Garden City, N.Y.: Doubleday Anchor Books, 1959.

Goldscheider, Ludwig (Editor), *Five Hundred Self-Portraits from Antique Times to the Present Day in Sculpture, Painting, Drawing, and Engraving*, translated by J. Byam Shaw, London: George Allen and Unwin, 1937.

Goldstein, Kurt, "The Smiling of the Infant and the Problem of Understanding the 'Other,'" *Journal of Psychology*, Vol. XLIV, 1957, pp. 175–191.

Goldstein, Leon J., "The Phenomenological and Naturalistic Approaches to the Social," in *Philosophy of the Social Sciences: A Reader* (edited by Maurice Natanson), New York: Random House, 1963, pp. 286–301.

Goldwater, Robert, and Marco Treves (Editors), *Artists on Art: From the XIV to the XX Century*, New York: Pantheon Books, 1958.

Gouldner, Alvin W., "Anti-Minotaur: The Myth of a Value-Free Sociology," in *Sociology on Trial* (edited by Maurice Stein and Arthur Vidich), Englewood Cliffs, N.J.: Prentice-Hall, 1963, pp. 35–52.

Grene, Marjorie, *Introduction to Existentialism*, Chicago: University of Chicago Press (Phoenix Books), 1959 (originally published as *Dreadful Freedom*).

————, *Martin Heidegger*, New York: Hillary House, 1958.

Gross, Llewellyn (Editor), *Symposium on Sociological Theory*, Evanston, Ill.: Row, Peterson, 1959.

Gross, Neal, Ward S. Mason, and Alexander W. McEachern, *Explorations in Role Analysis: Studies of the School Superintendency Role*, New York: John Wiley and Sons, 1957.

Gunther, John, *Death Be Not Proud: A Memoir*, with an Introduction by the author, New York: Modern Library, 1953.

Gurwitsch, Aron, *The Field of Consciousness*, Pittsburgh: Duquesne University Press, 1964.

————, *Studies in Phenomenology and Psychology*, Evanston, Ill.: Northwestern University Press, 1966.

Gusdorf, Georges, *Speaking (La Parole)*, translated with an Introduction by Paul T. Brockelman, Evanston, Ill.: Northwestern University Press, 1965.

Guttmann, Julius, *Philosophies of Judaism: The History of Jewish Philosophy from Biblical Times to Franz Rosenzweig*, translated by David W. Silverman with an Introduction by R. J. Zwi Werblowsky, Garden City, N.Y.: Doubleday Anchor Books, 1964.

Hall, Everett W., *Philosophical Systems: A Categorial Analysis*, Chicago: University of Chicago Press, 1960.

Hallie, Philip P., *Maine de Biran: Reformer of Empiricism, 1766–1824*, Cambridge, Mass.: Harvard University Press, 1959.

Hampshire, Stuart, "The Analogy of Feeling," in *Clarity Is Not Enough* (edited by H. D. Lewis), London: George Allen and Unwin, 1963, pp. 369–380.

————, *Thought and Action*, New York: Viking Press (Compass Book), 1967.

Hanson, Norwood R., *Patterns of Discovery: An Enquiry into the Conceptual Foundations of Science*, Cambridge: Cambridge University Press, 1961.

Harper, Ralph, *Existentialism: A Theory of Man*, Cambridge, Mass.: Harvard University Press, 1948.

Harries, Karsten, *The Meaning of Modern Art: A Philosophical Interpretation*, Evanston, Ill.: Northwestern University Press, 1968.

Hartshorne, Charles, and William L. Reese (Editors), *Philosophers Speak of God*, Chicago: University of Chicago Press (Phoenix Books), 1953.

Hayek, Friedrich A., *The Sensory Order: An Inquiry into the Foundations of Theoretical Psychology*, with an Introduction by Heinrich Klüver, Chicago: University of Chicago Press, 1963.

Hegel, G. W. F., *The Logic of Hegel*, translated by William Wallace, Oxford: Clarendon Press, 1892.

———, *The Phenomenology of Mind*, translated with an Introduction by J. B. Baille, with a new Introduction by George Lichtheim, New York: Harper Torch-books, 1967.

Heidegger, Martin, *Being and Time*, translated by John Macquarrie and Edward Robinson, New York: Harper, 1962.

———, "The Origin of the Work of Art," translated by Albert Hofstadter, in *Philosophies of Art and Beauty: Selected Readings in Aesthetics from Plato to Heidegger* (edited by Albert Hofstadter and Richard Kuhns), New York: Modern Library, 1964, pp. 649–701.

Hethmon, Robert H. (Editor), *Strasberg at the Actor's Studio: Tape-Recorded Sessions*, New York: Viking Press, 1965.

Hexter, J. H., "Historiography: The Rhetoric of History," *International Encyclopedia of the Social Sciences* (edited by David L. Sills), New York: Macmillan and Free Press, 1968, Vol. VI, pp. 368–394.

Hick, John, *Philosophy of Religion*, Englewood Cliffs, N.J.: Prentice-Hall, 1963.

——— (Editor), *Classical and Contemporary Readings in the Philosophy of Religion*, Englewood Cliffs, N.J.: Prentice-Hall, 1964.

——— (Editor), *The Existence of God: Readings*, New York: Macmillan, 1964.

Hocking, William E., "Marcel and the Ground Issues of Metaphysics," *Philosophy and Phenomenological Research*, Vol. XIV, 1954, pp. 439–469.

———, *The Self: Its Body and Freedom*, New Haven: Yale University Press, 1928.

Hofstadter, Albert, *Truth and Art*, New York: Columbia University Press, 1965.

———, and Richard Kuhns (Editors), *Philosophies of Art and Beauty: Selected Readings in Aesthetics from Plato to Heidegger*, New York: Modern Library, 1964.

Hohl, Hubert, *Lebenswelt und Geschichte: Grundzüge der Spätphilosophie E. Husserls*, Freiburg: Karl Alber, 1962.

Hollingdale, R. J., *Nietzsche: The Man and His Philosophy*, Baton Rouge: Louisiana State University Press, 1965.

Holmes, Urban Tigner, Jr., *Daily Living in the Twelfth Century, Based on the Observations of Alexander Neckam in London and Paris*, Madison: University of Wisconsin Press, 1953.

Homans, George C., *The Human Group*, New York: Harcourt, Brace, 1950.

———, *The Nature of Social Science*, New York: Harcourt, Brace and World, 1967.

————, *Social Behavior: Its Elementary Forms*, New York: Harcourt, Brace and World, 1961.

Hook, Sidney, *Education for Modern Man*, New York: Dial Press, 1946.

————, *The Hero in History: A Study in Limitation and Possibility*, Boston: Beacon Press, 1955.

————, *John Dewey: An Intellectual Portrait*, New York: John Day, 1939.

Hoselitz, Bert F. (Editor), *A Reader's Guide to the Social Sciences*, Glencoe, Ill.: Free Press, 1959.

Hospers, John, *An Introduction to Philosophical Analysis*, 2nd edition, Englewood Cliffs, N.J.: Prentice-Hall, 1967.

————, *Meaning and Truth in the Arts*, Chapel Hill: University of North Carolina Press, 1946.

————, "Problems of Aesthetics," in *The Encyclopedia of Philosophy* (edited by Paul Edwards), New York: Macmillan and Free Press, 1967, Vol. I, pp. 35–56.

Hume, David, *A Treatise of Human Nature*, edited by L. A. Selby-Bigge, Oxford: Clarendon Press, 1888.

Husserl, Edmund, *Cartesian Meditations: An Introduction to Phenomenology*, translated by Dorion Cairns, The Hague: Martinus Nijhoff, 1960.

————, *The Idea of Phenomenology*, translated by William P. Alston and George Nakhnikian, with an Introduction by the latter, The Hague: Martinus Nijhoff, 1964 (also included in *Readings in Twentieth Century Philosophy*, edited by William P. Alston and George Nakhnikian, New York: Free Press of Glencoe, 1963).

————, *Ideas: General Introduction to Pure Phenomenology*, translated by W. R. Boyce Gibson, New York: Macmillan, 1931.

————, *Die Krisis der europäischen Wissenschaften und die transzendentale Phänomenologie: eine Einleitung in die phänomenologische Philosophie*, herausgegeben von Walter Biemel, The Hague: Martinus Nijhoff, 1954.

————, *The Paris Lectures*, translated with an Introduction by Peter Koestenbaum, The Hague: Martinus Nijhoff, 1964.

————, "Phenomenology," translated by C. V. Salmon, *Encyclopaedia Britannica*, 14th edition, 1927, Vol. XVII, pp. 699–702 (also included in *Realism and the Background of Phenomenology*, edited by Roderick M. Chisholm, Glencoe, Ill.: Free Press of Glencoe, 1960).

————, "Phenomenology and Anthropology," translated by Richard G. Schmitt, in *Realism and the Background of Phenomenology* (edited by Roderick M. Chisholm), Glencoe, Ill.: Free Press of Glencoe, 1960, pp. 129–142.

————, *Phenomenology and the Crisis of Philosophy: Philosophy as Rigorous Science and Philosophy and the Crisis of European Man*, translated with an Introduction by Quentin Lauer, New York: Harper Torchbooks, 1965.

————, *The Phenomenology of Internal Time-Consciousness*, translated by James S. Churchill and edited by Martin Heidegger, with an Introduction by Calvin O. Schrag, Bloomington: Indiana University Press, 1964.

Hutchison, John A., *Faith, Reason, and Existence: An Introduction to Contemporary Philosophy of Religion*, New York: Oxford University Press, 1956.

Hyde, Lawrence, *I Who Am: A Study of the Self*, London: Omega Press, 1954.

James, William, *The Principles of Psychology*, 2 volumes, New York: Henry Holt, 1893.

————, *The Varieties of Religious Experience: A Study in Human Nature*, New York: Modern Library, 1929.

————, *The Writings of William James: A Comprehensive Edition, Including an Annotated Bibliography of the Writings of William James*, edited with an Introduction by John J. McDermott, New York: Modern Library, 1968.

Jameson, Frederic, *Sartre: The Origins of a Style*, New Haven: Yale University Press, 1961.

Jaspers, Karl, *General Psychopathology*, translated by J. Hoenig and Marian W. Hamilton, Chicago: University of Chicago Press, 1963.

————, *Man in the Modern Age*, translated by Eden and Cedar Paul, Garden City, N.Y.: Doubleday Anchor Books, 1957.

————, *The Origin and Goal of History*, translated by Michael Bullock, New Haven: Yale University Press, 1953.

————, *Three Essays: Leonardo, Descartes, Max Weber*, translated by Ralph Manheim, New York: Harcourt, Brace and World, 1964.

Johnstone, Henry W., Jr., "Persons and Selves," *Philosophy and Phenomenological Research*, Vol. XXVIII, 1967, pp. 205–212.

————, *Philosophy and Argument*, University Park: Pennsylvania State University Press, 1959.

———— (Editor), *What Is Philosophy?*, New York: Macmillan, 1965.

Jonas, Hans, *The Phenomenon of Life: Toward a Philosophical Biology*, New York: Harper and Row, 1966.

Jones, J. R., "Our Knowledge of Other Persons," *Philosophy*, Vol. XXV, 1950, pp. 134–148.

————, "The Self in Sensory Cognition," *Mind*, Vol. LVIII, 1949, pp. 40–61.

————, "Self-Knowledge," *Proceedings of the Aristotelian Society*, Supplement, Vol. XXX, 1956, pp. 120–142.

————, "'Selves': A Reply to Mr. Flew," *Mind*, Vol. LXIX, 1950, pp. 233–236.

Joseph, H. W. B., *An Introduction to Logic*, 2nd edition, Oxford: Clarendon Press, 1946.

Jung. Carl Gustav, *Psychology and Religion*, New Haven: Yale University Press, 1938.

Kahler, Erich, *Out of the Labyrinth: Essays in Clarification*, New York: George Braziller, 1967.

Kaiser, Charles Hillis, *An Essay on Method*, New Brunswick, N.J.: Rutgers University Press, 1952.

Kallen, Horace M., *Art and Freedom: A Historical and Biographical Interpretation of the Relations between the Ideas of Beauty, Use, and Freedom in Western Civilization from the Greeks to the Present Day*, 2 volumes, New York: Duell, Sloan and Pearce, 1942.

Kaplan, Abraham, *The Conduct of Inquiry: Methodology for Behavioral Science*, San Francisco: Chandler, 1964.

Kaufmann, Felix, *Methodology of the Social Sciences*, New York: Oxford University Press, 1944.

Kaufmann, Fritz, "The Phenomenological Approach to History," *Philosophy and Phenomenological Research*, Vol. II, 1941, pp. 159–172.

Kaufmann, Walter (Editor), *Existentialism: From Dostoevsky to Sartre*, New York: Meridian Books, 1956.

Keene, Donald, "Confessions of a Specialist," *The New York Times Book Review*, June 30, 1968, p. 2 and ff.

Kelsen, Hans, *Society and Nature: A Sociological Inquiry*, Chicago: University of Chicago Press, 1943.

Kemeny, John G., *A Philosopher Looks at Science*, Princeton, N.J.: D. Van Nostrand, 1959.

Kierkegaard, Søren, *Fear and Trembling: A Dialectical Lyric*, translated with an Introduction by Walter Lowrie, Princeton, N.J.: Princeton University Press, 1941.

————, *The Journals: A Selection*, translated and edited by Alexander Dru, London: Oxford University Press, 1938.

————, *Philosophical Fragments; or, A Fragment of Philosophy*, translated with an Introduction by David F. Swenson, Princeton, N.J.: Princeton University Press, 1944 (second edition, Princeton University Press, 1962).

————, *Training in Christianity, and the Edifying Discourse Which "Accompanied" It*, translated with an Introduction by Walter Lowrie, Princeton, N.J.: Princeton University Press, 1957.

Klein, Jacob, "Phenomenology and the History of Science," in *Philosophical Essays in Memory of Edmund Husserl* (edited by Marvin Farber), Cambridge, Mass.: Harvard University Press, 1940, pp. 143–163.

Klibansky, Raymond (Editor), *Philosophy in the Mid-Century*, Firenze: La Nuova Italia Editrice. Vol. I, *Logic and Philosophy of Science*, 1961; Vol. II, *Metaphysics and Analysis*, 1961; Vol. III, *Values, History, and Religion*, 1961; Vol. IV, *History of Philosophy: Contemporary Thought in Europe and Asia*, 1959.

Kockelmans, Joseph J. (Editor), *Phenomenology: The Philosophy of Edmund Husserl and Its Interpretation*, Garden City, N.Y.: Doubleday Anchor Books, 1967.

Koestler, Arthur, *Darkness at Noon*, translated by Daphne Hardy with a Foreword by Peter Viereck, New York: New American Library (Signet Classic), 1961.

Köhler, Wolfgang, *The Place of Value in a World of Facts*, New York: Liveright, 1938.

Kris, Ernst, *Psychoanalytic Explorations in Art*, London: George Allen and Unwin, 1953.

Kuhn, Helmut, *Encounter with Nothingness: An Essay on Existentialism*, Hinsdale, Ill.: Henry Regnery, 1949.

————, "The Phenomenological Concept of 'Horizon,'" in *Philosophical Essays in Memory of Edmund Husserl* (edited by Marvin Farber), Cambridge, Mass.: Harvard University Press, 1940, pp. 106–123.

Kuhn, Thomas S., *The Structure of Scientific Revolutions*, Chicago: University of Chicago Press (Phoenix Books), 1967.

Laguna, Grace A. de, *On Existence and the Human World*, New Haven: Yale University Press, 1966.

Laird, John, *Problems of the Self*, London: Macmillan, 1917.

Lamprecht, Sterling, *Our Philosophical Traditions: A Brief History of Philosophy in Western Civilization*, New York: Appleton-Century-Crofts, 1955.

Landgrebe, Ludwig, "The World as a Phenomenological Problem," translated by Dorion Cairns, *Philosophy and Phenomenological Research*, Vol. I, 1940, pp. 38–58.

Landsberg, Paul-Louis, *The Experience of Death*, together with *The Moral Problem of Suicide*, translated by Cynthia Rowland with a Foreword by Martin Jarrett-Kerr, New York: Philosophical Library, 1953 (note: "The Experience of Death" is reprinted in *Essays in Phenomenology*, edited by Maurice Natanson, The Hague: Martinus Nijhoff, 1966).

Langan, Thomas, *Merleau-Ponty's Critique of Reason*, New Haven: Yale University Press, 1966.

Langer, Susanne K., *Feeling and Form: A Theory of Art*, New York: Charles Scribner's Sons, 1953.

————, *Philosophy in a New Key: A Study in the Symbolism of Reason, Rite, and Art*, 2nd edition, New York: New American Library (Mentor Book), 1962.

————, *Problems of Art: Ten Philosophical Lectures*, New York: Charles Scribner's Sons, 1957.

Lavater, John Caspar, *Essays on Physiognomy, Designed to Promote the Knowledge and Love of Mankind*, translated by Henry Hunter, 5 volumes, London: Printed for John Murray, Bookseller, 1789–1798.

Lawrence, Nathaniel, and Daniel O'Connor (Editors), *Readings in Existential Phenomenology*, Englewood Cliffs, N.J.: Prentice-Hall, 1967.

Lee, Edward N., and Maurice Mandelbaum (Editors), *Phenomenology and Existentialism*, Baltimore: Johns Hopkins Press, 1967.

Lee, Grace Chin, *George Herbert Mead: Philosopher of the Social Individual*, New York: Kings Crown Press, 1945.

Lerner, Daniel (Editor), *The Human Meaning of the Social Sciences*, New York: Meridian Books, 1959.

Levich, Marvin (Editor), *Aesthetics and the Philosophy of Criticism*, New York: Random House, 1963.

Levinson, Daniel J., "Role, Personality, and Social Structure," in *Sociological Theory: A Book of Readings* (edited by Lewis A. Coser and Bernard Rosenberg), 2nd edition, New York: Macmillan, 1964, pp. 284–297.

Lévi-Strauss, Claude, *The Scope of Anthropology*, translated by Sherry Ortner Paul and Robert A. Paul, London: Jonathan Cape, 1967.

Levy, Marion J., Jr., *The Structure of Society*, Princeton, N.J.: Princeton University Press, 1952.

Lewin, Kurt, *Field Theory in Social Science: Selected Theoretical Papers*, edited by Dorwin Cartwright, New York: Harper Torchbooks, 1964.

Lichtenberg, Georg Christoph, *The Lichtenberg Reader: Selected Writings*, translated and edited with an Introduction by Franz H. Mautner and Henry Hatfield, Boston: Beacon Press, 1959.

Linschoten, Hans, *On the Way toward a Phenomenological Psychology: The Psychology of William James*, edited by Amedeo Giorgi, Pittsburgh: Duquesne University Press, 1968.

Linton, Ralph, *The Study of Man: An Introduction*, New York: D. Appleton-Century, 1936.

Lipman, Matthew, *What Happens in Art*, New York: Appleton-Century-Crofts, 1967.

Locke, Don, *Myself and Others: A Study in Our Knowledge of Minds*, Oxford: Clarendon Press, 1968.

Loewenberg, J., *Hegel's Phenomenology: Dialogues on the Life of Mind*, La Salle, Ill.: Open Court, 1965.

Loewenstein, Karl, *Max Weber's Political Ideas in the Perspective of Our Time*, translated by Richard and Clara Winston, Amherst: University of Massachusetts Press, 1966.

Loomis, Charles P., and Zona K. Loomis, *Modern Social Theories: Selected American Writers*, Princeton, N.J.: D. Van Nostrand, 1961.

Lord, James, *A Giacometti Portrait*, Garden City, N.Y.: Doubleday (Museum of Modern Art), 1965.

Löwith, Karl, *Das Individuum in der Rolle des Mitmenschen*, Darmstadt: Wissenschaftliche Buchgesellschaft, 1962.

————, *Meaning in History: The Theological Implications of the Philosophy of History*, Chicago: University of Chicago Press, 1949.

Lowrie, Walter, *Kierkegaard*, 2 volumes, New York: Harper Torchbooks, 1962.

Lucas, E. Louise, *Art Books: A Basic Bibliography on the Fine Arts*, Greenwich, Conn.: New York Graphic Society, 1968.

Lundberg, George A., *Can Science Save Us?*, New York: Longmans, Green, 1947.

————, *Foundations of Sociology*, New York: Macmillan, 1939.

Lynd, Robert S., *Knowledge for What?*, Princeton, N.J.: Princeton University Press, 1939.

————, *Middletown in Transition*, New York: Harcourt, Brace, 1937.

Lynd, Staughton, "A Profession of History," *New American Review*, No. 2, New York: New American Library, 1968, pp. 192–205 (this essay also appears as "Historical Past and Existential Present" in *The Dissenting Academy*, edited by Theodore Roszak, New York: Pantheon Books, 1967).

Macdonald, Margaret, "The Philosopher's Use of Analogy," in *Essays on Logic and Language* (edited with an Introduction by Antony Flew), New York: Philosophical Library, 1951, pp. 80–100.

McEwen, William P., *The Problem of Social-Scientific Knowledge*, Totowa, N.J.: Bedminster Press, 1963.

McGill, V. J., *Schopenhauer: Pessimist and Pagan*, New York: Brentano, 1931.

MacIver, Robert M., and Charles H. Page, *Society: An Introductory Analysis*, New York: Rinehart, 1962.

Macmurray, John, *Persons in Relation*, London: Faber and Faber, 1961.

————, *The Self as Agent*, London: Faber and Faber, 1957.

Madariaga, Salvador de, *Portrait of a Man Standing*, University: University of Alabama Press, 1968.

Madden, Edward H. (Editor), *The Structure of Scientific Thought: An Introduction to Philosophy of Science*, Boston: Houghton Mifflin, 1960.

Maimon, Solomon, *The Autobiography*, with an Essay on Maimon's Philosophy by Hugo Bergman, London: East and West Library, 1954.

Maine de Biran, Pierre, *Essai sur les fondements de la psychologie et sur ses rapports avec l'étude de la nature, Oeuvres de Maine de Biran* (edited by Pierre Tisserand), Vol. VIII and IX, Paris: Félix Alcan, 1932.

Malcolm, Norman, *Knowledge and Certainty: Essays and Lectures*, Englewood Cliffs, N.J.: Prentice-Hall, 1965.

————, *Ludwig Wittgenstein: A Memoir, with a Biographical Sketch by Georg Henrik von Wright*, New York: Oxford University Press, 1958.

Malinowski, Bronislaw, *A Scientific Theory of Culture, and Other Essays*, New York: Oxford University Press, 1960.

Mandelbaum, Maurice, *The Problem of Historical Knowledge: An Answer to Relativism*, with a new Preface by the author, New York: Harper Torchbooks, 1967.

————, Francis W. Gramlich, Alan Ross Anderson, and Jerome B. Schneewind (Editors), *Philosophic Problems: An Introductory Book of Readings*, 2nd edition, New York: Macmillan, 1967.

Mannheim, Karl, *Ideology and Utopia: An Introduction to the Sociology of Knowledge*, with a Preface by Louis Wirth, New York: Harcourt, Brace, 1949.

Manser, Anthony, *Sartre: A Philosophical Study*, London: University of London (Athlone Press), 1966.

Marcel, Gabriel, *Being and Having: An Existentialist Diary*, translated by Katherine Farrer, with an Introduction by James Collins, New York: Harper Torchbooks, 1965.

————, *Creative Fidelity*, translated with an Introduction by Robert Rosthal, New York: Noonday Press, 1964.

————, *The Existential Background of Human Dignity*, Cambridge, Mass: Harvard University Press, 1963.

————, *Homo Viator: Introduction to a Metaphysic of Hope*, translated by Emma Craufurd, New York: Harper Torchbooks, 1962.

————, *Metaphysical Journal*, translated by Bernard Wall, Chicago: Henry Regnery, 1952.

————, *The Mystery of Being*, 2 volumes, translated by G. S. Fraser, Chicago: Henry Regnery (Gateway Edition), 1960.

————, *The Philosophy of Existentialism*, translated by Manya Harari, New York: Citadel Press, 1961 (published in England as *The Philosophy of Existence*).

Marcuse, Herbert, *One Dimensional Man: Studies in the Ideology of Advanced Industrial Society*, Boston: Beacon Press, 1964.

————, "On Science and Phenomenology," followed by comments by Aron Gurwitsch, in *Boston Studies in the Philosophy of Science* (edited by Robert S. Cohen and Marx W. Wartofsky), New York: Humanities Press, 1965, Vol. II, pp. 279–290.

Margenau, Henry, *The Nature of Physical Reality: A Philosophy of Modern Physics*, New York: McGraw-Hill, 1950.

Margolis, Joseph (Editor), *An Introduction to Philosophical Inquiry: Contemporary and Classical Sources*, New York: Alfred A. Knopf, 1968.

———— (Editor), *Philosophy Looks at the Arts: Readings in Aesthetics*, New York: Charles Scribner's Sons, 1962.

Marías, Julián, *Reason and Life: The Introduction to Philosophy*, translated by Kenneth S. Reid and Edward Sarmiento, New Haven: Yale University Press, 1956.

Martin, C. B., *Religious Belief*, Ithaca, N.Y.: Cornell University Press, 1959.

Martindale, Don, *The Nature and Types of Sociological Theory*, Boston: Houghton Mifflin, 1960.

———, "Verstehen," in *International Encyclopedia of the Social Sciences* (edited by David L. Sills), New York: Macmillan and Free Press, 1968, Vol. XVI, pp. 308–313.

May, Rollo (Editor), *Existential Psychology*, New York: Random House, 1961.

———, Ernest Angel, and Henri F. Ellenberger (Editors), *Existence: A New Dimension in Psychiatry and Psychology*, New York: Basic Books, 1958.

Mayer-Gross, W., Eliot Slater, and Martin Roth, *Clinical Psychiatry*, London: Cassell, 1960.

Mead, George H., *Mind, Self, and Society: From the Standpoint of a Social Behaviorist*, edited with an Introduction by Charles W. Morris, Chicago: University of Chicago Press, 1934.

———, *The Philosophy of the Act*, edited with an Introduction by Charles W. Morris in collaboration with John M. Brewster, Albert M. Dunham, and David L. Miller, Chicago: University of Chicago Press, 1938.

———, *The Philosophy of the Present*, edited by Arthur E. Murphy with Prefatory Remarks by John Dewey, Chicago: Open Court, 1932.

Mehta, J. L., *The Philosophy of Martin Heidegger*, Varanasi: Banaras Hindu University Press, 1967.

Merlan, Philip, "Time Consciousness in Husserl and Heidegger," *Philosophy and Phenomenological Research*, Vol. VIII, 1947, pp. 23–53.

Merleau-Ponty, Maurice, *Phenomenology of Perception*, translated by Colin Smith, New York: Humanities Press, 1962.

———, *The Primacy of Perception, and Other Essays on Phenomenological Psychology, the Philosophy of Art, History, and Politics*, edited with an Introduction by James M. Edie, Evanston, Ill.: Northwestern University Press, 1964.

———, *Signs*, translated with an Introduction by Richard C. McCleary, Evanston, Ill.: Northwestern University Press, 1964.

Merton, Robert K., *Social Theory and Social Structure*, revised edition, Glencoe, Ill.: Free Press, 1957.

———, Leonard Broom, and Leonard S. Cottrell, Jr. (Editors), *Sociology Today: Problems and Prospects*, New York: Basic Books, 1959.

Meyerhoff, Hans, "'The New Yorker' in Hollywood," *Partisan Review*, Vol. XVIII, 1951, pp. 569–574.

——— (Editor), *The Philosophy of History in Our Time: An Anthology*, Garden City, N.Y.: Doubleday Anchor Books, 1959.

Mill, John Stuart, *Autobiography*, with an Introduction by Currin V. Shields, New York: Bobbs-Merrill, 1957.

———, *Utilitarianism*, edited by Oskar Piest, New York: Library of Liberal Arts, 1957.

Miller, Vassar, *Wage War on Silence: A Book of Poems*, Middletown, Conn.: Wesleyan University Press, 1960.

Mills, C. Wright, *The Sociological Imagination*, New York: Grove Press, 1961.

Minkowski, Eugène, *Le Temps vécu: études phénoménologiques et psychopathologiques*, Neuchatel: Delachaux et Niestlé, 1968.

————, *Traité de psychopathologie*, Paris: Presses Universitaires de France, 1966.

Minkus, P. A., *Philosophy of the Person*, New York: Humanities Press, 1960.

Mireaux, Émile, *Daily Life in the Time of Homer*, translated by Iris Sells, New York: Macmillan, 1960.

Mises, Ludwig von, *Human Action: A Treatise on Economics*, London: William Hodge, 1949.

Montaigne, Michel de, *The Autobiography*, edited by Marvin Lowenthal, New York: Vintage Books, 1935.

Moore, Asher, "Existential Phenomenology," followed by comments by Rollo Handy, *Philosophy and Phenomenological Research*, Vol. XXVII, 1967, pp. 408–414.

Moore, G. E., "An Autobiography," in *The Philosophy of G. E. Moore* (edited by Paul Arthur Schilpp), Chicago: Northwestern University, 1942, pp. 3–39.

Morris, Charles, *Signs, Language, and Behavior*, New York: Prentice-Hall, 1946.

Mukerji, A. C., *The Nature of Self*, Allahabad: The Indian Press, 1938.

Munby, A. N. L., *Portrait of an Obsession: The Life of Sir Thomas Phillipps, the World's Greatest Book Collector*, adapted by Nicolas Barker from the five volumes of *Phillipps Studies*, New York: G. P. Putnam's Sons, 1967.

Murdoch, Iris, *Sartre: Romantic Rationalist*, New Haven: Yale University Press, 1953.

Murdock, George P. (Editor), *Studies in the Science of Society: Presented to Albert Galloway Keller*, London: Oxford University Press, 1937.

Mure, G. R. G., *The Philosophy of Hegel*, London: Oxford University Press, 1965.

Nadel, S. F., *The Foundations of Social Anthropology*, London: Cohen and West, 1963.

————, *The Theory of Social Structure*, with a Memoir by Meyer Fortes, London: Cohen and West, 1965.

Nagel, Ernest, *The Structure of Science: Problems in the Logic of Scientific Explanation*, New York: Harcourt, Brace, 1961.

Natanson, Maurice, "Alfred Schutz," in *International Encyclopedia of the Social Sciences* (edited by David L. Sills), New York: Macmillan and Free Press, 1968, Vol. XIV, pp. 72–74.

————, "Alfred Schutz on Social Reality and Social Science," *Social Research*, Vol. XXXV, 1968, pp. 217–244.

————, "Alienation and Social Role," in *Phenomenology in America* (edited by James M. Edie), Chicago: Quadrangle Books, 1967, pp. 255–268.

————, "Anonymity and Recognition: Toward an Ontology of Social Roles," in *Conditio Humana: Erwin W. Straus on His 75th Birthday* (edited by Walter von Baeyer and Richard M. Griffith), Berlin: Springer, 1966, pp. 255–271.

————, *A Critique of Jean-Paul Sartre's Ontology*, Lincoln: University of Nebraska, 1951.

————, "The *Lebenswelt*," followed by comments by John Kuiper, in *Phenomenology: Pure and Applied, The First Lexington Conference* (edited by Erwin W. Straus), Pittsburgh: Duquesne University Press, 1964, pp. 75–93.

————, *Literature, Philosophy, and the Social Sciences: Essays in Existentialism and Phenomenology*, The Hague: Martinus Nijhoff, 1962.

————, "Man as an Actor," followed by comments by James M. Edie, in *Phenomenology of Will and Action: The Second Lexington Conference on Pure and Applied Phenomenology* (edited by Erwin W. Straus and Richard M. Griffith), Pittsburgh: Duquesne University Press, 1967, pp. 201–220.

————, "The Phenomenology of Alfred Schutz," *Inquiry*, Vol. XIX, 1966, pp. 147–155.

————, *The Social Dynamics of George H. Mead*, with an Introduction by Horace M. Kallen, Washington, D.C.: Public Affairs Press, 1956.

———— (Editor), *Essays in Phenomenology*, The Hague: Martinus Nijhoff, 1966.

———— (Editor), *Philosophy of the Social Sciences: A Reader*, New York: Random House, 1963.

————, and Henry W. Johnstone, Jr. (Editors), *Philosophy, Rhetoric, and Argumentation*, with a Foreword by Robert T. Oliver, University Park: Pennsylvania State University Press, 1965.

Nota, John H., *Phenomenology and History*, translated by Louis Grooten and the author, Chicago: Loyola University Press, 1967.

Nowicki, M., "Bibliography of Works in the Philosophy of History, 1958–1961," *History and Theory*, Beiheft 3, The Hague: Mouton, 1964.

Oakeshott, Michael, *Experience and Its Modes*, Cambridge: Cambridge University Press, 1933.

O'Connor, D. J. (Editor), *A Critical History of Western Philosophy*, New York: Free Press, 1964.

Olson, Robert G., *A Short Introduction to Philosophy*, New York: Harcourt, Brace and World, 1967.

Ortega y Gasset, José, *Man and People*, translated by Willard R. Trask, New York: W. W. Norton, 1957.

————, *Toward a Philosophy of History*, translated by Helene Weyl, New York: W. W. Norton, 1941 (republished in 1961 as *History as a System*).

————, *What Is Philosophy?*, translated by Mildred Adams, New York: W. W. Norton, 1960.

Otto, Rudolf, *The Idea of the Holy: An Inquiry into the Non-Rational Factor in the Idea of the Divine and Its Relation to the Rational*, translated by John W. Harvey, 2nd edition, London: Oxford University Press, 1957.

Panofsky, Erwin, *Meaning in the Visual Arts: Papers in and on Art History*, Garden City, N.Y.: Doubleday Anchor Books, 1955.

Parker, DeWitt H., *The Self and Nature*, Cambridge, Mass.: Harvard University Press, 1917.

Parmenter, Ross, *The Awakened Eye*, Middletown, Conn.: Wesleyan University Press, 1968.

Parsons, Talcott, *The Social System*, Glencoe, Ill.: Free Press, 1951.

———, *The Structure of Social Action: A Study in Social Theory with Special Reference to a Group of Recent European Writers*, with a new Introduction by the author, 2 volumes, New York: Free Press, 1968.

———, Edward Shils, Kaspar D. Naegele, and Jesse R. Pitts (Editors), *Theories of Society: Foundations of Modern Sociological Theory*, 2 volumes, New York: Free Press of Glencoe, 1961.

Passmore, John, *A Hundred Years of Philosophy*, revised edition, New York: Basic Books, 1966.

———, "The Idea of a History of Philosophy," *History and Theory*, Beiheft 5, The Hague: Mouton, 1965, pp. 1–32.

Paton, H. J., *In Defense of Reason*, London: Hutchinson's University Library, 1951.

———, *The Modern Predicament: A Study in the Philosophy of Religion*, New York: Macmillan, 1955.

Peirce, Charles Sanders, *Collected Papers:* Vol. VI, *Scientific Metaphysics*, edited by Charles Hartshorne and Paul Weiss, Cambridge, Mass.: The Belknap Press of Harvard University Press, 1960.

Penelhum, Terence, "Personal Identity," in *The Encyclopedia of Philosophy* (edited by Paul Edwards), New York: Macmillan and Free Press, 1967, Vol. VI, pp. 95–107.

Pepper, Stephen C., *The Basis of Criticism in the Arts*, Cambridge, Mass.: Harvard University Press, 1956.

———, *The Work of Art*, Bloomington: Indiana University Press, 1955.

Percy, Walker, "The Symbolic Structure of Interpersonal Process," *Psychiatry*, Vol. XXIV, 1961, pp. 39–52.

Perry, Ralph Barton, "The Ego-Centric Predicament," in *The Development of American Philosophy: A Book of Readings*, 2nd edition (edited by Walter G. Muelder, Laurence Sears, and Anne V. Schlabach), Boston: Houghton Mifflin, 1960, pp. 331–337.

Pfuetze, Paul E., *Self, Society, Existence: Human Nature in the Thought of George Herbert Mead and Martin Buber*, with a Foreword by H. Richard Niebuhr, New York: Harper Torchbooks, 1961.

Philipson, Morris (Editor), *Aesthetics Today*, New York: Meridian Books, 1961.

Phillips, William (Editor), *Art and Psychoanalysis*, New York: Meridian Books, 1963.

Picard, Max, *The Human Face*, translated by Guy Endore, New York: Farrar and Rinehart, 1930.

Pike, Nelson (Editor), *God and Evil: Readings in the Theological Problem of Evil*, Englewood Cliffs, N.J.: Prentice-Hall, 1964.

Piper, David, *The English Face*, London: Thames and Hudson, 1957.

Pirandello, Luigi, *Naked Masks: Five Plays*, edited by Eric Bentley, New York: E. P. Dutton (Dutton Paperback Edition), 1952.

————, *Saggi*, Milano: Mondadori, 1939.

Plato, *The Republic*, translated with an Introduction by Francis Macdonald Cornford, New York: Oxford University Press, 1945.

Polsky, Ned, *Hustlers, Beats, and Others*, Chicago: Aldine, 1967.

Preiss, Jack J., and Howard J. Ehrlich, *An Examination of Role Theory: The Case of the State Police*, Lincoln: University of Nebraska Press, 1966.

Prescott, William H., *History of the Conquest of Mexico*, edited by Wilfred Harold Munro with Notes by John Foster Kirk, Montezuma Edition, Vol. I, Philadelphia: J. B. Lippincott, 1904.

Price, H. H., "Our Evidence for the Existence of Other Minds," *Philosophy*, Vol. XIII, 1938, pp. 425–456.

————, "Our Knowledge of Other Minds," *Proceedings of the Aristotelian Society*, Vol. XXXII, 1932, pp. 53–78.

Rabil, Albert, Jr., *Merleau-Ponty: Existentialist of the Social World*, New York: Columbia University Press, 1967.

Rader, Melvin (Editor), *A Modern Book of Aesthetics: An Anthology*, 3rd edition, New York: Holt, Rinehart and Winston, 1960.

Radnitzky, Gerard, *Contemporary Schools of Metascience*, Göteborg: Akademiförlaget, 1968. Vol. I, *Anglo-Saxon Schools of Metascience;* Vol. II, *Continental Schools of Metascience*.

Raju, P. T., *Indian Idealism and Modern Challenges*, Chandigarh: Panjab University Publication Bureau, 1961.

Randall, John Herman, Jr., *The Career of Philosophy*, New York: Columbia University Press. Vol. I, *From the Middle Ages to the Enlightenment*, 1962; Vol. II, *From the German Enlightenment to the Age of Darwin*, 1965.

Rank, Otto, *Art and Artist: Creative Urge and Personality Development*, translated by Charles Francis Atkinson with a Preface by Ludwig Lewisohn, New York: Alfred A. Knopf, 1932.

Rapaport, David (Translator and Editor), *Organization and Pathology of Thought: Selected Sources*, New York: Columbia University Press, 1951.

Reinhardt, Kurt F., *The Existentialist Revolt: The Main Themes and Phases of Existentialism—Kierkegaard, Nietzsche, Heidegger, Jaspers, Sartre, Marcel—with an Appendix on Existentialist Psychotherapy*, New York: Frederick Ungar, 1960.

Renier, G. J., *History: Its Purpose and Method*, London: George Allen and Unwin, 1961.

Rice, John Andrew, *I Came Out of the Eighteenth Century*, New York: Harper, 1942.

Rice, Philip Blair, "Existentialism and the Self," in *The Kenyon Critics: Studies in Modern Literature* (edited by John Crowe Ransom), New York: World, 1951, pp. 200–224.

Richardson, Maurice, and Philip Toynbee, *Thanatos: A Modern Symposium*, London: Victor Gollancz, 1963.

Richardson, William J., *Heidegger: Through Phenomenology to Thought*, 2nd edition, with a Preface by Martin Heidegger, The Hague: Martinus Nijhoff, 1967.

Ricoeur, Paul, *History and Truth*, translated with an Introduction by Charles A. Kelbley, Evanston, Ill.: Northwestern University Press, 1965.

———, *Husserl: An Analysis of His Phenomenology*, translated by Edward G. Ballard and Lester E. Embree, Evanston, Ill.: Northwestern University Press, 1967.

Riezler, Kurt, *Man, Mutable and Immutable: The Fundamental Structure of Social Life*, Chicago: Henry Regnery, 1950.

Ritchie, Benbow, "The Formal Structure of the Aesthetic Object," in *The Problems of Aesthetics: A Book of Readings* (edited by Eliseo Vivas and Murray Krieger), New York: Holt, Rinehart and Winston, 1960, pp. 225–233.

Robertiello, Richard C., David Friedman, and Bertram Pollens, *The Analyst's Role*, New York: Citadel Press, 1963.

Rocheblave-Spenlé, Anne-Marie, *La Notion de rôle en psychologie sociale*, Paris: Presses Universitaires de France, 1962.

Rodman, Selden, *Conversations with Artists*, with an Introduction by Alexander Eliot, New York: Devin-Adair, 1957.

Roethke, Theodore, *The Collected Poems of Theodore Roethke*, New York: Doubleday, 1966.

Rogers, Carl, *On Becoming a Person: A Therapist's View of Psychotherapy*, Boston: Houghton Mifflin, 1961.

Rollins, C. D., "Solipsism," in *The Encyclopedia of Philosophy* (edited by Paul Edwards), New York: Macmillan and Free Press, 1967, Vol. VII, pp. 487–491.

Romains, Jules, *The Death of a Nobody*, translated by Desmond MacCarthy and Sidney Waterlow, with an Introduction by the author translated by Haakon Chevalier and an Afterword by Maurice Natanson, New York: New American Library (Signet Classic), 1961.

Romero, Francisco, *Theory of Man*, translated by William F. Cooper with an Introduction by William J. Kilgore, Berkeley: University of California Press, 1964.

Ross, Lillian, *Portrait of Hemingway*, New York: Simon and Schuster, 1961.

Rotenstreich, Nathan, *Between Past and Present: An Essay on History*, with a Foreword by Martin Buber, New Haven: Yale University Press, 1958.

Roth, Henry, *Call It Sleep*, with an Afterword by Walter Allen, New York: Avon Books, 1964.

Roth, Philip, "Civilization and Its Discontents," *New American Review*, No. 3, New York: New American Library, 1968, pp. 7–81.

Rousseau, Jean-Jacques, *The Confessions*, New York: Modern Library, 1945.

Rudich, Norman, "The Dialectics of Poesis: Literature as a Mode of Cognition," in *Boston Studies in the Philosophy of Science* (edited by Robert S. Cohen and Marx W. Wartofsky), New York: Humanities Press, 1965, Vol. II, pp. 343–400.

Rudner, Richard S., *Philosophy of Social Science*, Englewood Cliffs, N.J.: Prentice-Hall, 1966.

Ruesch, Jurgen, and Gregory Bateson, *Communication: The Social Matrix of Psychiatry*, New York: W. W. Norton, 1968.

Ruitenbeek, Hendrik M. (Editor), *Varieties of Classic Social Theory*, New York: E. P. Dutton, 1963.

——— (Editor), *Varieties of Modern Social Theory*, New York: E. P. Dutton, 1963.

Rule, John C., "Bibliography of Works in the Philosophy of History, 1945–1957," *History and Theory*, Beiheft 1, The Hague: Mouton, 1961.

Russell, Bertrand, *The Autobiography*, Boston: Little, Brown. Vol. I, *1872–1914*, 1967; Vol. II, *1914–1944*, 1968.

———, *A History of Western Philosophy, and Its Connection with Political and Social Circumstances from the Earliest Times to the Present Day*, New York: Simon and Schuster, 1945.

———, *Human Knowledge: Its Scope and Limits*, New York: Simon and Schuster, 1948.

———, *The Problems of Philosophy*, New York: Oxford University Press, 1959.

Ryle, Gilbert, *The Concept of Mind*, New York: Barnes and Noble, 1950.

Santayana, George, *The Letters*, edited with an Introduction by Daniel Cory, New York: Charles Scribner's Sons, 1955.

———, *Persons and Places*, with an Introduction by Daniel Cory, New York: Charles Scribner's Sons, 1963.

———, *Realms of Being*, Vol. XIV of the Triton Edition of the *Works of George Santayana*, New York: Charles Scribner's Sons, 1937.

———, *Scepticism and Animal Faith: Introduction to a System of Philosophy*, New York: Dover, 1955.

———, *The Sense of Beauty: Being the Outlines of Aesthetic Theory*, with a Foreword by Philip Blair Rice, New York: Modern Library, 1955.

Sarbin, Theodore R., "Role: Psychological Aspects," in *International Encyclopedia of the Social Sciences* (edited by David L. Sills), New York: Macmillan and Free Press, 1968, Vol. XIII, pp. 546–552.

———, and Vernon L. Allen, "Role Theory," in *The Handbook of Social Psychology* (edited by Gardner Lindzey and Elliot Aronson), Reading, Mass.: Addison-Wesley, 1954, Vol. I, pp. 223–258: 2nd ed. 1968, Vol. I, pp. 488–567.

Sartre, Jean-Paul, *Anti-Semite and Jew*, translated by George J. Becker, New York: Schocken Books, 1948.

———, *Being and Nothingness: An Essay on Phenomenological Ontology*, translated with an Introduction by Hazel E. Barnes, New York: Philosophical Library, 1956.

———, *The Emotions: Outline of a Theory*, translated by Bernard Frechtman, New York: Philosophical Library, 1948.

———, "Existentialism and Humanism," translated by Philip Mairet, in *Existentialism from Dostoevsky to Sartre* (edited by Walter Kaufmann), New York: Meridian Books, 1956, pp. 287–311 (note: Also available as a book, *Existentialism and Humanism*, London: Methuen, 1948 and published in the United States in a different translation as *Existentialism*).

———, "Faces, Preceded by Official Portraits," translated by Anne P. Jones, in *Essays in Phenomenology* (edited by Maurice Natanson), The Hague: Martinus Nijhoff, 1966, pp. 157–163.

———, *Imagination: A Psychological Critique*, translated with an Introduction by Forrest Williams, Ann Arbor: University of Michigan Press, 1962.

———, *Literary and Philosophical Essays*, translated by Annette Michelson, London: Rider, 1955.

———, *The Philosophy of Jean-Paul Sartre*, edited with an Introduction by Robert Denoon Cumming, New York: Random House, 1965.

———, *The Psychology of Imagination*, New York: Philosophical Library, 1948.

———, *Search for a Method*, translated with an Introduction by Hazel E. Barnes, New York: Alfred A. Knopf, 1963.

———, *Situations*, translated by Benita Eisler, New York: George Braziller, 1965.

———, *The Transcendence of the Ego: An Existentialist Theory of Consciousness*, translated with an Introduction by Forrest Williams and Robert Kirkpatrick, New York: Noonday Press, 1957.

———, *What Is Literature?*, translated by Bernard Frechtman, New York: Philosophical Library, 1949.

———, *The Words*, translated by Bernard Frechtman, New York: George Braziller, 1964.

Scheler, Max, *On the Eternal in Man*, translated by Bernard Noble, New York: Harper, 1960.

———, *Man's Place in Nature*, translated with an Introduction by Hans Meyerhoff, Boston: Beacon Press, 1961.

———, *The Nature of Sympathy*, translated by Peter Heath with an Introduction by W. Stark, New Haven: Yale University Press, 1954.

———, *Die Wissensformen und die Gesellschaft*, Leipzig: Neue-Geist, 1926.

Schmitt, Richard, "Phenomenology," in *The Encyclopedia of Philosophy* (edited by Paul Edwards), New York: Macmillan and Free Press, 1967, Vol. VI, pp. 135–151.

Schoeck, Helmut, and James W. Wiggins (Editors), *Scientism and Values*, Princeton, N.J.: D. Van Nostrand, 1960.

Schrader, George Alfred, Jr. (Editor), *Existential Philosophers: Kierkegaard to Merleau-Ponty*, New York: McGraw-Hill, 1967.

Schrag, Calvin O., *Existence and Freedom: Towards an Ontology of Human Finitude*, with a Foreword by John Wild, Evanston, Ill.: Northwestern University Press, 1961.

Schutz, Alfred, *Collected Papers:* Vol. I, *The Problem of Social Reality*, edited with an Introduction by Maurice Natanson, with a Preface by H. L. Van Breda, The Hague: Martinus Nijhoff, 1962.

———, *Collected Papers:* Vol. II, *Studies in Social Theory*, edited with an Introduction by Arvid Brodersen, The Hague: Martinus Nijhoff, 1964.

———, *Collected Papers:* Vol. III, *Studies in Phenomenological Philosophy*, edited by I. Schutz with an Introduction by Aron Gurwitsch, The Hague: Martinus Nijhoff, 1966.

———, *The Phenomenology of the Social World*, translated by George Walsh and Frederick Lehnert, with an Introduction by George Walsh, Evanston, Ill.: Northwestern University Press, 1967.

Scott, Nathan A., Jr. (Editor), *The Modern Vision of Death*, Richmond, Va.: John Knox Press, 1967.

Scriven, Michael, *Primary Philosophy*, New York: McGraw-Hill, 1966.

Shahn, Ben, *The Shape of Content*, New York: Vintage Books, 1960.

Shaw, Charles Gray, *The Ego and Its Place in the World*, New York: Macmillan, 1913.

Sheets, Maxine, *The Phenomenology of Dance*, Madison: University of Wisconsin Press, 1966.

Sherrington, Charles, *Man on His Nature*, 2nd edition, Cambridge: Cambridge University Press, 1963.

Shestov, Leon, "In Memory of a Great Philosopher: Edmund Husserl," translated by George L. Kline, in *Russian Philosophy* (edited by James M. Edie, James P. Scanlan, and Mary-Barbara Zeldin with the collaboration of George L. Kline), Chicago: Quadrangle Books, 1965, Vol. III, pp. 248–276.

Shoemaker, Sydney, *Self-Knowledge and Self-Identity*, Ithaca, N.Y.: Cornell University Press, 1963.

Shorter, J. M., "Other Minds," in *The Encyclopedia of Philosophy* (edited by Paul Edwards), New York: Macmillan and Free Press, 1967, Vol. VI, pp. 7–13.

Sills, David L. (Editor), *International Encyclopedia of the Social Sciences*, 17 volumes, New York: Macmillan and Free Press, 1968.

Simmel, Georg, *Fragmente und Aufsätze: Aus dem Nachlass und Veröffentlichungen des letzten Jahre*, herausgegeben mit einem Vorwort von Gertrud Kantorowicz, Hildesheim: Georg Olms, 1967.

————, *The Sociology of Georg Simmel*, translated and edited with an Introduction by Kurt H. Wolff, Glencoe, Ill.: Free Press, 1950.

Smith, Page, *The Historian and History*, New York: Alfred A. Knopf, 1964.

Smith, T. V., and Marjorie Grene (Editors), *Philosophers Speak for Themselves*, 4 volumes, Chicago: University of Chicago Press (Phoenix Books), 1966. Vol. I, *From Thales to Plato;* Vol. II, *From Aristotle to Plotinus;* Vol. III, *From Descartes to Locke;* Vol. IV, *Berkeley, Hume, and Kant.*

Smythies, J. R. (Editor), *Brain and Mind: Modern Concepts of the Nature of Mind*, New York: Humanities Press, 1965.

Sonnemann, Ulrich, *Existence and Therapy: An Introduction to Phenomenological Psychology and Existential Analysis*, New York: Grune and Stratton, 1954.

Spanos, William V. (Editor), *A Casebook on Existentialism*, New York: Thomas Y. Crowell, 1966.

Spender, Stephen, *World Within World*, New York: Harcourt, Brace, 1948.

Spiegelberg, Herbert, "Husserl's Phenomenology and Existentialism," *Journal of Philosophy*, Vol. LVII, 1960, pp. 62–74.

————, *The Phenomenological Movement: A Historical Introduction*, 2 volumes, 2nd edition, The Hague: Martinus Nijhoff, 1965.

————, "The 'Reality-Phenomenon' and Reality," in *Philosophical Essays in Memory of Edmund Husserl* (edited by Marvin Farber), Cambridge, Mass.: Harvard University Press, 1940, pp. 84–105.

Spinoza, *The Correspondence*, translated and edited with an Introduction by A. Wolf, London: George Allen and Unwin, 1928.

Spitzer, Leo, "*Milieu* and *Ambiance:* An Essay in Historical Semantics," *Philosophy and Phenomenological Research*, Vol. III, 1942, pp. 169–218.

Sprott, W. J. H., *Sociology*, London: Hutchinson's University Library, 1959.

Stace, W. T., *The Theory of Knowledge and Existence*, Oxford: Clarendon Press, 1932.

Stanislavski, Konstantin, *An Actor Prepares*, translated by Elizabeth Hapgood with an Introduction by John Gielgud, New York: Theatre Arts Books, 1948.

Staude, John R., *Max Scheler: An Intellectual Portrait*, New York: Free Press, 1967.

Stearns, Isabel, "The Person," *Review of Metaphysics*, Vol. III, 1950, pp. 427–436.

Stein, Maurice, and Arthur Vidich (Editors), *Sociology on Trial*, Englewood Cliffs, N.J.: Prentice-Hall, 1963.

Stern, Alfred, *Philosophy of History and the Problem of Values*, The Hague: Mouton, 1962.

Stern, Fritz (Editor), *The Varieties of History: From Voltaire to the Present*, New York: Meridian Books, 1956.

Stevens, Wallace, *The Necessary Angel: Essays on Reality and the Imagination*, New York: Vintage Books, 1965.

Still, James, *Hounds on the Mountain*, New York: Viking Press, 1937.

Stolnitz, Jerome, *Aesthetics and Philosophy of Art Criticism: A Critical Introduction*, Boston: Houghton Mifflin, 1960.

―――― (Editor), *Aesthetics*, New York: Macmillan, 1965.

Stonier, Alfred, and Karl Bode, "A New Approach to the Methodology of the Social Sciences," *Economica*, New Series, Vol. IV, 1937, pp. 406–424.

Strasser, Stephan, *Phenomenology and the Human Sciences: A Contribution to a New Scientific Ideal*, Pittsburgh: Duquesne University Press, 1963.

――――, *The Soul in Metaphysical and Empirical Psychology*, Pittsburgh: Duquesne University Press, 1957.

Straus, Erwin W., *On Obsession: A Clinical and Methodological Study*, New York: Nervous and Mental Disease Monographs, 1948.

――――, *Phenomenological Psychology: Selected Papers*, translated, in part, by Erling Eng, New York: Basic Books, 1966.

――――, *The Primary World of Senses: A Vindication of Sensory Experience*, translated by Jacob Needleman, New York: Free Press of Glencoe, 1963.

Strauss, Anselm L., *Mirrors and Masks*, Glencoe, Ill.: Free Press, 1959.

Strauss, Leo, *Natural Right and History*, Chicago: University of Chicago Press, 1953.

Strawson, P. F., *Individuals: An Essay in Descriptive Metaphysics*, Garden City, N.Y.: Doubleday Anchor Books, 1963.

Stroud, Robert, *Stroud's Digest on the Diseases of Birds*, Jersey City, N.J.: T.F.H. Publications, 1964.

Sumner, William Graham, *Folkways: A Study of the Sociological Importance of Manners, Customs, Mores, and Morals*, New York: Ginn, 1906.

Symonds, Percival M., *The Ego and the Self*, New York: Appleton-Century-Crofts, 1951.

Tagiuri, Renato, and Luigi Petrullo (Editors), *Person Perception and Interpersonal Behavior*, Stanford: Stanford University Press, 1958.

Tatarkiewicz, Ladislas, "The History of Philosophy and the Art of Writing It," translated by Elaine P. Halperin, *Diogenes*, No. 20, 1957, pp. 52–67.

Taylor, A. E., *Elements of Metaphysics*, London: Methuen, 1946.

Tejera, Victorino, *Art and Human Intelligence*, New York: Appleton-Century-Crofts, 1965.

Theunissen, Michael, *Der Andere: Studien zur Sozialontologie der Gegenwart*, Berlin: Walter de Gruyter, 1965.

Thévenaz, Pierre, *What Is Phenomenology?, and Other Essays*, translated by James M. Edie, Charles Courtney, and Paul Brockelman, edited with an Introduction by James M. Edie, Chicago: Quadrangle Books, 1962.

Thilly, Frank, and Ledger Wood, *A History of Philosophy*, 3rd edition, New York: Henry Holt, 1957.

Thody, Philip, *Jean-Paul Sartre: A Literary and Political Study*, New York: Macmillan, 1960.

Thomas, Anne Lloyd, Review of *Philosophical Essays* by O. K. Bouwsma, *Mind*, Vol. LXXVI, 1967, pp. 606–608.

Thomas, W. I., and Dorothy S. Thomas, *The Child in America: Behavior Problems and Programs*, New York: Alfred A. Knopf, 1928.

Thompson, D'Arcy Wentworth, *On Growth and Form*, 2 volumes, Cambridge: Cambridge University Press, 1963.

Tillich, Paul, *Dynamics of Faith*, New York: Harper Torchbooks, 1958.

Tillman, Frank A., "On Perceiving Persons," in *Phenomenology in America*, edited with an Introduction by James M. Edie, Chicago: Quadrangle Books, 1967, pp. 161–172.

Timasheff, Nicholas, *Sociological Theory*, revised edition, New York: Random House, 1966.

Tolstoy, Leo, *The Death of Ivan Ilych, and Other Stories*, title story translated by Aylmer Maude, with an Afterword by David Magarshack, New York: New American Library (Signet Classic), 1964.

————, *What Is Art?, and Essays on Art*, translated by Aylmer Maude, London: Oxford University Press, 1959.

Tomas, Vincent (Editor), *Creativity in the Arts*, Englewood Cliffs, N.J.: Prentice-Hall, 1964.

Toulemont, René, *L'Essence de la société selon Husserl*, Paris: Presses Universitaires de France, 1962.

Trilling, Lionel, "Of This Time, Of That Place," in *The Experience of Literature: A Reader with Commentaries* (edited by Lionel Trilling), New York: Holt, Rinehart and Winston, 1967, pp. 755–781.

Turner, Ralph H., "Role: Sociological Aspects," in *International Encyclopedia of the Social Sciences* (edited by David L. Sills), New York: Macmillan and Free Press, 1968, Vol. XIII, pp. 552–556.

Tymieniecka, Anna-Teresa, *Phenomenology and Science in Contemporary European Thought*, with a Foreword by I. M. Bocheński, New York: Farrar, Straus, and Cudahy, 1962.

Udy, Stanley H., Jr., "Social Structure: Social Structural Analysis," in *International Encyclopedia of the Social Sciences* (edited by David L. Sills), New York: Macmillan and Free Press, 1968, Vol. XIV, pp. 489–495.

Uexküll, J. von, *Theoretical Biology*, New York: Harcourt, Brace, 1926.

Unamuno, Miguel de, *The Tragic Sense of Life*, translated by J. E. Crawford Flitch with an Introduction by Salvador de Madariaga, New York: Dover, 1954.

Van Den Berg, J. H., *The Phenomenological Approach to Psychiatry: An Introduction to Recent Phenomenological Psychopathology*, Springfield, Ill.: Charles C. Thomas, 1955.

Van Der Leeuw, G., *Religion: In Essence and Manifestation*, translated by J. E. Turner, London: George Allen and Unwin, 1938.

Van Gogh, Vincent, *The Complete Letters of Vincent Van Gogh, with Reproductions of All the Drawings in the Correspondence*, 3 volumes, Greenwich, Conn.: New York Graphic Society, 1959.

Varet, Gilbert, *Manuel de bibliographie philosophique*, 2 volumes, Paris: Presses Universitaires de France, 1956. Vol. I, *Les Philosophes classiques;* Vol. II, *Les Sciences philosophiques.*

Victoroff, David, *G. H. Mead: Sociologue et philosophe*, Paris: Presses Universitaires de France, 1953.

Vivas, Eliseo, and Murray Krieger (Editors), *The Problems of Aesthetics: A Book of Readings*, New York: Holt, Rinehart and Winston, 1960.

Voegelin, Eric, *The New Science of Politics: An Introduction*, Chicago: University of Chicago Press, 1952.

———, *Order and History*, Baton Rouge: Louisiana State University Press. Vol. I, *Israel and Revelation*, 1956; Vol. III, *Plato and Aristotle*, 1957.

Volkart, Edmund H. (Editor), *Social Behavior and Personality: Contributions of W. I. Thomas to Theory and Social Research*, New York: Social Science Research Council, 1951.

Waelhens, Alphonse de, "The Phenomenology of the Body," in *Readings in Existential Phenomenology* (edited by Nathaniel Lawrence and Daniel O'Connor), Englewood Cliffs, N.J.: Prentice-Hall, 1967, pp. 149–167.

Wahl, Jean, *The Philosopher's Way*, New York: Oxford University Press, 1948.

Wain, John, *Sprightly Running: Part of an Autobiography*, New York: St. Martin's Press, 1963.

Waismann, Friedrich, "How I See Philosophy," in *Logical Positivism* (edited by A. J. Ayer), New York: Free Press, 1959, pp. 345–380.

Walsh, W. H., *Philosophy of History: An Introduction*, New York: Harper Torchbooks, 1960.

Wann, T. W. (Editor), *Behaviorism and Phenomenology: Contrasting Bases for Modern Psychology*, Chicago: University of Chicago Press (Phoenix Books), 1965.

Wartofsky, Marx W., *Conceptual Foundations of Scientific Thought: An Introduction to the Philosophy of Science*, New York: Macmillan, 1968.

Watson, J. D., *The Double Helix*, New York: Atheneum, 1968.

Webb, Clement C. J., *A History of Philosophy*, London: Oxford University Press, 1964.

———, *Our Knowledge of One Another*, New York: Oxford University Press, 1930.

Weber, Max, *On the Methodology of the Social Sciences*, translated and edited by Edward A. Shils and Henry A. Finch, with a Foreword by Edward A. Shils, Glencoe, Ill.: Free Press, 1949.

———, *The Theory of Social and Economic Organization*, translated by A. M. Henderson and Talcott Parsons, edited with an Introduction by Talcott Parsons, New York: Oxford University Press, 1947.

Weil, Simone, *Waiting for God*, translated by Emma Craufurd with an Introduction by Leslie A. Fiedler, New York: Capricorn Books, 1959.

Weiss, Paul, *History: Written and Lived*, Carbondale: Southern Illinois University Press, 1962.

———, *The World of Art*, Carbondale: Southern Illinois University Press, 1961.

Weitz, Morris (Editor), *Problems in Aesthetics: An Introductory Book of Readings*, New York: Macmillan, 1959.

Weizsäcker, C. F. von, *The History of Nature*, Chicago: University of Chicago Press, 1949.

Wellek, René, and Austin Warren, *Theory of Literature*, New York: Harcourt, Brace (Harvest Book), 1956.

Wells, Donald A., *God, Man, and the Thinker: Philosophies of Religion*, New York: Random House, 1962.

Werkmeister, W. H., *The Basis and Structure of Knowledge*, New York: Harper, 1948.

———, "On 'Describing a World,'" *Philosophy and Phenomenological Research*, Vol. XI, 1951, pp. 303–325.

———, *A Philosophy of Science*, Lincoln: University of Nebraska Press, 1965.

Wertenbaker, Lael Tucker, *Death of a Man*, New York: Random House, 1957.

Wheelwright, Philip, *The Burning Fountain: A Study in the Language of Symbolism*, revised edition, Bloomington: Indiana University Press, 1968.

White, Leonard D. (Editor), *The State of the Social Sciences*, Chicago: University of Chicago Press, 1956.

White, Morton G., *Foundations of Historical Knowledge*, New York: Harper, 1965.

Whitehead, Alfred North, *Dialogues*, recorded by Lucien Price, New York: New American Library (Mentor Book), 1956.

———, *Symbolism: Its Meaning and Effect*, New York: Macmillan, 1958.

Wiesel, Elie, in "Jewish Values in the Post-Holocaust Future: A Symposium," *Judaism*, Vol. XVI, 1967, pp. 266–299.

Wild, John D., *The Challenge of Existentialism*, Bloomington: Indiana University Press, 1959.

———, "Contemporary Phenomenology and the Problem of Existence," *Philosophy and Phenomenological Research*, Vol. XX, 1959, pp. 166–180.

———, *Human Freedom and Social Order: An Essay in Christian Philosophy*, Durham, N.C.: Duke University Press, 1959.

———, "Husserl's Life-World and the Lived Body," followed by comments by Jesse De Boer, in *Phenomenology: Pure and Applied, the First Lexington Conference* (edited by Erwin W. Straus), Pittsburgh: Duquesne University Press, 1964, pp. 10–28.

Wilde, Jean T., and William Kimmel (Editors), *The Search for Being: Essays from Kierkegaard to Sartre on the Problem of Existence*, with an Introduction by William Kimmel and a Preface by Martin C. D'Arcy, New York: Twayne, 1962.

Willett, John (Translator and Editor), *Brecht on Theatre: The Development of an Aesthetic*, New York: Hill and Wang, 1964.

Williams, Heathcote, *The Speakers*, New York: Grove Press, 1967.

Williams, John A., *The Man Who Cried I Am*, Boston: Little, Brown, 1967.

Wilson, Edmund, *Europe without Baedeker: Sketches among the Ruins of Italy, Greece, and England, Together with Notes from a European Diary, 1963–1964*, New York: Farrar, Straus and Giroux, 1966.

Wilson, G. A., *The Self and Its World*, New York: Macmillan, 1926.

Winch, Peter, *The Idea of a Social Science, and Its Relation to Philosophy*, New York: Humanities Press, 1960.

Wisdom, John, *Other Minds*, New York: Philosophical Library, 1952.

Wittgenstein, Ludwig, *Philosophical Investigations*, translated by G. E. M. Anscombe, 3rd edition, New York: Macmillan, 1968.

———, *Tractatus Logico-Philosophicus*, with an Introduction by Bertrand Russell, New York: Harcourt, Brace, 1947.

Wolff, Kurt H. (Editor), *Georg Simmel, 1858–1918: A Collection of Essays, with Translations and a Bibliography*, Columbus: Ohio State University Press, 1959.

Woolf, Virginia, *To the Lighthouse*, New York: Harcourt, Brace and World (Harvest Book), 1955.

Wright, Richard, *Black Boy: A Record of Childhood and Youth*, with an Afterword by John Reilly, New York: Harper and Row (Perennial Classic), 1966.

Wurgaft, Lewis D., "Bibliography of Works in the Philosophy of History, 1962–1965," *History and Theory*, Beiheft 7, Middletown, Conn.: Wesleyan University Press, 1967.

Wyschogrod, Michael, *Kierkegaard and Heidegger: The Ontology of Existence*, New York: Humanities Press, 1954.

Zaner, Richard M., *The Problem of Embodiment: Some Contributions to a Phenomenology of the Body*, The Hague: Martinus Nijhoff, 1964.

————, "Theory of Intersubjectivity: Alfred Schutz," *Social Research*, Vol. XXVIII, 1961, pp. 71–93.

Zilboorg, Gregory, *Mind, Medicine, and Man*, with a Foreword by Arthur H. Ruggles, New York: Harcourt, Brace, 1943.

Znaniecki, Florian, *Cultural Sciences: Their Origin and Development*, Urbana: University of Illinois Press, 1963.

————, *Social Relations and Social Roles: The Unfinished Systematic Sociology*, San Francisco: Chandler, 1965.

Zweig, Stefan, *Master Builders: A Typology of the Spirit*, translated by Eden and Cedar Paul, New York: Viking Press, 1939.